THE LEGAL AND ETHICAL DIMENSIONS OF GLOBAL BUSINESS

DON MAYER, J.D.,
LL.M. (INTERNATIONAL AND COMPARATIVE LAW)
UNIVERSITY OF DENVER

TABLE OF CONTENTS

CHAPTER ONE:

INTRODUCTION TO INTERNATIONAL LAW

I. WHAT IS INTERNATIONAL LAW?

International law is not like "domestic law" (which is sometimes call "municipal law"). Domestic law governs legal relations within a sovereign nation state. Beyond the borders of the U.S., there is no single "law giver" or sovereign that sets the rules of the economic game for business. Instead, there are numerous nation-states, all with different rules and regulations and customary ways of doing business. In the age of global business and international trade, understanding international law is essential.

Let's venture a short definition: international law is comprised of all the written rules and principles that govern how nations deal with one another, the relations between citizens of one state and citizens of another state, and the relations between citizens of one state and the government of a different state. It also includes the rules of interaction between international organizations and the various nation-states in "the international community." (Actually, using the word "community" suggests a stronger kind of agreement on values than is currently evident among all the nation-states.)

Public international law concerns itself only with questions of rights and obligations between and among several nations or nations and the citizens or subjects of other nations. In contrast, *private international law* deals with controversies between private persons and firms. These controversies arise out of situations which have a significant relationship to multiple nations. In recent years the line between public and private international law has become increasingly blurred. Issues of private international law may also implicate issues of public international law, and many matters of private international law have substantial international significance politically. In this course and in these materials, we will mostly focus on private international law issues.

Notice that international law — unlike the law of any sovereign state —is essentially law by voluntary agreement or customary practice. Because there is no world government there is no "top down" enforcement. If a sovereign state decides to depart from a treaty (an agreement it has made with another nation) or from customary practice, it is free to do so, but it can expect that other sovereign states will react negatively to a departure from what has been agreed upon or is considered a "norm" in international relations.

The actions of Vladimir Putin to invade Ukraine, for example, are both a departure from earlier agreements between the Ukraine and Russia (the Minsk Agreements),[1] and are certainly contrary to the norms of "self-determination" established after World War II as a key value in the U.N. Charter. "All peoples have the right to self-determination. By virtue of that right they freely determine their political status and freely pursue their economic, social and cultural development."[2] In departing from international norms, Putin has risked isolation from "the international community."[3] Other

---

[1] Reuters: *What are the Minsk Agreements on the Ukraine Conflict?* (Dec. 6, 2021). https://www.reuters.com/world/europe/what-are-minsk-agreements-ukraine-conflict-2021-12-06/
[2] https://unpo.org/article/4957
[3] This is a common phrase, but does not represent a real, tangible community in the usual sense of the word "community."

nations quickly imposed sanctions against Russia and its oligarchs, including Putin, taking back earlier established gains and benefits to Russia that require mutuality and reciprocity.

Apart from these many sanctions, which clearly affect how business can be done (or undone) between companies in "Western" nations and companies in Russia, there is a basic question of whether the invasion of Ukraine is a violation of international law. The Council of Foreign Relations publishes an excellent journal, Foreign Affairs, and their website has this informative article, free of charge:

https://www.cfr.org/article/how-russias-invasion-ukraine-violates-international-law

Later we will have the opportunity to discuss the "sanctions" imposed by the U.S., what authority a U.S. President has to impose those without Congressional approval, how the law provides for those, and the impacts of those sanctions on companies doing business with or in Russia. We will also examine Putin's threat to "nationalize" (take government control of) U.S. businesses that sought to leave Russia after the invasion, and how those companies responded.

II.   **SOURCES OF INTERNATIONAL LAW**

The International Court of Justice (ICJ) was formed in 1945 as the primary judicial arm of the United nations. It is the ultimate arbiter of international law disputes between nations—cases brought by nations against nations. It sits at The Hague, Netherlands, and bases its work on the statute of the international Court of Justice, which lists the following as traditional sources of international law.

A.   Treaties and Conventions

A treaty is an agreement between two or more nations to set rules for their interactions. In the US, a treaty has the same status as any legislation that is signed by the president and becomes law. If promises are made to be broken, then treaties are made to be broken but you might be surprised to find that many treaties have proven quite durable. Most common kind of treaty between two nations is a Treaty of friendship commerce and navigation (an "FCN treaty"). Such treaties usually provide for consular relations (embassies, diplomatic recognition, etc), commercial relations, and rights to enter by sea or air.

The U.S. State department maintains a list of all treaties in force:
https://www.state.gov/wp-content/uploads/2020/08/TIF-2020-Full-website-view.pdf

Also common are bilateral investment treaties (BITs), which establish the conditions for free trade and investment between two nations. A larger grouping of nations could create a multilateral treaty that But allow for a common market. Indeed that is how the European Union got started, with the European Coal and Steel community treaty in 1951.

https://en.wikipedia.org/wiki/European_Coal_and_Steel_Community

A convention is a multilateral treaty that is sponsored by an international organization (IO), but sometimes "international treaty" and "international convention" are used interchangeably.

See https://www.law.cornell.edu/wex/international_conventions

What is the legal effect of a treaty on a country's "domestic law"?

To use the lingo of international business la, it's customary to talk about "domestic law" or "municipal law" as the law of a sovereign state that has force and effect within that sovereign state's territorial boundaries. In other words, the domestic law of The United states is what you have studied in earlier law courses, so the question becomes how treaties are incorporated into the domestic law of this or any other country.

If a treaty is "self-executing" it is one that automatically creates rights that are enforceable in the courts of that country without further legislative action. A non-self-executing treaty or one without direct effect is one that requires some additional legislative act before it becomes enforceable in domestic law. In this chapter we will see the case of Sei Fujii v. California, in which a US court determined that the UN charter was not self-executing.

It's important to remember that any law can be repealed in whole or in part and any treaty can be abrogated in whole or in part. The usual rule in US courts is that statutes and are equal in force and effect. But a statute passed after a treaty is concluded could amend or revoke a prior treaty. Likewise, a Treaty concluded might effectively amend or modify a prior piece of legislation. In other words, the courts will give effect to the most recent statute or treaty, rending inoperative anything inconsistent in the prior treaties and statutes of U.S. domestic law. This is known as the last in time rule.

B.   Custom and "Customary International Law

There were a lot more multilateral treaties after WWII; before that, international law consisted primarily of bilateral treaties and customary practices. Custom has evolved through a long historical process by which state practices and recognition of the binding character of those practices have become normative rules. The rationale for custom is that it rests on the consent of sovereign or equal states. The creation of custom can be slow and its content uncertain, and it has been replaced to a large extent by multilateral treaties, but custom nonetheless continues to contribute significantly to international law.

Historically, examples of customary international law include rules for prosecuting the crimes of slavery, piracy, or genocide, rules for diplomatic immunity and the protection of ambassadors, rules for the inviolability of embassies, rules that protect civilians during war, or rules governing the seizure of private vessels during war time.

In recent years there has been increasing debate over whether customary international law is part of American law, and if so, which customs and norms are part of it and which are not. US judges, including the Supreme Court, generally accept customary international law as a part of American law, as long as there is no contradictory statute or treaty and where there is no other way to resolve the case other than by applying customary norms. The following well known decision of US Supreme Court from 1900 reflects this view.

Case 1-1

<u>The Paquette Habana</u>
175 U.S. 677 (1900)
U.S. Supreme Court

Facts. This appeal of a district court decree, which condemned two fishing vessels and their cargoes as prizes of war, was brought by the owners of two separate fishing vessels. Each of the vessel running in and out of Havana and sailing under the Spanish flag was a fishing smack which regularly engaged in fishing on the coast of Cuba. Inside the vessels were fresh fish which the crew had caught.

The owners of the vessels were not aware of the existence of a war until they were stopped by a U.S. patrol. No incriminating material like arms were found on the fishermen and they did not make any attempt to run the blockade after learning of its existence not did they resist their arrest. When the owners appealed, they argued that both customary international law and writings of leading international scholars recognized an exemption from seizure at wartime of coastal fishing vessels.

Issue. Are coastal fishing vessels with their cargoes and crews excluded from prizes of war?

Held. (Gray, J.). Yes. Coastal fishing vessels with their cargoes and crews are excluded from prizes of war. The doctrine that exempts coastal fishermen with their vessels and crews from capture as prizes of war has been known by the U.S. from the time of the War of Independence and has been recognized explicitly by the French and British governments. It is an established rule of international law that coastal fishing vessels with their equipment and supplies, cargoes and crews, unarmed and honestly pursuing their peaceful calling of catching and bringing in fish are exempt from capture as prizes of war. Reversed.

C.   <u>Jus Cogens</u>

When courts are required to decide international disputes, they frequently rely on the general principles of law that are common to the legal systems of the world. Indeed, although there are more than 200 states in the world today, there are, in practical terms, only two major legal systems: the Anglo-American common law system and the Romano-Germanic civil law system; and the two are remarkably similar in their basic procedures and substantive rules. It is this similarity that provides courts with the general principles they can use in deciding many problems that arise in international disputes.

The idea of international *jus cogens* as a body of higher law for the international community has achieved some currency in the late twentieth century. First embodied in the 1969 Vienna Convention on the Law of Treaties, it was confirmed in Article 53 of the 1986 Vienna Convention on the Law of Treaties (see the box on Article 53). In its judgment in the *Nicaragua Case*[4] in 1986, the ICJ affirmed *jus cogens* as an accepted doctrine in international law. The ICJ relied on the prohibition on the use of force as being 'a conspicuous example of a rule of international law having the character of *jus cogens*.

---

[4] https://h2o.law.harvard.edu/text_blocks/29108

The doctrine of international *jus cogens* was developed under the strong influence of natural law concepts. In contrast to positivists, who predicate international law on freedom of contract, naturalists (or cosmopolitans) believe that states cannot be absolutely free in their contractual relations but must respect certain fundamental principles deeply rooted in the international community.

At the 1969 Vienna Conference on the Law of Treaties, a number of states spoke of *jus cogens* having its origin in concepts of natural law.

Article 53
Treaties conflicting with a peremptory norm of general international law (*jus cogens*)

A treaty is void if, at the time of its conclusion, it conflicts with a peremptory norm of general international law. For the purposes of the present Convention, a peremptory norm of general international law is a norm accepted and recognized by the international community of States as a whole as a norm from which no derogation is permitted and which can be modified only by a subsequent norm of general international law having the same character.

The following video is required viewing, and explains natural law.

https://www.youtube.com/watch?v=r_UfYY7aWKo

In practice, though, "peremptory norms" can quickly be forgotten where a nation, or its leader, determines to violate those norms. If it ever came to a court case, however, the International Court of Justice could (and would) determine that the nation-state departing from peremptory norms would be on the wrong side of international law.

But the ICJ only hears cases when two nation-states agree that the ICJ should hear the case. In the case of Nicaragua v. U.S., for example, the U.S. refused to participate or obey the determination of the court. In other cases, however, two nation-states agree to hear a dispute, and the ICJ more or less acts as an arbitrator between the two States and his decision is complied with. In setting fishing boundaries between the U.S. and Canada, for example, both states have complied. See, for example, the following NY Times article if you have access:

https://www.nytimes.com/1984/10/13/world/world-court-settles-dispute-on-us-canada-boundary.html

In Chapter Two we will look at "universal jurisdiction" and "crimes against humanity," as there is now an international court to bring those who commit such crimes to justice. You are hearing a lot about "war crimes" right now, but, as you might expect, bringing war criminals" to a court with jurisdiction has its challenges.

III. INTERNATIONAL PERSONS

The personalities of international law are states and their subdivisions, international organizations, businesses, and individuals.

A.   <u>States</u>

States are political entities that have a territory, a population, a government capable of entering into international relations, and a government capable of controlling its territory and peoples.

Independent states are free from the political control of other states and free to enter into agreements with other international persons. Dependent states have formally surrendered some aspect of their political and governmental functions to another state. Some states that have achieved independence, and recognition by other states in the international community, may lose some control of substantial parts of its populace or parts of its territory. These are referred to as the inchoate states.

For a state to exist in the international community, it must be recognized by other states. Recognition comes about by a unilateral declaration, and it can be either explicit (express) or implicit (tacit). Once given, it implies that the recognized state or government is entitled to the rights and privileges granted by international law.

A state is recognized when an identifiable government, people, and territory first come into existence.

2022 Query: What countries have diplomatically recognized Donbask and Luhansk, the "breakaway Republics" in Ukraine? Could they be considered "nation-states" as of mid-2022? What would status as a nation-state in the international order require? Would they be eligible for admission to the United Nations?

Two theories serve as guidelines for when a government should be recognized. The <u>declaratory doctrine</u> holds that the legal existence of a government happens automatically by operation of law whenever a government is capable of controlling a territory and its people. The <u>constitutive doctrine</u> states that a government does not truly come into existence until such time as it is recognized by other states and participates in the international arena.

Territorial Sovereignty – Sovereignty is the right to exercise the functions of a state within a territory. This right, however, may not be absolute. Other states may obtain servitudes, either by treaty or practice, to a limited use of certain territory.

Negative Servitudes: Air and Water Pollution – Negative servitudes prevent one state from doing something within its territory that causes injury to a second state. Transboundary pollution can also involve water pollution. Under the Helsinki rules, only material damage can be the basis of a state's liability in a case wherein activity lawful *per se* brings about the pollution of the waters of an international river basin.

Case 1-2
The Trail Smelter Arbitration
(United States v. Canada)

American–Canadian International Joint Commission, Arbitral Tribunal, 1938 and 1941.

Facts: A Canadian lead and zinc smelter at Trail, British Columbia, was polluting the waters of the Columbia River that then ran into the state of Washington. After negotiations between the U.S. and Canada, the latter agreed to refer the matter to an International Joint Commission. The Commission's Arbitral Tribunal awarded the U.S. $350,000 in damages, but did not order the smelter to cease operations. In 1941, the U.S. sought to have the operation of the smelter enjoined.

Issue: Can Canada be enjoined from causing harm to a U.S. river?

Holding: Canada may be enjoined from polluting U.S. rivers.

Law: International law establishes that "A state owes at all times a duty to protect other states against injurious acts by individuals from within its jurisdiction." In a case decided by the Federal Court of Switzerland between two Swiss cantons, it enjoined the use of a shooting establishment that had endangered the territory of the other. It said: "This right (sovereignty) excludes ... not only the usurpation and exercise of sovereign rights (of another state) ... but also an actual encroachment which might prejudice the natural use of the territory and the free movement of its inhabitants." Cases decided by the U.S. Supreme Court (which may by analogy be applied in the international arena) have held that no state has the right to use or permit the use of its territory in such a manner as to cause injury by fumes in or to the territory of another or the properties or persons therein, when the consequences are serious and the injury is established by clear and convincing evidence.

Explanation: Canada is responsible in international law for the conduct of the Trail Smelter.

Order: Canada must undertake to stop the pollution caused by the smelter at Trail, British Columbia.

To have territorial sovereignty, a state must first acquire territory. This is done either by: (1) the occupation of land not claimed by another sovereign, (2) the voluntary transfer of territory from one sovereign to another, and (3) the conquest and continued occupation of the territory of another sovereign. Once territory is acquired, a state's title is affirmed either by the formal recognition of other states or by a process of estoppel. Estoppel arises when a state fails to speak up and object to another's exercise of sovereignty when it would be reasonable to do so.

Changes in Territorial Sovereignty: When there is a change in sovereignty over territory, several legal consequences arise. As to treaty rights and obligations, successor states must observe treaties that implement general rules of international law, and they are bound by dispositive treaties—that is, treaties concerned with rights over territory, such as boundaries and servitudes.

When a new state comes into being through decolonization, its obligation to observe the treaties made by its colonial parent state are determined by the Clean Slate Doctrine, which essentially allows a nation freed from colonial rule to start fresh; it need not be bound by agreements made by the colonized nation.

B.   International Organizations

Public or intergovernmental organizations (IGOs) are permanent organizations set up by two or more states to carry on activities of common interest. An IGO is created much in the fashion of a corporation. Its aims and objectives, internal structure, resources, and express powers are set out in a constituent instrument, or charter, which is drafted and adopted by the organization's member states.

For an IGO to have the legal capacity to deal with other international persons—including the capacity to carry on diplomatic relations with a state or to sue or be sued in an international or municipal court—it must be recognized. As for establishing the legal capacity of an IGO vis-à-vis its nonmember states, recognition is also required. In some states, an IGO is essentially seen as an agency of its members and recognition of the IGO will be implied if its member states are recognized. In other countries, recognition requires specific certification from the government.

The United Nations

The most important IGO is the United Nations. Its goals are the maintenance of peace and security in the world, the promotion of economic and social cooperation, and the protection of human rights. The organs of the United Nations are the General Assembly, the Security Council, the Secretariat, the International Court of Justice, the Trusteeship Council, and the Economic and Social Council.

The General Assembly is the main deliberative organ of the UN. Its function is to discuss and vote on any question or matter within the scope of the charter.

The Security Council is made up of representatives of 15 member states, 5 of which are permanent member states: China, Russia, the United States, England, and France. It is these countries that emerged from World War II as "victors" over the fascists (Italy), the Nazis (Germany, also fascist) and the militarism of Prime Minister Tojo in Japan. Decisions on procedural matters are made by an affirmative vote of at least 9 of the 15 members. Decisions on substantive matters require nine votes, including the concurring votes of all five permanent members. This is the rule of "great Power unanimity," often referred to as the "veto" power.

The Secretariat is the administrative arm of the United Nations, responsible for making reports and recommendations to the General Assembly and the Security Council.

The International Court of Justice is the United Nations' principal judicial body. More on the "ICJ" later on, but be aware that the ICJ only hears cases where the nations have agreed that it can, and that its decisions are essentially advisory; the UN does not enforce its judgments.

The Economic and Social Council, which comprises 54 member states elected by the General Assembly, is responsible for promoting economic, social, health, cultural, and educational progress as well as respect for human rights.

The United Nations System is the name given to various autonomous agencies concerned with a wide range of economic and social problems that have entered into agreements with the United Nations to become United Nations specialized agencies. The World Trade Organization (WTO) and the International Atomic Energy Agency (IAEA), although not specialized agencies, have entered into similar relationships with the United Nations.

A very large number of companies collaborate to some degree or another with the United Nations. The UN has sponsored a Global Compact for businesses to join in support of the Millennium Development Goals. We will be looking at the Global Compact and the Millennium Development Goals toward the end of this course, when we consider issues of corruption, public governance and sustainability.

The European Union

The European Union (EU), with 27 member states, covers a large part of the continent of Europe. The EU already has a population of over half a billion, the largest population in the world after China and India. The founding states created the EU in order to integrate their economies and political institutions.

[Optional wiki-read: https://en.wikipedia.org/wiki/Member_state_of_the_European_Union]

Supranational Powers: EU law within its scope of applicability is superior to the laws of the member states. This supremacy principle has two consequences: (1) the member states are required to bring their internal laws into compliance with EU law and (2) EU law is directly effective within the member states.

Import Restrictions. Before the E.U., nations could restrict imports for any number of reasons. Because I like beer, I have found the case of German beer purity a good example of how "union" worked to undo the German beer purity law of 1616. What follows is a brief description of that venerable old law and how it fit (or didn't) with the integration of the E.U.'s trade and commerce.

On April 23, 2016, breweries all over Germany and especially in Bavaria celebrated the 500 year anniversary of the enactment of the Bavarian *Reinheitsgebot* (beer purity law); a regulation that mandates which ingredients are allowed for the brewing of beer. The *Reinheitsgebot* is one of the oldest food regulations in the world that is still in effect and it has played a crucial role in establishing German beer's worldwide reputation for taste and quality. In part because of the rising popularity of craft brewing, this centuries-old law is still being discussed today.

In 1516, the Dukes of Bavaria, the brothers Wilhelm IV and Ludwig X, decreed a new general ordinance for all of Bavaria at a meeting of the Estates of Bavaria. The section of the ordinance titled "*Wie das Bier Sommer und Winter auf dem Land soll geschenkt und gebraut werden*" (How beer shall be served and brewed in summer and winter in the countryside) stipulated that only barley, hops, and water could be used to brew beer. This came to be known as the "Bavarian *Reinheitsgebot*". Yeast was not yet used for fermentation and therefore was not added to the list of allowed ingredients until 1906.

The rationale behind the enactment of the *Reinheitsgebot* is not quite clear. Different theories have been discussed, among them the effort to prevent competition for grains that were used for bread making in order to keep the price of food down, or the preservation of public health by making the brew less diluted.

After economic integration, the EU found that the 1616 law was an impermissible import restriction to brewers in other EU nations that wanted to sell beer in Germany.

"In 1984, the European Commission sued Germany in the European Court of Justice (CJEU) because of the application of the *Reinheitsgebot* to beers imported from other member states. The CJEU held in 1987 that the German law provisions prohibiting the import of beers that do not conform to the *Reinheitsgebot* constituted a barrier to the free movement of goods according to Article 30 of the Treaty on the Functioning of the European Union. Furthermore, the prohibition was not justified on grounds of the protection of public health under Article 36 TFEU due to a lack of proportionality."[5]

Here is a link to the treaty, with Article 30's provisions. It runs 344 pages.

https://eur-lex.europa.eu/legal-content/EN/TXT/PDF/?uri=CELEX:12012E/TXT&from=EN

The Institutions of the European Union – The main institutions of the EU are (1) the Council of the European Union and the European Council, (2) the European Parliament, and (3) the European Commission.

The Council of the European Union and the European Council

Council of the European Union: The Council of the European Union is the main decision-making body of the EU. Its role is to (1) adopt legislation in conjunction with the Parliament, (2) adopt an annual budget, also in conjunction with Parliament, (3) adopt international agreements, and (4) coordinate the economic policies of the member states.

European Council: The European Council consists of the heads of state of the member states, along with its own president and the president of the European Commission (nonvoting). The European Council focuses on establishing general policies and goals for the EU.

European Commission

The European Commission is the EU's executive branch, but also has some legislative functions. It drafts legislation for submission to the Council and the Parliament, and once the legislation is adopted it is responsible for its implementation. Commission decisions are made collegially, even though each commissioner is given responsibility for specific activities.

The European Parliament

At first only a deliberative body, the Parliament now has three main roles: (1) it has oversight authority over all EU institutions, (2) it shares legislative power with the Council of the EU, and (3) it determines the EU's annual budget in conjunction with the Council of the EU.

For certain kinds of legislation, Parliament only has a veto right: it may not amend or modify a commission proposal. This power, known as assent, applies to proposals for the accession of new members, to the adoption of certain international agreements, and to certain rules relating to the European Central Bank.

---

[5] Jenny Gesley, 500 Year Anniversary of the Bavarian Beer Purity Law of 1516 ("Reinheitsgebot"), Library of Congress,
April 21, 2016. Retrieved from https://blogs.loc.gov/law/2016/04/500-year-anniversary-of-the-bavarian-beer-purity-law-of-1516-reinheitsgebot/

European Court of Justice: Eight advocates-general assist the 27 judges of the Court of Justice in carrying out their duties. The Court will sit as a full court, in a Grand Chamber of 13 judges or in Chambers of three or five judges. The Court also sits in Grand Chamber when a member state or an institution that is a party to the proceedings so requests, and in particularly complex or important cases.

The full Court will sit in plenary sessions for contentious cases. It hears four kinds of contentious cases: (1) appeals from the Court of First Instance; (2) complaints brought by the commission or by one member state against another member state for failure of the latter to meet its obligations under EU law; (3) complaints brought by a member state against an EU institution or its servants for failing to act or for injuries they may have caused; and (4) actions brought by a member state, the council, the commission, or Parliament seeking the annulment of an EU legal measure.

European Economic and Social Committee: This consultative body is an institutionalized lobby. Its 222 members represent a wide range of special-interest groups, including employers, trade unions, consumers, farmers, and so on.

European Court of First Instance: It is the EU's trial court for cases brought by member states against the European Commission, cases seeking compensation for damage caused by the European Community institutions or their staff, cases relating to community trademarks, cases where individuals challenge legislation or actions taken by the EU institutions or challenge an institution's failure to act, and cases deciding employment disputes between EU institutions and their employees.

European Central Bank: The European Central Bank (ECB) is responsible for carrying out the EU's monetary policy. The ECB's decision-making bodies are a governing council and an executive board.

European Court of Auditors: It supervises the EU budget. The Court of Auditors has wide-ranging powers to examine the legality and regularity of EU receipts and expenditures and to ensure the sound financial management of the budget.

Other IGOs

General IGOs: Three prominent regional general IGOs are devoted to political cooperation, security, and the promotion of economic, social, and cultural development. Each limits membership to states from its region. The Council of Europe has stressed legal, social, and cultural matters; the Organization of American States (OAS) has emphasized issues of peace and security; and the newly established African Union (AU) is concentrating on political cooperation.

In addition to these three regional general IGOs, there are three nonregional general IGOs: the Commonwealth of Nations, the Arab League, and the Commonwealth of Independent States. Each of these organizations encourages cooperation among its members but, unlike the Council of Europe or the OAS, which perform many service functions, they are primarily forum organizations.

Specialized IGOs: There is a whole range of specialized IGOs that deal with a wide variety of issues of mutual interest to their members. Examples are the European Space Agency, the International Coffee Organization, the International Criminal Police Organization (INTERPOL), and the International Institute for the Unification of Private Law (UNIDROIT).

One important group of specialized IGOs promotes economic cooperation and development. Customs unions are intended to eliminate trade barriers between their members and to establish common external tariffs. Examples include the EU.

Free Trade Areas (FTAs) are set up to eliminate trade barriers between member states without establishing a common external tariff. Examples include the Association of Southeast Asian Nations Free Trade Area (ASEAN-FTA), the Central European Free Trade Area (CEFTA), the European Free Trade Association (EFTA), the Southern Cone Common Market (MERCOSUR), and the North American Free Trade Agreement (NAFTA).

The functions of an economic consultative association are to gather and exchange statistics and information, to coordinate the economic policies of member states, and to promote mutual trade cooperation. Examples are the Organization for Economic Cooperation and Development (OECD), the Colombo Plan for Cooperative Economic and Social Development in Asia and the Pacific (Colombo Plan), the Group of 77 (G-77), and the Organization of Petroleum Exporting Countries (OPEC).

Nongovernmental Organizations: Nonprofit nongovernmental organizations (NGOs) serve as coordinating agencies for private national groups in international affairs. Examples of nonprofit NGOs are the International Air Transport Association, the International Bar Association, Amnesty International, the International Committee of the Red Cross, Greenpeace, and Transparency International.

A multinational or transnational corporations (MNEs or TNCs, as they are sometime abbreviated) are clearly not governmental, but are sometimes called "for profit NGOs."

IV.   INTERNATIONAL LEGAL TRADITIONS

The study, analysis, and comparison of the different municipal law systems is known as comparative law. Comparative law scholars classify countries into legal families. The two most widely distributed legal families are the Romano-Germanic civil law and the Anglo-American common law. Another family that has become important internationally in recent years is the Islamic law. In addition, many legal systems are hybrids. Some legal practices are unique to a particular country.

The Romano-Germanic Civil Law System – The oldest and most influential legal family is the Romano-Germanic legal system, commonly called the civil law. The compilation and codification of all Roman law under the direction of the Byzantine Emperor Justinian was the most significant event in the historical development of the civil law. This code, known as the Corpus Juris Civilis, was compiled between 528 and 534 A.D. It was important because it preserved in written form the ancient legal system.

The medieval Roman Catholic Church also played an important role in preserving the ancient law. Canon law, the law used in the church's courts, was based on Roman law.

Students from throughout Europe who traveled to Italy to study returned to their own countries to establish the new profession of law. They set up new universities and found work both in the church and as advisors to princes and municipalities. Their common background led to the creation of a new civil law, one based on the Roman law, canon law, and the huge body of writings created by the glossators and commentators. This was called the *jus commune*, or the common law of Europe.

Lex mercatoria (the law merchant), was an international body of generally accepted commercial rules that transcended national boundaries, one that proved to be more influential than even the civil law.

In the sixteenth and seventeenth centuries, the new study of the *jus commune* was carried on by French Humanists and Dutch Naturalists. Along with the development of a theory of law, other events would eventually lead to the disappearance of the *jus commune* as the common law of Europe. The appearance of national states, with national literatures written in national languages, led to aspirations for systems of national law. In many of the states of continental Europe, legal nationalism found its embodiment in national codes.

Both the French Civil Code of 1804 and the German Civil Code of 1896 were models for most of the other contemporary civil codes. The French Civil Code is often referred to as the Code Napoléon, because of the extensive involvement of Napoléon Bonaparte (1769–1821) in its writing. It incorporated the principal ideas of the French Revolution, including the right to possess private property, the freedom to contract, and the autonomy of the patriarchal family.

Because the French Civil Code was written in a remarkably short period of time—at the insistence of Napoléon—its authors relied heavily on the *jus commune,* French royal ordinances, academic writings, and customary law. Unlike the German Civil Code, however, the style and form of the French Civil Code are straightforward, easy to read, and understandable to everyone—in many respects, it reminds one of the U.S. Constitution.

The authors of the French Civil Code realized that they could not foresee every possible legal eventuality, so they set out flexible general rules rather than detailed provisions.

The German Civil Code was enacted almost a century later, partly because Germany first had to take shape as a nation and partly because of the influence of a group of German scholars known as Pandectists.

The German Civil Code's organization and form are extremely precise and technical. Special terminology was devised. Legal concepts were defined and then used the same way throughout the entire code. Unlike the French Civil Code, the German Civil Code was meant for the use of trained experts.

In the twentieth century, changes in France and Germany—as well as in the other civil law countries—had profound effects on civil law. For one, there was a movement away from relying only on the civil code. Special legislation and judicial interpretations became more influential. There was also some revision of the codes themselves, especially in Germany.

The Anglo-American Common Law System – In 1066, the Normans conquered England and William the Conqueror began to centralize the governmental administration of his new kingdom. The name "common law" is derived from the theory that the king's courts represented the common custom of the realm, as opposed to the local customary law practiced in the county and manorial courts.

Development of the enduring principles of the common law was largely the product of three courts created by Henry II. The Court of Exchequer settled tax disputes; the Court of Common Pleas dealt with matters that did not involve a direct interest of the king, such as title to land, enforcement of promises, and payment of debts; and the Court of King's Bench handled cases of direct royal interest, such as the issuance of *writs* to control unruly public officials. Eventually, the jurisdiction of the King's Bench was used to control abuses of power by the king himself, establishing a fundamental doctrine of the common law: the supremacy of the law.

The common law is based on the customary practice of the courts. The common law must also be distinguished from the law that evolved out of equity and out of admiralty and from other specialized jurisdictions. The common law's basis in court decisions, or precedent, is also the principal factor distinguishing it from the Romano-Germanic civil law, where the grounds for deciding cases are found in codes, statutes, and prescribed texts.

In each of the principal nations in which the common law developed—Australia, Canada, India, Ireland, New Zealand, and the United States—there was a direct political linkage to England.

The Islamic Law System – The Islamic legal system is known as Shari'a. It is derived from the following sources, in the order of their importance: (1) the Koran, (2) the Sunna or traditional teachings and practices of the Prophet Muhammad (570–632 A.D.), (3) the writings of Islamic scholars who derived rules by analogy from the principles established in the Koran and the Sunna, and (4) the consensus of the legal community.

In the tenth century A.D., three centuries after the founding of Islam, the legal community decided that further improvement of the scholars' analysis of divine law was impossible. They decided at that time to "close the door of *ijtihad* (independent reasoning)," freezing the evolution of Islamic law. As a consequence, Shari'a judges and scholars may only apply the law as it was set down by the early writers. They may not change, modify, or extend that law.

The Shari'a is primarily a moral code, more concerned with ethics than with the promotion of commerce or international relations. Nonetheless, many principles of the Shari'a are not unlike the principles found in the civil law and the common law.

Newt Gingrich, former Speaker of the House in the 1990s, and pivotal politician for the "Contract with America" and the Clinton Impeachment, wants laws passed to prevent any U.S. judge from using Shari'a as a basis for any ruling. In 2010, he said "We should have a federal law that says under no circumstances in any jurisdiction in the United States will Sharia [law] be used in any court to apply to any judgment made about American law." In Oklahoma, in 2010, the voters approved such a measure. See: Andy Barr, Oklahoma Bans Sharia Law.

https://www.politico.com/story/2010/11/oklahoma-bans-sharia-law-044630

Current Query: Should your state pass a law like Oklahoma's? Do you believe that any judge — state or federal —would actually invoke Shari'a law as a basis for a ruling in a court case? Why do you think so, or think not?

Note to students: Gingrich (and many others) want "America to be America," not Europe or (worse) Islamic. Communism, for example, is usually considered "un-American," as it runs counter to "the free enterprise system." So, for that reason, and for the threat of the former USSR's nuclear arsenal, and the growing influence of communist thinking around the globe, the U.S. fought the "Cold War" with the Soviet Union to defeat communism. (Some politicians will try to paint "liberalism" and "socialism" as variants of communism, but this is deliberately misleading, as there are big differences.[6]) Clearly, pride in one's nation and its culture, even its ways of doing business, is natural. The notion of "nationhood" as a geographic territory with specific values is common to many societies, so it makes sense that people will argue over what the nation's values are. Related to "nationhood" is "nationalism," an important topic for consideration in international affairs and international law.

Nationalism can sometimes morph into an attitude of "my country, right or wrong," or even jingoism[7] and militarism, such as Hitler's embrace of a "greater destiny" for Germany, or Putin's embrace of a "greater destiny" for Russia. In fairness, we should note that in the U.S., "manifest destiny" was a slogan that somehow made it morally right displace the Native Indian population and restrict them to reservations; some estimates suggest that European settlement may have cut the Native American population by more than 70% between Columbus' discovery of "the New World" and the end of the 19th Century.[8]

We will briefly consider "nationalism" in the links below, still a major force in international relations, both trade relations and otherwise. "America First," resonates with "nationalism," and national pride (and perhaps arrogance as well) motivated Japan's Prime Minister Tojo's decision to make war on the United States. See https://www.history.com/topics/world-war-ii/tojo-hideki

All of this raises the question for "public international law" of what is a just war? When is it "just" to wage war on other nations or peoples? World War II is considered a classic case of a just war, owing to Hitler's aggression in Europe (and towards Russia), and Tojo's aggression toward the U.S. resulting in Pearl Harbor and the war in the Pacific during World War II. But armed conflicts in Vietnam, the invasion of Iraq, and the lengthy military engagement in Afghanistan are less clear-cut in terms of national security interests of the U.S.

V.   CASES AND MATERIALS

Cases:

On Comity: Ignacio Sequihua et al. v. Texaco, Inc. et al.

On Self-Executing Treaties: Sei Fujii v. California

Links:
Nationalism
Colonialism and Imperialism
Sovereignty
Self-determination
Separatist movements

---

[6] https://cole.house.gov/media-center/weekly-columns/socialism-un-american
[7] "Jingoism" is nationalism in the form of aggressive and proactive foreign policy, such as a country's advocacy for the use of threats or actual force, as opposed to peaceful relations, in efforts to safeguard what it perceives as its national interests. Jingoism can also be excessive bias in judging one's own country as superior to others – an extreme type of nationalism.
[8] National Geographic, Native Americans in Colonial America.
https://www.nationalgeographic.org/encyclopedia/native-americans-colonial-america/

IGNACIO SEQUIHUA, ct al., Plaintiffs, v. TEXACO, INC., et al., Defendants.

United States District Court for the Southern District of Texas, Houston Division

847 F. Supp. 61 (1994)

Background: Texaco began drilling for oil in the Ecuadorian Amazon rain forest in 1964. Later, a "consortium" was established whereby Petro Ecuador became a joint venture partner with Texaco, with Texaco responsible for the drilling operations. Texaco ceased its operations in 1992, and Petro Ecuador took over. Various lawsuits were filed in the United States by indigenous peoples from Ecuador and Peru in the 1990s, alleging serious negligence on the part of Texaco and other consortium members in their operations in the Oriente region of Ecuador's rainforest.

The Consortium's operations allegedly resulted in twenty-six million gallons of crude oil and toxic wastewater discharged into the surrounding environment. Some 2.5 million acres may have been impacted by oil-related discharges into wetlands, streams and rivers; discharges leeching into the soil and groundwater and combustion of crude oil and the flaring of natural gas allegedly caused both environmental and health harms. Allegations from various lawsuits filed in the 1990s claimed that the Consortium dug and operated hundreds of unlined pits, which were used to store toxic chemicals utilized in drilling operations as well as other runoff. The failure of Texaco and/or its partners with regard to "production water" and "formation water" were of particular concern. Additional sources of environmental contamination included the burning of crude oil, gas flaring, and spraying of roads with crude oil for maintenance and dust control.

The Sequihua case was the first to be filed against Texaco, which later was bought by Chevron. (Typically, a corporation will buy not only the assets, but any pending liabilities as well.) Chevron has spent nearly 30 years fighting off a very large judgment from an Ecuador court after the case below was dismissed on the grounds of "comity" and "forum non conveniens." Those interested in the long, tortured history of this case can watch the video on You Tube, "Chevron punished for Texaco oil pollution in Ecuador."

https://www.youtube.com/watch?v=5Uj6LqPRSDk

See also

https://www.theguardian.com/commentisfree/2020/sep/17/chevron-amazon-oil-toxic-waste-dump-ecuador-boycott

Opinion and Order, Judge Norman Black

Plaintiffs, residents of Ecuador and a community in that country, filed this action is state court asserting a variety of causes of action arising out of the alleged contamination of the air, ground and water in Ecuador. In addition to monetary relief, Plaintiffs seek an injunction requiring Defendants to return the land to its former condition and the imposition of a "trust fund" to be administered by the Court.

.

MOTION TO REMAND

Removal of this case from state court was based on both diversity and federal question jurisdiction. Plaintiffs moved to remand, asserting that this Court lacks jurisdiction. Defendants, in their response in opposition to the motion to remand, argue that the Court has federal question jurisdiction because the lawsuit "not only raises questions of international law, but threatens to create an international incident." In this regard, the Court notes that the Republic of Ecuador has officially protested this litigation, asserting that it will do "violence" to the international legal system, and has asked that the case be dismissed.

Plaintiffs in their complaint assert injuries that arose solely in Ecuador to as many as 500,000 Ecuadorans in an area that covers 1/3 of Ecuador. Plaintiffs complain about conduct which is regulated by the government in Ecuador, which is a country with its own environmental laws and regulations, a nation that owns the land at issue, and that treats all petroleum exploration and development as a "public utility" controlled by the government. Such matters affecting international law and the relationship between the United States and foreign governments give rise to federal question jurisdiction

Additionally, there are essential elements of Plaintiffs' claims which, if "well-pleaded", require the application and resolution of the federal common law regarding foreign relations. Plaintiffs' claims of nuisance and injunctive relief require them as part of their prima facie case to challenge the policies and regulations of Ecuador,

as well as the approvals from Ecuador that Defendants received, in order to show that the conduct was improper on land owned by Ecuador. Federal question jurisdiction clearly exists where, as here, the essential elements of Plaintiffs' prima facie case necessarily involve federal international relations, such as the international law relating to the control by a foreign country over its own resources.

Lastly, Plaintiffs' request for a trust fund asks this Court to step into the shoes of the Ecuadoran Health Ministry and supervise a medical monitoring scheme of unknown cost, scope or duration for as many as 500,000 Ecuadoran citizens over the protest of the government of Ecuador. It is incomprehensible that Plaintiffs could argue this does not fully and completely involve the relationship between the United States through this Court and the Republic of Ecuador.

Based upon the important foreign policy implications of this case, upon the international legal principle that each country has the right to control its own natural resources, and the strong opposition expressed by the Republic of Ecuador to this litigation, the Court finds without reservation that Plaintiffs' state law claims, if well-pleaded, raise issues of international relations which implicate federal common law. Consequently, this Court has federal question jurisdiction and the motion to remand must be denied.

MOTIONS TO DISMISS

Defendants have moved to dismiss on a number of grounds. On the basis of the comity of nations and the doctrine of *forum non conveniens,* the Court should not exercise its jurisdiction over this case and the motions to dismiss should be granted.

Comity of Nations

Under the doctrine known as comity of nations, a court should decline to exercise jurisdiction under certain circumstances in deference to the laws and interests of another foreign country.

. . .Consideration of these factors leads to the inescapable conclusion that the Court should decline to exercise jurisdiction over this case. The challenged activity and the alleged harm occurred entirely in Ecuador; Plaintiffs are all residents of Ecuador; Defendants are not residents of Texas; enforcement in Ecuador of any judgment issued by this Court is questionable at best; the challenged conduct is regulated by the Republic of Ecuador and exercise of jurisdiction by this Court would interfere with Ecuador's sovereign right to control its own environment and resources; and the Republic of Ecuador has expressed its strenuous objection to the exercise of jurisdiction by this Court. Indeed, none of the factors favor the exercise of jurisdiction. Accordingly, the case should be dismissed under the doctrine of comity of nations.

Forum Non Conveniens

Defendants have also moved to dismiss on the basis of *forum non conveniens,* asserting that the convenience of the parties and the Court and the interests of justice require that the case be tried in Ecuador. *See Piper Aircraft Co. v. Reyno, 454 U.S. 235, 70 L. Ed. 2d 419, 102 S. Ct. 252 (1981)*. A federal district court must apply federal law in deciding *forum non conveniens* issues. Movants bear the burden of proof as to all elements of a motion to dismiss based on *forum non conveniens.*

Initially, Defendants must show that an adequate and available forum exists. In this case, it is clear from the affidavits of two former Ecuadoran Supreme Court justices that an adequate forum is available in Ecuador. Plaintiffs are residents of Ecuador, and Defendants are alleged to have conducted business in that country. Ecuador provides private remedies for tortious conduct and maintains an independent judicial system with adequate procedural safeguards. Therefore, Ecuador is an adequate and available forum even though it may not provide the same benefits as the American system.

Having found that the courts in Ecuador provide an adequate and available forum, the Court must now consider the relevant private interest factors, including Plaintiffs' choice of forum. *Id.*

Obviously, Plaintiffs have chosen Texas as their forum. Their initial choice, however, was not the United States District Court, but was Harris County District Court from which the case was removed. Also, a foreign plaintiff's choice of an American forum is entitled to less deference than a plaintiff's selection of his home forum. *Piper Aircraft, 454 U.S. at 255-56*.

Other private interest factors weigh heavily in favor of the foreign forum. Access to all evidence and the availability of compulsory process would be present in Ecuador, not in the Southern District of Texas. The cost of obtaining the attendance of willing witnesses would be much greater in this district than in Ecuador. Either all witnesses would be required to travel here from outside the district, or all American attorneys would be required to travel to Ecuador at great expense. A view of the premises, likely in a pollution case such as this, would be possible only in Ecuador. As discussed previously, enforcement in Ecuador of a judgment by this Court is questionable. These factors weigh heavily in favor of the courts in Ecuador.

As noted above, Plaintiffs attempt to delay the Court's ruling on the motions to dismiss arguing that they need time for discovery on the *forum non conveniens* issues. The only discovery they mention, however, is whether the defense witnesses are in Ecuador or in the United States. It is undisputed that the Plaintiffs all reside in Ecuador, that their medical records are in Ecuador, and that the subject land, air and water are in Ecuador. There is no assertion that witnesses or documents may be located in the Southern District of Texas. Also, as noted above, Plaintiffs received an extension of time to respond to the motions, which have been pending for over a month. Plaintiffs' request to delay this case while it attempts to determine if any witnesses or documents are located anywhere in the United States is without merit.

Although the private considerations strongly favor dismissal, the Court will also address the public interest factors described in *In re Air Crash Disaster, 821 F.2d at 1162-63*. The administrative difficulties flowing from court congestion favors the foreign forum. Second, Ecuador clearly has a

18

local interest in having controversies regarding its air, land and water resolved at home. This, while otherwise readily apparent, is made more clear by the strong objection of the Republic of Ecuador to the exercise of jurisdiction by this Court. This district does not have any direct interest in this case, and its citizens should not bear the burden of jury service in litigation which has no relation to their community. Dismissal would also serve to avoid unnecessary parallel litigation in Ecuador and to avoid problems in conflicts of law or in the application of foreign law. These important public interests weigh so heavily in favor of the Ecuadoran forum that they require dismissal.

Based on its consideration of the interests described by the Fifth Circuit in *In re Air Crash Disaster* as discussed above, the Court finds without reservation that dismissal on the basis of *forum non conveniens* will "best serve the convenience of the parties and the ends of justice." Consequently, Defendants' motions to dismiss or, alternatively, for summary judgment must be granted. An appropriate final order consistent herewith shall be issued this day.

SIGNED this 26th day of January, 1994, at Houston, Texas.

NORMAN W. BLACK

CHIEF JUDGE

A note to students on "comity." The notion of international comity encompasses forms of conduct in relations between sovereign States which are based on courtesy, tradition, goodwill, or utility. Though not being legally binding, comity is enshrined in rules, albeit of tradition or usage, and not of international law. This is judicial, not legislative, and judicial decisions about "comity" are varied and sometimes inconsistent. In this case, the "strong objection" of Ecuador to the jurisdiction of the U.S. court was definitive — since the Ecuador courts were available to hear the dispute and Ecuador objected to US jurisdiction, the "comity" issue was an easy call for the court.

Case Comments and Questions:

1.   Plaintiffs filed this lawsuit in a Texas state court. The case was "removed" to a federal district court. Why would the defendant oil company prefer to be in federal court? Why would the plaintiff file in state court, rather than federal court? Do both courts have "subject matter jurisdiction" over this case?

Answer: Both courts have subject matter jurisdiction over the case. In the US federal system, states retain considerable powers and responsibilities. The US Constitution specifies that only federal courts can hear certain kinds of cases such as patent disputes, admiralty cases, and cases against the US government. (For a complete list, see the US Constitution, Article III.)

All other cases can be heard by state courts, but, if there is a "federal question" — meaning, a question that involves US federal law — defendants can request removal to the federal court. This is usually done for strategic reasons; attorneys for the defendant may be far more familiar with federal procedural laws, and put the plaintiff's attorneys at a disadvantage.

In a footnote, the court comments that, "Having found federal question jurisdiction, the Court need not address the arguments regarding diversity jurisdiction." Federal courts also have jurisdiction over cases that involve parties from different states, in the hopes of providing a more neutral forum that favors neither party. A Nebraska plaintiff suing a defendant from Maine in a tort case, for example, might put the non-resident at a disadvantage.

2.   Why would the government of Ecuador want the case tried in Ecuador? What did it tell the court?

3.   What if Texaco's oil drilling operations had damaged the natural environment in Texas, and injured residents of Texas? Plaintiffs would all be Texas residents, and Defendant would also be a "resident" of Texas. This is a non-criminal "tort" case: harm has been done, there is no contract between the parties, and one party wants compensation and more. If all this happened in Texas with Texas litigants, would there be a "federal question" in this case?

4.   What is "federal common law"?

Answer: Federal common law is applied primarily in admiralty and maritime cases, disputes between states, matters of international relations, and in cases regarding the proprietary interests of the U.S. Federal common law is used when federal statutory law does not completely address an issue or problem.

In Zschernig v. Miller (1968) the Supreme Court affirmed the supremacy of federal law in the area of foreign relations. Zschernig invalidated an Oregon statute that, as applied, prevented foreigners from inheriting if their home country did not recognize reciprocal inheritance rights for United States citizens. The Court declared that the statute was "an intrusion by the State into the field of foreign affairs,"" and that such an intrusion was inadmissible because "the statute as construed seems to make unavoidable judicial criticism of nations established on a more authoritarian basis than our own."" The statute as applied did, "indeed, illustrate the dangers which are involved if each State, speaking through its probate courts, is permitted to establish its own foreign policy."' Zschernig did not itself create federal common law; it did, however, recognize that state law "must bow to superior federal policy."'

State law needed to give way as long as the state law might "disturb foreign relations.' '0 6 In determining the content of those relations and the potential for state law to disturb them, the Court seems engaged in a form of federal common lawmaking. The most recent Restatement of Foreign Relations Law confirms the supremacy of federal common law (in the absence of a federal treaty or statute) in matters of foreign relations. Section 112 provides, in relevant part, that "[t]he determination and interpretation of international law present federal questions and their disposition by the United States Supreme Court is conclusive for other courts in the United States."' The comments to that section explain, "The conclusive authority of the United States Supreme Court to determine and interpret international law for all courts in United States derives from the character of that law as federal law."

SEI FUJII, Appellant, v. THE STATE OF CALIFORNIA, Respondent.

Supreme Court of California (1952)

Background:

Born in Yamaguchi Prefecture, Japan, in 1882, Sei Fujii was the eldest son in his family. In 1903, he immigrated to the United States to seek his future. He was an intelligent young man; his family recognized his potential and generously gave him money to pay for his passage.

Fujii graduated from USC Law School in 1911, but he was denied admission to the State Bar and a license to practice law because he was not, nor could he become, a naturalized US citizen.

After graduating, Fujii sought the assistance of a fellow USC law school graduate, J. Marion Wright (class of 1913), who could legally do what he himself could not do. Wright was the grandson of an immigrant and thus, sympathetic to the problems facing the Japanese on the West Coast. The two would partner together to serve the Japanese community for the next four decades. Fujii was determined to legally challenge the Alien Land Law, and he waited for a favorable opening in California's social and legal climates.

The Naturalization Act of 1870, a federal law, limited citizenship to "Free White Persons and Africans" thereby prohibiting persons of other ethnicities from becoming citizens. It was created specifically in response to anti-Chinese unrest. Under California's Alien Land Law, non-white and non-black persons were further denied the right "to acquire, possess, enjoy, use, cultivate, occupy, transfer, transmit and inherit real property, or any interests therein." This law and subsequent revisions were passed in response to anti-Japanese hysteria spurred by the economic success of Japanese truck farmers. (To partially circumvent the Alien Land Law, first-generation Japanese farmers—the Issei—put their properties in the names of their children, the Nisei, who were citizens by birth.)

Sei Fujii, the plaintiff here, is an "alien" (Japanese) who was not eligible for US citizenship. He appeals from a judgment that certain land purchased by him in 1948 had escheated to the state. (Escheat is a process that gives land to the State when there is no will and no heirs under the "intestacy" laws of a state; intestacy laws specify which family members have claims on an estate when there is no will, or when someone does "intestate.") There is no treaty between the U.S. and Japan that would give plaintiff the right to own land, and the sole question presented on this appeal is the validity of the California Alien Land Law.

OPINION

GIBSON, Chief Judge

United Nations Charter

It is first contended that the land law has been invalidated and superseded by the provisions of the United Nations Charter pledging the member nations to promote the observance of human rights and fundamental freedoms without distinction as to race. Plaintiff relies on statements in the preamble and in articles 1, 55 and 56 of the charter.

It is not disputed that the charter is a treaty, and our federal Constitution provides that treaties made under the authority of the United States are part of the supreme law of the land and that the judges in every state are bound thereby. (U.S. Const., art. VI)

A treaty, however, does not automatically supersede local laws that are inconsistent with it unless the treaty provisions are self-executing. In the words of Chief Justice Marshall: A treaty is "to be regarded in courts of justice as equivalent to an act of the Legislature, whenever it operates of itself, without the aid of any legislative provision. But when the terms of the stipulation import a contract—when either of the parties engages to perform a particular act, the treaty addresses itself to the political, not the judicial department; and the Legislature must execute the contract, before it can become a rule for the court." Foster v. Neilson (1829).

In determining whether a treaty is self-executing courts look to the intent of the signatory parties as manifested by the language of the instrument, and, if the instrument is uncertain, recourse may be had to the circumstances surrounding its execution.

In order for a treaty provision to be operative without the aid of implementing legislation and to have the force and effect of a statute, it must appear that the framers of the treaty intended to prescribe a rule that, standing alone, would be enforceable in the courts. (See Head Money Cases, Edye v. Robertson, 112 U.S. 580 (1884) and others.

It is clear that the provisions of the preamble and of article 1 of the charter which are claimed to be in conflict with the alien land law are not self-executing. They state general purposes and objectives of the United Nations Organization and do not purport to impose legal obligations on the individual member nations or to create rights in private persons.

It is equally clear that none of the other provisions relied on by plaintiff is self-executing. Article 55 declares that the United Nations "shall promote ... universal respect for, and observance of, human rights and fundamental freedoms for all without distinction as to race, sex, language, or religion," and in article 56, the member nations "pledge themselves to take joint and separate action in cooperation with the Organization for the achievement of the purposes set forth in Article 55." Although the member nations have obligated themselves to cooperate with the international organization in promoting respect for, and observance of, human rights, it is plain that it was contemplated that future legislative action by the several nations would be required to accomplish the declared objectives, and there is nothing to

indicate that these provisions were intended to become rules of law for the courts of this country upon the ratification of the charter.

The language used in articles 55 and 56 is not the type customarily employed in treaties which have been held to be self-executing and to create rights and duties in individuals. For example, the treaty involved in Clark v. Allen 331 U.S. 503 (1947), relating to the rights of a national of one country to inherit real property located in another country, specifically provided that "such national shall be allowed a term of three years in which to sell the property ... and withdraw the proceeds ..." free from any discriminatory taxation. In Nielsen v. Johnson, 279 U.S. 47, 50 [49 S. Ct. 223, 73 L. Ed. 607], the provision treated as being self-executing was equally definite. There each of the signatory parties agreed that "no higher or other duties, charges, or taxes of any kind, shall be levied" by one country on removal of property therefrom by citizens of the other country "than are or shall be payable in each State, upon the same, when removed by a citizen or subject of such state respectively." In other instances treaty provisions were enforced without implementing legislation where they prescribed in detail the rules governing rights and obligations of individuals or specifically provided that citizens of one nation shall have the same rights while in the other country as are enjoyed by that country's own citizens.

It is significant to note that when the framers of the charter intended to make certain provisions effective without the aid of implementing legislation they employed language which is clear and definite and manifests that intention. For example, article 104 provides: "The Organization shall enjoy in the territory of each of its Members such legal capacity as may be necessary for the exercise of its functions and the fulfillment of its purposes." Article 105 provides: "1. The Organization shall enjoy in the territory of each of its Members such privileges and immunities as are necessary for the fulfillment of its purposes. 2. Representatives of the Members of the United Nations and officials of the Organization shall similarly enjoy such privileges and immunities as are necessary for the independent exercise of their functions in connection with the Organization." In Curran v. City of New York, 77 N.Y.S.2d 206, 212, these articles were treated as being self-executory. (See, also, Balfour, Guthrie & Co. v. United States, 90 F. Supp. 831, 832.)

The provisions in the charter pledging cooperation in promoting observance of fundamental freedoms lack the mandatory quality and definiteness which would indicate an intent to create justiciable rights in private persons immediately upon ratification. Instead, they are framed as a promise of future action by the member nations. Secretary of State Stettinius, chairman of the United States delegation at the San Francisco Conference where the charter was drafted, stated in his report to President Truman that article 56 "pledges the various countries to cooperate with the organization by joint and separate action in the achievement of the economic and social objectives of the organization without infringing upon their right to order their national affairs according to their own best ability, in their own way, and in accordance with their own political and economic institutions and processes." (Report to the President on the Results of the San Francisco Conference by the Chairman of the United States Delegation, the Secretary of State, Department of State Publication 2349, Conference Series 71, p. 115; Hearings before the Committee on Foreign Relations, United States Senate [Revised] July 9-13, 1945, p. 106.) The same view was repeatedly expressed by delegates of other nations in the debates attending the drafting of article 56. (See U.N.C.I.O. Doc. 699, II/3/40, May 30, 1945, pp. 1-3; U.N.C.I.O. Doc. 684, II/3/38, May 29, 1945, p. 4; Kelsen, The Law of the United Nations [1950], footnote 9, pp. 100-102.)

The humane and enlightened objectives of the United Nations Charter are, of course, entitled to respectful consideration by the courts and legislatures of every member nation, since that document expresses the universal desire of thinking men for peace and for equality of rights and opportunities. The charter represents a moral commitment of foremost importance, and we must not permit the spirit of our pledge to be compromised or disparaged in either our domestic or foreign affairs.

We are satisfied, however, that the charter provisions relied on by plaintiff were not intended to supersede existing domestic legislation, and we cannot hold that they operate to invalidate the Alien Land Law.

Fourteenth Amendment of the Federal Constitution

The next question is whether the alien land law violates the due process and equal protection clauses of the Fourteenth Amendment [of the United States Constitution]....

...The California alien land law is obviously designed and administered as an instrument for effectuating racial discrimination, and the most searching examination discloses no circumstances justifying classification on that basis. There is nothing to indicate that those alien residents who are racially ineligible for citizenship possess characteristics which are dangerous to the legitimate interests of the state, or that they, as a class, might use the land for purposes injurious to public morals, safety or welfare. Accordingly, we hold that the alien land law is invalid as in violation of the Fourteenth Amendment.

[The judgment of the intermediate appellate court was reversed in part and affirmed in part. Although the United Nations Charter established no rights that applied directly to the plaintiff, the due process and equal protection clauses of the Fourteenth Amendment of the U.S. Constitution forbade racial discrimination of the kind contained in the California alien land law.]

Case Questions:

1. What if Texas enacted legislation that made it illegal for Muslims to own land in Texas, and the legislation provided that all lands owned by Muslims would be claimed by the State of Texas. What are the constitutional arguments against such a law?

2. The Court said, "The provisions in the charter pledging cooperation in promoting observance of fundamental freedoms lack the mandatory quality and definiteness which would indicate an intent to create justiciable rights in private persons immediately upon ratification." (a) For you, what freedoms would be "fundamental"? (b) Is a "right" to own property fundamental, or are there more fundamental rights? (c) What does "justiciable" mean in the sentence above?

3. Who is protected by the 14th Amendment? Only citizens, or are "aliens" protected, too?

4. Research question #1: In general — What rights do U.S. citizens have that "aliens" do not?

5. Research question #2: Why did people in California, and their politicians, dislike Japanese people so much that they passed the law early in the 20th Century — even before the Japanese declared war on the U.S. — that forbade land ownership by Asians?

Those who have studied ethics in general, or "business ethics" in particular, know that all of us (individuals, corporations, and nations) have a built-in bias toward our own interests; the behavioral psychologists call this the "self-serving bias." "Nationalism" means that we protect what is ours, but, in the case of World War II and Japanese bombardment of Pearl Harbor on Dec. 7, 1941, the "pride" of (or wish for) national supremacy led Japan into a war that it lost. For centuries, "sovereigns" have been waging war, or using force, to take lands owned or inhabited by others. (The U.S. is no exception here, considering the genocide against Native Americans.) Each nation seeks to extend its "sphere of influence," even though the principle of "self-determination" (see below) is central to the rule of international law. The opposition of NATO allies to Russian "incursions" into the Ukraine is based on the concepts of sovereignty and self-determination for the Ukrainian people. Vladimir Putin's nationalism seeks to extend Russia's land ownership and influence beyond its current borders, and justifies its current actions based on historical "ownership" of Ukraine.

A. Nationalism

https://www.britannica.com/topic/nationalism

Read through the first few entries, up to the photo of Charles DeGaulle.

B. Colonialism and Imperialism

https://www.youtube.com/watch?v=x1ROXlmpDI0

C. Sovereignty

From the Stanford Encyclopedia of Philosophy:

https://plato.stanford.edu/entries/sovereignty/

D.   Self-determination

https://unpo.org/article/4957

https://www.youtube.com/watch?v=_0sjrdR4EWE

E.   Separatist Movements

SIGNIFICANT SEPARATIST MOVEMENTS

CHAPTER TWO:

JURISDICTION AND DISPUTE SETTLEMENT

I. INTRODUCTION

These materials assume that you have had some background in basic US "domestic" law. That includes basic civil procedure, like the important questions around which courts have subject matter jurisdiction and personal jurisdiction over the case and over the parties to the lawsuit. Without the power to hear and decide a case (i.e., subject matter jurisdiction), any case will be dismissed, no matter how meritorious. And, unless there is at least one defendant over whom the court can constitutionally claim personal jurisdiction, any case will be dismissed in its entirety. But you can always file a new complaint in a court that does have subject matter jurisdiction and personal jurisdiction over at least one defendant — as long as the statute of limitations has not "run" (meaning thatthe legislated time period to file has ended).

This chapter can be summed up simply: if you're in business internationally, you have to look carefully at each potential contract you or your firm makes so that you know where any dispute will be resolved — that might be a court somewhere, but where? And, it might be an arbitrator or arbitral panel. This chapter will make you aware of all the possibilities, but will also give you some expertise in managing business to business or business to consumer relations so that you will have the "venue" (the court or arbitration tribunal) that you would prefer if things get messy.

First, here are some key basics to review, on subject matter jurisdiction and personal jurisdiction. They are not the same!

When all of the parties to a lawsuit are located in the same state within the U.S., and the lawsuit is about questions of state law, subject matter jurisdiction and personal jurisdiction are seldom contested by the plaintiff or defendant. But a lot of litigation in U.S. courts involves individuals and firms from different states, and that often brings up the basic question of whether it is fair to make a defendant in one state come to a court in another U.S. state. See, for example, Carnival Cruise versus Shute in this chapter. In that case, a man and wife from Washington State wanted to sue Carnival Cruise lines, whose principal place of business was in Florida. U.S. courts have long had to decide whether it is "fair" to make defendants travel from their usual location to a distant (or even nearby state). That becomes a question of whether the court has "personal jurisdiction" over the defendant. In a global context, the personal jurisdiction issue comes up all the time: we will see plaintiffs from one nation suing defendants from another nation, and personal jurisdiction will almost always be an issue — unless the parties have agreed at the time of contracting on a suitable forum to resolve their disputes.

Subject matter jurisdiction is often a major issue in U.S. lawsuits, because we have two court systems: state and federal. Sometimes a lawsuit is appropriate for either court system but sometimes it must exclusively be heard in federal courts. (This was true in Carnival Cruise versus Shute, for example; only federal courts are empowered to hear "admiralty" cases.) In lawsuits between parties from different nations, however, the issue of subject matter jurisdiction is less common: you could sue a Netherlands corporation in either Colorado state court or federal court, and the judge would have subject matter jurisdiction. In international business disputes, the most likely questions about subject matter jurisdiction will deciding whether the the national court system chosen by plaintiff keeps the case or dismisses it to a forum contractually selected by plaintiff and defendant before the dispute came to be.

Suppose your lawsuit relates the contract between you and your supplier, and includes an agreement to arbitrate disputes that might arise later from the business relationship; that clause will mean that judges have no subject matter jurisdiction; the arbitrator we'll hear and decide the case and make a final and binding award, which the courts will ordinarily enforce.

II. PERMISSIBLE BASES FOR NATIONS TO ASSERT PERSONAL JURISDICTION OVER FOREIGN PARTIES

Under customary international law, nations with well-developed legal systems will generally enforce a judgment from another nation's judiciary, provided that nation follows customary practice by only asserting personal jurisdiction over the citizens/nationals of another nation where one of the following categories applies.

Territorial jurisdiction: Do something that creates a cause of action in a foreign country, and that country's laws (and judicial system) has jurisdiction over you. For example, if you went to Italy on vacation and committed a crime or a tort, under customary international law Italy would have every right and reason to assert jurisdiction over you. If you were back in the U.S. when the lawsuit was filed, you could be served with process here and the court case in Italy would proceed with you or without you. A default judgment would occur if you did not participate in the court case.

But suppose you did go to Italy, contested the case, and lost; then, a judgment from Italy would be recognized in US courts as being fair, since you did the acts complained of in Italy, and, since you showed up for the trial, you basically consented to Italy's jurisdiction. (You will notice in the Bremen case how Unterweser's attorneys worked very hard not to say that the firm's participation in preliminary federal court hearings in Tampa was a consent to jurisdiction of the court.)

Nationality jurisdiction: if you and your friend go to Italy on vacation and s/he commits a crime or you are injured by a "tort" s/he commits — let's say s/he drives negligently and as a passenger, you are seriously injured — then US courts would have acceptable jurisdiction under international law because the two of you are both U S citizens/ nationals. The case could be heard in US courts. (You could bring a lawsuit in Italy, but why? If there was evidence there that could only be accessed by having a trial there, it might make sense, but modern technologies have lessened the need for that kind of proximity.)

Objective territoriality (or protective jurisdiction — these two phrases mean essentially the same thing.) Suppose an Italian business person or firm defrauds you and or a U.S. company using the internet or the telephone, and you suffer financial losses here, international law would recognize the fairness of your bringing a legal action in the United States, since the Italian person or firm had directly dealt with you as a U.S. citizen. The fact they are there and you are here does not insulate them from a lawsuit. If they don't show up here in the US, the question becomes whether the default judgment obtained in a U.S. court is enforceable in Italy. Provided that it is clear that the Italian person or firm clearly aimed to "do business" in the US, then the judgment would ordinarily be upheld by a court in Italy. We examine this issue further in Koster v. Automark, below.

International law also has the curious phenomenon of what is known as universal jurisdiction for certain criminal acts; that is, some acts are so contrary to the norms of civilized behavior that any nation's legal system can here and decide such a case.

Please read the material at this website:

https://ijrcenter.org/cases-before-national-courts/domestic-exercise-of-universal-jurisdiction/

You will also want to view this short video — What is Universal Jurisdiction?

https://www.youtube.com/watch?v=x3Q6zw8LnDU

"War crimes," much in the news in 2022 after Putin's invasion of Ukraine, are supposed to be crimes against humanity, invoking universal jurisdiction. But bringing war criminals to justice is easier said than done.

III.   LEGAL SETTLEMENT OF INTERNATIONAL DISPUTES

The case of Scherk v. Alberto Culver Co. shows us how the U.S. Supreme Court is willing to let parties arbitrate important issues of public concern, rather than go through a lengthy court battle. This case will require several re-readings for you to really understand what's going on. It is also one of those 5 to 4 decisions where the Court is almost evenly split as to how the law should apply to the facts in the case.

Scherk v. Alberto Culver Co.
417 U.S. 506 (1974)

MR. JUSTICE STEWART delivered the opinion of the Court.

Alberto-Culver Co., the respondent, is an American company incorporated in Delaware with its principal office in Illinois. It manufactures and distributes toiletries and hair products in this country and abroad. During the 1960's Alberto-Culver decided to expand its overseas operations, and as part of this program it approached the petitioner Fritz Scherk, a German citizen residing at the time of trial in Switzerland. Scherk was the owner of three interrelated business entities, organized under the laws of Germany and Liechtenstein, that were engaged in the manufacture of toiletries and the licensing of trademarks for such toiletries. An initial contact with Scherk was made by a representative of Alberto-Culver in Germany in June, 1967, and

negotiations followed at further meetings in both Europe and the United States during 1967 and 1968. In February 1969 a contract was signed in Vienna, Austria, which provided for the transfer of the ownership of Scherk's enterprises to Alberto-Culver, along with all rights held by these enterprises to trademarks in cosmetic goods. The contract contained a number of express warranties whereby Scherk guaranteed the sole and unencumbered ownership of these trademarks. In addition, the contract contained an arbitration clause providing that "any controversy or claim [that] shall arise out of this agreement or the breach thereof" would be referred to arbitration before the International Chamber of Commerce in Paris, France, and that "the laws of the State of

Illinois, U. S. A. shall apply to and govern this agreement, its interpretation and performance." [1]

The closing of the transaction took place in Geneva, Switzerland, in June 1969. Nearly one year later Alberto-Culver allegedly discovered that the trademark rights purchased under the contract were subject to substantial encumbrances that threatened to give others superior rights to the trademarks and to restrict or preclude Alberto-Culver's use of them. Alberto-Culver thereupon tendered back to Scherk the property that had been transferred to it and offered to rescind the contract. Upon Scherk's refusal, Alberto-Culver commenced this action for damages and other relief in a Federal District Court in Illinois, contending that Scherk's fraudulent representations concerning the status of the trademark rights constituted violations of § 10 (b) of the Securities Exchange Act of 1934, 48 Stat. 891, 15 U.S.C. §78j(b) and Rule 10b-5, promulgated thereunder, 17 CFR §140.10b-5.

In response, Scherk filed a motion to dismiss the action for want of personal and subject-matter jurisdiction as well as on the basis of *forum non conveniens*, or, alternatively, to stay the action pending arbitration in Paris pursuant to the agreement of the parties. Alberto-Culver, in turn, opposed this motion and sought a preliminary injunction restraining the prosecution of arbitration proceedings. [2] On December 2, 1971, the District Court denied Scherk's motion to dismiss, and, on January 14, 1972, it granted a preliminary order enjoining Scherk from proceeding with arbitration. In taking these actions the court relied entirely on this Court's decision in Wilko v. Swan, 346 U.S. 427, which held that an agreement to arbitrate could not preclude a buyer of a security from seeking a judicial remedy under the Securities Act of 1933, in view of the language of § 14 of that Act, barring "any condition, stipulation, or provision binding any person acquiring any security to waive compliance with any provision of this subchapter . . . ." 48 Stat. 84, 15 U.S.C. §77n. The Court of Appeals for the Seventh Circuit, with one judge dissenting, affirmed, upon what it considered the controlling authority of the *Wilko* decision. Because of the importance of the question presented we granted Scherk's petition for a writ of certiorari.

_____

[1] The arbitration clause relating to the transfer of one of Scherk's business entities, similar to the clauses covering the other two, reads in its entirety as follows:
"The parties agree that if any controversy or claim shall arise out of this agreement or the breach thereof and either party shall request that the matter shall be settled by arbitration, the matter shall be settled exclusively by arbitration in accordance with the rules then obtaining of the International Chamber of Commerce, Paris, France, by a single arbitrator, if the parties shall agree upon one, or by one arbitrator appointed by each party and a third arbitrator appointed by the other arbitrators. In case of any failure of a party to make an appointment referred to above within four weeks after notice of the controversy, such appointment shall be made by said Chamber. All arbitration proceedings shall be held in Paris, France, and each party agrees to comply in all respects with any award made in any such proceeding and to the entry of a judgment in any jurisdiction upon any award rendered in such proceeding. The laws of the State of Illinois, U. S. A. shall apply to and govern this agreement, its interpretation and performance."
[2] Scherk had taken steps to initiate arbitration in Paris in early 1971. He did not, however, file a formal request for arbitration with the International Chamber of Commerce until November 9, 1971, almost five months after the filing of Alberto-Culver's complaint in the Illinois federal court.

I.

The United States Arbitration Act, now 9 U.S.C. § 1 et seq., reversing centuries of judicial hostility to arbitration agreements, [4] was designed to allow parties to avoid "the costliness and delays of litigation," and to place arbitration agreements "upon the same footing as other contracts . . . ." H. R. Rep. No. 96, 68th Cong., 1st Sess., 1, 2 (1924); see also S. Rep. No. 536, 68th Cong., 1st Sess. (1924). Accordingly, the Act provides that an arbitration agreement such as is here involved "shall be valid, irrevocable, and enforceable, save upon such grounds as exist at law or in equity for the revocation of any contract." 9 U.S.C. § 2.[5] The Act also provides in § 3 for a stay of proceedings in a case where a court is satisfied that the issue before it is arbitrable under the agreement, and § 4 of the Act directs a federal court to order parties to proceed to arbitration if there has been a "failure, neglect, or refusal" of any party to honor an agreement to arbitrate.

In Wilko v. Swan, this Court acknowledged that the Act reflects a legislative recognition of the "desirability of arbitration as an alternative to the complications of litigation," but nonetheless declined to apply the Act's provisions. That case involved an agreement between Anthony Wilko and Hayden, Stone & Co., a large brokerage firm, under which Wilko agreed to purchase on margin a number of shares of a corporation's common stock. Wilko alleged that his purchase of the stock was induced by false representations on the part of the defendant concerning the value of the shares, and he brought suit for damages under § 12 (2) of the Securities Act of 1933, 15 U.S.C. § 77l. The defendant responded that Wilko had agreed to submit all controversies arising out of the purchase to arbitration, and that this agreement, contained in a written margin contract between the parties, should be given full effect under the Arbitration Act.

. . . Alberto-Culver's contract to purchase the business entities belonging to Scherk was a truly international agreement. Alberto-Culver is an American corporation with its principal place of business and the vast bulk of its activity in this country, while Scherk is a citizen of Germany whose companies were organized under the laws of Germany and Liechtenstein. The negotiations leading to the signing of the contract in Austria and to the closing in Switzerland took place in the United States, England, and Germany, and involved consultations with legal and trademark experts from each of those countries and from Liechtenstein. Finally, and most significantly, the subject matter of the contract concerned the sale of business enterprises organized under the laws of and primarily situated in European countries, whose activities were largely, if not entirely, directed to European markets.

Such a contract involves considerations and policies significantly different from those found controlling in *Wilko*. In *Wilko*, quite apart from the arbitration provision, there was no question but that the laws of the United States generally, and the federal securities laws in particular, would govern disputes arising out of the stock-purchase agreement. The parties, the negotiations, and the subject matter of the contract were all situated in this country, and no credible claim could have been entertained that any international conflict-of-laws problems would arise. In this case, by contrast, in the absence of the arbitration

---

[4] English courts traditionally considered irrevocable arbitration agreements as "ousting" the courts of jurisdiction, and refused to enforce such agreements for this reason. This view was adopted by American courts as part of the common law up to the time of the adoption of the Arbitration Act. See H. R. Rep. No. 96, 68th Cong., 1st Sess., 1, 2 (1924); Sturges & Murphy, Some Confusing Matters Relating to Arbitration under the United States Arbitration Act, 17 Law & Contemp. Prob. 580.

[5] Section 2 of the Arbitration Act renders "valid, irrevocable, and enforceable" written arbitration provisions "in any maritime transaction or a contract evidencing a transaction involving commerce . . . ," as those terms are defined in. § 1. In Bernhardt v. Polygraphic Co. 350 U.S. 198 (1956) this Court held that the stay provisions of § 3 apply only to the two kinds of contracts specified in § 1 and § 2. Since the transaction in this case constituted "commerce . . . with foreign nations," the Act clearly covers this agreement.

provision considerable uncertainty existed at the time of the agreement, and still exists, concerning the law applicable to the resolution of disputes arising out of the contract.

Such uncertainty will almost inevitably exist with respect to any contract touching two or more countries, each with its own substantive laws and conflict-of-laws rules. A contractual provision specifying in advance the forum in which disputes shall be litigated and the law to be applied is, therefore, an almost indispensable precondition to achievement of the orderliness and predictability essential to any international business transaction. Furthermore, such a provision obviates the danger that a dispute under the agreement might be submitted to a forum hostile to the interests of one of the parties or unfamiliar with the problem area involved.

A parochial refusal by the courts of one country to enforce an international arbitration agreement would not only frustrate these purposes, but would invite unseemly and mutually destructive jockeying by the parties to secure tactical litigation advantages. In the present case, for example, it is not inconceivable that if Scherk had anticipated that Alberto-Culver would be able in this country to enjoin resort to arbitration he might have sought an order in France or some other country enjoining Alberto-Culver from proceeding with its litigation in the United States. Whatever recognition the courts of this country might ultimately have granted to the order of the foreign court, the dicey atmosphere of such a legal no-man's-land would surely damage the fabric of international commerce and trade, and imperil the willingness and ability of businessmen to enter into international commercial agreements.

The exception to the clear provisions of the Arbitration Act carved out by *Wilko* is simply inapposite to a case such as the one before us. In *Wilko* the Court reasoned that "when the security buyer, prior to any violation of the Securities Act, waives his right to sue in courts, he gives up more than would a participant in other business transactions. The security buyer has a wider choice of courts and venue. He thus surrenders one of the advantages the Act gives him . . . ." In the context of an international contract, however,

these advantages become chimerical since, as indicated above, an opposing party may by speedy resort to a foreign court block or hinder access to the American court of the purchaser's choice.

Two Terms ago in The Bremen v. Zapata Off-Shore Co., 407 U.S. 1, rejected the doctrine that a forum-selection clause of a contract, although voluntarily adopted by the parties, will not be respected in a suit brought in the United States "'unless the selected state would provide a more convenient forum than the state in which suit is brought.'" Rather, we concluded that a "forum clause should control absent a strong showing that it should be set aside." We noted that "much uncertainty and possibly great inconvenience to both parties could arise if a suit could be maintained in any jurisdiction in which an accident might occur or if jurisdiction were left to any place [where personal or *in rem* jurisdiction might be established]. The elimination of all such uncertainties by agreeing in advance on a forum acceptable to both parties is an indispensable element in international trade, commerce, and contracting."

An agreement to arbitrate before a specified tribunal is, in effect, a specialized kind of forum-selection clause that posits not only the situs of suit but also the procedure to be used in resolving the dispute. The invalidation of such an agreement in the case before us would not only allow the respondent to repudiate its solemn promise but would, as well, reflect a "parochial concept that all disputes must be resolved under our laws and in our courts. . . . We cannot have trade and commerce in world markets and international waters exclusively on our terms, governed by our laws, and resolved in our courts." (Citing *Bremen v. Zapata.*)

For all these reasons we hold that the agreement of the parties in this case to arbitrate any dispute arising out of their international commercial transaction is to be respected and enforced by the federal courts in accord with the explicit provisions of the Arbitration Act. [15]

Accordingly, the judgment of the Court of Appeals is reversed and the case is remanded to that court with directions to remand to the District Court for further proceedings consistent with this opinion.

It is so ordered.

<u>Note to Students</u>: *Scherk was a 5 – 4 decision. The Dissent has a lot to say. By in large, the Supreme Court has consistently favored arbitration of international business disputes.*

MR. JUSTICE DOUGLAS, with whom MR. JUSTICE BRENNAN, MR. JUSTICE WHITE, and MR. JUSTICE MARSHALL concur, dissenting.

Respondent (Alberto-Culver) is a publicly held corporation whose stock is traded on the New York Stock Exchange and is a Delaware corporation with its principal place of business in Illinois. Petitioner (Scherk) owned a business in Germany, Firma Ludwig Scherk, dealing with cosmetics and toiletries. Scherk owned various trademarks and all outstanding securities of a Liechtenstein corporation (SEV) and of a German corporation, Lodeva. Scherk also owned various trademarks which were licensed to manufacturers and distributors in Europe and in this country. SEV collected the royalties on those licenses.

Alberto-Culver undertook to purchase from Scherk the entire establishment - the trademarks and the stock of the two corporations; and later, alleging it had been defrauded, brought this suit in the United States District Court in Illinois to

---

[15] Our conclusion today is confirmed by international developments and domestic legislation in the area of commercial arbitration subsequent to the *Wilko* decision. On June 10, 1958, a special conference of the United Nations Economic and Social Council adopted the Convention on the Recognition and Enforcement of Foreign Arbitral Awards. In 1970 the United States acceded to the treaty, [1970] 21 U. S. T. (pt. 3) 2517, T. I. A. S. No. 6997, and Congress passed Chapter 2 of the United States Arbitration Act, 9 U.S.C. §201 *et seq.* in order to implement the Convention. Section 1 of the new chapter, 9 U.S.C. §201, provides unequivocally that the Convention "shall be enforced in United States courts in accordance with this chapter."

The goal of the Convention, and the principal purpose underlying American adoption and implementation of it, was to encourage the recognition and enforcement of commercial arbitration agreements in international contracts and to unify the standards by which agreements to arbitrate are observed and arbitral awards are enforced in the signatory countries. . . . .Article II (1) of the Convention provides:

"Each Contracting State shall recognize an agreement in writing under which the parties undertake to submit to arbitration all or any differences which have arisen or which may arise between them in respect of a defined legal relationship, whether contractual or not, concerning a subject matter capable of settlement by arbitration."

In their discussion of this Article, the delegates to the Convention voiced frequent concern that courts of signatory countries in which an agreement to arbitrate is sought to be enforced should not be permitted to decline enforcement of such agreements on the basis of parochial views of their desirability or in a manner that would diminish the mutually binding nature of the agreements. See G. Haight, Convention on the Recognition and Enforcement of Foreign Arbitral Awards: Summary Analysis of Record of United Nations Conference, May/June 1958, pp. 24-28 (1958).

Without reaching the issue of whether the Convention, apart from the considerations expressed in this opinion, would require of its own force that the agreement to arbitrate be enforced in the present case, we think that this country's adoption and ratification of the Convention and the passage of Chapter 2 of the United States Arbitration Act provide strongly persuasive evidence of congressional policy consistent with the decision we reach today.

rescind the agreement and to obtain damages. [417 U.S. 506, 522]

The only defense material at this stage of the proceeding is a provision of the contract providing that if any controversy or claim arises under the agreement the parties agree it will be settled "exclusively" by arbitration under the rules of the International Chamber of Commerce, Paris, France.

The basic dispute between the parties concerned allegations that the trademarks which were basic assets in the transaction were encumbered and that their purchase was induced through serious instances of fraudulent representations and omissions by Scherk and his agents within the jurisdiction of the United States. If a question of trademarks were the only one involved, the principle of The Bremen v. Zapata Off-Shore Co., would be controlling.

We have here, however, questions under the Securities Exchange Act of 1934, which in 3 (a) (10) defines "security" as including any "note, stock, treasury stock, bond, debenture, certificate of interest or participation in any profit-sharing agreement . . . ." 15 U.S.C. 78c (a) (10). We held in Tcherepnin v. Knight, 389 U.S. 332, as respects 3 (a) (10):

> "[R]emedial legislation should be construed broadly to effectuate its purposes. The Securities Exchange Act quite clearly falls into the category of remedial legislation. One of its central purposes is to protect investors through the requirement of full disclosure by issuers of securities, and the definition of security in 3 (a) (10) necessarily determines the classes of investments and investors which will receive the Act's protections. Finally, we are reminded that, in searching for the meaning and scope of the word `security' in the Act, form should be disregarded for substance and the emphasis should be on economic reality." Id., at 336. (Footnote omitted.)

Section 10 (b) of the 1934 Act makes it unlawful for any person by use of agencies of interstate commerce or the mails "[t]o use or employ, in connection with the purchase or sale of any security," whether or not registered on a national securities exchange, "any manipulative or deceptive device or contrivance in contravention of such rules and regulations as the Commission may prescribe." 15 U.S.C. 78j (b).

Alberto-Culver, as noted, is not a private person but a corporation with publicly held stock listed on the New York Stock Exchange. If it is to be believed, if in other words the allegations made are proved, the American company has been defrauded by the issuance of "securities" (promissory notes) for assets which are worthless or of a much lower value than represented. Rule 10b-5 of the Securities and Exchange Commission states:

> "It shall be unlawful for any person, directly or indirectly, by the use of any means or instrumentality of interstate commerce, or of the mails or of any facility of any national securities exchange,
> "(a) To employ any device, scheme, or artifice to defraud,
> "(b) To make any untrue statement of a material fact or to omit to state a material fact necessary in order to make the statements made, in the light of the circumstances under which they were made, not misleading, or
> "(c) To engage in any act, practice, or course of business which operates or would operate as a fraud or deceit upon any person,
> "in connection with the purchase or sale of any security." 17 CFR 240.10b-5. [417 U.S. 506, 524]
> Section 29 (a) of the Act provides:
> "Any condition, stipulation, or provision binding any person to waive compliance with any provision of this chapter or of any rule or regulation thereunder, or of any rule of an exchange required thereby shall be void." 15 U.S.C. 78cc (a).

And 29 (b) adds that "[e]very contract" made in violation of the Act "shall be void." No exception is made for contracts which have an international character.

The Securities Act of 1933, 48 Stat. 84, 15 U.S.C. 77n, has a like provision:

> "Any condition, stipulation, or provision binding any person acquiring any security to waive compliance with any provision of this subchapter or of the rules and regulations of the Commission shall be void."

In Wilko v. Swan, a customer brought suit against a brokerage house alleging fraud in the sale of stock. A motion was made to stay the trial until arbitration occurred under the United States Arbitration Act, 9 U.S.C. 3, as provided in the customer's contract. The Court held that an agreement for arbitration was a "stipulation" within the meaning of the statute which sought to "waive" compliance with the Securities Act. We accordingly held that the courts, not the arbitration tribunals, had jurisdiction over suits under that Act. The arbitration agency, we held, was bound by other standards which were not necessarily consistent with the 1933 Act. We said:

> "As the protective provisions of the Securities Act require the exercise of judicial direction to fairly assure their effectiveness, it seems to us that Congress must have intended 14 . . . to apply to waiver of judicial trial and review

Wilko was held by the Court of Appeals to control this case - and properly so.

The Court does not consider the question whether a "security" is involved in this case, saying it was not raised by petitioner. A respondent, however, has the right to urge any argument to support the judgment in his favor . . . . The Court of Appeals held that "securities" within the meaning of the 1934 Act were involved here. The brief of the respondent is based on the premise that "securities" are involved here; and petitioner has not questioned that ruling of the Court of Appeals.

It could perhaps be argued that Wilko does not govern because it involved a little customer pitted against a big brokerage house, while we deal here with sophisticated buyers and sellers: Scherk, a powerful German operator, and Alberto-Culver, an American business surrounded and protected by lawyers and experts. But that would miss the point of the problem. The Act does not speak in terms of "sophisticated" as opposed to "unsophisticated" people dealing in securities. The rules when the giants play are the same as when the pygmies enter the market.

If there are victims here, they are not Alberto-Culver the corporation, but the thousands of investors who are the security holders in Alberto-Culver. If there is fraud and the promissory notes are excessive, the impact is on the equity in Alberto-Culver.

. . .

There has been much support for arbitration of disputes; and it may be the superior way of settling some disagreements. If A and B were quarreling over a trademark and there was an arbitration clause in the contract, the policy of Congress in implementing the United Nations Convention on the Recognition and Enforcement of Foreign Arbitral Awards, as it did in 9 U.S.C. 201 et seq., would prevail. But the Act does not substitute an arbiter for the settlement of disputes under the 1933 and 1934 Acts. Art. II (3) of the Convention says:

> "The court of a Contracting State, when seized[9] of an action in a matter in respect of which the parties have made an agreement within the meaning of this article, shall, at the request of one of the parties, refer the parties to arbitration, unless it finds that the said agreement is null and void, inoperative or incapable of

---

[9] "Seized of" here just means "having jurisdiction over"

being performed." 5 1970. 3 U.S. T. 2517, 2519, T. I. A. S. No. 6997.

But 29 (a) of the 1934 Act makes agreements to arbitrate liabilities under 10 of the Act "void" and "inoperative." Congress has specified a precise way whereby big and small investors will be protected and the rules under which the Alberto-Culvers of this Nation shall operate. They or their lawyers cannot waive those statutory conditions, for our corporate giants are not principalities of power but guardians of a host of wards unable to care for themselves. It is these wards that the 1934 Act tries to protect. Not a word in the Convention governing awards adopts the standards which Congress has passed to protect the investors under the 1934 Act. It is peculiarly appropriate that we adhere to Wilko - more so even than when Wilko was decided. Huge foreign investments are being made in our companies. It is important that American standards of fairness in security dealings govern the destinies of American investors until Congress changes these standards.

The Court finds it unnecessary to consider Scherk's argument that this case is distinguishable from Wilko in that Wilko involved parties of unequal bargaining strength. Ante, at 512-513, n. 6. Instead, the Court rests its conclusion on the fact that this was an "international" agreement, with an American corporation investing in the stock and property of foreign businesses, and speaks favorably of the certainty which inheres when parties specify an arbitral forum for resolution of differences in "any contract touching two or more countries."

This invocation of the "international contract" talisman might be applied to a situation where, for example, an interest in a foreign company or mutual fund was sold to an utterly unsophisticated American citizen, with material fraudulent misrepresentations made in this country. The arbitration clause could appear in the fine print of a form contract, and still be sufficient to preclude recourse to our courts, forcing the defrauded citizen to arbitration in Paris to vindicate his rights.

It has been recognized that the 1934 Act, including the protections of Rule 10b-5, applies when foreign defendants have defrauded American investors, particularly when, as alleged here, they have profited by virtue of proscribed conduct within our boundaries. This is true even when the defendant is organized under the laws of a foreign country, is conducting much of its activity outside the United States, and is therefore governed largely by foreign law. The language of 29 of the 1934 Act does not immunize such international transactions, and the United Nations Convention provides that a forum court in which a suit is brought need not enforce an agreement to arbitrate which is "void" and "inoperative" as contrary to its public policy. When a foreign corporation undertakes fraudulent action which subjects it to the jurisdiction of our federal securities laws, nothing justifies the conclusion that only a diluted version of those laws protects American investors.

Section 29 (a) of the 1934 Act provides that a stipulation binding one to waive compliance with "any provision" of the Act shall be void, and the Act expressly provides that the federal district courts shall have "exclusive jurisdiction" over suits brought under the Act. 15 U.S.C. 78aa. The Court appears to attach some significance to the fact that the specific provisions of the 1933 Act involved in Wilko are not duplicated in the 1934 Act, which is involved in this case. While Alberto-Culver would not have the right to sue in either a state or federal forum as did the plaintiff in Wilko, the Court deprives it of its right to have its Rule 10b-5 claim heard in a federal court. We spoke at length in Wilko of this problem, elucidating the undesirable effects of remitting a securities plaintiff to an arbitral, rather than a judicial, forum. Here, as in Wilko, the allegations of fraudulent misrepresentation will involve "subjective findings on the purpose and knowledge" of the defendant, questions ill-determined by arbitrators without judicial instruction on the law.[10] See *id.* at 435. An arbitral

---

[10] Here, Justice Douglas implies that federal judges are better at judging federal laws than arbitrators.

award can be made without explication of reasons and without development of a record, so that the arbitrator's conception of our statutory requirement may be absolutely incorrect yet functionally unreviewable, even when the arbitrator seeks to apply our law. We recognized in Wilko that there is no judicial review corresponding to review of court decisions. Id., at 436-437. The extensive pretrial discovery provided by the Federal Rules of Civil Procedure for actions in district court would not be available. And the wide choice of venue provided by the 1934 Act, 15 U.S.C. 78aa, would be forfeited. See Wilko v. Swan, supra, at 431, 435. The loss of the proper judicial forum carries with it the loss of substantial rights.

When a defendant, as alleged here, has, through proscribed acts within our territory, brought itself within the ken of federal securities regulation, a fact not disputed here, those laws - including the controlling principles of Wilko - apply whether the defendant is foreign or American, and whether or not there are transnational elements in the dealings. Those laws are rendered a chimera when foreign corporations or funds - unlike domestic defendants - can nullify them by virtue of arbitration clauses which send defrauded American investors to the uncertainty of arbitration on foreign soil, or, if those investors cannot afford to arbitrate their claims in a far-off forum, to no remedy at all.

Moreover, the international aura which the Court gives this case is ominous. We now have many multinational corporations in vast operations around the world - Europe, Latin America, the Middle East, and Asia. The investments of many American investors turn on dealings by these companies. Up to this day, it has been assumed by reason of Wilko that they were all protected by our various federal securities Acts. If these guarantees are to be removed, it should take a legislative enactment. I would enforce our laws as they stand, unless Congress makes an exception. [417 U.S. 506, 534]

The virtue of certainty in international agreements may be important, but Congress has dictated that when there are sufficient contacts for our securities laws to apply, the policies expressed in those laws take precedence. Section 29 of the 1934 Act, which renders arbitration clauses void and inoperative, recognizes no exception for fraudulent dealings which incidentally have some international factors. The Convention makes provision for such national public policy in Art. II (3). Federal jurisdiction under the 1934 Act will attach only to some international transactions, but when it does, the protections afforded investors such as Alberto-Culver can only be full-fledged.

The famous Bremen case is next. Here, a U.S. company was contracting with a German company to two a drilling rig from Texas to the Adriatic Sea. A storm arose in the Gulf of Mexico, damaging the rig. The Bremen, owned by the German company, stopped in Tampa, Florida, and the boat was "arrested" — served with a summons (!) — as was the German firm, Unterweser, claiming negligence in the towing of the drilling rig. What follows was the first time the Supreme Court recognized and enforced a "forum selection clause." Forum selection clauses, including arbitration clauses, which effectively select a non-judicial forum, are now standard in international business transactions

THE BREMEN ET AL. v. ZAPATA OFF-SHORE CO.

U.S. Supreme Court, 407 U.S. 1 (1972)

Burger, C. J., delivered the opinion of the Court, in which Brennan, Stewart, White, Marshall, Blackmun, Powell, and Rehnquist, JJ., joined.. Douglas, J., filed a dissenting opinion.

MR. CHIEF JUSTICE BURGER delivered the opinion of the Court.

We granted certiorari to review a judgment of the United States Court of Appeals for the Fifth Circuit declining to enforce a forum-selection clause governing disputes arising under an international towage contract between petitioners and respondent. The circuits have differed in their approach to such clauses. For the reasons stated here, we vacate the judgment of the Court of Appeals.

In November 1967, Zapata Offshore Company, a Houston-based American corporation, contracted with petitioner Unterweser, a German corporation, to tow Zapata's ocean-going, self-elevating drilling rig *Chaparral* from Louisiana to a point off Ravenna, Italy, in the Adriatic Sea, where Zapata had agreed to drill certain wells.

Zapata had solicited bids for the towage, and several companies including Unterweser had responded. Unterweser was the low bidder and Zapata requested it to submit a contract, which it did. The contract submitted by Unterweser contained the following provision:

> "Any dispute arising must be treated before the London Court of Justice."

In addition the contract contained two clauses purporting to exculpate Unterweser from liability for damages to the towed barge. (Note: exculpate means "to excuse.") The General Towage Conditions of the contract included the following:

> "1. . . . [Unterweser and its] masters and crews are not responsible for defaults and/or errors in the navigation of the tow.
>
> "2. . . .
>
> "b) Damages suffered by the towed object are in any case for account of its Owners."

In addition, the contract provided that any insurance of the *Chaparral* was to be "for account of" Zapata. Unterweser's initial telegraphic bid had also offered to "arrange insurance covering towage risk for rig if desired." Zapata chose to be self-insured on all its rigs, so the loss in this case was not compensated by insurance.

After reviewing the contract and making several changes, but without any alteration in the forum-selection or exculpatory clauses, a Zapata vice president executed the contract and forwarded it to Unterweser in Germany, where Unterweser accepted the changes, and the contract became effective.

On January 5, 1968, Unterweser's deep sea tug *Bremen* departed Venice, Louisiana, with the *Chaparral* in tow bound for Italy. On January 9, while the flotilla was in international waters in the middle of the Gulf of Mexico, a severe storm arose. The sharp roll of the *Chaparral* in Gulf waters caused its elevator legs, which had been raised for the voyage, to break off and fall into the sea, seriously damaging the *Chaparral*. In this emergency situation Zapata instructed the *Bremen* to tow its damaged rig to Tampa, Florida, the nearest port of refuge.

On January 12, Zapata, ignoring its contract promise to litigate "any dispute arising" in the English courts, commenced a suit in admiralty in the United States District Court at Tampa, seeking $3,500,000 damages against Unterweser *in personam* and the *Bremen in rem*, alleging negligent towage and breach of contract.[11] Unterweser responded by invoking the forum clause of the towage contract, and moved to dismiss for lack of jurisdiction or on *forum non conveniens* grounds, or in the alternative to stay the action pending submission of the dispute to the "London Court of Justice." Shortly thereafter, in February, before the District Court had ruled on its motion to stay or dismiss the United States action, Unterweser commenced an action against Zapata seeking damages for breach of the towage contract in the High Court of Justice in London, as the contract provided. Zapata appeared in that court to contest jurisdiction, but its challenge was rejected, the English courts holding that the contractual forum provision conferred jurisdiction.

(Unterweser also wanted to take advantage of a "limitation action" under US admiralty law, and filed that before a six-month period expired. That court entered the customary injunction against proceedings outside the limitation court, and Zapata refilled its initial claim in the limitation action. Zapata would argue that Unterweser's filing waived its claim that the forum selection clause in the contract must be enforced, but the Supreme Court did not agree.)

On July 29, after the six-month period for filing the limitation action had run, that the District Court denied Unterweser's January motion to dismiss or stay Zapata's initial action. In denying the motion, that court relied on the prior decision of the Court of Appeals in *Carbon Black Export, Inc.* v. *The Monrosa*, 254 F.2d 297 (CA5 1958), cert. dismissed, 359 U.S. 180 (1959). In that case the Court of Appeals had held a forum-selection clause unenforceable, reiterating the traditional view of many American courts that "agreements in advance of controversy whose object is to oust the jurisdiction of the courts are contrary to public policy and will not be enforced." 254 F.2d, at 300-301. Apparently concluding that it was bound by the *Carbon Black* case, the District Court gave the forum-selection clause little, if any, weight. Instead, the court treated the motion to dismiss under normal *forum non conveniens* doctrine applicable in the absence of such a clause, citing *Gulf Oil Corp.* v. *Gilbert*, 330 U.S. 501 (1947). Under that doctrine "unless the balance is strongly in favor of the defendant, the plaintiff's

---

[11] The *Bremen* was arrested by a United States marshal acting pursuant to Zapata's complaint immediately upon her arrival in Tampa. The tug was subsequently released when Unterweser furnished security in the amount of $ 3,500,000.

choice of forum should rarely be disturbed." *Id.*, at 508. The District Court concluded: "The balance of conveniences here is not strongly in favor of [Unterweser] and [Zapata's] choice of forum should not be disturbed."

Thereafter, on January 21, 1969, the District Court denied another motion by Unterweser to stay the limitation action pending determination of the controversy in the High Court of Justice in London and granted Zapata's motion to restrain Unterweser from litigating further in the London court. The District Judge ruled that, having taken jurisdiction in the limitation proceeding, he had jurisdiction to determine all matters relating to the controversy. He ruled that Unterweser should be required to "do equity" by refraining from also litigating the controversy in the London court, not only for the reasons he had previously stated for denying Unterweser's first motion to stay Zapata's action, but also because Unterweser had invoked the United States court's jurisdiction to obtain the benefit of the Limitation Act.

On appeal, a divided panel of the Court of Appeals affirmed, and on rehearing *en banc* the panel opinion was adopted, with six of the 14 *en banc* judges dissenting. As had the District Court, the majority rested on the *Carbon Black* decision, concluding that "'at the very least'" that case stood for the proposition that a forum-selection clause "'will not be enforced unless the selected state would provide a more convenient forum than the state in which suit is brought.'" From that premise the Court of Appeals proceeded to conclude that, apart from the forum-

selection clause, the District Court did not abuse its discretion in refusing to decline jurisdiction on the basis of *forum non conveniens*. It noted that (1) the flotilla never "escaped the Fifth Circuit's mare nostrum[12], and the casualty occurred in close proximity to the district court"; (2) a considerable number of potential witnesses, including Zapata crewmen, resided in the Gulf Coast area; (3) preparation for the voyage and inspection and repair work had been performed in the Gulf area; (4) the testimony of the *Bremen* crew was available by way of deposition; (5) England had no interest in or contact with the controversy other than the forum-selection clause. The Court of Appeals majority further noted that Zapata was a United States citizen and "the discretion of the district court to remand the case to a foreign forum was consequently limited" -- especially since it appeared likely that the English courts would enforce the exculpatory clauses. [8] In the Court of Appeals' view, enforcement of such clauses would be contrary to public policy in American courts under *Bisso* v. *Inland Waterways Corp.*, 349 U.S. 85 (1955), and *Dixilyn Drilling Corp.* v. *Crescent Towing & Salvage Co.*, 372 U.S. 697 (1963). Therefore, "the district court was entitled to consider that remanding Zapata to a foreign forum, with no practical contact with the controversy, could raise a bar to recovery by a United States citizen which its own convenient courts would not countenance."(The record contains an undisputed affidavit of a British solicitor stating an opinion that the exculpatory clauses of the contract would be held "prima facie valid and enforceable" against Zapata in any action maintained in England in which

---

[12] Latin, for "our sea." The court here is just saying that the Gulf of Mexico is proximate to the U.S., and that such proximity makes it possible for Unterweser to invoke the Limitation Act in the US Code, and for the court to consider Tampa to be the more convenient place to try the issues in the case.

Zapata alleged that defaults or errors in Unterweser's tow caused the casualty and damage to the *Chaparral*.

In addition, it is not disputed that while the limitation fund in the District Court in Tampa amounts to $ 1,390,000, the limitation fund in England would be only slightly in excess of $ 80,000 under English law. The Court of Appeals also indicated in passing that even if it took the view that choice-of-forum clauses were enforceable unless "unreasonable" it was "doubtful" that enforcement would be proper here because the exculpatory clauses would deny Zapata relief to which it was "entitled" and because England was "seriously inconvenient" for trial of the action.

We hold, with the six dissenting members of the Court of Appeals, that far too little weight and effect were given to the forum clause in resolving this controversy. For at least two decades we have witnessed an expansion of overseas commercial activities by business enterprises based in the United States. The barrier of distance that once tended to confine a business concern to a modest territory no longer does so. Here we see an American company with special expertise contracting with a foreign company to tow a complex machine thousands of miles across seas and oceans. The expansion of American business and industry will hardly be encouraged if, notwithstanding solemn contracts, we insist on a parochial concept that all disputes must be resolved under our laws and in our courts. (emphasis added) Absent a contract forum, the considerations relied on by the Court of Appeals would be persuasive reasons for holding an American forum convenient in the traditional sense, but in an era of expanding world trade and commerce,

the absolute aspects of the doctrine of the *Carbon Black* case have little place and would be a heavy hand indeed on the future development of international commercial dealings by Americans. We cannot have trade and commerce in world markets and international waters exclusively on our terms, governed by our laws, and resolved in our courts. (emphasis added)

Forum-selection clauses have historically not been favored by American courts. Many courts, federal and state, have declined to enforce such clauses on the ground that they were "contrary to public policy," or that their effect was to "oust the jurisdiction" of the court. Although this view apparently still has considerable acceptance, other courts are tending to adopt a more hospitable attitude toward forum-selection clauses.

. . .

This approach is substantially that followed in other common-law countries including England. It is the view advanced by noted scholars and that adopted by the Restatement of the Conflict of Laws. It accords with ancient concepts of freedom of contract and reflects an appreciation of the expanding horizons of American contractors who seek business in all parts of the world. Not surprisingly, foreign businessmen prefer, as do we, to have disputes resolved in their own courts, but if that choice is not available, then in a neutral forum with expertise in the subject matter. Plainly, the courts of England meet the standards of neutrality and long experience in admiralty litigation. The choice of that forum was made in an arm's-length negotiation by experienced and sophisticated businessmen, and absent some compelling and countervailing reason it should be honored by the parties and enforced by the courts.

The argument that such clauses are improper because they tend to "oust" a court of jurisdiction is hardly more than a vestigial legal fiction. It appears to rest at core on historical judicial resistance to any attempt to reduce the power and business of a particular court and has little place in an era when all courts are overloaded and when businesses once essentially local now operate in world markets. It reflects something of a provincial attitude regarding the fairness of other tribunals. No one seriously contends in this case that the forum-selection clause "ousted" the District Court of jurisdiction over Zapata's action. The threshold question is whether that court should have exercised its jurisdiction to do more than give effect to the legitimate expectations of the parties, manifested in their freely negotiated agreement, by specifically enforcing the forum clause.

There are compelling reasons why a freely negotiated private international agreement, unaffected by fraud, undue influence, or overweening bargaining power,[13] such as that involved here, should be given full effect. In this case, for example, we are concerned with a far from routine transaction between companies of two different nations contemplating the tow of an extremely costly piece of equipment from Louisiana across the Gulf of Mexico and the Atlantic Ocean, through the Mediterranean Sea to its final destination in the Adriatic Sea. In the course of its voyage, it was to traverse the waters of many jurisdictions. The *Chaparral* could have been damaged at any point along the route, and there were countless possible ports of refuge. That the accident occurred in the Gulf of Mexico and the barge was towed to Tampa in an emergency were mere fortuities. It cannot be doubted for a moment that the parties sought to provide for a neutral forum for the resolution of any disputes arising during the tow. Manifestly much uncertainty and possibly great inconvenience to both parties could arise if a suit could be maintained in any jurisdiction in which an accident might occur or if jurisdiction were left to any place where the *Bremen* or Unterweser might happen to be found. The elimination of all such uncertainties by agreeing in advance on a forum acceptable to both parties is an indispensable element in international trade, commerce, and contracting. There is strong evidence that the forum clause was a vital part of the agreement,[14] and it would be unrealistic to think that the parties did

---

[13] "Zapata has neither presented evidence of nor alleged fraud or undue bargaining power in the agreement. Unterweser was only one of several companies bidding on the project. No evidence contradicts its Managing Director's affidavit that it specified English courts 'in an effort to meet Zapata Off-Shore Company half way.' Zapata's Vice President has declared by affidavit that no specific negotiations concerning the forum clause took place. But this was not simply a form contract with boilerplate language that Zapata had no power to alter. The towing of an oil rig across the Atlantic was a new business. Zapata did make alterations to the contract submitted by Unterweser. The forum clause could hardly be ignored. It is the final sentence of the agreement, immediately preceding the date and the parties' signatures. . . ." 428 F.2d 888, 907.

[14] Zapata has denied specifically discussing the forum clause with Unterweser, but, as Judge Wisdom pointed out, Zapata made numerous changes in the contract without altering the forum clause, which could hardly have escaped its attention. Zapata is clearly not unsophisticated in such matters. The contract of its wholly owned subsidiary with an Italian corporation covering the contemplated drilling operations in the Adriatic Sea provided that all disputes were to be settled by arbitration in London under English law, and contained broad exculpatory clauses. App. 306-311.

not conduct their negotiations, including fixing the monetary terms, with the consequences of the forum clause figuring prominently in their calculations. Under these circumstances, as Justice Karminski reasoned in sustaining jurisdiction over Zapata in the High Court of Justice, "the force of an agreement for litigation in this country, freely entered into between two competent parties, seems to me to be very powerful."

The record here refutes any notion of overweening bargaining power. Judge Wisdom, dissenting, in the Court of Appeals noted:

The record contains an affidavit of a Managing Director of Unterweser stating that Unterweser considered the choice-of-forum provision to be of "overriding importance" to the transaction. He stated that Unterweser towage contracts ordinarily provide for exclusive German jurisdiction and application of German law, but that "in this instance, in an effort to meet [Zapata] half way, [Unterweser] proposed the London Court of Justice. Had this provision not been accepted by [Zapata], [Unterweser] would not have entered into the towage contract . . . ." He also stated that the parties intended, by designating the London forum, that English law would be applied. A responsive affidavit by Hoyt Taylor, a vice president of Zapata, denied that there were any discussions between Zapata and Unterweser concerning the forum clause or the question of the applicable law.

Thus, in the light of present-day commercial realities and expanding international trade we conclude that the forum clause should control absent a strong showing that it should be set aside. Although their opinions are not altogether explicit, it seems reasonably

clear that the District Court and the Court of Appeals placed the burden on Unterweser to show that London would be a more convenient forum than Tampa, although the contract expressly resolved that issue. The correct approach would have been to enforce the forum clause specifically unless Zapata could clearly show that enforcement would be unreasonable and unjust, or that the clause was invalid for such reasons as fraud or overreaching. Accordingly, the case must be remanded for reconsideration.

Courts have also suggested that a forum clause, even though it is freely bargained for and contravenes no important public policy of the forum, may nevertheless be "unreasonable" and unenforceable if the chosen forum is *seriously* inconvenient for the trial of the action. Of course, where it can be said with reasonable assurance that at the time they entered the contract, the parties to a freely negotiated private international commercial agreement contemplated the claimed inconvenience, it is difficult to see why any such claim of inconvenience should be heard to render the forum clause unenforceable. We are not here dealing with an agreement between two Americans to resolve their essentially local disputes in a remote alien forum. In such a case, the serious inconvenience of the contractual forum to one or both of the parties might carry greater weight in determining the reasonableness of the forum clause. The remoteness of the forum might suggest that the agreement was an adhesive[15] one, or that the parties did not have the particular controversy in mind when they made their agreement; yet even there the party claiming should bear a heavy burden of proof. Similarly, selection of a remote forum to apply differing foreign law to an essentially American controversy might contravene an important public policy of the forum. For example, so long as *Bisso* governs American courts with respect to the towage business in American waters, it would quite arguably be improper to permit an American tower to avoid that policy by providing a foreign forum for resolution of his disputes with an Amcrican towee.

This case, however, involves a freely negotiated international commercial transaction between a German and an American corporation for towage of a vessel from the Gulf of Mexico to the Adriatic Sea. As noted, selection of a London forum was clearly a reasonable effort to bring vital certainty to this international transaction and to provide a neutral forum experienced and capable in the resolution of admiralty litigation. Whatever "inconvenience" Zapata would suffer by being forced to litigate in the contractual forum as it agreed to do was clearly foreseeable at the time of contracting. In such circumstances it should be incumbent on the party seeking to escape his contract to show that trial in the contractual forum will be so gravely difficult and inconvenient that he will for all practical purposes be deprived of his day in court. Absent that, there is no basis for concluding that it would be unfair, unjust, or unreasonable to hold that party to his bargain.

In the course of its ruling on Unterweser's second motion to stay the proceedings in Tampa, the District Court did make a conclusory finding that the balance of convenience was "strongly" in favor of litigation in Tampa. However, as previously noted,

in making that finding the court erroneously placed the burden of proof on Unterweser to show that the balance of convenience was strongly in its favor.

Moreover, the finding falls far short of a conclusion that Zapata would be effectively deprived of its day in court should it be forced to litigate in London. Indeed, it cannot even be assumed that it would be placed to the expense of transporting its witnesses to London. It is not unusual for important issues in international admiralty cases to be dealt with by deposition. Both the District Court and the Court of Appeals majority appeared satisfied that Unterweser could receive a fair hearing in Tampa by using deposition testimony of its witnesses from distant places, and there is no reason to conclude that Zapata could not use deposition testimony to equal advantage if forced to litigate in London as it bound itself to do. Nevertheless, to allow Zapata opportunity to carry its heavy burden of showing not only that the balance of convenience is strongly in favor of trial in Tampa (that is, that it will be far more inconvenient for Zapata to litigate in London than it will be for Unterweser to litigate in Tampa), but also that a London trial will be so manifestly and gravely inconvenient to Zapata that it will be effectively deprived of a meaningful day in court, we remand for further proceedings.

Zapata's remaining contentions do not require extended treatment. . . . . .

The judgment of the Court of Appeals is vacated and the case is remanded for further proceedings consistent with this opinion.

---

[15] In a contract of "adhesion," one party is confronted with (essentially) no choice and no bargaining ability. Courts treat contracts of adhesion differently, depending on the jurisdiction. And a contract of adhesion is different from a contract tainted by fraud or duress.

Vacated and remanded.

MR. JUSTICE DOUGLAS, dissenting.

Petitioner Unterweser contracted with respondent to tow respondent's drilling barge from Louisiana to Italy. The towage contract contained a "forum selection clause" providing that any dispute must be litigated before the High Court of Justice in London, England. While the barge was being towed in the Gulf of Mexico a casualty was suffered. The tow made for Tampa Bay, the nearest port, where respondent brought suit for damages in the District Court.

Petitioners sued respondent in the High Court of Justice in London, which denied respondent's motion to dismiss.

Petitioners, having previously moved the District Court to dismiss, filed a complaint in that court seeking exoneration or limitation of liability as provided in 46 U. S. C. ß 185. Respondent filed its claim in the limitation proceedings, asserting the same cause of action as in its original action. Petitioners then filed objections to respondent's claim and counterclaimed against respondent, alleging the same claims embodied in its English action, plus an additional salvage claim.

Respondent moved for an injunction against petitioners' litigating further in the English case and the District Court granted the injunction pending determination of the limitation action. Petitioners moved to stay their own limitation proceeding pending a resolution of the suit in the English court. That motion was denied. 296 F.Supp. 733.

That was the posture of the case as it reached the Court of Appeals, petitioners appealing from the last two orders. The Court of Appeals affirmed. 428 F.2d 888, 446 F.2d 907.

Chief Justice Taft in *Hartford Accident Co.* v. *Southern Pacific*, 273 U.S. 207, 214, in discussing the Limitation of Liability Act said that "the great object of the statute was to encourage shipbuilding and to induce the investment of money in this branch of industry, by limiting the venture of those who build the ship to the loss of the ship itself or her freight then pending, in cases of damage or wrong, happening without the privity or knowledge of the ship owner, and by the fault or neglect of the master or other persons on board; that the origin of this proceeding for limitation of liability is to be found in the general maritime law, differing from the English maritime law; and that such a proceeding is entirely within the constitutional grant of power to Congress to establish courts of admiralty and maritime jurisdiction."

Chief Justice Taft went on to describe how the owner of a vessel who, in case the vessel is found at fault, may limit his liability to the value of the vessel and may bring all claimants "into concourse in the proceeding, by monition" and they may be enjoined from suing the owner and the vessel on such claims in any other court. *Id.*, at 215.

Chief Justice Taft concluded: "This Court has by its rules and decisions given the statute a very broad and equitable construction for the purpose of carrying out its purpose and for facilitating a settlement of the whole controversy over such losses as are comprehended within it, and that all the ease with which rights can be adjusted in equity is intended to be given to the proceeding. It is the administration of equity in an admiralty court. . . . The proceeding partakes in a way of the features of a bill to enjoin a multiplicity of suits, a bill in the nature of an interpleader, and a creditor's bill. It looks to a complete and just disposition of a many cornered controversy, and is applicable to proceedings *in rem* against the ship as well as to proceedings *in personam* against the owner, the limitation extending to the owner's property as well as to his person." *Id.*, at 215-216.

The Limitation Court is a court of equity and traditionally an equity court may enjoin litigation in another court where equitable considerations indicate that the other litigation might prejudice the proceedings in the Limitation Court. Petitioners' petition for limitation subjects them to the full equitable powers of the Limitation Court.

Respondent is a citizen of this country. Moreover, if it were remitted to the English court, its substantive rights would be adversely affected. Exculpatory provisions in the towage control provide (1) that petitioners, the masters and the crews "are not responsible for defaults and/or errors in the navigation of the tow" and (2) that "damages suffered by the towed object are in any case for account of its Owners."

Under our decision in *Dixilyn Drilling Corp* v. *Crescent Towing & Salvage Co.*, 372 U.S. 697, 698, "a contract which exempts the tower from liability for its own negligence" is not enforceable, though there is evidence in the present record that it is enforceable in England. That policy was first announced in *Bisso* v. *Inland Waterways Corp.*, 349 U.S. 85; and followed in *Boston Metals Co.* v. *The Winding Gulf*, 349 U.S. 122; *Dixilyn, supra;* and other cases cited here by Douglas, J.

Moreover, the casualty occurred close to the District Court, a number of potential witnesses, including respondent's crewmen, reside in that area, and the inspection and repair work were done there. The testimony of the tower's crewmen, residing in Germany, is already available by way of depositions taken in the proceedings.

All in all, the District Court judge exercised his discretion wisely in enjoining petitioners from pursuing the litigation in England. [*]

[*] It is said that because these parties specifically agreed to litigate their disputes before the London Court of Justice, the District Court, absent "unreasonable" circumstances, should have honored that choice by declining to exercise its jurisdiction. The forum-selection clause, however, is part and parcel of the exculpatory provision in the towing agreement which, as mentioned in the text, is not enforceable in American courts. For only by avoiding litigation in the United States could petitioners hope to evade the *Bisso* doctrine.

Judges in this country have traditionally been hostile to attempts to circumvent the public policy against exculpatory agreements. For example, clauses specifying that the law of a foreign place (which favors such releases) should control have regularly been ignored. Thus, in *The Kensington*, 183 U.S. 263, 276, the Court held void an exemption from liability despite the fact that the contract provided that it should be construed under Belgian law which was more tolerant. And see *E. Gerli & Co.* v. *Cunard S. S. Co.*, 48 F.2d 115, 117 (CA2); *Oceanic Steam Nav. Co.* v. *Corcoran*, 9 F.2d 724, 731 (CA2); *In re Lea Fabrics, Inc.*, 226 F.Supp. 232, 237 (NJ); *F. A. Straus & Co.* v. *Canadian P. R. Co.*, 254 N. Y. 407, 173 N. E. 564; *Siegelman* v. *Cunard White Star*, 221 F.2d 189, 199 (CA2) (Frank, J., dissenting). 6A A. Corbin on Contracts ß 1446 (1962).

The instant stratagem of specifying a foreign forum is essentially the same as invoking a foreign law of construction except that the present circumvention also requires the American party to travel across an ocean to seek relief. Unless we are prepared to overrule *Bisso* we should not countenance devices designed solely for the purpose of evading its prohibition.

45

It is argued, however, that one of the rationales of the *Bisso* doctrine, "to protect those in need of goods or services from being overreached by others who have power to drive hard bargains" (349 U.S., at 91), does not apply here because these parties may have been of equal bargaining stature. Yet we have often adopted prophylactic rules rather than attempt to sort the core cases from the marginal ones. In any event, the other objective of the *Bisso* doctrine, to "discourage negligence by making wrongdoers pay damages" (*ibid.*) applies here and in every case regardless of the relative bargaining strengths of the parties.

I would affirm the judgment below.

Here is some interesting background on the Zapata company:

Zapata got its start in 1953 as an independent oil and gas venture launched by future President of the United States, George Bush. Bush, in his years before entering the national political spotlight, formed the company with the help of another distinguished individual, Pennzoil chairman J. Hugh Liedtke. Together, the pair set in motion a corporate entity that matured into a sprawling force in international energy-processing, with corporate reaches into a spectrum of diversified businesses, including natural-gas compression, off-shore drilling, and coal mining. At its peak as a global conglomerate, Zapata collected as much as $350 million in annual sales, exerting itself as a formidable force in its various industries. However, the most intriguing chapter in the company's history began when its encouraging success started to unravel at an alarming speed, long after both Bush (who cashed in his stake in 1966) and Liedtke had left Zapata to pursue other interests. In the wake of the company's sanguine years, debt accrued to a deleterious magnitude, touching off a two-decade period that saw the company scramble to forestall bankruptcy while it grappled with shaping a new identity for itself over and over again. The search to find a solution to its profound problems steered Zapata far away from its original business, into a field Bush and Liedtke could never had imagined.

https://companies.jrank.org/pages/4911/Zapata-Corporation.html

---

Notice that in both <u>Scherk</u> and <u>Bremen v. Zapata,</u> the Court decides that it does not have subject matter jurisdiction over the case. In <u>Scherk</u>, the parties had chosen arbitration instead; in Bremen, the parties had chosen another court system, one in England. In Pebble Beach v. Caddy, the court has subject matter jurisdiction, but has to decide if it is fair to make and enforce a judgment against a foreign national, Michael Caddy, when his actual contacts with the United States are very limited.

Pebble Beach v. Michael Caddy

453 F.3d 1151 (2006)
United States Court of Appeals for the Ninth Circuit

Procedural Posture

Appellant Pebble Beach, a California golf course resort, sued appellee Michael Caddy, a British bed and breakfast (B & B) owner. The causes of action were based on federal and state law alleging intentional infringement and dilution of its trademark. The United States District Court for the Northern District of California dismissed the complaint for lack of personal jurisdiction and denied the resort's motion for additional discovery. The resort sought review.

Judges: Before: Mary M. Schroeder, Chief Judge, Stephen S. Trott and Andrew J. Kleinfeld, Circuit Judges. Opinion by Judge Trott.

(Note to students: it is typical for an appellate court to have three judges, so that there are no "ties." Unanimous and 2-1 decisions are thus the usual outcome There was no dissent in this case, so it was 3 - 0.)

TROTT, Circuit Judge:

Pebble Beach Company ("Pebble Beach"), a golf course resort in California, appeals the dismissal for lack of jurisdiction of its complaint against Michael Caddy ("Caddy"), a small-business owner located in southern England. . . .Because Caddy did not expressly aim his conduct at California or the United States, we hold that the district court determined correctly that it lacked personal jurisdiction. . . . Thus, we affirm.

I

Pebble Beach is a well-known golf course and resort located in Monterey County, California. The golf resort has used "Pebble Beach" as its trade name for 50 years. Pebble Beach contends that the trade name has acquired secondary meaning[16] in the United States and the United Kingdom. Pebble Beach operates a website located at *www.pebblebeach.com*.

Caddy, a dual citizen of the United States and the United Kingdom, occupies and runs a three-room bed and breakfast, restaurant, and bar located in southern England. Caddy's business operation is located on a cliff overlooking the pebbly beaches of England's south shore, in a town called Barton-on-Sea. The name of Caddy's operation is "Pebble Beach," which, given its location, is no surprise. Caddy advertises his services, which do not include a golf course, at his website, https://www.pebblebeach-uk.com/. Caddy's website includes general information about the accommodations he provides, including lodging rates in pounds sterling, a menu, and a wine list. The website is not interactive. Visitors to the website who have questions about Caddy's services may fill out an on-line inquiry form. However, the website does not have a reservation system, nor does it allow potential guests to book rooms or pay for services on-line.

---

[16] Note to students: "secondary meaning" is an important phrase in trademark law, as we'll see in the Chapter on Intellectual Property. Trademarks, to be protected under federal law, must be distinctive, unique, fanciful, or at least not "descriptive" of what the mark designates. Thus, "Holiday Inn" could only be protected once that phrase had acquired "secondary meaning" to consumers meaning that consumers routinely identified a certain company (Holiday Inns, Inc. of Memphis TN) as being behind that mark. If Pebble Beach were an identifiable place geographically, near Carmel, California, some might argue that a course located there would not be entitled to a "mark" that was unique or fanciful.

Except for a brief time when Caddy worked at a restaurant in Carmel, California, his domicile has been in the United Kingdom.

On October 8, 2003, Pebble Beach sued Caddy under the Lanham Act and the California Business and Professions Code for intentional infringement and dilution of its "Pebble Beach" mark. Caddy moved to dismiss the complaint for lack of personal jurisdiction and insufficiency of service of process. On March 1, 2004, the district court granted Caddy's motion on personal jurisdiction grounds, without addressing the insufficiency of service of process issue. The district court denied also Pebble Beach's request for additional discovery. Pebble Beach timely appealed to the Ninth Circuit.

II

We review de novo[17] the district court's determination that it does not have personal jurisdiction over Caddy. Caddy contends that the district court may not assert personal jurisdiction over him, and, consequently, that the complaint against him was properly dismissed. Pebble Beach argues that Caddy is subject to specific personal jurisdiction in California, or, alternatively, in any forum in the United States, because he has expressly aimed tortious conduct at California and the United States. [1] Pebble Beach asserts that it may look to the entire United States as a litigation forum pursuant to Federal Rules of Civil Procedure Rule 4(k)(2) if Caddy's contacts with California are insufficient to warrant jurisdiction.

When a defendant moves to dismiss for lack of personal jurisdiction, the plaintiff bears the burden of demonstrating that the court has jurisdiction over the defendant. However, this demonstration requires that the plaintiff make only a prima facie showing of jurisdictional facts to withstand the motion to dismiss.

The general rule is that personal jurisdiction over a defendant is proper if it is permitted by a long-arm statute and if the exercise of that jurisdiction does not violate federal due process.

For due process to be satisfied, a defendant, if not present in the forum, must have "minimum contacts" with the forum state such that the assertion of jurisdiction "does not offend traditional notions of fair play and substantial justice." (citing to International Shoe Co. v. Washington, 326 U.S. 310 (1945).

The "minimum contacts" test is satisfied when,

> (1) the defendant has performed some act or consummated some transaction within the forum or otherwise purposefully availed himself of the privileges of conducting activities in the forum, (2) the claim arises out of or results from the defendant's forum-related activities, and (3) the exercise of jurisdiction is reasonable.

Under the first prong of the "minimum contacts" test, Pebble Beach has the burden of establishing that Caddy "has performed some act or consummated some transaction within the forum or otherwise purposefully availed himself of the privileges of conducting activities in the forum." We have refined this to mean whether Caddy has either (1) "purposefully availed" himself of the privilege of conducting activities in the forum, or (2) "purposefully directed" his activities toward the forum. Although we sometimes use the phrase "purposeful availment" to include both purposeful availment and direction, availment and direction are, in fact, two distinct concepts.

Thus, in order to satisfy the first prong of the "minimum contacts" test, Pebble Beach must establish either that Caddy (1) purposefully availed himself of the privilege of conducting activities in California, or the United States as a

---

[17] "De novo" is a Latin expression meaning "anew" or "from the beginning." In terms of appellate review, de novo review just means that the appellate court will give a "fresh look" to the issue on appeal, and give any weight to the lower court's decision.

[1] Caddy's contacts with California or the United States are not continuous or substantial enough to establish general jurisdiction. Thus, we consider only the question of whether Caddy's contacts are sufficient to establish specific jurisdiction.

whole, or (2) that he purposefully directed its activities toward one of those two forums. *Id.*

1. Purposeful Availment

Pebble Beach fails to identify any conduct by Caddy that took place in California or in the United States that adequately supports the availment concept. Evidence of availment is typically action taking place in the forum that invokes the benefits and protections of the laws in the forum. Evidence of direction generally consists of action taking place outside the forum that is directed at the forum. *Id.* (suggesting evidence of purposeful direction includes activities such as distribution and advertising). All of Caddy's action identified by Pebble Beach is action taking place outside the forum. Accordingly, we reject Pebble Beach's assertion that Caddy has availed himself of the jurisdiction of the district court *under both concepts* and proceed only to determine whether Caddy has purposefully directed his action toward one of two applicable forums.

2. Purposeful Direction: California

In *Calder v. Jones*, the Supreme Court held that a foreign act that is both aimed at and has effect in the forum satisfies the first prong of the specific jurisdiction analysis. 465 U.S. 783 (1984). We have commonly referred to this holding as the "*Calder* effects test." To satisfy this test the defendant "must have (1) committed an intentional act, which was (2) expressly aimed at the forum state, and (3) caused harm, the brunt of which is suffered and which the defendant knows is likely to be suffered in the forum state. However, referring to the *Calder* test as an "effects" test can be misleading. For this reason, we have warned courts not to focus too narrowly on the test's third prong—the effects prong—holding that "something more" is needed in addition to a mere foreseeable effect.

We conclude that Caddy's actions were not expressly aimed at California. The only acts identified by Pebble Beach as being directed at California are the website and the use of the name

"Pebble Beach" in the domain name. These acts were not aimed at California and, regardless of foreseeable effect, are insufficient to establish jurisdiction.

In support of its contention that Caddy has expressly aimed conduct at California, Pebble Beach identifies a list of cases where we have found that a defendant's actions have been expressly aimed at the forum state sufficient to establish jurisdiction over the defendant. Pebble Beach asserts that these cases show that Caddy's website and domain name, coupled by his knowledge of the golf resort as a result of his working in California, are sufficient to satisfy the express aiming standard that it is required to meet. We disagree. If anything, these cases establish that "something more"--the express aiming requirement--has not been met by Pebble Beach.

In *Panavision Limited v. Toeppen*, the defendant, a cybersquatter, registered the plaintiff's trademark as part of a domain name. 141 F.3d 1316 (1998). The use of the domain name by the defendant prevented the plaintiff from registering its own domain name and was part of a plan to obtain money from the plaintiff in exchange for the rights to the domain name. *Id.* The court found personal jurisdiction, not merely because [of the domain name use, but because the plan was expressly aimed at the plaintiff:

> [The Defendant] did considerably more than simply register Panavision's trademarks as his domain names on the Internet. He registered those names as part of a scheme to obtain money from Panavision. Pursuant to that scheme, he demanded $ 13,000 from Panavision to release the domain names to it. His acts were aimed at Panavision in California, and caused it to suffer injury there. Id.,at 1318.

Here, Caddy has hatched no such plan directed at Pebble Beach. He is not a cybersquatter trying to obtain money from Pebble Beach. His operation is legitimate and his website relates directly to that end.

In *Metropolitan Life Insurance Co. v. Neaves,* similar to *Panavision,* the defendant's alleged plan to defraud the insurance company involved direct interaction with the forum state. We held that the action at issue satisfied *Calder*'s "effects test" because the defendant sent a letter to the forum state addressed to the plaintiff, thereby defrauding a forum state entity.

In *Bancroft & Masters, Inc. v. Augusta National Inc.*, a dispute over the domain name *www.masters.org* was triggered by a letter sent by Augusta that required Bancroft & Masters, a computer corporation in California, to sue or lose the domain name. *223 F.3d 1082 (9th Cir. 2000)*. We stated that the "expressly aiming" standard was satisfied when "individualized targeting was present." *Id. at 1088*. We reasoned that specific jurisdiction was proper and that the expressly aiming requirement was satisfied because the letter sent by Augusta constituted "individualized targeting." *Id.*

The defendant in both *Bancroft* and *Metropolitan Life* did "something more" than commit a "foreign act with foreseeable effects in the forum state." *Id. at 1087*. In both cases this "individualized targeting" was correspondence that was a clear attempt to force the plaintiff to act. Here, Caddy engaged in no "individualized targeting." There is no letter written by Caddy forcing Pebble Beach to act. The only substantial action is a domain name and non-interactive informative web site along with the extraneous fact that Caddy had worked, at some point in his past, in California. This does not constitute "individualized targeting." Indeed, to hold otherwise would be contrary to what we have suggested in earlier case law.

These cases establish two salient points. First, there can be no doubt that we still require "something more" than just a foreseeable effect to conclude that personal jurisdiction is proper. (citing Bancroft, above). Second, an internet domain name and passive website alone are not "something more," and, therefore, alone are not enough to subject a party to jurisdiction.

In contrast to those cases where jurisdiction was proper because "something more" existed, the circumstances here are more analogous to Schwarzenegger v. Fred Martin Motor Co., 374

F.3d 797 (9th Circ. 2004). There, "the Terminator" (Arnold Schwarzenegger) brought an action in California claiming that an Ohio car dealership impermissibly used his "Terminator" image in a newspaper advertisement in Akron, Ohio. The federal district court in California dismissed the complaint for lack of personal jurisdiction. Applying the *Calder* "effects test," we affirmed, concluding that even though the advertisement might lead to eventual harm in California this "foreseeable effect" was not enough because the advertisement was expressly aimed at Ohio rather than California. We concluded that, without "something more" than possible effect, there was simply no individualized targeting of California, or the type of wrongful conduct, that could be construed as being directed at the forum state. We held that Schwarzenegger had not established the California court's personal jurisdiction over the car dealership.

Pebble Beach, like Schwarzenegger, relies almost exclusively on the possible foreseeable effects. Like Schwarzenegger, Pebble Beach's arguments depend on the possible effects of a non-interactive advertisement—here, Caddy's passive website. Notably absent in both circumstances is action that can be construed as being expressly aimed at California. The fact that Caddy once lived in California and therefore has knowledge of the Pebble Beach golf resort goes to the foreseeable effect prong of the "effects test" and is not an independent act that can be interpreted as being expressly aimed at California.

3. Purposeful Direction: United States

Even if Pebble Beach is unable to show purposeful direction as to California, Pebble Beach can still establish personal jurisdiction if Caddy purposefully directed his action at the United States. This ability to look to the aggregate contacts of a defendant with the United States as a whole, instead of a particular state forum, is a product of Rule 4(k)(2). Rule 4(k)(2) is commonly referred to as the federal long-arm statute.

The exercise of Rule 4(k)(2) as a federal long-arm statute requires the plaintiff to prove three factors. First, the claim against the defendant must arise under federal law. Second, the defendant must not be subject to the personal jurisdiction of any state court of general jurisdiction. Third, the federal court's exercise of personal jurisdiction must comport with due process. Here, the first factor is satisfied because Pebble Beach's claims arises under the Lanham Act. And, as established above, the second factor is satisfied as Caddy is not subject to personal jurisdiction of California, or any state court.

That leaves the third factor--due process. The due process analysis is identical to the one discussed above when the forum was California, except here the relevant forum is the entire United States. And, as with the foregoing analysis, our resolution here depends on whether Caddy's actions were purposefully directed at the United States. Pebble Beach contends that the "purposeful direction" requirement is satisfied under the *Calder* "effects test" because Caddy's operation is expressly aimed at the United States. Pebble Beach makes four arguments.

First, Pebble Beach claims that because Caddy selected a ".com" domain name it shows that the United States was his "primary" market and that he is directly advertising his services to the United States. Second, Pebble Beach asserts that his selection of the name "Pebble Beach" shows the United States is his primary target because "Pebble Beach" is a famous United States trademark. Third, Pebble Beach asserts that Caddy's intent to advertise to the United States is bolstered by the fact that Caddy's facilities are located in a resort town that caters to foreigners, particularly Americans. Finally, Pebble Beach asserts that a majority of Caddy's business in the past has been with Americans.

As before, Pebble Beach's arguments focus too much on the effects prong and not enough on the "something more" requirement. First, following the rationale articulated in cases like Cybersell, Rio Properties and Panavision, we conclude that the selection of a particular domain name is insufficient by itself to confer jurisdiction over a non-resident defendant, even under Rule 4(k)(2), where the forum is the United States. The fact that the name "Pebble Beach" is a famous mark known

world-wide is of little practical consequence when deciding whether action is directed at a particular forum via the world wide web. Also of minimal importance is Caddy's selection of a ".com" domain name instead of a more specific United Kingdom or European Union domain. To suggest that ".com" is an indicator of express aiming at the United States is even weaker than the counter assertion that having "U.K." in the domain name, which is the case here, is indicative that Caddy was only targeting his services to the United Kingdom. Neither provides much more than a slight indication of where a website may be located and does not establish to whom the website is directed. Accordingly, we reject these arguments.

This leaves Pebble Beach's arguments that because Caddy's business is located in an area frequented by Americans, and because he occasionally services Americans, jurisdiction is proper. These arguments fail for the same reasons; they go to effects rather than express aiming. Pebble Beach's arguments do have intuitive appeal—they suggest a real effect on Americans. However, as reiterated throughout this opinion, showing "effect" satisfies only the third prong of the *Calder* test; it is not the "something more" that is required. In *Bancroft*, we stated that foreseeable effects alone are not sufficient to exercise jurisdiction, that "something more" is required and that "'something more' is what the Supreme Court described as 'express aiming' at the forum state." Bancrof, 223 F.3d at 1087. The "something more" additional requirement is important simply because the effects cited may not have been caused by the defendant's actions of which the plaintiff complains. Here, although Caddy may serve vacationing Americans, there is not a scintilla of evidence indicating that this patronage is related to either Caddy's choice of a domain name or the posting of a passive website. Accordingly, we find no action on the part of Caddy expressly directed at the United States and conclude that an exercise of personal jurisdiction over Caddy would offend due process.

51

III

Caddy did not expressly aim his conduct at California or the United States and therefore is not subject to the personal jurisdiction of the district court. A passive website and domain name alone do not satisfy the *Calder* effects test and there is no other action expressly aimed at California or the United States that would justify personal jurisdiction.

Case Questions

1.   You are general manager for Pebble Beach Golf Course and Resort. You notice a "Pebbles" resort website: https://gopebbles.com/

Would you be concerned that this might deprive your operation of customers?

Here is Mr. Caddy's current site: https://www.pebblebeach-uk.com/

Notice that you still cannot make a reservation on this website. Do you think it would, or should, make a legal difference if people in the U.S. could interact with his website and make a reservation?

2.   Do you see any difference between the court's thinking about purposeful availment" in California and its thinking about purposeful availment in the US more generally? What?

3.   Do you think Pebble Beach Company might have been overly "litigious"? Trademark law (see Chapter Six in this book) is meant to protect the intellectual property of people and businesses, so that customers are not confused as to the origin of certain goods and services. If you were going to Caddy's website, do you think you might confuse his business operation with the world-famous golf course near Carmel, California?

4.   If the case were heard in the U.S., what kind of damages, if any, would you award to Pebble Beach Golf Club and Resort?

5.   Suppose that Caddy had been served with the summons and complaint, a U.S. court were to hear this case, without Caddy appearing before the court personally and without his attorneys agreeing that the court had personal jurisdiction. Suppose also that the court agreed with plaintiffs that there was both subject matter and personal jurisdiction. If there were a judgment against Caddy, how would it be enforced, if Caddy had no assets in the U.S.?

   a.   If there were to be a money judgment awarded to Pebble Beach by the U.S. court, would an English court enforce the award? Why should or shouldn't it?

   b.   If the U.S. court agreed to enjoin (block) Caddy from using the phrase "Pebble Beach" on his website, how could a U.S. court enforce that? Would an English court enforce that? Suppose that a U.S. company, Amazon Web Services, were hosting Caddy's website in "the cloud" (using a server farm in Utah). Should AWS end hosting of Caddy's website, or block access to his website from U.S. customers? Would https://gopebbles.com/ also be blocked, or just Caddy's "pebble" website?

In the Koster v. Automark case, Mr. Koster (from the Netherlands) wanted to enforce a default judgment from that legal system in Illinois, hoping to have the Dutch court's judgment enforced where Automark had assets that could be attached. He was unsuccessful in convincing the Illinois court that the Netherlands court had personal jurisdiction over Automark.

KOSTER v. AUTOMARK INDUSTRIES, INC.
640 F.2d 77 (1981)

Hendrik KOSTER, a Citizen of the Netherlands, Plaintiff-Appellee, v. AUTOMARK INDUSTRIES, INCORPORATED, a Delaware Corporation, Defendant-Appellant.
United States Court of Appeals, Seventh Circuit.

HARLINGTON WOOD, Jr., Circuit Judge.

This diversity case involves the appeal of defendant Automark Industries, Inc. ("Automark"), a corporation doing business in Illinois, from the district court's determination on motion for summary judgment in favor of plaintiff Hendrik Koster, a citizen of the Netherlands. The district court's decision granted enforcement of a default judgment obtained in district court in Amsterdam by Koster against Automark in a case brought on a claimed breach of contract. Finding that Automark did not have sufficient contact with the Netherlands to vest that country's courts with personal jurisdiction over Automark so as to permit enforcement of the default judgment in United States courts, we reverse.

Whether a court may, under American law, assert jurisdiction over a foreign defendant-company depends upon whether the company "purposefully avails itself of the privilege of conducting activities within the forum State." *Shaffer v. Heitner,* 433 U.S. 186, 216, 97 S.Ct. 2569, 2586, 53 L.Ed.2d 683 (1977). This means that the company must pass a threshold of minimum contacts with the forum state so that it is fair to subject it to the jurisdiction of that state's courts. *World-Wide Volkswagen Corp. v. Woodson,* 444 U.S. 286, 292, 100 S.Ct. 559, 564, 62 L.Ed.2d 490 (1980); *International Shoe v. Washington,* 326 U.S. 310, 66 S.Ct. 154, 90 L.Ed. 95 (1945).

The parties agree that the document alleged to be Automark's contract to purchase up to 600,000 units of Koster's valve cap gauges was executed in Milan, Italy.[1] The Milan meeting between Koster and Automark followed preliminary inquiry and discussion between the two parties during a period of five months. The discussion was carried on via mail between Koster's Amsterdam office and Automark's Illinois address. Automark began the exchange of letters in June, 1970 with a one-sentence request for "descriptive material and prices" of Koster's product. Automark subsequently expressed interest in marketing the tire gauges, but stated that it needed to know the details of such important factors as Koster's relationship with the Swiss factory that produced the gauges, Koster's present patent rights, and his rights to worldwide distribution of the total output of the Swiss factory. Automark expressly disclaimed willingness to negotiate and conclude a contract through the mail.[2]

In early November, 1970, Automark's vice-president, J. L. Bohmrich, wrote that he would like to meet with Koster in Amsterdam or at the Swiss factory during a European trip Bohmrich planned to take later in the month. Koster replied that he would instead be willing to meet in Milan, and would telephone Bohmrich's Illinois office to make arrangements. As noted, the Milan meeting resulted in execution of the document involved in this case. So far as the record shows, Automark never ordered Koster's gauges, and Koster never shipped any gauges.

The business contacts described above are insufficient to reach the minimum level needed to satisfy due process requirements prerequisite to enforcement of the Dutch default judgment. A recent opinion of this court, *Lakeside Bridge & Steel Co. v. Mountain State Construction Co.,* 597 F.2d 596 (7th Cir. 1979), thoroughly analyzed the due process requirements of minimum contacts in concluding that a federal court sitting in a diversity case arising in Wisconsin did not have personal jurisdiction of a West Virginia defendant. Whether it be Wisconsin or the Netherlands, the standard of minimum contacts is the same. . . . The facts in the *Lakeside* case were similar to those involved here, and if anything, presented a more compelling case for recognizing personal jurisdiction.

In *Lakeside,* the defendant construction company had ordered structural assemblies from plaintiff Lakeside, a Wisconsin company. Several letters and telephone calls had been exchanged between the two businesses, and a contract concluded by mail. The assemblies were delivered, and Lakeside sued when the defendant withheld part of the purchase price. The court assumed that the defendant believed that Lakeside would perform the contract in Wisconsin, the forum state. Focusing on the nature and quality of the contacts between the two companies, the court nevertheless concluded that Wisconsin could not assert jurisdiction over the West Virginia company because the defendant's Wisconsin contacts did not show that it "purposefully avail[ed] itself of the privilege of conducting activities within the forum state." 597 F.2d at 603.

The document at issue in the case before us was executed in Italy and involved the purchase of goods manufactured in Switzerland. While the document contains language that might be construed as an agreement to pay, which payment Koster claims was to take place in the Netherlands, such a promise even if so interpreted is not sufficient contact to confer personal jurisdiction. *Kulko v. California Superior Court,* 436 U.S. 84, 93 n.6, 98 S.Ct. 1690, 1697, n.6, 56 L.Ed.2d 132 (1978) (child-support payments required under separation agreement to spouse living in California insufficient contact to confer jurisdiction on that state).

In comparison to the facts in the *Lakeside* case, Automark's *only* contacts with the Netherlands were eight letters, and possibly a telegram and a transatlantic telephone call all preliminary to the meeting in Italy. In *Lakeside,* 597 F.2d at 604, the court notes that such contacts cannot be held to satisfy jurisdictional requirements, otherwise "[u]se of the interstate telephone and mail service to communicate with [an out-of-state] plaintiff, if constituting contacts supporting jurisdiction, would give jurisdiction to any state into which communications were directed." Such a result would make virtually every business subject to suit in any state with which it happened to communicate in some manner. That clearly would not satisfy the demands of due process.

Lakeside emphasizes that "the best interests of the international and state systems" of commerce should be considered when making determinations about minimum contacts in individual cases. 597 F.2d at 603, *quoting Restatement (Second) of Conflict of Laws* § 37, Comment *a* (1971). This consideration weighs in favor of Automark, since it "is based on the proposition that `[a] state should not improperly impinge upon the interests of other states by trying in its courts a case with which it has no adequate relationship.'" 597 F.2d at 603, *quoting Restatement, supra,* § 24, Comment *b.* The Netherlands lacks an adequate relationship to defendant's presence and conduct to justify trial of the case in that country. The interests of international business are better served by protecting potential international purchasers from being unreasonably called to defend suits commenced in foreign courts which lack jurisdiction according to our recognized standards of due process. *See* 597 F.2d at 603 n.12.

Moreover, the *Lakeside* opinion stresses that where the nature of a defendant's business contact in the forum state does not involve activities dangerous to persons and property, the propriety of vesting personal jurisdiction in that state must be considered in light of its relationship with the defendant other than that at issue in the lawsuit. 597 F.2d at 603. The purchase and shipment of valve gauges is not a dangerous activity. And here, there are no allegations that Automark had any relationship with the Netherlands beyond the letters, telegram and telephone call involved in its business contact with Koster.

On these facts, Automark did not have the minimum contacts necessary to show that it purposefully utilized the privilege to conduct business activities in the Netherlands sufficient to confer on that country's courts personal jurisdiction over Automark. The district court concluded that cases decided under the Illinois long-arm statute, Ill.Rev.Stat.Ch. 110, § 17(a), supported his finding that Automark satisfied the requirement of minimum contacts to support the Dutch court's jurisdiction. We disagree. We note that the Illinois courts have held that the state long-arm statute is intended to assert jurisdiction over non-resident defendants only "to the extent permitted by the due process clause." *Colony Press, Inc. v. Fleeman,* 17 Ill.App.3d 14, 19, 308 N.E.2d 78 (1974). The *Lakeside* court's discussion of the application of Wisconsin's long-arm statute to a decision on the basis of federal due process rights is pertinent. The court noted that the Wisconsin law "was intended by the state legislature to reach only so far as permitted by the due process clause.... In these circumstances we are interpreting the statute, not ruling on its constitutionality, when we decide the due process question; yet we are of course not bound by the [state courts'] determination of that federal question". 597 F.2d at 599. Likewise, in the case before us we are not bound by Illinois judicial determinations on the requirements of due process to support personal jurisdiction. This is especially true where we are considering the powers of a court in a jurisdiction other than Illinois.

At any rate, the cases relied upon by the district court for its determination that the Dutch court was vested with personal jurisdiction do not detract from our holding here. Thus, in *Colony Press, supra,* the state court noted that the "essential points" for purposes of its determination that an Ohio corporation was subject to a suit brought in Illinois courts by an Illinois company were that the contract was accepted in Illinois and performance thereunder was expected to occur wholly within that state. 17 Ill.App.3d at 18, 308 N.E.2d 78. As our discussion indicates, the document involved in this case was executed in Italy, and the goods to which it related were to be produced in Switzerland: the Netherlands was not the situs of either activity.

And the other case relied upon by the district judge, *Cook Associates, Inc. v. Colonial Broach & Machine Co.,* 14 Ill.App.3d 965, 304 N.E.2d 27 (1973), dealt with a service contract involving an out-of-state company that had used the services of an Illinois employment agency via a single telephone call. This satisfied the requirements for minimum contacts under the circumstances of that case since "that call was all that was necessary for defendant to achieve its [business] purpose", *i. e.,* obtaining the names of prospective employees. 14 Ill.App.3d at 970, 304 N.E.2d 27. The conclusion and performance of the contract were carried out in Illinois via that telephone call, unlike the situation before us where neither activity occurred in the Netherlands.

Absent personal jurisdiction over Automark in the Dutch case that resulted in a default judgment, the courts of this country lack jurisdiction to enforce the foreign default judgment. The decision of the district court accordingly is reversed and the case is remanded with directions to dismiss the complaint.[3]

55

Footnotes to Koster v. Automark:

1. There apparently was some disagreement before the district court as to where this document was executed, since it bears the handwritten words "Scope [Koster's company] Amsterdam, Neth." The briefs of both parties on appeal agree that the document was executed in Milan, Italy.
The text of the handwritten document, which serves as the alleged contract, reads as follows:
We agree to purchase up to 600,000 pieces of Amico valve cap gauges bulkpacked from you at $0.11 each C.I.T. N.Y. within the 12 mos. period beginning 1/1/71.
It is signed by Automark's vice-president. It is questionable whether the document represents a valid contract, as it contains no corresponding promise by Koster. In light of our disposition of this case, however, we need not reach the question of the sufficiency of the document to satisfy the prerequisites to a binding contract.

2. Automark's letter to Koster of September 22, 1970 reads in pertinent part as follows: Anyone who will conclude a major international marketing program by mail is not, in our opinion, worth doing business with and we wonder why you are so anxious to sign up anyone so long as it is done in a matter of days. If and when we get into a program with you, it will be because we have met you personally and come to a meeting of the minds and because we have subsequently committed major marketing funds and energies to an AMICO program. If you are interested in a hit and miss, catch as catch can program (unfortunately these are American colloquial expressions but I do not know what to replace them with), then we have no place in your program and you should proceed without us.

3. Automark raised another issue which because of our resolution of the case becomes a collateral matter.
Automark contends that the Dutch statute governing service of process on defendants who reside in foreign countries provides insufficient assurances of actual notice to comport with American due process requirements. Absence of personal jurisdiction in the Netherlands courts would prevent a court in this country from enforcing a judgment rendered in the Netherlands. *Hilton v. Guyot,* 159 U.S. 113, 184, 202, 16 S.Ct. 139, 151, 158, 40 L.Ed. 95 (1895).   (Note to students: the rest of the footnote goes way too deep into the weeds for reproduction here.)

Note to students re <u>Carnival Cruise</u>: Admiralty cases involve the navigable waters of the U.S. (including navigable rivers, bays, lakes, etc.) as well as all waters adjacent to the U.S. states (e.g. Gulf of Mexico, or along the Pacific Coast, and all maritime cases generally; these are to be heard exclusively in federal courts, and never state courts.

CARNIVAL CRUISE LINES, INC. v. SHUTE et vir

U.S. Supreme Court, 499 U.S. 585 (1991)

PRIOR HISTORY: CERTIORARI TO THE UNITED STATES COURT OF APPEALS FOR THE NINTH CIRCUIT.

DISPOSITION: 897 F. 2d 377, reversed.

JUDGES: Blackmun, J., delivered the opinion of the Court, in which Rehnquist, C. J., and White, O'Connor, Scalia, Kennedy, and Souter, JJ., joined. Stevens, J., filed a dissenting opinion, in which Marshall, J., joined.

OPINION BY: BLACKMUN

[1A] In this admiralty case we primarily consider whether the United States Court of Appeals for the Ninth Circuit correctly refused to enforce a forum-selection clause contained in tickets issued by petitioner Carnival Cruise Lines, Inc., to respondents Eulala and Russel Shute.
I
The Shutes, through an Arlington, Wash., travel agent, purchased passage for a 7-day cruise on petitioner's ship, the *Tropicale*. Respondents paid the fare to the agent who forwarded the payment to petitioner's headquarters in Miami, Fla. Petitioner then prepared the tickets and sent them to respondents in the State of Washington. The face of each ticket, at its left-hand lower corner, contained this admonition:
"SUBJECT TO CONDITIONS OF CONTRACT ON LAST PAGES **IMPORTANT!** PLEASE READ CONTRACT -- ON LAST PAGES 1, 2, 3" App. 15.
The following appeared on "contract page 1" of each ticket:
"*TERMS AND CONDITIONS OF PASSAGE CONTRACT TICKET*

. . . .

"3. (a) The acceptance of this ticket by the person or persons named hereon as passengers shall be deemed to be an acceptance and agreement by each of them of all of the terms and conditions of this Passage Contract Ticket.

. . . .

"8. It is agreed by and between the passenger and the Carrier that all disputes and matters whatsoever arising under, in connection with or incident to this Contract shall be litigated, if at all, in and before a Court located in the State of Florida, U. S. A., to the exclusion of the Courts of any other state or country."

II

Respondents boarded the *Tropicale* in Los Angeles, Cal. The ship sailed to Puerto Vallarta, Mexico, and then returned to Los Angeles. While the ship was in international waters off the Mexican coast, respondent Eulala Shute was injured when she slipped on a deck mat during a guided tour of the ship's galley. Respondents filed suit against petitioner in the United States District Court for the Western District of Washington, claiming that Mrs. Shute's injuries had been caused by the negligence of Carnival Cruise Lines and its employees. *Id.*, at 4.

Petitioner moved for summary judgment, contending that the forum clause in respondents' tickets required the Shutes to bring their suit against petitioner in a court in the State of Florida. Petitioner contended, alternatively, that the District Court lacked personal jurisdiction over petitioner because petitioner's contacts with the State of Washington were insubstantial. The District Court granted the motion, holding that petitioner's contacts with Washington were constitutionally insufficient to support the exercise of personal jurisdiction. See App. to Pet. for Cert. 60a.

The Court of Appeals reversed. Reasoning that "but for" petitioner's solicitation of business in Washington, respondents would not have taken the cruise and Mrs. Shute would not have been injured, the court concluded that petitioner had sufficient contacts with Washington to justify the District Court's exercise of personal jurisdiction. 897 F. 2d 377, 385-386 (CA9 1990).

Turning to the forum-selection clause, the Court of Appeals acknowledged that a court concerned with the enforceability of such a clause must begin its analysis with *The Bremen* v. *Zapata Off-Shore Co.*, 407 U.S. 1 (1972), where this Court held that forum-selection clauses, although not "historically . . . favored," are "prima facie valid." *Id.*, at 9-10. See 897 F. 2d, at 388. The appellate court concluded that the forum clause should not be enforced because it "was not freely bargained for." *Id.* at 389. As an "independent justification" for refusing to enforce the clause, the Court of Appeals noted that there was evidence in the record to indicate that "the Shutes are physically and financially incapable of pursuing this litigation in Florida" and that the enforcement of the clause would operate to deprive them of their day in court and thereby contravene this Court's holding in *The Bremen*. 897 F. 2d, at 389.

We granted certiorari to address the question whether the Court of Appeals was correct in holding that the District Court should hear respondents' tort claim against petitioner. 498 U.S. 807-808 (1990).Because we find the forum-selection clause to be dispositive of this question, we need not consider petitioner's constitutional argument as to personal jurisdiction. See *Ashwander* v. *TVA*, 297 U.S. 288, 347 (1936) (Brandeis, J., concurring) ("'It is not the habit of the Court to decide questions of a constitutional nature unless absolutely necessary to a decision of the case,'" quoting *Burton* v. *United States*, 196 U.S. 283, 295 (1905)).

III

We begin by noting the boundaries of our inquiry. First, this is a case in admiralty, and federal law governs the enforceability of the forum-selection clause we scrutinize. . . .Second, we do not address the question whether respondents had sufficient notice of the forum clause before entering the contract for passage. Respondents essentially have conceded that they had notice of the forum-selection provision. Brief for Respondents 26 ("The respondents do not contest the incorporation of the provisions nor [*sic*] that the forum selection clause was reasonably communicated to the respondents, as much as three pages of fine print can be communicated"). . ..

Within this context, respondents urge that the forum clause should not be enforced because, contrary to this Court's teachings in *The Bremen*, the clause was not the product of negotiation, and enforcement effectively would deprive respondents of their day in court. Additionally, respondents contend that the clause violates the Limitation of Vessel Owner's Liability Act, 46 U. S. C. App. ß 183c. We consider these arguments in turn.

IV

A

Both petitioner and respondents argue vigorously that the Court's opinion in *The Bremen* governs this case, and each side purports to find ample support for its position in that opinion's broadranging language. This seeming paradox derives in large part from key factual differences between this case and *The Bremen*, differences that preclude an automatic and simple application of *The Bremen*'s general principles to the facts here.

In *The Bremen*, this Court addressed the enforceability of a forum-selection clause in a contract between two business corporations. An American corporation, Zapata, made a contract with Unterweser, a German corporation, for the towage of Zapata's oceangoing drilling rig from Louisiana to a point in the Adriatic Sea off the coast of Italy. The agreement provided that any dispute arising under the contract was to be resolved in the London Court of Justice. After a storm in the Gulf of Mexico seriously damaged the rig, Zapata ordered Unterweser's ship to tow the rig to Tampa, Fla., the nearest point of refuge. Thereafter, Zapata sued Unterweser in admiralty in federal court at Tampa. Citing the forum clause, Unterweser moved to dismiss. The District Court denied Unterweser's motion, and the Court of Appeals for the Fifth Circuit, sitting en banc on rehearing, and by a sharply divided vote, affirmed. *In re Complaint of Unterweser Reederei, GmBH*, 446 F. 2d 907 (1971).

This Court vacated and remanded, stating that, in general, "a freely negotiated private international agreement, unaffected by fraud, undue influence, or overweening bargaining power, such as that involved here, should be given full effect." The Court further generalized that "in the light of present-day commercial realities and expanding international trade we conclude that the forum clause should control absent a strong showing that it should be set aside." The Court did not define precisely the circumstances that would make it unreasonable for a court to enforce a forum clause. Instead, the Court discussed a number of factors that made it reasonable to enforce the clause at issue in *The Bremen* and that, presumably, would be pertinent in any determination whether to enforce a similar clause.

In this respect, the Court noted that there was "strong evidence that the forum clause was a vital part of the agreement, and [that] it would be unrealistic to think that the parties did not conduct their negotiations, including fixing the monetary terms, with the consequences of the forum clause figuring prominently in their calculations." Further, the Court observed that it was not "dealing with an agreement between two Americans to resolve their essentially local disputes in a remote alien forum," and that in such a case, "the serious inconvenience of the contractual forum to one or both of the parties might carry greater weight in determining the reasonableness of the forum clause." The Court stated that even where the forum clause establishes a remote forum for resolution of conflicts, "the party claiming [unfairness] should bear a heavy burden of proof."

In applying *The Bremen*, the Court of Appeals in the present litigation took note of the foregoing "reasonableness" factors and rather automatically decided that the forum-selection clause was unenforceable because, unlike the parties in *The Bremen*, respondents are not business persons and did not negotiate the terms of the clause with petitioner. Alternatively, the Court of Appeals ruled that the clause should not be enforced because enforcement effectively would deprive respondents of an opportunity to litigate their claim against petitioner.

The Bremen concerned a "far from routine transaction between companies of two different nations contemplating the tow of an extremely costly piece of equipment from Louisiana across the Gulf of Mexico and the Atlantic Ocean, through the Mediterranean Sea to its final destination in the Adriatic Sea." These facts suggest that, even apart from the evidence of negotiation regarding the forum clause, it was entirely reasonable for the Court in *The Bremen* to have expected Unterweser and Zapata to have negotiated with care in selecting a forum for the resolution of disputes arising from their special towing contract.

[1B] In contrast, respondents' passage contract was purely routine and doubtless nearly identical to every commercial passage contract issued by petitioner and most other cruise lines. See, *e. g., Hodes* v. *S. N. C. Achille Lauro ed Altri-Gestione*, 858 F. 2d 905, 910 (CA3 1988), cert. dism'd, 490 U.S. 1001 (1989). In this context, it would be entirely unreasonable for us to assume that respondents -- or any other cruise passenger -- would negotiate with petitioner the terms of a forum-selection clause in an ordinary commercial cruise ticket. Common sense dictates that a ticket of this kind will be a form contract the terms of which are not subject to negotiation, and that an individual purchasing the ticket will not have bargaining parity with the cruisw line. But by ignoring the crucial differences in the business contexts in which the respective contracts were executed, the Court of Appeals' analysis seems to us to have distorted somewhat this Court's holding in *The Bremen*.

In evaluating the reasonableness of the forum clause at issue in this case, we must refine the analysis of *The Bremen* to account for the realities of form passage contracts. As an initial matter, we do not adopt the Court of Appeals' determination that a nonnegotiated forum-selection clause in a form ticket contract is never enforceable simply because it is not the subject of bargaining. Including a reasonable forum clause in a form contract of this kind well may be permissible for several reasons: First, a cruise line has a special interest in limiting the fora in which it potentially could be subject to suit. Because a cruise ship typically carries passengers from many locales, it is not unlikely that a mishap on a cruise could subject the cruise line to litigation in several diffcrent fora. See *The Bremen*, 407 U.S., at 13, and n. 15; *Hodes*, 858 F. 2d, at 913. Additionally, a clause establishing *ex ante* the forum for dispute resolution has the salutary effect of dispelling any confusion about where suits arising from the contract must be brought and defended, sparing litigants the time and expense of pretrial motions to determine the correct forum and conserving judicial resources that otherwise would be devoted to deciding those motions. See *Stewart Organization*, 487 U.S., at 33 (concurring opinion). Finally, it stands to reason that passengers who purchase tickets containing a forum clause like that at issue in this case benefit in the form of reduced fares reflecting the savings that the cruise line enjoys by limiting the fora in which it may be sued. Cf. *Northwestern Nat. Ins. Co.* v. *Donovan*, 916 F. 2d 372, 378 (CA7 1990).

We also do not accept the Court of Appeals' "independent justification" for its conclusion that *The Bremen* dictates that the clause should not be enforced because "there is evidence in the record to indicate that the Shutes are physically and financially incapable of pursuing this litigation in Florida." 897 F. 2d, at 389. We do not defer to the Court of Appeals' findings of fact. In dismissing the case for lack of personal jurisdiction over petitioner, the District Court made no finding regarding the physical and financial impediments to the Shutes' pursuing their case in Florida. The Court of Appeals' conclusory reference to the record provides no basis for this Court to validate the finding of inconvenience. Furthermore, the Court of Appeals did not place in proper context this Court's statement in *The Bremen* that "the serious inconvenience of the contractual forum to one or both of the parties might carry greater weight in determining the reasonableness of the forum clause." 407 U.S., at 17. The Court made this statement in evaluating a hypothetical "agreement between two Americans to resolve their essentially local disputes in a remote alien forum."

In the present case, Florida is not a "remote alien forum," nor -- given the fact that Mrs. Shute's accident occurred off the coast of Mexico -- is this dispute an essentially local one inherently more suited to resolution in the State of Washington than in Florida. In light of these distinctions, and because respondents do not claim lack of notice of the forum clause, we conclude that they have not satisfied the "heavy burden of proof," *ibid.*, required to set aside the clause on grounds of inconvenience.

It bears emphasis that forum-selection clauses contained in form passage contracts are subject to judicial scrutiny for fundamental fairness. In this case, there is no indication that petitioner set Florida as the forum in which disputes were to be resolved as a means of discouraging cruise passengers from pursuing legitimate claims. Any suggestion of such a bad-faith motive is belied by two facts: Petitioner has its principal place of business in Florida, and many of its cruises depart from and return to Florida ports. Similarly, there is no evidence that petitioner obtained respondents' accession to the forum clause by fraud or overreaching. Finally, respondents have conceded that they were given notice of the forum provision and, therefore, presumably retained the option of rejecting the contract with impunity. In the case before us, therefore, we conclude that the Court of Appeals erred in refusing to enforce the forum-selection clause.

B

Respondents also contend that the forum-selection clause at issue violates 46 U. S. C. App. ß 183c. That statute, enacted in 1936, see ch. 521, 49 Stat. 1480, provides:

"It shall be unlawful for the . . . owner of any vessel transporting passengers between ports of the United States or between any such port and a foreign port to insert in any rule, regulation, contract, or agreement any provision or limitation (1) purporting, in the event of loss of life or bodily injury arising from the negligence or fault of such owner or his servants, to relieve such owner . . . from liability, or from liability beyond any stipulated amount, for such loss or injury, or (2) purporting in such event to lessen, weaken, or avoid the right of any claimant to a trial by court of competent jurisdiction on the question of liability for such loss or injury, or the measure of damages therefor. All such provisions or limitations contained in any such rule, regulation, contract, or agreement are hereby declared to be against public policy and shall be null and void and of no effect."

By its plain language, the forum-selection clause before us does not take away respondents' right to "a trial by [a] court of competent jurisdiction" and thereby contravene the explicit proscription of Section §183c. Instead, the clause states specifically that actions arising out of the passage contract shall be brought "if at all," in a court "located in the State of Florida," which, plainly, is a "court of competent jurisdiction" within the meaning of the statute.
Respondents appear to acknowledge this by asserting that although the forum clause does not directly prevent the determination of claims against the cruise line, it causes plaintiffs

unreasonable hardship in asserting their rights and therefore violates Congress' intended goal in enacting §183c. Significantly, however, respondents cite no authority for their contention that Congress' intent in enacting §183c was to avoid having a plaintiff travel to a distant forum in order to litigate. The legislative history of §183c suggests instead that this provision was enacted in response to passenger-ticket conditions purporting to limit the shipowner's liability for negligence or to remove the issue of liability from the scrutiny of any court by means of a clause providing that "the question of liability and the measure of damages shall be determined by arbitration." . . .. There was no prohibition of a forum-selection clause. Because the clause before us allows for judicial resolution of claims against petitioner and does not purport to limit petitioner's liability for negligence, it does not violate §183c.

V

The judgment of the Court of Appeals is reversed.
It is so ordered.

DISSENT BY: STEVENS; MARSHALL

Justice Stevens, with whom Justice Marshall joins, dissenting.

The Court prefaces its legal analysis with a factual statement that implies that a purchaser of a Carnival Cruise Lines passenger ticket is fully and fairly notified about the existence of the choice of forum clause in the fine print on the back of the ticket. See *ante*, at 587-588. Even if this implication were accurate, I would disagree with the Court's analysis. But, given the Court's preface, I begin my dissent by noting that only the most meticulous passenger is likely to become aware of the forum-selection provision. I have therefore appended to this opinion a facsimile of the relevant text, using the type size that actually appears in the ticket itself. A careful reader will find the forum-selection clause in the 8th of the 25 numbered paragraphs.

Of course, many passengers, like the respondents in this case, will not have an opportunity to read paragraph 8 until they have actually purchased their tickets. By this point, the passengers will already have accepted the condition set forth in paragraph 16(a), which provides that "the Carrier shall not be liable to make any refund to passengers in respect of . . . tickets wholly or partly not used by a passenger." Not knowing whether or not that provision is legally enforceable, I assume that the average passenger would accept the risk of having to file suit in Florida in the event of an injury, rather than canceling -- without a refund -- a planned vacation at the last minute. The fact that the cruise line can reduce its litigation costs, and therefore its liability insurance premiums, by forcing this choice on its passengers does not, in my opinion, suffice to render the provision reasonable. Cf. *Steven* v. *Fidelity & Casualty Co. of New York*, 58 Cal. 2d 862, 883, 377 P. 2d 284, 298 (1962) (refusing to enforce limitation on liability in insurance policy because insured "must purchase the policy before he even knows its provisions").

Even if passengers received prominent notice of the forum-selection clause before they committed the cost of the cruise, I would remain persuaded that the clause was unenforceable under traditional principles of federal admiralty law and is "null and void" under the terms of Limitation of Vessel Owner's Liability Act, ch. 521, 49 Stat. 1480, 46 U. S. C. App. §183c, which was enacted in 1936 to invalidate expressly stipulations limiting shipowners' liability for negligence.

Exculpatory clauses in passenger tickets have been around for a long time. These clauses are typically the product of disparate bargaining power between the carrier and the passenger, and they undermine the strong public interest in deterring negligent conduct. For these reasons, courts long before the turn of the century consistently held such clauses unenforceable under federal admiralty law. Thus, in a case involving a ticket provision purporting to limit the shipowner's liability for the negligent handling of baggage, this Court wrote:

"It is settled in the courts of the United States that exemptions limiting carriers from responsibility for the negligence of themselves or their servants are both unjust and unreasonable, and will be deemed as wanting in the element of voluntary assent; and, besides, that such conditions are in conflict with public policy. This doctrine was announced so long ago, and has been so frequently reiterated, that it is elementary. We content ourselves with referring to the cases of the *Baltimore & Ohio &c. Railway* v. *Voigt*, 176 U.S. 498, 505, 507, and *Knott* v. *Botany Mills*, 179 U.S. 69, 71, where the previously adjudged cases are referred to and the principles by them expounded are restated." *The Kensington*, 183 U.S. 263, 268 (1902).

Clauses limiting a carrier's liability or weakening the passenger's right to recover for the negligence of the carrier's employees come in a variety of forms. Complete exemptions from liability for negligence or limitations on the amount of the potential damage recovery, requirements that notice of claims be filed within an unreasonably short period of time, provisions mandating a choice of law that is favorable to the defendant in negligence cases, and forum-selection clauses are all similarly designed to put a thumb on the carrier's side of the scale of justice. [4]

See 46 U. S. C. App. §183c:

"It shall be unlawful for the . . . owner of any vessel transporting passengers between ports of the United States or between any such port and a foreign port to insert in any rule, regulation, contract, or agreement any provision or limitation (1) purporting, in the event of loss of life or bodily injury arising from the negligence or fault of such owner or his servants, to relieve such owner . . . from liability, or from liability beyond any stipulated amount, for such loss or injury. . . ."

See 46 U. S. C. App. ß 183b(a):
Forum-selection clauses in passenger tickets involve the intersection of two strands of traditional contract law that qualify the general rule that courts will enforce the terms of a contract as written. Pursuant to the first strand, courts traditionally have reviewed with heightened scrutiny the terms of contracts of adhesion, form contracts offered on a take-or-leave basis by a party with stronger bargaining power to a party with weaker power. Some commentators have questioned whether contracts of adhesion can justifiably be enforced at all under traditional contract theory because the adhering party generally enters into them without manifesting knowing and voluntary consent to all their terms.

The common law, recognizing that standardized form contracts account for a significant portion of all commercial agreements, has taken a less extreme position and instead subjects terms in contracts of adhesion to scrutiny for reasonableness. Judge J. Skelly Wright set out the state of the law succinctly in *Williams* v. *Walker-Thomas Furniture Co.*, 121 U. S. App. D. C. 315, 319-320, 350 F. 2d 445, 449-450 (1965) (footnotes omitted):

"Ordinarily, one who signs an agreement without full knowledge of its terms might be held to assume the risk that he has entered a one-sided bargain. But when a party of little bargaining power, and hence little real choice, signs a commercially unreasonable contract with little or no knowledge of its terms, it is hardly likely that his consent, or even an objective manifestation of his consent, was ever given to all of the terms. In such a case the usual rule that the terms of the agreement are not to be questioned should be abandoned and the court should consider whether the terms of the contract are so unfair that enforcement should be withheld."

The second doctrinal principle implicated by forum-selection clauses is the traditional rule that "contractual provisions, which seek to limit the place or court in which an action may . . . be brought, are invalid as contrary to public policy." See Dougherty, Validity of Contractual Provision Limiting Place or Court in Which Action May Be Brought, 31 A. L. R. 4th 404, 409, §3 (1984). . . .Although adherence to this general rule has declined in recent years, particularly following our decision in *The Bremen* v. *Zapata Off-Shore Co.*, 407 U.S. 1 (1972), the prevailing rule is still that forum-selection clauses are not enforceable if they were not freely bargained for, create additional expense for one party, or deny one party a remedy. . . .A forum-selection clause in a standardized passenger ticket would clearly have been unenforceable under the common law before our decision in *The Bremen*, see 407 U.S., at 9, and n. 10, and, in my opinion, remains unenforceable under the prevailing rule today.

The Bremen, which the Court effectively treats as controlling this case, had nothing to say about stipulations printed on the back of passenger tickets. That case involved the enforceability of a forum-selection clause in a freely negotiated international agreement between two large corporations providing for the towage of a vessel from the Gulf of Mexico to the Adriatic Sea. The Court recognized that such towage agreements had generally been held unenforceable in American courts, [5] but held that the doctrine of those cases did not extend to commercial arrangements between parties with equal bargaining power.

5 "In [*Carbon Black Export, Inc.* v. *The Monrosa*, 254 F. 2d 297 (CA5 1958), cert. dism'd, 359 U.S. 180 (1959),] the Court of Appeals had held a forum-selection clause unenforceable, reiterating the traditional view of many American courts that 'agreements in advance of controversy whose object is to oust the jurisdiction of the courts are contrary to public policy and will not be enforced.' 254 F. 2d, at 300-301." *The Bremen* v. *Zapata Off-Shore Co.*, 407 U.S. 1, 6 (1972).

The federal statute that should control the disposition of the case before us today was enacted in 1936 when the general rule denying enforcement of forum-selection clauses was indisputably widely accepted. The principal subject of the statute concerned the limitation of shipowner liability, but as the following excerpt from the House Report explains, the section that is relevant to this case was added as a direct response to shipowners' ticketing practices.

"During the course of the hearings on the bill (H. R. 9969) there was also brought to the attention of the committee a practice of providing on the reverse side of steamship tickets that in the event of damage or injury caused by the negligence or fault of the owner or his servants, the liability of the owner shall be limited to a stipulated amount, in some cases $ 5,000, and in others substantially lower amounts, or that in such event the question of liability and the measure of damages *shall be determined by arbitration*. The amendment to chapter 6 of title 48 of the Revised Statutes proposed to be made by section 2 of the committee amendment is intended to, and in the opinion of the committee will, *put a stop to all such practices and practices of a like "character."* H. R. Rep. No. 2517, 74th Cong., 2d Sess., 6-7 (1936) (emphasis added); see also S. Rep. No. 2061, 74th Cong., 2d Sess., 6-7 (1936).

The intent to "put a stop to all such practices and practices of a like character" was effectuated in the second clause of the statute. It reads:

"It shall be unlawful for the manager, agent, master, or owner of any vessel transporting passengers between ports of the United States or between any such port and a foreign port to insert in any rule, regulation, contract, or agreement any provision or limitation (1) purporting, in the event of loss of life or bodily injury arising from the negligence or fault of such owner or his servants, to relieve such owner, master, or agent from liability, or from liability beyond any stipulated amount, for such loss or injury, or (2) *purporting in such event to lessen, weaken, or avoid the right of any claimant to a trial by court of competent jurisdiction on the question of liability for such loss or injury, or the measure of damages therefor.* All such provisions or limitations contained in any such rule, regulation, contract, or agreement are declared to be against public policy and shall be null and void and of no effect." 46 U. S. C. App. §183c (emphasis added).

The stipulation in the ticket that Carnival Cruise sold to respondents certainly lessens or weakens their ability to recover for the slip and fall incident that occurred off the west coast of Mexico during the cruise that originated and terminated in Los Angeles, California. It is safe to assume that the witnesses -- whether other passengers or members of the crew -- can be assembled with less expense and inconvenience at a west coast forum than in a Florida court several thousand miles from the scene of the accident.

A liberal reading of the 1936 statute is supported by both its remedial purpose and by the legislative history's general condemnation of "all such practices." Although the statute does not specifically mention forum-selection clauses, its language is broad enough to encompass them. The absence of a specific reference is adequately explained by the fact that such clauses were already unenforceable under common law and would not often have been used by carriers, which were relying on stipulations that purported to exonerate them from liability entirely. Cf. *Moskal v. United States*, 498 U.S. 103, 110-113 (1990).

(Footnote from Justice Stevens) "The Court does not make clear whether the result in this case would also apply if the clause required Carnival passengers to sue in Panama, the country in which Carnival is incorporated."

Under these circumstances, the general prohibition against stipulations purporting "to lessen, weaken, or avoid" the passenger's right to a trial certainly should be construed to apply to the manifestly unreasonable stipulation in these passengers' tickets. Even without the benefit of the statute, I would continue to apply the general rule that prevailed prior to our decision in *The Bremen* to forum-selection clauses in passenger tickets.

I respectfully dissent.

Case Questions:

1. Do you understand why this case had to be heard in federal court?
2. Do you think this decision is fair to Mr. and Mrs. Shute?
3. If there had been no forum selection clause, do you think the court in Washington should take personal jurisdiction over Carnival Cruise Lines?
4. What are some of the differences between the Bremen case and in this case? do you think the majority is correct in thinking those differences should not lead to a different result?
5. How is it "just" to have a major corporation dictate the terms of dispute resolution to its customers and to have the U.S. court system back them up?

CHAPTER THREE:

NATIONAL LAWMAKING POWERS AND THE REGULATION OF INTERNATIONAL BUSINESS

Contents:

I.   TREATIES AND THE U.S. CONSTITUTION

A.   Introduction

Under international law, a treaty is any agreement concluded between two nation-states if the agreement is intended to have international legal effect.

"Treaty" has a much more restricted meaning under the constitutional law of the United States. It is an international agreement that has received the "advice and consent" (in practice, just the consent) of two-thirds of the Senate and that has been ratified by the President.

The Senate does not ratify treaties. When the Senate gives its consent, the President--acting as the chief diplomat of the United States--has discretion whether or not to ratify the instrument. Several instruments that have received the Senate's consent have nonetheless remained unratified. Those instruments are not in force for the United States, despite the Senate's consent to them.

Not all international agreements negotiated by the Executive Branch are submitted to the Senate for its consent. Quite often, the Executive Branch negotiates agreements that are intended to be binding without the consent of two-thirds of the Senate. Sometimes these agreements are entered into with the concurrence of a simple majority of both houses of Congress ("Congressional-Executive agreements"); on other occasions the President simply enters into an agreement without the intended or actual participation of either house of Congress. This is known as a "Presidential agreement," or "Sole Executive" agreement. The extent of the President's authority to enter into Sole Executive agreements is controversial.

Clearly, the President has some authority to make agreements in his capacities as commander in chief of the armed forces and as "chief diplomat." Thus, armistice agreements and certain agreements incidental to the operation of foreign embassies in the United States could be done as Sole Executive Agreements. The agreement-making scope of these two sources of Presidential authority is nevertheless somewhat vague.

Congress has attempted to curb the President's claimed authority as commander in chief to commit U.S. armed forces to positions of peril. Over a presidential veto, Congress passed the War Powers Joint Resolution in 1973, which has had the effect of inducing Presidents to consult with —and report to —Congress when U. S. armed forces are used in combat situations, but it has not significantly limited the President's practical power to commit the United States to use military force.

As a matter of domestic law within the United States, Congress may override a pre-existing treaty or Congressional-Executive agreement of the United States. To do so, however, would place the United States in breach of the obligation owed under international law to its treaty partner(s) to honor the treaty or agreement in good faith. Consequently, courts in the United States are disinclined to find that Congress has actually intended to override a treaty or other internationally binding obligation. Instead, they struggle to interpret the Congressional act and/or the international instrument in such a way as to reconcile the two.

B.   "Self-executing" treaties

Recall the Sei Fujii case from Chapter One. Provisions in treaties and other international agreements are given effect as law in domestic courts of the United States only if they are "self-executing" or if they have been implemented by an act (such as an act of Congress) having the effect of federal law. Courts in this country have been reluctant to find various treaty provisions self-executing, but on several occasions they have found them so —sometimes simply by giving direct effect to the provisions without expressly saying that they are self-executing. There are varying formulations as to what tends to make a treaty provision self-executing or non-self-executing, but within constitutional constraints (such as the requirement that appropriations of money originate in the House of Representatives) the primary consideration is the intent —or lack thereof—that the provision become effective as judicially-enforceable domestic law without implementing legislation.

For the most part, the more specific the provision is and the more it reads like an act of Congress, the more likely it is to be treated as self-executing.

Remember: Whether it is a treaty that has been consented to by the Senate, or a Congressional-Executive agreement (approved by a majority of the Senate), either has the same force and effect as legislation passed by Congress and signed into law by the President. Of course, like any legislation, Congress can amend or abolish that law. Whatever legislation passes both houses and is signed into law will supersede prior laws, treaties, or agreements. This is the "last in time" rule that courts use when laws and treaties and agreements are in any kind of conflict.

C.   <u>Examples of Congressional-Executive agreements:</u>

The North American Free Trade Agreement (NAFTA)
The U.S.-Canada-Mexico Free Trade Agreement (USMCA)(replacing NAFTA)
U.S. membership in the World Trade Organization (WTO)

In part because the enumerated powers of Congress and the president have been interpreted broadly, most agreements that are proposed as treaties could also have been proposed as congressional-executive agreements. For that reason, the U.S. government has frequently chosen to use congressional-executive agreements rather than treaties for controversial agreements that are unlikely to gain the required supermajority of 67 votes (2/3rds of the Senators). In this way, these agreements are exactly like any other legislation passed by both Houses of Congress and signed by the President.

II.   STATE VS. FEDERAL POWERS

<u>Introduction</u>: Although we still hear about "states rights" in our federal system, the federal government is the proper government entity to deal with other nation-states, so that there is one foreign policy rather than 51. But, states will still always be tempted to pass laws that make a political statement, and push the boundaries of what the Constitution allows states to do, and this often means that the Supreme Court must define (and re-define) what those boundaries are. In the following case, the State of Massachusetts chose to limit the state's agencies from dealing with the government of Myannmar. The State did not disallow private businesses in that state from dealing with Myanmar's government. Still, the Court had reason to disallow the Massachusetts law; declared unconstitutional by the Court, the law could have no effect in Massachusetts or anywhere else, and similar laws passed by other states would have no effect, either.

A.   <u>State interference in foreign affairs</u>

Stephen P. Crosby, Secretary of Administration and Finance of Massachusetts et al. v. National Foreign Trade Council
U.S. Supreme Court (2000)

Justice Souter delivered the opinion of the Court.

I.

In June 1996, Massachusetts adopted "An Act Regulating State Contracts with Companies Doing Business with or in Burma (Myanmar)." The statute generally bars state entities from buying goods or services from any person (defined to include a business organization) identified on a "restricted purchase list" of those doing business with Burma.

'Doing business with Burma' is defined broadly to cover any person

"(a) having a principal place of business, place of incorporation or its corporate headquarters in Burma (Myanmar) or having any operations, leases, franchises, majority-owned subsidiaries, distribution agreements, or any other similar agreements in Burma (Myanmar), or being the majority-owned subsidiary, licensee or franchise of such a person;

"(b) providing financial services to the government of Burma (Myanmar), including providing direct loans, underwriting government securities, providing any consulting advice or assistance, providing brokerage services, acting as a trustee or escrow agent, or otherwise acting as an agent pursuant to a contractual agreement;

"(c) promoting the importation or sale of gems, timber, oil, gas or other related products, commerce in which is largely controlled by the government of Burma (Myanmar), from Burma (Myanmar);

"(d) providing any goods or services to the government of Burma (Myanmar)." §7:22G.

. . .

In September 1996, three months after the Massachusetts law was enacted, Congress passed a statute imposing a set of mandatory and conditional sanctions on Burma. See Foreign Operations, Export Financing, and Related Programs Appropriations Act, 1997, §570, 110 Stat. 3009—166 to 3009—167 (enacted by the Omnibus Consolidated Appropriations Act, 1997, §101(c), 110 Stat. 3009—121 to 3009—172). The federal Act has five basic parts, three substantive and two procedural.

First, it imposes three sanctions directly on Burma. It bans all aid to the Burmese Government except for humanitarian assistance, counter-narcotics efforts, and promotion of human rights and democracy. §570(a)(1). The statute instructs United States representatives to international financial institutions to vote against loans or other assistance to or for Burma, §570(a)(2), and it provides that no entry visa shall be issued to any Burmese government official unless required by treaty or to staff the Burmese mission to the United Nations, §570(a)(3). These restrictions are to remain in effect "[u]ntil such time as the President determines and certifies to Congress that Burma has made measurable and substantial progress in improving human rights practices and implementing democratic government." §570(a).

Second, the federal Act authorizes the President to impose further sanctions subject to certain conditions. He may prohibit "United States persons" from "new investment" in Burma, and shall do so if he determines and certifies to Congress that the Burmese Government has physically harmed, rearrested, or exiled Daw Aung San Suu Kyi (the opposition leader selected to receive the Nobel Peace Prize), or has committed "large-scale repression of or violence against the Democratic opposition." §570(b).

Third, the statute directs the President to work to develop "a comprehensive, multilateral strategy to bring democracy to and improve human rights practices and the quality of life in Burma." §570(c). He is instructed to cooperate with members of the Association of Southeast Asian Nations (ASEAN) and with other countries having major trade and investment interests in Burma to devise such an approach, and to pursue the additional objective of fostering dialogue between the ruling State Law and Order Restoration Council (SLORC) and democratic opposition groups.

…..

On May 20, 1997, the President issued the Burma Executive Order, Exec. Order No. 13047, 3 CFR 202 (1997 Comp.). He certified for purposes of §570(b) that the

Government of Burma had "committed large-scale repression of the democratic opposition in Burma" and found that the Burmese Government's actions and policies constituted "an unusual and extraordinary threat to the national security and foreign policy of the United States," a threat characterized as a national emergency. The President then prohibited new investment in Burma "by United States persons," Exec. Order No. 13047, §1, any approval or facilitation by a United States person of such new investment by foreign persons, §2(a), and any transaction meant to evade or avoid the ban, §2(b). The order generally incorporated the exceptions and exemptions addressed in the statute. §§3, 4. Finally, the President delegated to the Secretary of State the tasks of working with ASEAN and other countries to develop a strategy for democracy, human rights, and the quality of life in Burma, and of making the required congressional reports. §5.

II.

Respondent National Foreign Trade Council (Council) is a nonprofit corporation representing companies engaged in foreign commerce; 34 of its members were on the Massachusetts restricted purchase list in 1998. *National Foreign Trade Council* v. *Natsios*, 181 F.3d 38, 48 (CA1 1999). Three withdrew from Burma after the passage of the state Act, and one member had its bid for a procurement contract increased by 10 percent under the provision of the state law allowing acceptance of a low bid from a listed bidder only if the next-to-lowest bid is more than 10 percent higher.

In April 1998, the Council filed suit in the United States District Court for the District of Massachusetts, seeking declaratory and injunctive relief against the petitioner state officials charged with administering and enforcing the state Act (whom we will refer to simply as the State).

The Council argued that the state law unconstitutionally infringed on the federal foreign affairs power, violated the Foreign Commerce Clause, and was preempted by the federal Act. After detailed stipulations, briefing, and argument, the District Court permanently enjoined enforcement of the state Act, holding that it "unconstitutionally impinge[d] on the federal government's exclusive authority to regulate foreign affairs." (citing *National Foreign Trade Council* v. *Baker*, 26 F. Supp. 2d 287, 291 (Mass. 1998)).

The United States Court of Appeals for the First Circuit affirmed on three independent grounds. . . . The State's petition for certiorari challenged the decision on all three grounds and asserted interests said to be shared by other state and local governments with similar measures. Though opposing certiorari, the Council acknowledged the significance of the issues and the need to settle the constitutionality of such laws and regulations. We granted certiorari to resolve these important questions, and now affirm.

III.

A fundamental principle of the Constitution is that Congress has the power to preempt state law. Art. VI, cl. 2. Even without an express provision for preemption, we have found that state law must yield to a congressional Act in at least two circumstances. When Congress intends federal law to "occupy the field," state law in that area is preempted. .... And even if Congress has not occupied the field, state law is naturally preempted to the extent of any conflict with a federal statute. . . . . We will find preemption where it is impossible for a private party to comply with both state and federal law, . . . and where "under the circumstances of [a] particular case, [the challenged state law] stands as an obstacle to the accomplishment and execution of the full purposes and objectives of Congress." What is a sufficient obstacle is a matter of judgment, to be informed by examining the federal statute as a whole and identifying its purpose and intended effects:

"For when the question is whether a Federal act overrides a state law, the entire scheme of the statute must of course be considered and that which needs must be implied is of no less force than that which is expressed. If the purpose of the act cannot otherwise be accomplished–if its operation within its chosen field else must be frustrated and its provisions be refused their natural effect–the state law must yield to the regulation of Congress within the sphere of its delegated power." *Savage, supra,* 533, quoted in *Hines, supra*, at 67, n. 20.

Applying this standard, we see the state Burma law as an obstacle to the accomplishment of Congress's full objectives under the federal Act.7 We find that the state law undermines the intended purpose and "natural effect" of at least three provisions of the federal Act, that is, its delegation of effective discretion to the President to control economic sanctions against Burma, its limitation of sanctions solely to United States persons and new investment, and its directive to the President to proceed diplomatically in developing a comprehensive, multilateral strategy towards Burma.

(The rest of the opinion by Justice Souter is omitted.)

Case Questions:

1.	What if the Governor of Colorado decided in 2022 that the state would no longer sponsor any trade missions to Myannmar as a result of the military coup in 2021? Is that unconstitutional?

2.	What if neither the Governor nor the Colorado legislature made changes to Colorado's laws, but Western Union, headquartered in the Denver Tech Center, decided that it would no longer handle transactions between the U.S. and Myannmar? Are there any Constitutional issues?

3.	Could the Colorado legislature decide that companies like Western Union could no longer "do business" in Myannmar? Could Congress? Suppose that a 2009 DU graduate has a Colorado based business importing Russian nesting dolls,[18] and that Colorado's legislature (or Congress, or the President by executive order) has effectively deprived her of substantial income. If half of her income were from Russian imports, would she have a cause of action against the government of Colorado? Or Congress? Why or why not?

4.	Suppose Congress does nothing and says nothing about the military's coup in Myannmar. Would the U.S. President be able to put "sanctions" on Myannmar's leaders, doing so by "executive order"? If so, and if Western Union's business in

_____

[18] The Russian Store, website, https://www.therussianstore.com/nesting-dolls.html

Myannmar was profitable, could the company challenge the President's executive order in court? On what grounds? What would be the result?

5. In Myannmar, a government in exile has been formed — called the national unity government (or NUG for short) — which is comprised mainly of elected representatives of former leader Aung San Suu Kyi's deposed government and ethnic minority groups.[19] It claims to be the legitimate government of Myanmar and should be able to appoint the country's ambassadors. Civil society groups in Myanmar have sent a letter to the General Assembly urging it to retain current UN ambassador Kyaw Moe Tun, who opposed the coup and is a vocal critic of the junta. Should the U.S. recognize the NUG? Should the U.N.?

6. A large amount of cash is frozen in U.S. banks.[20] Should the banks give the money to the Myannmar military or the government in exile? Do they have to ask the U.S. government before they dispense any of the frozen money? By what legal mechanism was the money frozen in the first place?

B. Federal Pre-emption of State Law:

U.S. v. Locke
529 U.S. 89 (2000)

Facts: In the aftermath of the Exxon Valdez oil spill, the State of Washington created the Office of Marine Safety, which was directed to establish standards to provide the "best achievable protection" (BAP) from oil spill damage. The agency promulgated tanker design, equipment, reporting, and operating requirements. The International Association of Independent Tanker Owners (Intertanko), a trade association of tanker operators, filed suit against the state and local officials responsible for enforcing the BAP regulations. The state official, Gary Locke, was governor of Washington at the time.

Intertanko argued that Washington's BAP standards had entered an area occupied by the federal government and imposed unique requirements in an area where national uniformity was mandated. Further, Intertanko argued that if every political subdivision were to promulgate such maritime regulations, the goal of national governments to develop effective international environmental and safety would be undermined. The District Court upheld Washington's regulations. Thereafter, the Federal Government intervened on Intertanko's behalf, contending that the District Court's ruling failed to give sufficient weight to the substantial foreign affairs interests of the Federal Government. The Court of Appeals affirmed.

---

[19] Two governments claim to run Myanmar. So, who gets the country's seat at the UN? The Conversation. Sep. 23, 2021. https://theconversation.com/two-governments-claim-to-run-myanmar-so-who-gets-the-countrys-seat-at-the-un-167885

[20] Simon Lewis & Humeyra Pamuk, *U.S. blocked Myanmar junta attempt to empty $1 billion New York Fed account*, Reuters. Mar. 4, 2021 https://www.reuters.com/article/us-myanmar-politics-usa-fed-exclusive-idUSKCN2AW2MD

Question
Are the State of Washington's maritime regulations on tanker design, equipment, reporting, and operating requirements pre-empted by federal law?

Conclusion

Yes. In a unanimous opinion delivered by Justice Anthony Kennedy, the Court held that Washington's regulations regarding general navigation watch procedures, crew English-language skills and training, and maritime casualty reporting are pre-empted by the comprehensive federal regulatory scheme governing oil tankers. "The State of Washington has enacted legislation in an area where the federal interest has been manifest since the beginning of our Republic and is now well established," wrote Justice Kennedy for the Court. Justice Kennedy also noted that States may regulate their own ports and waterways so long as the rules are based on "the peculiarities of local waters" and do not conflict with federal regulation.

Optional: For the full opinion, you can follow this link:

https://supreme.justia.com/cases/federal/us/471/84/

III. EXECUTIVE VS. LEGISLATIVE POWERS —PRESIDENTIAL POWERS

In the area of trade and foreign affairs, the U.S. President (according to our courts) has express powers granted by the Constitution, as well as inherent powers and implied powers.

A.   Inherent Powers

The President is "commander in chief," and has "inherent powers" because of that Constitutional provision. The Korean War left North and South Korea divided, a fact we are still dealing with today. As you can tell from the following five minute You Tube video (optional), the Korean War required a great deal of resources and personnel. U.S. losses were far from trivial. In the Youngstown case, below, the Justices of the US Supreme Court were divided as to whether or not the President had inherent power to order the end of a strike at a U.S. steel mill, or whether Congressional actions expressly or impliedly gave him that power.

Video: Five Crucial Facts about the Korean War

https://www.youtube.com/watch?v=30sECZAwZAw

Youngstown Sheet & Tube Co. v. Sawyer
343 U.S. 579 (1952)

Appeal from the D.C. Circuit Court of Appeals

Synopsis

To avert a nationwide strike of steel workers in April 1952, which he believed would jeopardize national defense, the President issued an Executive Order directing the Secretary of Commerce to seize and operate most of the steel mills. The Order was not based upon any specific statutory authority, but was based generally upon all powers vested in the President by the Constitution and laws of the United States and as President of the United States and Commander in Chief of the Armed Forces. The Secretary issued an order seizing the steel mills and directing their presidents to operate them as operating managers for the United States in accordance with his regulations and directions. The President promptly reported these events to Congress; but Congress took no action. It had provided other methods of dealing with such situations, and had refused to authorize governmental seizures of property to settle labor disputes. The steel companies sued the Secretary in a Federal District Court, praying for a declaratory judgment and injunctive relief. The District Court issued a preliminary injunction, which the Court of Appeals stayed.

MR. JUSTICE BLACK delivered the opinion of the Court.

We are asked to decide whether the President was acting within his constitutional power when he issued an order directing the Secretary of Commerce to take possession of and operate most of the Nation's steel mills. The mill owners argue that the President's order amounts to lawmaking, a legislative function which the Constitution has expressly confided to the Congress, and not to the President. The Government's position is that the order was made on findings of the President that his action was necessary to avert a national catastrophe which would inevitably result from a stoppage of steel production, and that, in meeting this grave emergency, the President was acting within the aggregate of his constitutional powers as the Nation's Chief Executive and the Commander in Chief of the Armed Forces of the United States. The issue emerges here from the following series of events:

In the latter part of 1951, a dispute arose between the steel companies and their employees over terms and conditions that should be included in new collective bargaining agreements. Long-continued conferences failed to resolve the dispute. On December 18, 1951, the employees' representative, United Steelworkers of America, CIO, gave notice of an intention to strike when the existing bargaining agreements expired on December 31. The Federal Mediation and Conciliation Service then intervened in an effort to get labor and management to agree. This failing, the President on December 22, 1951, referred the dispute to the Federal Wage Stabilization

Board to investigate and make recommendations for fair and equitable terms of settlement. This Board's report resulted in no settlement. On April 4, 1952, the Union gave notice of a nationwide strike called to begin at 12:01 a.m. April 9. The indispensability of steel as a component of substantially all weapons and other war materials led the President to believe that the proposed work stoppage would immediately jeopardize our national defense and that governmental seizure of the steel mills was necessary in order to assure the continued availability of steel. Reciting these considerations for his action, the President, a few hours before the strike was to begin, issued Executive Order 10340, a copy of which is attached as an appendix, *post,* p. 343 U. S. 589. The order directed the Secretary of Commerce to take possession of most of the steel mills and keep them running. The Secretary immediately issued his own possessory orders, calling upon the presidents of the various seized companies to serve as operating managers for the United States. They were directed to carry on their activities in accordance with regulations and directions of the Secretary. The next morning the President sent a message to Congress reporting his action. Cong.Rec. April 9, 1952, p. 3962. Twelve days later, he sent a second message. Cong.Rec. April 21, 1952, p. 4192. Congress has taken no action.

Obeying the Secretary's orders under protest, the companies brought proceedings against him in the District Court. Their complaints charged that the seizure was not authorized by an act of Congress or by any constitutional provisions. The District Court was asked to declare the orders of the President and the Secretary invalid and to issue preliminary and permanent injunctions restraining their enforcement. Opposing the motion for preliminary injunction, the United States asserted that a strike disrupting steel production for even a brief period would so endanger the wellbeing and safety of the Nation that the President had "inherent power" to do what he had done -- power "supported by the Constitution, by historical precedent, and by court decisions." The Government also contended that, in any event, no preliminary injunction should be issued, because the companies had made no showing that their available legal remedies were inadequate or that their injuries from seizure would be irreparable. Holding against the Government on all points, the District Court, on April 30, issued a preliminary injunction restraining the Secretary from "continuing the seizure and possession of the plants . . . and from acting under the purported authority of Executive Order No. 10340." 103 F. Supp. 569. On the same day, the Court of Appeals stayed the District Court's injunction. 197 F.2d 582. Deeming it best that the issues raised be promptly decided by this Court, we granted certiorari on May 3 and set the cause for argument on May 12.

Two crucial issues have developed: *First.* Should final determination of the constitutional validity of the President's order be made in this case which has proceeded no further than the preliminary injunction stage? *Second.* If so, is the seizure order within the constitutional power of the President?

I

It is urged that there were nonconstitutional grounds upon which the District Court could have denied the preliminary injunction, and thus have followed the customary judicial practice of declining to reach and decide constitutional questions until compelled to do so. On this basis, it is argued that equity's extraordinary injunctive relief should have been denied because (a) seizure of the companies' properties did not inflict irreparable damages, and (b) there were available legal remedies adequate to afford compensation for any possible damages which they might suffer. While separately argued by the Government, these two contentions are here closely related, if not identical. Arguments as to both rest in large part on the Government's claim that, should the seizure ultimately be held unlawful, the companies could recover full compensation in the Court of Claims for the unlawful taking. Prior cases in this Court have cast doubt on the right to recover in the Court of Claims on account of properties unlawfully taken by government officials for public use as these properties were alleged to have been. *See e.g., Hooe v. United States,* 218 U. S. 322, 218 U. S. 335-336; *United States v. North American Co.,* 253 U. S. 330, 253 U. S. 333. *But see Larson v. Domestic & Foreign Corp.,* 337 U. S. 682, 337 U. S. 701-702. Moreover, seizure and governmental operation of these going businesses were bound to result in many present and future damages of such nature as to be difficult, if not incapable, of measurement. Viewing the case this way, and in the light of the facts presented, the District Court saw no reason for delaying decision of the constitutional validity of the orders. We agree with the District

Court, and can see no reason why that question was not ripe for determination on the record presented. We shall therefore consider and determine that question now.

II

The President's power, if any, to issue the order must stem either from an act of Congress or from the Constitution itself. There is no statute that expressly authorizes the President to take possession of property as he did here. Nor is there any act of Congress to which our attention has been directed from which such a power can fairly be implied. Indeed, we do not understand the Government to rely on statutory authorization for this seizure. There are two statutes which do authorize the President to take both personal and real property under certain conditions. However, the Government admits that these conditions were not met, and that the President's order was not rooted in either of the statutes. The Government refers to the seizure provisions of one of these statutes (§ 201(b) of the Defense Production Act) as "much too cumbersome, involved, and time-consuming for the crisis which was at hand."

Moreover, the use of the seizure technique to solve labor disputes in order to prevent work stoppages was not only unauthorized by any congressional enactment; prior to this controversy, Congress had refused to adopt that method of settling labor disputes. When the Taft-Hartley Act was under consideration in 1947, Congress rejected an amendment which would have authorized such governmental seizures in cases of emergency. Apparently it was thought that the technique of seizure, like that of compulsory arbitration, would interfere with the process of collective bargaining. Consequently, the plan Congress adopted in that Act did not provide for seizure under any circumstances. Instead, the plan sought to bring about settlements by use of the customary devices of mediation, conciliation, investigation by boards of inquiry, and public reports. In some instances, temporary injunctions were authorized to provide cooling-off periods. All this failing, unions were left free to strike after a secret vote by employees as to whether they wished to accept their employers' final settlement offer.

It is clear that, if the President had authority to issue the order he did, it must be found in some provision of the Constitution. And it is not claimed that express constitutional language grants this power to the President. The contention is that presidential power should be implied from the aggregate of his powers under the Constitution. Particular reliance is placed on provisions in Article II which say that "The executive Power shall be vested in a President . . ."; that "he shall take Care that the Laws be faithfully executed", and that he "shall be Commander in Chief of the Army and Navy of the United States."

The order cannot properly be sustained as an exercise of the President's military power as Commander in Chief of the Armed Forces. The Government attempts to do so by citing a number of cases upholding broad powers in military commanders engaged in day-to-day fighting in a theater of war. Such cases need not concern us here. Even though "theater of war" be an expanding concept, we cannot with faithfulness to our constitutional system hold that the Commander in Chief of the Armed Forces has the ultimate power as such to take possession of private property in order to keep labor disputes from stopping production. This is a job for the Nation's lawmakers, not for its military authorities.

Nor can the seizure order be sustained because of the several constitutional provisions that grant executive power to the President. In the framework of our Constitution, the President's power to see that the laws are faithfully executed refutes the idea that he is to be a lawmaker. The Constitution limits his functions in the lawmaking process to the recommending of laws he thinks wise and the vetoing of laws he thinks bad. And the Constitution is neither silent nor equivocal about who shall make laws which the President is to execute. The first section of the first article says that "All legislative Powers herein granted shall be vested in a Congress of the United States. . . ." After granting many powers to the Congress, Article I goes on to provide that Congress may

"make all Laws which shall be necessary and proper for carrying into Execution the foregoing Powers, and all other Powers vested by this Constitution in the Government of the United States, or in any Department or Officer thereof."

The President's order does not direct that a congressional policy be executed in a manner prescribed by Congress -- it directs that a presidential policy be executed in a manner prescribed by the President. The preamble of the order itself, like that of many statutes, sets out reasons why the President believes certain policies should be adopted, proclaims these policies as rules of conduct to be followed, and again, like a statute, authorizes a government official to promulgate additional rules and regulations consistent with the policy proclaimed and needed to carry that policy into execution. The power of Congress to adopt such public policies as those proclaimed by the order is beyond question. It can authorize the taking of private property for public use. It can make laws regulating the relationships between employers and employees, prescribing rules designed to settle labor disputes, and fixing wages and working conditions in certain fields of our economy. The Constitution does not subject this lawmaking power of Congress to presidential or military supervision or control.

It is said that other Presidents, without congressional authority, have taken possession of private business enterprises in order to settle labor disputes. But even if this be true, Congress has not thereby lost its exclusive constitutional authority to make laws necessary and proper to carry out the powers vested by the Constitution "in the Government of the United States, or any Department or Officer thereof."

The Founders of this Nation entrusted the lawmaking power to the Congress alone in both good and bad times. It would do no good to recall the historical events, the fears of power, and the hopes for freedom that lay behind their

choice. Such a review would but confirm our holding that this seizure order cannot stand.

The judgment of the District Court is

Affirmed.

DISSENT (the Chief Justice and two Associate Justices)

MR. CHIEF JUSTICE **VINSON**, with whom MR. JUSTICE **REED** and MR. JUSTICE **MINTON** join, dissenting.

The President of the United States directed the Secretary of Commerce to take temporary possession of the Nation's steel mills during the existing emergency because "a work stoppage would immediately jeopardize and imperil our national defense and the defense of those joined with us in resisting aggression, and would add to the continuing danger of our soldiers, sailors, and airmen engaged in combat in the field." The District Court ordered the mills returned to their private owners on the ground that the President's action was beyond his powers under the Constitution.

This Court affirms. Some members of the Court are of the view that the President is without power to act in time of crisis in the absence of express statutory authorization. Other members of the Court affirm on the basis of their reading of certain statutes. Because we cannot agree that affirmance is proper on any ground, and because of the transcending importance of the questions presented not only in this critical litigation but also to the powers of the President and of future Presidents to act in time of crisis, we are compelled to register this dissent.

I.

In passing upon the question of Presidential powers in this case, we must first consider the context in which those powers were exercised.

Those who suggest that this is a case involving extraordinary powers should be mindful that these are extraordinary times. A world not yet recovered from the devastation of World War II has been forced to face the threat of another and more terrifying global conflict.

Accepting in full measure its responsibility in the world community, the United States was instrumental in securing adoption of the United Nations Charter, approved by the Senate by a vote of 89 to 2. The first purpose of the United Nations is to "maintain international peace and security, and to that end: to take effective collective measures for the prevention and removal of threats to the peace, and for the suppression of acts of aggression or other breaches of the peace, ..." In 1950, when the United Nations called upon member nations "to render every assistance" to repel aggression in Korea, the United States furnished its vigorous support. For almost two full years, our armed forces have been fighting in Korea, suffering casualties of over 108,000 men. Hostilities have not abated. The "determination of the United Nations to continue its action in Korea to meet the aggression" has been reaffirmed. Congressional support of the action in Korea has been manifested by provisions for increased military manpower and equipment and for economic stabilization. . .

Further efforts to protect the free world from aggression are found in the congressional enactments of the Truman Plan for assistance to Greece and Turkey and the Marshall Plan for economic aid needed to build up the strength of our friends in Western Europe. In 1949, the Senate approved the North Atlantic Treaty under which each member nation agrees that an armed attack against one is an armed attack against all. Congress immediately implemented the North Atlantic Treaty by authorizing military assistance to nations dedicated to the principles of mutual security under the United Nations Charter. The concept of mutual security recently has been extended by treaty to friends in the Pacific.

Our treaties represent not merely legal obligations but show congressional recognition that mutual security for the free world is the best security against the threat of aggression on a global scale. The need for mutual security is shown by the very size of the armed forces outside the free world. *Defendant's brief informs us that the Soviet Union maintains the largest air force in the world and maintains ground forces much larger than those presently available to the United States and the countries joined with us in mutual security arrangements. Constant international tensions are cited to demonstrate how precarious is the peace.*

Even this brief review of our responsibilities in the world community discloses the enormity of our undertaking. Success of these measures may, as has often been observed, dramatically influence the lives of many generations of the world's peoples yet unborn. Alert to our responsibilities, which coincide with our own self-preservation through mutual security, Congress has enacted a large body of implementing legislation. As an illustration of the magnitude of the over-all program, Congress has appropriated $ 130 billion for our own defense and for military assistance to our allies since the June, 1950, attack in Korea.

In the Mutual Security Act of 1951, Congress authorized "military, economic, and technical assistance to friendly countries to strengthen the mutual security and individual and collective defenses of the free world, . . ." Over $ 5 1/2 billion were appropriated for military assistance for fiscal year 1952, the bulk of that amount to be devoted to purchase of military equipment. A request for over $ 7 billion for the same purpose for fiscal year 1953 is currently pending in Congress. In addition to direct shipment of military equipment to nations of the free world, defense production in those countries relies upon shipment of machine tools and allocation of steel tonnage from the United States.

Congress also directed the President to build up our own defenses. Congress, recognizing the "grim fact . . . that the United States is now engaged in a struggle for survival" and that "it is imperative that we now take those necessary steps to make our strength equal to the peril of the hour," granted authority to draft men into the armed forces. As a result, we now have over 3,500,000 men in our armed forces.

Appropriations for the Department of Defense, which had averaged less than $ 13 billion per year for the three years before attack in Korea, were increased by Congress to $ 48 billion for fiscal year 1951 and to $ 60 billion for fiscal year 1952. A request for $ 51 billion for the Department Defense for fiscal year 1953 is currently pending in Congress. The bulk of the increase is for military equipment and supplies -- guns, tanks, ships, planes and ammunition -- all of which require steel. Other defense programs requiring great quantities of steel include the large scale expansion of facilities for the Atomic Energy Commission and the expansion of the Nation's productive capacity affirmatively encouraged by Congress.

Congress recognized the impact of these defense programs upon the economy. Following the attack in Korea, the President asked for authority to requisition property and to allocate and fix priorities for scarce goods. In the Defense Production Act of 1950, Congress granted the powers requested and, *in addition*, granted power to stabilize prices and wages and to provide for settlement of labor disputes arising in the defense program.

. . .

Even before Korea, steel production at levels above theoretical 100% capacity was not capable of supplying civilian needs alone. Since Korea, the tremendous military demand for steel has far exceeded the increases in productive capacity. This Committee emphasized that the shortage of steel, even with the mills operating at full capacity, coupled with increased civilian purchasing power, presented grave danger of disastrous inflation. [21]

The President has the duty to execute the foregoing legislative programs. Their successful execution depends upon continued production of steel and stabilized prices for steel. Accordingly, when the collective bargaining agreements

---

[21] *Id., at 8-9*.

between the Nation's steel producers and their employees, represented by the United Steel Workers, were due to expire on December 31, 1951, and a strike shutting down the entire basic steel industry was threatened, the President acted to avert a complete shutdown of steel production. On December 22, 1951, he certified the dispute to the Wage Stabilization Board, requesting that the Board investigate the dispute and promptly report its recommendation as to fair and equitable terms of settlement. The Union complied with the President's request and delayed its threatened strike while the dispute was before the Board. After a special Board panel had conducted hearings and submitted a report, the full Wage Stabilization Board submitted its report and recommendations to the President on March 20, 1952.

The Board's report was acceptable to the Union but was rejected by plaintiffs. The Union gave notice of its intention to strike as of 12:01 a. m., April 9, 1952, but bargaining between the parties continued with hope of settlement until the evening of April 8, 1952. After bargaining had failed to avert the threatened shutdown of steel production, the President issued the following Executive Order:

The language of the Executive Order is mostly omitted here, but, these paragraphs provide the essence of the E.O.:

"WHEREAS in order to assure the continued availability of steel and steel products during the existing emergency, it is necessary that the United States take possession of and operate the plants, facilities, and other property of the said companies as hereinafter provided:

"NOW, THEREFORE, by virtue of the authority vested in me by the Constitution and laws of the United States, and as President of the United States and Commander in Chief of the armed forces of the United States, it is hereby ordered as follows:

"1. The Secretary of Commerce is hereby authorized and directed to take possession of all or such of the plants, facilities, and other property of the companies named in the list attached hereto, or any part thereof, as he may deem necessary in the interests of national defense; and to operate or to arrange for the operation thereof and to do all things necessary for, or incidental to, such operation. . . ." [22]

The next morning, April 9, 1952, the President addressed the following Message to Congress:

"*To the Congress of the United States*:

"The Congress is undoubtedly aware of the recent events which have taken place in connection with the management-labor dispute in the steel industry. These events culminated in the action which was taken last night to provide for temporary operation of the steel mills by the Government.

"I took this action with the utmost reluctance. The idea of Government operation of the steel mills is thoroughly distasteful to me and I want to see it ended as soon as possible. However, in the situation which confronted me yesterday, I felt that I could make no other choice. The other alternatives appeared to be even worse -- so much worse that I could not accept them.

"One alternative would have been to permit a shutdown in the steel industry. The effects of such a shut-down would have been so immediate and damaging with respect to our efforts to support our Armed Forces and to protect our national security that it made this alternative unthinkable.

"The only way that I know of, other than Government operation, by which a steel shut-down could have been avoided was to grant the demands of the steel industry for a large price increase. I believed and the officials in charge of our stabilization agencies believed that this would have wrecked our stabilization program. I was unwilling to accept the incalculable damage which might be done to our country by following such a course.

---

[22] Exec. Order 10340, *17 Fed. Reg. 3139 (1952)*.

"Accordingly, it was my judgment that Government operation of the steel mills for a temporary period was the least undesirable of the courses of action which lay open. In the circumstances, I believed it to be, and now believe it to be, my duty and within my powers as President to follow that course of action.

"It may be that the Congress will deem some other course to be wiser. It may be that the Congress will feel we should give in to the demands of the steel industry for an exorbitant price increase and take the consequences so far as resulting inflation is concerned.

"It may be that the Congress will feel the Government should try to force the steel workers to continue to work for the steel companies for another long period, without a contract, even though the steel workers have already voluntarily remained at work without a contract for 100 days in an effort to reach an orderly settlement of their differences with management.

"It may even be that the Congress will feel that we should permit a shut-down of the steel industry, although that would immediately endanger the safety of our fighting forces abroad and weaken the whole structure of our national security.

"I do not believe the Congress will favor any of these courses of action, but that is a matter for the Congress to determine.

"It may be, on the other hand, that the Congress will wish to pass legislation establishing specific terms and conditions with reference to the operation of the steel mills by the Government. Sound legislation of this character might be very desirable.

"On the basis of the facts that are known to me at this time, I do not believe that immediate congressional action is essential; but I would, of course, be glad to cooperate in developing any legislative proposals which the Congress may wish to consider.

"If the Congress does not deem it necessary to act at this time, I shall continue to do all that is within my power to keep the steel industry operating and at the same time make every effort to bring about a settlement of the dispute so the mills can be returned to their private owners as soon as possible."

Twelve days passed without action by Congress. On April 21, 1952, the President sent a letter to the President of the Senate in which he again described the purpose and need for his action and again stated his position that "The Congress can, if it wishes, reject the course of action I have followed in this matter." Congress has not so acted to this date.

Meanwhile, plaintiffs instituted this action in the District Court to compel defendant to return possession of the steel mills seized under Executive Order 10340. . . . .

Secretary of Defense Lovett swore that "a work stoppage in the steel industry will result immediately in serious curtailment of production of essential weapons and munitions of all kinds." He illustrated by showing that 84% of the national production of certain alloy steel is currently used for production of military-end items and that 35% of total production of another form of steel goes into ammunition, 80% of such ammunition now going to Korea. The Secretary of Defense stated that: "We are holding the line [in Korea] with ammunition and not with the lives of our troops."

. . . .

Plaintiffs do not remotely suggest any basis for rejecting the President's finding that *any* stoppage of steel production would immediately place the Nation in peril. Moreover, even self-generated doubts that *any* stoppage of steel production constitutes an emergency are of little comfort here. The Union and the plaintiffs bargained for 6 months with over 100 issues in dispute -- issues not limited to wage demands but including the union shop and other matters of principle between the parties. At the time of seizure there was not, and there is not now, the slightest evidence to justify the belief that any strike will be of short duration. The Union and the steel companies may well engage in a lengthy struggle. Plaintiffs' counsel tells us that "sooner or later" the mills will operate again.

82

That may satisfy the steel companies and, perhaps, the Union. But our soldiers and our allies will hardly be cheered with the assurance that the ammunition upon which their lives depend will be forthcoming -- "sooner or later," or, in other words, "too little and too late."

Accordingly, if the President has any power under the Constitution to meet a critical situation in the absence of express statutory authorization, there is no basis whatever for criticizing the exercise of such power in this case.

II. (Omitted)

III.

(The dissent then goes on for several pages citing many examples of Presidential actions that were taken for reasons of exigency but without express authorization from Congress.)

This is but a cursory summary of executive leadership. But it amply demonstrates that Presidents have taken prompt action to enforce the laws and protect the country whether or not Congress happened to provide in advance for the particular method of execution. At the minimum, the executive actions reviewed herein sustain the action of the President in this case. And many of the cited examples of Presidential practice go far beyond the extent of power necessary to sustain the President's order to seize the steel mills. The fact that temporary executive seizures of industrial plants to meet an emergency have not been directly tested in this Court furnishes not the slightest suggestion that such actions have been illegal. Rather, the fact that Congress and the courts have consistently recognized and given their support to such executive action indicates that such a power of seizure has been accepted throughout our history.

History bears out the genius of the Founding Fathers, who created a Government subject to law but not left subject to inertia when vigor and initiative are required.

IV.

Focusing now on the situation confronting the President on the night of April 8, 1952, we cannot but conclude that the President was performing his duty under the Constitution to "take Care that the Laws be faithfully executed" -- a duty described by President Benjamin Harrison as "the central idea of the office." [83]

The President reported to Congress the morning after the seizure that he acted because a work stoppage in steel production would immediately imperil the safety of the Nation by preventing execution of the legislative programs for procurement of military equipment. And, while a shutdown could be averted by granting the price concessions requested by plaintiffs, granting such concessions would disrupt the price stabilization program also enacted by Congress. Rather than fail to execute either legislative program, the President acted to execute both.

Much of the argument in this case has been directed at straw men. We do not now have before us the case of a President acting solely on the basis of his own notions of the public welfare. Nor is there any question of unlimited executive power in this case. The President himself closed the door to any such claim when he sent his Message to Congress stating his purpose to abide by any action of Congress, whether approving or disapproving his seizure action. Here, the President immediately made sure that Congress was fully informed of the temporary action he had taken only to preserve the legislative programs from destruction until Congress could act.

The absence of a specific statute authorizing seizure of the steel mills as a mode of executing the laws -- both the military procurement program and the anti-inflation program -- has not until today been thought to prevent the President from executing the laws.

. . . .And the Defense Production Act authorizes the President to requisition equipment and

---

[83] Harrison, This Country of Ours (1897), 98.

condemn real property needed without delay in the defense effort. Where Congress authorizes seizure in instances not necessarily crucial to the defense program, it can hardly be said to have disclosed an intention to prohibit seizures where essential to the execution of that legislative program.

Whatever the extent of Presidential power on more tranquil occasions, and whatever the right of the President to execute legislative programs as he sees fit without reporting the mode of execution to Congress, the single Presidential purpose disclosed on this record is to faithfully execute the laws by acting in an emergency to maintain the status quo, thereby preventing collapse of the legislative programs until Congress could act. The President's action served the same purposes as a judicial stay entered to maintain the status quo in order to preserve the jurisdiction of a court. In his Message to Congress immediately following the seizure, the President explained the necessity of his action in executing the military procurement and anti-inflation legislative programs and expressed his desire to cooperate with any legislative proposals approving, regulating or rejecting the seizure of the steel mills. Consequently, there is no evidence whatever of any Presidential purpose to defy Congress or act in any way inconsistent with the legislative will.

. . .The Framers knew, as we should know in these times of peril, that there is real danger in Executive weakness. There is no cause to fear Executive tyranny so long as the laws of Congress are being faithfully executed. Certainly there is no basis for fear of dictatorship when the Executive acts, as he did in this case, only to save the situation until Congress could act.

V. (Mostly omitted)

When the President acted on April 8, he had exhausted the procedures for settlement available to him. Taft-Hartley was a route parallel to, not connected with, the WSB procedure. The strike had been delayed 99 days as contrasted with the maximum delay of 80 days under Taft-Hartley. There had been a hearing on the issues in dispute and bargaining which promised settlement up to the very hour before seizure had broken down. Faced with immediate national peril through stoppage in steel production on the one hand and faced with destruction of the wage and price legislative programs on the other, the President took temporary possession of the steel mills as the only course open to him consistent with his duty to take care that the laws be faithfully executed.

Plaintiffs' property was taken and placed in the possession of the Secretary of Commerce to prevent any interruption in steel production. It made no difference whether the stoppage was caused by a union-management dispute over terms and conditions of employment, a union-Government dispute over wage stabilization or a management-Government dispute over price stabilization. The President's action has thus far been effective, not in settling the dispute, but in saving the various legislative programs at stake from destruction until Congress could act in the matter.

VI.

The diversity of views expressed in the six opinions of the majority, the lack of reference to authoritative precedent, the repeated reliance upon prior dissenting opinions, the complete disregard of the uncontroverted facts showing the gravity of the emergency and the temporary nature of the taking all serve to demonstrate how far afield one must go to affirm the order of the District Court.

The broad executive power granted by Article II to an officer on duty 365 days a year cannot, it is said, be invoked to avert disaster. Instead, the President must confine himself to sending a message to Congress recommending action. Under this messenger-boy concept of the Office, the President cannot even act to preserve legislative programs from destruction so that Congress will have something left to act upon. There is no judicial finding that the executive action was unwarranted because there was in fact no basis for the President's finding of the existence of an emergency for, under this view, the gravity of the emergency and the immediacy of the threatened disaster are considered irrelevant as a matter of law.

Seizure of plaintiffs' property is not a pleasant undertaking. Similarly unpleasant to a free country are the draft which disrupts the home and military procurement which causes economic dislocation and compels adoption of price controls, wage stabilization and allocation of materials. The President informed Congress that even a temporary Government operation of plaintiffs' properties was "thoroughly distasteful" to him, but was necessary to prevent immediate paralysis of the mobilization program. Presidents have been in the past, and any man worthy of the Office should be in the future, free to take at least interim action necessary to execute legislative programs essential to survival of the Nation. A sturdy judiciary should not be swayed by the unpleasantness or unpopularity of necessary executive action, but must independently determine for itself whether the President was acting, as required by the Constitution, to "take Care that the Laws be faithfully executed."

As the District Judge stated, this is no time for "timorous" judicial action. But neither is this a time for timorous executive action. Faced with the duty of executing the defense programs which Congress had enacted and the disastrous effects that any stoppage in steel production would have on those programs, the President acted to preserve those programs by seizing the steel mills. There is no question that the possession was other than temporary in character and subject to congressional direction -- either approving, disapproving or regulating the manner in which the mills were to be administered and returned to the owners. The President immediately informed Congress of his action and clearly stated his intention to abide by the legislative will. No basis for claims of arbitrary action, unlimited powers or dictatorial usurpation of congressional power appears from the facts of this case. On the contrary, judicial, legislative and executive precedents throughout our history demonstrate that in this case the President acted in full conformity with his duties under the Constitution. Accordingly, we would reverse the order of the District Court.

A note on "emergency powers." Many who follow politics and the three branches of government have noted that the Executive Branch has grown in size and influence. All Presidents since George H.W. Bush (1989-1993) have claimed powers that had not been previously exercised. No Presidential candidate has ever campaigned on the promise to reduce, rather than expand, executive power. Truman saw in Korea and the steel industry a "national emergency." When can a President simply declare "an emergency" and claim unusual powers?

See the Brennan Center's report here:

https://www.brennancenter.org/our-work/research-reports/guide-emergency-powers-and-their-use

Questions on Youngstown Sheet and Tube v. Sawyer

1. Does the majority opinion agree, or disagree, that President Truman had the power under the Constitution to have the government seize and operate the steel mills?
2. What was the basis, in terms of legislation from Congress, that made Truman think he had the express power to seize and operate the steel mills?
3. In your opinion, was this an "emergency" for the nation?
4. Why did the majority on the Court, and the trial court, think that the owners of the mills would have a hard time claiming damages later on, after the government relinquished control of the mills?
5. Reflect a bit on the actions (or inactions) of Congress here; did they meet their legislative responsibilities to the nation?
6. Summarize the main points of the dissenting Justices Vinson, Reed, and Minton.

Goldwater et al. v. Carter
SUPREME COURT OF THE UNITED STATES (1979)

Introductory Note, from Wikipedia:

Goldwater v. Carter, 444 U.S. 996 (1979), was a US Supreme Court case which was the result of a lawsuit filed by Senator Barry Goldwater and other members of the U.S. Congress, challenging the right of Preisent Jimmy Carter to unilaterally nullify the Sino-American Mutual Defense Treaty, which the U.S. had signed with the Republic of China, so that relations could instead be established with the People's Republic of China. Goldwater and his co-filers claimed that the President required Senate approval to take such an action, under Article II, Seciton II of the Constitution, and that, by not doing so, President Carter had acted beyond the powers of his office.

Granting a petition for certiorari, but without hearing oral arguments, the court vacated a court of appeals ruling and remanded the case to a federal district court with directions to dismiss the complaint. A majority of six Justices ruled that the case should be dismissed without hearing an oral argument. Justices Powell and Rehnquist issued two separate concurring opinions on the case. Rehnquist claimed that the issue concerned how foreign affairs were conducted between Congress and the President, and was essentially political, not judicial; therefore, it was not eligible to be heard by the court. Powell, while agreeing that the case did not merit judicial review, believed that the issue itself, the powers of the President to break treaties without congressional approval, would have been arguable had Congress issued a formal opposition through a resolution to the termination of the treaty.. (The Senate had drafted such a resolution, but not voted upon it.) This would have turned the case into a constitutional debate between the executive powers granted to the President and the legislative powers granted to Congress. As the case stood, however, it was simply a dispute among unsettled, competing political forces within the legislative and executive branches of government, and hence still political in nature due to the lack of majority or supermajority vote in the Senate speaking officially as a constitutional institution. Today, the case is considered a textbook example of the political question doctrine in U.S. constitutional law.

* * *

Students: In view of the ongoing and current tensions between Congress and the Executive branch, this case presents issues that are important both now and in the future. E.g. imagine if both House and Senate had instructed the President not to impose sanctions on Iran, Russia, or China but the President ignored Congress and instructed the Depts. Of Commerce and Treasury to impose sanctions, or suppose Congress wants tougher sanctions imposed on Russia, passes a law detailing such sanctions, but the President only orders some of the sanctions.

The key question not fully answered in this case is whether the Supreme Court is willing to be a referee in the case of a true impasse between Congress and the Executive Branch, or whether it will essentially "recuse itself" by claiming that the impasse is a "political question." Its "political question" doctrine keeps the Court at a distance from such disputes, and is often used to avoid answering questions that really should be answered.

Goldwater v. Carter
U.S. Supreme Court

444 U.S. 996 (1979)

Certiorari granted, judgment vacated, and case remanded with directions to dismiss the complaint. MR. JUSTICE MARSHALL concurs in the result. MR. JUSTICE POWELL concurs in the judgment and filed a statement. MR. JUSTICE REHNQUIST concurs in the judgment and filed a statement in which THE CHIEF JUSTICE, MR. JUSTICE STEWART, and MR. JUSTICE STEVENS join. MR. JUSTICE WHITE and MR. JUSTICE BLACKMUN join in the grant of the petition for writ of certiorari but would set the case for argument and give it plenary consideration. MR. JUSTICE BLACKMUN filed a statement in which MR. JUSTICE WHITE joins. MR. JUSTICE BRENNAN would grant the petition for writ of certiorari and affirm the judgment of the Court of Appeals and filed a statement.

MR. JUSTICE POWELL, concurring.

Although I agree with the result reached by the Court, I would dismiss the complaint as not ripe for judicial review.

I

This Court has recognized that an issue should not be decided if it is not ripe for judicial review. Buckley v. Valeo , 424 U.S. 1, 113-114 (1976) Prudential considerations persuade me that a dispute between Congress and the President is not ready for judicial review unless and until each branch has taken action asserting its constitutional authority. Differences between the President and the Congress are commonplace under our system. The differences should, and almost invariably do, turn on political rather than legal considerations. The Judicial Branch should not decide issues affecting the allocation of power between the President and Congress until the political branches reach a constitutional impasse. Otherwise, we would encourage small groups or even individual Members of Congress to seek judicial resolution of issues before the normal political process has the opportunity to resolve the conflict.

In this case, a few Members of Congress claim that the President's action in terminating the treaty with Taiwan has deprived them of their constitutional role with respect to a change in the supreme law of the land. Congress has taken no official action. In the present posture of this case, we do not know whether there ever will be an actual confrontation between the Legislative and Executive Branches. Although the Senate has considered a resolution declaring that Senate approval is necessary for the termination of any mutual defense treaty, see 125 Cong. Rec. S7015, S7038-S7039 (June 6, 1979), no final vote has been taken on the resolution. See id ., at S16683-S16692 (Nov. 15, 1979). Moreover, it is unclear whether the resolution would have retroactive effect. See id ., at S7054-S7064 (June 6, 1979); id ., at S7862 (June 18, 1979). It cannot be said that either the Senate or the House has rejected the President's claim. If the Congress chooses not to confront the President, it is not our task to do so. I therefore concur in the dismissal of this case.

II

MR. JUSTICE REHNQUIST suggests, however, that the issue presented by this case is a nonjusticiable political question which can never be considered by this Court. I cannot agree. In my view, reliance upon the political-question doctrine is inconsistent with our precedents. As set forth in the seminal case of Baker v. Carr , 369 U.S. 186, 217 (1962), the doctrine incorporates three inquiries: (i) Does the issue involve resolution of questions committed by the text of the Constitution to a coordinate branch of Government? (ii) Would resolution of the question demand that a court move beyond areas of judicial expertise? (iii) Do prudential considerations counsel against judicial intervention? In my opinion the answer to each of these inquiries would require us to decide this case if it were ready for review.

First, the existence of "a textually demonstrable constitutional commitment of the issue to a coordinate political department," turns on an examination of the constitutional provisions governing the exercise of the power in question. Powell v. McCormack , 395 U.S. 486, 519 (1969).

No constitutional provision explicitly confers upon the President the power to terminate treaties. Further, Art. II, ß 2, of the Constitution authorizes the President to make treaties with the advice and consent of the Senate. Article VI provides that treaties shall be a part of the supreme law of the land. These provisions add support to the view that the text of the Constitution does not unquestionably commit the power to terminate treaties to the President alone. Cf. Gilligan v. Morgan , 413 U.S. 1, 6 (1973); Luther v. Borden , 7 How. 1, 42 (1849).

Second, there is no "lack of judicially discoverable and manageable standards for resolving" this case; nor is a decision impossible "without an initial policy determination of a kind clearly for nonjudicial discretion." Baker v. Carr, supra, at 217. We are asked to decide whether the President may terminate a treaty under the Constitution without congressional approval. Resolution of the question may not be easy, but it only requires us to apply normal principles of interpretation to the constitutional provisions at issue. The present case involves neither review of the President's activities as Commander in Chief nor impermissible interference in the field of foreign affairs. Such a case would arise if we were asked to decide, for example, whether a treaty required the President to order troops into a foreign country. But "it is error to suppose that every case or controversy which touches foreign relations lies beyond judicial cognizance." Baker v. Carr, supra, at 211. This case "touches" foreign relations, but the question presented to us concerns only the constitutional division of power between Congress and the President.

A simple hypothetical demonstrates the confusion that I find inherent in MR. JUSTICE REHNQUIST'S opinion concurring in the judgment. Assume that the President signed a mutual defense treaty with a foreign country and announced that it would go into effect despite its rejection by the Senate. Under MR. JUSTICE REHNQUIST'S analysis that situation would present a political question even though Art. II, ß 2, clearly would resolve the dispute. Although the answer to the hypothetical case seems self-evident because it demands textual rather than interstitial analysis, the nature of the legal issue presented is no different from the issue presented in the case before us. In both cases, the Court would interpret the Constitution to decide whether congressional approval is necessary to give a Presidential decision on the validity of a treaty the force of law. Such an inquiry demands no special competence or information beyond the reach of the Judiciary. Cf. Chicago & Southern Air Lines v. Waterman S.S. Corp ., 333 U.S. 103, 111 (1948). [1]

1 The Court has recognized that, in the area of foreign policy, Congress may leave the President with wide discretion that otherwise might run afoul of the nondelegation doctrine. United States v. Curtiss-Wright Export Corp ., 299 U.S. 304 (1936). As stated in that case, "the "President alone has the power to speak or listen as a representative of the Nation. He makes treaties with the advice and consent of the Senate; but he alone

negotiates." Id ., at 319 (emphasis in original). Resolution of this case would interfere with neither the President's ability to negotiate treaties nor his duty to execute their provisions. We are merely being asked to decide whether a treaty, which cannot be ratified without Senate approval, continues in effect until the Senate or perhaps the Congress take further action.

Finally, the political-question doctrine rests in part on prudential concerns calling for mutual respect among the three branches of Government. Thus, the Judicial Branch should avoid "the potentiality of embarrassment [that would result] from multifarious pronouncements by various departments on one question." Similarly, the doctrine restrains judicial action where there is an "unusual need for unquestioning adherence to a political decision already made." Baker v. Carr, supra at 217.

If this case were ripe for judicial review, none of these prudential considerations would be present. Interpretation of the Constitution does not imply lack of respect for a coordinate branch. Powell v. McCormack, supra , at 548. If the President and the Congress had reached irreconcilable positions, final disposition of the question presented by this case would eliminate, rather than create, multiple constitutional interpretations. The specter of the Federal Government brought to a halt because of the mutual intransigence of the President and the Congress would require this Court to provide a resolution pursuant to our duty "'to say what the law is.'" United States v. Nixon , 418 U.S. 683, 703 (1974), quoting Marbury v. Madison , 1 Cranch 137, 177 (1803).

III

In my view, the suggestion that this case presents a political question is incompatible with this Court's willingness on previous occasions to decide whether one branch of our Government has impinged upon the power of another. See Buckley v. Valeo , 424 U.S., at 138; United States v. Nixon, supra , at 707; The Pocket Veto Case , 279 U.S. 655, 676-678 (1929); Myers v. United States , 272 U.S. 52 (1926). [2] Under the criteria enunciated in Baker v. Carr , we have the responsibility to decide whether both the Executive and Legislative Branches have constitutional roles to play in termination of a treaty. If the Congress, by appropriate formal action, had challenged the President's authority to terminate the treaty with Taiwan, the resulting uncertainty could have serious consequences for our country. In that situation, it would be the duty of this Court to resolve the issue.

 MR. JUSTICE REHNQUIST, with whom THE CHIEF JUSTICE, MR. JUSTICE STEWART, and MR. JUSTICE STEVENS join, concurring in the judgment.

I am of the view that the basic question presented by the petitioners in this case is "political" and therefore nonjusticiable because it involves the authority of the President in the conduct of our country's foreign relations and the extent to which the Senate or the Congress is authorized to negate the action of the President. In Coleman v. Miller , 307 U.S. 433 (1939), a case in which members of the Kansas Legislature brought an action attacking a vote of the State Senate in favor of the ratification of the Child Labor Amendment, Mr. Chief Justice Hughes wrote in what is referred to as the "Opinion of the Court":

"We think that... the question of the efficacy of ratifications by state legislatures, in the light of previous rejection or attempted withdrawal, should be regarded as a political question pertaining to the political departments, with the ultimate authority in the Congress in the exercise of its control over the promulgation of the adoption of the Amendment.

"The precise question as now raised is whether, when the legislature of the State, as we have found, has actually ratified the proposed amendment, the Court should] restrain the state officers from certifying the ratification to the Secretary of State, because of an earlier rejection, and thus prevent the question from coming before the political departments. We find no basis in either Constitution or statute for such judicial action. Article V, speaking solely of ratification, contains no provision as to rejection...." Id ., at 450.

Thus, Mr. Chief Justice Hughes' opinion concluded that "Congress in controlling the promulgation of the adoption of a constitutional amendment has the final determination of the question whether by lapse of time its proposal of the amendment had lost its vitality prior to the required ratifications." Id ., at 456.

I believe it follows a fortiori from Coleman that the controversy in the instant case is a nonjusticiable political dispute that should be left for resolution by the Executive and Legislative Branches of the Government. Here, while the Constitution is express as to the manner in which the Senate shall participate in the ratification of a treaty, it is silent as to that body's participation in the abrogation of a treaty. In this respect the case is directly analogous to Coleman, supra . As stated in Dyer v. Blair, 390 F. Supp. 1291, 1302 (ND Ill. 1975) (three-judge court):

"A question that might be answered in different ways for different amendments must surely be controlled by political standards rather than standards easily characterized as judicially manageable." In light of the absence of any constitutional provision governing the termination of a treaty, and the fact that different termination procedures may be appropriate for different treaties, the instant case in my view also "must surely be controlled by political standards."

I think that the justification for concluding that the question here is political in nature are even more compelling than in Coleman because it involves foreign relations -- specifically a treaty commitment to use military force in the defense of a foreign government if attached. In United States v. Curtiss-Wright Corp ., 299 U.S. 304 (1936), this Court said:

"Whether, if the Joint Resolution had related solely to internal affairs it would be open to the challenge that it constituted an unlawful delegation of legislative power to the Executive, we find it unnecessary to determine. The whole aim of the resolution is to affect a situation entirely external to the United States, and falling within the category of foreign affairs...." Id ., at 315.

The present case differs in several important respects from Youngstown Sheet & Tube Co. v. Sawyer , 343 U.S. 579 (1952), cited by petitioners as authority both for reaching the merits of this dispute and for reversing the Court of Appeals. In Youngstown , private litigants brought a suit contesting the President's authority under his war powers to seize the Nation's steel industry, an action of profound and demonstrable domestic impact. Here, by contrast, we are asked to settle a dispute between coequal branches of our Government, each of which has resources available to protect and assert its interests, resources not available to private litigants outside the judicial forum. [1] Moreover, as in Curtiss-Wright , the effect of this action, as far as we can tell, is "entirely external to the United States, and [falls] within the category of foreign affairs." Finally, as already noted, the situation presented here is closely akin to that presented in Coleman , where the Constitution spoke only to the procedure for ratification of an amendment, not to its rejection.

Having decided that the question presented in this action is nonjusticiable, I believe that the appropriate disposition is for this Court to vacate the decision of the Court of

90

Appeals and remand with instructions for the District Court to dismiss the complaint. This procedure derives support from our practice in disposing of moot actions in federal courts. For more than 30 years, we have instructed lower courts to vacate any decision on the merits of an action that has become moot prior to a resolution of the case in this Court. United States v. Munsingwear, Inc ., 340 U.S. 36 (1950). The Court has required such decisions to be vacated in order to "prevent a judgment, unreviewable because of mootness, from spawning any legal consequences." Id ., at 41. It is even more imperative that this Court invoke this procedure to ensure that resolution of a "political question," which should not have been decided by a lower court, does not "spawn any legal consequences." An Art. III court's resolution of a question that is "political" in character can create far more disruption among the three coequal branches of Government than the resolution of a question presented in a moot controversy. Since the political nature of the questions presented should have precluded the lower courts from considering or deciding the merits of the controversy, the prior proceedings in the federal courts must be vacated, and the complaint dismissed.

DISSENT BY: BLACKMUN (In Part); BRENNAN

MR. JUSTICE BLACKMUN, with whom MR. JUSTICE WHITE joins, dissenting in part.

In my view, the time factor and its importance are illusory; if the President does not have the power to terminate the treaty (a substantial issue that we should address only after briefing and oral argument), the notice of intention to terminate surely has no legal effect. It is also indefensible, without further study, to pass on the issue of justiciability or on the issues of standing or ripeness. While I therefore join in the grant of the petition for certiorari, I would set the case for oral argument and give it the plenary consideration it so obviously deserves.

MR. JUSTICE BRENNAN, dissenting.

I respectfully dissent from the order directing the District Court to dismiss this case, and would affirm the judgment of the Court of Appeals insofar as it rests upon the President's well-established authority to recognize, and withdraw recognition from, foreign governments.

In stating that this case presents a nonjusticiable "political question." MR. JUSTICE REHNQUIST, in my view, profoundly misapprehends the political-question principle as it applies to matters of foreign relations. Properly understood, the political-question doctrine restrains courts from reviewing an exercise of foreign policy judgment by the coordinate political branch to which authority to make that judgment has been "constitutional[ly] commit[ted]." Baker v. Carr, 369 U.S. 186, 211-213, 217 (1962). But the doctrine does not pertain when a court is faced with the antecedent question whether a particular branch has been constitutionally designated as the repository of political decision making power. Cf. Powell v. McCormack , 395 U.S. 486, 519-521 (1969). The issue of decision making authority must be resolved as a matter of constitutional law, not political discretion; accordingly, it falls within the competence of the courts.

The constitutional question raised here is prudently answered in narrow terms. Abrogation of the defense treaty with Taiwan was a necessary incident to Executive recognition of the Peking Government, because the defense treaty was predicated upon the now-abandoned view that the Taiwan Government was the only legitimate political authority in China. Our cases firmly establish that the Constitution commits to the President alone the power to recognize, and withdraw recognition from, foreign regimes. See Banco Nacional de Cuba v. Sabbatino , 376 U.S. 398, 410 (1964); Baker v. Carr, supra , at 212; United

States v. Pink , 315 U.S. 203, 228-230 (1942). That mandate being clear, our judicial inquiry into the treaty rupture can go no further. See Baker v. Carr, supra , at 212; United States v. Pink, supra , at 229.

DISSENT by MacKINNON in the Court of Appeals' decision.

Simply put, McKinnon is disturbed by his colleagues' willingness to say, on the one hand, that the president has the power to terminate this treaty, but that this decision should not be meant to be a precedent regarding the termination of other treaties. He brings up the possibility of a president terminating, for example, the NATO treaty.

He believes that his colleagues have deliberately ignored the necessary and proper clause in the constitution and believes that termination of treaties is an implied power vested in the government. The necessary and proper clause appears in article I section 8. Article I deals with legislative powers. He concludes that it is Congress that has the power to make laws, including treaties, and that a treaty is to be terminated in the same manner as any other law — by a formal act of Congress approved by the President.

He is clearly concerned that the Executive, given greater and greater power in international affairs, could alter the balance of power between the main branches of government.

But, two Justices (White and Blackmun) would set the case for argument, rather than dismiss the complaint. Justice Brennan would affirm the judgment of the Court of Appeals (meaning that he agrees with their analysis, and finds that the President alone had the power to terminate this treaty).

Questions on Goldwater v. Carter

1.   How important is it to U.S. and global commerce that Taiwan retains some independence from Beijing? What would be the effect on the U.S. (and U.S. companies) if Xi Jinping were to launch a successful invasion of Taiwan? Should U.S. businesses even care?

2. What if the U.S. President ordered U.S. armed forces to defend Taiwan? Would s/he need Congressional authorization?

3. What diplomatic agreements have the U.S. and China reached regarding Taiwan?

Here's what a former ambassador said about China and Taiwan:

Q. Why does China feel so strongly that Taiwan independence would be an act of war by Taiwan?

A.   Because Taiwan is part of China. It has been part of China since ancient times, and it's just because of some of the separatist attempts of certain people on Taiwan and the interference from foreign forces that Taiwan is still separated from the motherland.

I think that people can understand that when a country is divided its people will like to see the country reunite, especially in the case of China, which has suffered so much in the past. So I believe that what we are doing has the support of the peace-loving people in the world and we are seeking peaceful unification -- one country, two systems, is our basic policy. Of course, we will not make a commitment to go to the use of force. We do not make this kind of commitment precisely because we want to see the peaceful reunification of the country.

And there are some events in Taiwan which really cause us grave concern. Some people are openly campaigning for Taiwan independence and, of course, we have also been concerned by U.S. arms sales to Taiwan and other things. We have urged the American side to abide by the three joint communiqués between the two countries and to stop selling weapons to Taiwan.

Students: does this mean that Beijing does not recognize Taiwan's "sovereignty"? Under International Law, is it obligated to respect Taiwanese "nationalism" and "self-determination"?

IV. TRADE RELATIONS AND PRESIDENTIAL POWER

Expressly delegated powers

The President is "Commander in Chief," and this explains why President Truman intervened in the steel dispute in Youngstown case. Other than those inherent powers, also exercised in the Goldwater v. Carter case, Congress has often created laws that require executive action be taken, delegating power to the President to take action on his/her own. For example, the International Emergency Economic Powers Act, or the Economic Espionage Act, the Export Control Act, or the Trading with the Enemy Act. Here, we will just skim the provisions of "IEEPA" as an example of how Congress has often delegated power to the President. President Biden has issued Executive Orders against Russia for "cyber-hacking" and "cyber espionage," and has also issued Executive Orders under IEPPA for Russia's invasion of Ukraine. In doing so, he is using Congressionally delegated powers under IEPPA.

CHAPTER 35—INTERNATIONAL EMERGENCY ECONOMIC POWERS ACT

§1701. Unusual and extraordinary threat; declaration of national emergency; exercise of Presidential authorities

(a) Any authority granted to the President by section 1702 of this title may be exercised to deal with any unusual and extraordinary threat, which has its source in whole or substantial part outside the United States, to the national security, foreign policy, or economy of the United States, if the President declares a national emergency with respect to such threat.

(b) The authorities granted to the President by section 1702 of this title may only be exercised to deal with an unusual and extraordinary threat with respect to which a national emergency has been declared for purposes of this chapter and may not be exercised for any other purpose. Any exercise of such authorities to deal with any new threat shall be based on a new declaration of national emergency which must be with respect to such threat.

(Pub. L. 95–223, title II, §202, Dec. 28, 1977, 91 Stat. 1626.)

§1708. Actions to address economic or industrial espionage in cyberspace

(a) Report required

(1) In general

Not later than 180 days after December 19, 2014, and annually thereafter through 2020, the President shall submit to the appropriate congressional committees a report on foreign economic and industrial espionage in cyberspace during the 12-month period preceding the submission of the report that-

(A) identifies-

(i) foreign countries that engage in economic or industrial espionage in cyberspace with respect to trade secrets or proprietary information owned by United States persons;

(ii) foreign countries identified under clause (i) that the President determines engage in the most egregious economic or industrial espionage in cyberspace with respect to such trade secrets or proprietary information (to be known as "priority foreign countries");

(iii) categories of technologies or proprietary information developed by United States persons that-

(I) are targeted for economic or industrial espionage in cyberspace; and

(II) to the extent practicable, have been appropriated through such espionage;

(iv) articles manufactured or otherwise produced using technologies or proprietary information described in clause (iii)(II); and

(v) to the extent practicable, services provided using such technologies or proprietary information;

(B) describes the economic or industrial espionage engaged in by the foreign countries identified under clauses (i) and (ii) of subparagraph (A); and

(C) describes-

(i) actions taken by the President to decrease the prevalence of economic or industrial espionage in cyberspace; and

(ii) the progress made in decreasing the prevalence of such espionage.

(2) Determination of foreign countries engaging in economic or industrial espionage in cyberspace

For purposes of clauses (i) and (ii) of paragraph (1)(A), the President shall identify a foreign country as a foreign country that engages in economic or industrial espionage in cyberspace with respect to trade secrets or proprietary information owned by United States persons if the government of the foreign country-

(A) engages in economic or industrial espionage in cyberspace with respect to trade secrets or proprietary information owned by United States persons; or

(B) facilitates, supports, fails to prosecute, or otherwise permits such espionage by-

(i) individuals who are citizens or residents of the foreign country; or

(ii) entities that are organized under the laws of the foreign country or are otherwise subject to the jurisdiction of the government of the foreign country.

(3). omitted

(b) Imposition of sanctions

(1) In general

The President may, pursuant to the International Emergency Economic Powers Act (50 U.S.C. 1701 et seq.), block and prohibit all transactions in all property and interests in property of each person described in paragraph (2), if such property and interests in property are in the United States, come within the United States, or are or come within the possession or control of a United States person.

(2) Persons described

A person described in this paragraph is a foreign person the President determines knowingly requests, engages in, supports, facilitates, or benefits from the significant appropriation, through economic or industrial espionage in cyberspace, of technologies or proprietary information developed by United States persons.

(3) Exception – omitted - omitted

(4) Implementation; penalties

(c) Omitted

(d) Definitions - omitted

(Pub. L. 113–291, div. A, title XVI, §1637, Dec. 19, 2014, 128 Stat. 3644 .)

From the law firm Mayer/Brown: Biden Administration Announces Expansion of Sanctions. .

https://www.mayerbrown.com/en/perspectives-events/publications/2021/04/biden-administration-announces-expansion-of-sanctions-against-russia-and-signals-potential-additional-restrictions-following-solarwinds-cyber-attack

Blocking Property With Respect To Specified Harmful Foreign Activities of the Government of the Russian Federation

Vol. 86, No. 073, Monday, April 19, 2021

Presidential Documents

86 Federal Register (2021) 20249

Blocking Property With Respect To Specified Harmful Foreign Activities of the Government of the Russian Federation

By the authority vested in me as President by the Constitution and the laws of the United States of America, including the International Emergency Economic Powers Act (*50 U.S.C. 1701 et seq.*) (IEEPA), the National Emergencics Act (*50 U.S.C. 1601 et seq.*) (NEA), section 212(f) of the Immigration and Nationality Act of 1952 (*8 U.S.C. 1182(f)*), and section 301 of title 3, United States Code,

I, JOSEPH R. BIDEN JR., ***President of the United States*** of America, find that specified harmful foreign activities of the Government of the Russian Federation—in particular, efforts to undermine the conduct of free and fair democratic elections and democratic institutions in the United States and its allies and partners; to engage in and facilitate malicious cyber-enabled activities against the United States and its allies and partners; to foster and use transnational corruption to influence foreign governments; to pursue extraterritorial activities targeting dissidents or journalists; to undermine security in countries and regions important to United States national security; and to violate well-established principles of international law, including respect for the territorial integrity of states—constitute an unusual and extraordinary threat to the national security, foreign policy, and economy of the United States. I hereby declare a national emergency to deal with that threat.

Accordingly, I hereby order:

Section 1. All property and interests in property that are in the United States, that hereafter come within the United States, or that are or hereafter come within the possession or control of any United States person of the following persons are blocked and may not be transferred, paid, exported, withdrawn, or otherwise dealt in:

(a) any person determined by the Secretary of the Treasury, in consultation with the Secretary of State, and, with respect to subsection (a)(ii) of this section, in consultation with the Attorney General, or by the Secretary of State, in consultation with the Secretary of the Treasury, and, with respect to subsection (a)(ii) of this section, in consultation with the Attorney General:

(i) to operate or have operated in the technology sector or the defense and related materiel sector of the Russian Federation economy, or any other sector of the Russian Federation economy as may be determined by the Secretary of the Treasury, in consultation with the Secretary of State;

(ii) to be responsible for or complicit in, or to have directly or indirectly engaged or attempted to engage in, any of the following for or on behalf of, or for the benefit of, directly or indirectly, the Government of the Russian Federation:

(A) malicious cyber-enabled activities;

(B) interference in a United States or other foreign government election;

(C) actions or policies that undermine democratic processes or institutions in the United States or abroad;

(D) transnational corruption;

(E) assassination, murder, or other unlawful killing of, or infliction of other bodily harm against, a United States person or a citizen or national of a United States ally or partner;

(F) activities that undermine the peace, security, political stability, or territorial integrity of the United States, its allies, or its partners; or

(G) deceptive or structured transactions or dealings to circumvent any United States sanctions, including through the use of digital currencies or assets or the use of physical assets;

(iii) to be or have been a leader, official, senior executive officer, or member of the board of directors of:

(A) the Government of the Russian Federation;

(B) an entity that has, or whose members have, engaged in any activity described in subsection (a)(ii) of this section; or

(C) an entity whose property and interests in property are blocked pursuant to this order;

(iv) to be a political subdivision, agency, or instrumentality of the Government of the Russian Federation;

(v) to be a spouse or adult child of any person whose property and interests in property are blocked pursuant to subsection (a)(ii) or (iii) of this section;

(vi) to have materially assisted, sponsored, or provided financial, material, or technological support for, or goods or services to or in support of:

(A) any activity described in subsection (a)(ii) of this section; or

(B) any person whose property and interests in property are blocked pursuant to this order; or

(vii) to be owned or controlled by, or to have acted or purported to act for or on behalf of, directly or indirectly, the Government of the Russian Federation or any person whose property and interests in property are blocked pursuant to this order.

(b) any person determined by the Secretary of the Treasury, in consultation with the Secretary of State, to have materially assisted, sponsored, or provided financial, material, or technological support for, or goods or services to or in support of, a government whose property and interests in property are blocked pursuant to chapter V of title 31 of the Code of Federal Regulations or another Executive Order, and to be:

(i) a citizen or national of the Russian Federation;

(ii) an entity organized under the laws of the Russian Federation or any jurisdiction within the Russian Federation (including foreign branches); or

(iii) a person ordinarily resident in the Russian Federation.

(c) any person determined by the Secretary of State, in consultation with the Secretary of the Treasury, to be responsible for or complicit in, or to have directly or indirectly engaged in or attempted to engage in, cutting or disrupting gas or energy supplies to Europe, the Caucasus, or Asia, and to be:

(i) an individual who is a citizen or national of the Russian Federation; or

(ii) an entity organized under the laws of the Russian Federation or any jurisdiction within the Russian Federation (including foreign branches).

(d) The prohibitions in subsections (a), (b), and (c) of this section apply except to the extent provided by statutes, or in regulations, orders, directives, or licenses that may be issued pursuant to this order, and notwithstanding any contract entered into or any license or permit granted before the date of this order.

Sec. 2. The prohibitions in section 1 of this order include:

(a) the making of any contribution or provision of funds, goods, or services by, to, or for the benefit of any person whose property and interests in property are blocked pursuant to this order; and

(b) the receipt of any contribution or provision of funds, goods, or services from any such person.

Sec. 3. (a) The unrestricted immigrant and nonimmigrant entry into the United States of noncitizens determined to meet one or more of the criteria in section 1 of this order would be detrimental to the interests of the United States, and the entry of such persons into the United States, as immigrants or nonimmigrants, is hereby suspended, except when the Secretary of State or the Secretary of Homeland Security, as appropriate, determines that the person's entry would not be contrary to the interests of the United States, including when the Secretary of State or the Secretary of Homeland Security, as appropriate, so determines, based on a recommendation of the Attorney General, that the person's entry would further important United States law enforcement objectives.

(b) The Secretary of State shall implement this authority as it applies to visas pursuant to such procedures as the Secretary of State, in consultation with the Secretary of Homeland Security, may establish.

(c) The Secretary of Homeland Security shall implement this order as it applies to the entry of noncitizens pursuant to such procedures as the Secretary of Homeland Security, in consultation with the Secretary of State, may establish.

(d) Such persons shall be treated by this section in the same manner as persons covered by section 1 of *Proclamation* 8693 of July 24, 2011 (Suspension of Entry of Aliens Subject to United Nations Security Council Travel Bans and International Emergency Economic Powers Act Sanctions).

Sec. 4. (a) Any transaction that evades or avoids, has the purpose of evading or avoiding, causes a violation of, or attempts to violate any of the prohibitions set forth in this order is prohibited.

(b) Any conspiracy formed to violate any of the prohibitions set forth in this order is prohibited.

Sec. 5. I hereby determine that the making of donations of the types of articles specified in section 203(b)(2) of IEEPA (*50 U.S.C. 1702(b)(2)*) by, to, or for the benefit of any person whose property and interests in property are blocked pursuant to this order would seriously impair my ability to deal with the national emergency declared in this order, and I hereby prohibit such donations as provided by section 1 of this order.

Sec. 6. For the purposes of this order:

(a) the term "entity" means a partnership, association, trust, joint venture, corporation, group, subgroup, or other organization;

(b) the term "Government of the Russian Federation" means the Government of the Russian Federation, any political subdivision, agency, or instrumentality thereof, including the Central Bank of the Russian Federation, and any person owned, controlled, or directed by, or acting for or on behalf of, the Government of the Russian Federation;

(c) the term "noncitizen" means any person who is not a citizen or noncitizen national of the United States;

(d) the term "person" means an individual or entity; and

(e) the term "United States person" means any United States citizen, lawful permanent resident, entity organized under the laws of the United States or any jurisdiction within the United States (including foreign branches), or any person in the United States.

Sec. 7. For those persons whose property and interests in property are blocked pursuant to this order who might have a constitutional presence in the United States, I find that because of the ability to transfer funds or other assets instantaneously, prior notice to such persons of measures to be taken pursuant to this order would render those measures ineffectual. I therefore determine that for these measures to be effective in addressing the national emergency declared in this order, there need be no prior notice of a listing or determination made pursuant to section 1 of this order.

Sec. 8. The Secretary of the Treasury, in consultation with the Secretary of State, is hereby authorized to take such actions, including the promulgation of rules and regulations, and to employ all powers granted to the President by IEEPA, as may be necessary to carry out the purposes of this order. The Secretary of the Treasury may, consistent with applicable law, redelegate any of these functions within the Department of the Treasury. All departments and agencies of the United States shall take all appropriate measures within their authority to carry out the provisions of this order.

Sec. 9. Nothing in this order shall prohibit transactions for the conduct of the official business of the Federal Government or the United Nations (including its specialized agencies, programs, funds, and related organizations) by employees, grantees, and contractors thereof.

Sec. 10. The Secretary of the Treasury, in consultation with the Secretary of State, is hereby authorized to submit recurring and final reports to the Congress on the national emergency declared in this order, consistent with section 401(c) of the NEA (_50 U.S.C. 1641(c)_) and section 204(c) of IEEPA (_50 U.S.C. 1703(c)_).

Sec. 11. (a) Nothing in this order shall be construed to impair or otherwise affect:

(i) the authority granted by law to an executive department or agency, or the head thereof; or

(ii) the functions of the Director of the Office of Management and Budget relating to budgetary, administrative, or legislative proposals.

(b) This order shall be implemented consistent with applicable law and subject to the availability of appropriations.

(c) This order is not intended to, and does not, create any right or benefit, substantive or procedural, enforceable at law or in equity by any party against the United States, its departments, agencies, or entities, its officers, employees, or agents, or any other person.

THE WHITE HOUSE

99

V. Executive Powers and Current Events (2022)

A. Powers of the Presidency

President Biden, as of this writing, appears poised to invoke the heaviest of sanctions on Russia in the event that Russia invades Ukraine.

1. How are U.S. businesses being hurt by Russian sanctions?
2. Could Congress object to how the President is carrying out IEEPA with sanctions?
3. How often have Presidents used their power under IEEPA? With what consequences for U.S. businesses?
4. Sanctions are not "cost-free," either to US citizens or people and companies in other nations. Should the broad powers of the President be curtailed somewhat by Congress through amending the IEEPA?

Andrew Boyle: Reining in the President's Powers
Brennan Center for Justice
Aug. 4, 2021

For the U.S. government, sanctions are an attractive response to a wide range of foreign policy problems. Support for international terrorism? Sanctions. Interference in U.S. elections? Sanctions. Narcotics trafficking? Sanctions. As Deputy Secretary Treasury Wally Adeyemo recently admitted recently, sanctions have become America's "tool of first resort."

Key points:

1. Most U.S. sanctions regimes are imposed by the president, not by Congress, under the International Emergency Economic Powers Act (IEEPA).

2. When Congress passed IEEPA in 1977, it was with the expectation that national emergencies requiring peacetime sanctions programs would be "rare and brief" and would not be "equated with normal ongoing problems." The precipitating events would be ones that truly represented a threat to the United States.

3. IEEPA has become a routine instrument of foreign policy, invoked 65 times since the law's enactment. Sanctions programs regularly last for years or even decades. The president's reports to Congress are cursory, pro forma documents that give Congress no meaningful basis to evaluate the sanctions' effectiveness.

4. There are humanitarian consequences to sanctions that target an entire country. By one estimate, there have been tens of thousands of deaths due to sanctions.

5. There is also a financial cost, U.S. businesses must expend significant resources on ensuring compliance, as well as often pay hefty fines for failures to comply, even when those failures are inadvertent.

Boyle recommends remedial legislation to limit sweeping Presidential authority to impose sanctions under IEPPA. The entire article can be read at:

https://www.brennancenter.org/our-work/analysis-opinion/reining-presidents-sanctions-powers

Questions about Andrew Boyle's article, *Reining in the President's Sanctions Powers: Used widely since 9/11, the benefits of sanctions often don't outweigh the costs.*, Brennan Center, Aug. 4, 2021.

1. How can we, or the government, actually determine if the benefits of imposing sanctions outweigh the costs? In short, how useful is utilitarian analysis in this?
2. Is the U.S. Government actually doing a cost-benefit analysis on its sanctions as a whole, or not? If not, why not? If so, what do those analyses show?
3. Why would sanctions against an "authoritarian" regime be likely to fail, according to Boyle?
4. Would you agree with Boyle that, at least, some greater "transparency" is needed about the kind of sanctions and the effectiveness of those sanctions? What about periodic approval from Congress of existing sanctions? Should IEPPA based sanctions be mandatorily reviewed every five years? Every ten years?
5. The title of IEPPA includes the word "emergency." If sanctions against another nation are imposed for over ten years, has there been an "emergency" the entire time? Would the sanctions be legal constitutionally even though there is no emergency?

Presidential Trade Authority

Congress has repeatedly delegated authority in trade matters to the President. In the context of trade agreements, an important one is the so-called Trade Promotion Authority (TPA), also known as a "fast-track authority". Under a TPA, the President can negotiate and enter into international trade agreements. He is however required to submit the agreement to Congress for approval and for vote on legislation appropriate and necessary for the agreement to be implemented.

B.   Federal Agencies Affecting Trade

U.S. Department of Commerce

This department has broad authority over many international trade issues. The department's functions are fostering trade and promoting exports of US goods and services (trade promotion), investigating and resolving complaints by US firms that foreign governments are unfairly blocking access to foreign markets (market access), administering US unfair import laws (import administration), issuing export licenses for certain products, developing US international trade statistical information, and many other functions.

U.S. Department of Homeland Security

After 9/11, the Department of Homeland Security brought together many existing government agencies in 2003 with a common responsibility for protecting the American "homeland." The key agencies of Homeland Security are Customs and Border protection, US Immigration and Customs enforcement (ICE), the U.S. citizen immigration and services, the Transportation Security

Administration, the Federal Emergency Management Agency, the US Coast Guard and several others.

U.S. Trade Representative
A listing of bilateral investment treaties can be found at:

https://ustr.gov/trade-agreements/bilateral-investment-treaties

U.S. Department of the Treasury

Because of its control of currency, the Treasury Department has a significant impact on international business transactions. Since 2001, the Department's role has grown considerably in fighting the "global war on terror" (GWOT) by disrupting the flow of money to terrorist groups. FinCEN (the Bureau of Financial Crimes Enforcement Network) fosters domestic and international cooperation among law enforcement agencies in dealing with financial crimes. The Office of Foreign Assets Control (OFAC) administers US trade and financial sanctions, such as those imposed on Russia in 2022 after its invasion of Ukraine. Sanctions are targeted against illicit arms dealers, international drug traffickers, cyber-criminals, and illicit arms dealers (such as those who traffic in weapons of mass destruction).

International Trade Commission

The International Trade Commission was created by Congress in 1916 as an independent agency. The Commission maintains a highly trained group of professional economists and researchers; they conduct investigations and prepare reports on matters related to international economics and trade. They do so for Congress and for the President. Some of these investigations are highly political: they relate to the impact of imported goods on U S domestic industry. Accordingly, the ITC is a bipartisan agency: the members of the Commission are appointed by the president from both political parties and are subject to Senate confirmation.

U.S. Court of International Trade

The Court of International Trade consists of nine judges who hear cases that arise from trade or tariff laws of the United states. For example, you might appeal from a US Customs and Border Protection ruling on duties for imported goods, or might appeal from decisions of the International Trade Commission. Appeals from the Court of International Trade go to the Court of Appeals for the Federal Circuit and to the U S Supreme Court. The court has exclusive jurisdiction over all civil actions commenced against the United states involving (1) revenue from imports, (2) tariffs ,duties ,fees or other taxes on the importation of merchandise, and (3) embargoes or other quantitative restrictions on the importation of merchandise for reasons other than the protection of public health and safety. The court is located in New York City.

CHAPTER FOUR:

INTERNATIONAL TRADE IN GOODS AND SERVICES

I. HISTORY OF CONTEMPORARY INTERNATIONAL TRADE LAW

International trade has grown dramatically in the past 60 years. In great measure, this is because the world's nations have cooperated in eliminating protectionist domestic legislation and in promoting the free exchange of goods.

The several GATT treaties, the EU, the WTO, and many other international agreements and organizations have resulted in a dramatic lowering of tariffs—each nation giving up a little in order to get reciprocal reductions—and a tremendous increase in international trade.

Certain public interest and labor groups have complained that "free trade" ignores important environmental and labor issues, with dire consequences for the environment and workers in developing countries. Employee organizations in developed nations argue that free trade and globalization have led to the loss of thousands of good jobs, as manufacturing plants are moved and work is outsourced to lower-wage nations.

While "globalization" is under attack from a number of quarters, and the Bretton Woods System (see below) seems to be breaking down from a departure from the gold standard, nations that try to cheat the WTO's free trade system, and a deepening division between democratically ruled nations of "the West" and a growing array of allied authoritarian regimes, the basic rules are still in place, and, for those interested in global business, worth studying.

Protectionism – The Great Depression of the 1930s in many ways was a direct consequence of protectionism. Recovery from the Great Depression was U.S. President Franklin Roosevelt's main goal upon his election in 1932, and liberalization of international trade was at the heart of his program for achieving that end.

During World War II, the protectionist sentiments of the 1930s were rejected as destructive, and they were swept aside in a rush to arrange a comprehensive network of multilateral agreements to settle the world's political and economic problems.

The Bretton Woods System – The negotiators who met for the United Nations Monetary and Financial Conference in Bretton Woods in July 1944 were determined to create a system that would promote trade liberalization and multilateral economic cooperation. The Bretton Woods System was meant to be an integrated undertaking by the international community to establish a multilateral institutional framework of rules and obligations.

https://www.youtube.com/watch?v=RtFz9q26t5A

The Bretton Woods System was to have had at its core three major international organizations: the International Monetary Fund (IMF), the International Bank for Reconstruction and Development (IBRD or World Bank), and the ill-fated International Trade Organization (ITO). The Articles of Agreement of the IMF were adopted at Bretton Woods and ratified in 1945.

The 1947 General Agreement on Tariffs and Trade – GATT 1947 was a multilateral treaty that set out the principles under which its contracting states, on the basis of "reciprocity and mutual advantage," were to negotiate "a substantial reduction in customs tariffs and other impediments to trade."

The main principles of GATT 1947 were as follows:
- Trade discrimination was forbidden.
- The only barriers that one contracting state could use to limit the importation of goods from another contracting state were customs tariffs.
- The trade regulations of contracting states had to be transparent.
- Customs unions and free trade agreements between contracting states were regarded as legitimate means for liberalizing trade.
- GATT-contracting states were allowed to levy only certain charges on imported goods.

The legal framework established at Geneva in 1947 remained essentially unchanged until the creation of the World Trade Organization (WTO) in 1994.

Multilateral Trade Negotiations – To keep GATT 1947 up-to-date, the contracting parties regularly participated in multilateral trade negotiations (informally called rounds).

Since one of the main purposes of the GATT agreement was to reduce tariffs, the first five rounds were devoted almost exclusively to tariff reductions, while the last three completed rounds (the Kennedy, Tokyo, and Uruguay Rounds) expanded their agendas to nontariff matters.

More comprehensive negotiating techniques were proposed and used for the first time in the Kennedy Round (1964–1967). In addition to the negotiations on tariffs, the Kennedy Round dealt with the problems of nonreciprocity for developing states and with nontariff obstacles.

The next multilateral trade negotiations, known as the Tokyo Round (1973–1979), were characterized by an ambitious agenda and the participation of non-GATT states. The Tokyo Round produced several special agreements (popularly known as codes) to regulate nontariff matters as well as several sectoral agreements to promote trade in particular commodities.

The Uruguay Round – The Uruguay Round (1986–1994) brought about a major change in the institutional structure of the GATT, replacing the informal GATT institution with a new institution: the World Trade Organization.

The Uruguay Round Final Act is made up of three parts that together form a single whole. The first part, the formal Final Act itself, is a one-page "umbrella" that introduces the other two parts. The second part of the Final Act is made up of the WTO Agreement and its annexes, of which there are two kinds: Multilateral Trade Agreements and Plurilateral Trade Agreements. The third and final part comprises the ministerial declarations, decisions, and understandings.

II.   THE WORLD TRADE ORGANIZATION

The World Trade Organization (WTO) is meant to provide the "common institutional framework" for the implementation of the agreements that came out of the Uruguay Round of MTNs. Functions served by the WTO include:
- to implement, administer, and carry out the WTO Agreement and its annexes,
- to act as a forum for ongoing multilateral trade negotiations,

- to serve as a tribunal for resolving disputes, and
- to review the trade policies and practices of member states.

The WTO Agreement – The Agreement Establishing the World Trade Organization (WTO Agreement) has been described as a "mini-charter" because it is much less complex than the ITO's Havana Charter. The provisions of the WTO Agreement are exclusively institutional and procedural. The Agreement establishes a legal framework to bring together the various trade pacts that were negotiated under GATT 1947. The WTO is to be guided by the procedures, customary practices, and decisions of the old GATT.

Membership of the WTO – In order to join the WTO, a nation must complete an "accession agreement" which must be approved by all WTO members. The negotiations with the many nations and various groupings within the WTO are lengthy and complex.

Cape Verde and the Ukraine joined the WTO in 2010, bringing its total membership to 153. During 2011, the WTO approved the membership of Montenegro, Russia, Samoa, and Vanuatu. Since then, even more have joined, bringing the current total (Sept. 2020) to 164. See the Wikipedia entry on the WTO, which includes the following:

The WTO has 164 members and 24 observer governments. Liberia became the 163rd member on 14 July 2016, and Afghanistan became the 164th member on 29 July 2016. In addition to states, the European Union, and each EU country in its own right, is a member. WTO members do not have to be fully independent states; they need only be a customs territory with full autonomy in the conduct of their external commercial relations. Thus Hong Kong has been a member since 1995 (as "Hong Kong, China" since 1997) predating the People's Republic of China, which joined in 2001 after 15 years of negotiations. The Republic of China (Taiwan) acceded to the WTO in 2002 as "Separate Customs Territory of Taiwan, Penghu, Kinmen, and Matsu, despite its disputed status.

As of 2007, WTO member states represented 96.4% of global trade and 96.7% of global GDP. Iran, followed by Algeria, are the economies with the largest GDP and trade outside the WTO, using 2005 data. With the exception of the Holy See, observers must start accession negotiations within five years of becoming observers. A number of international intergovernmental organizations have also been granted observer status to WTO bodies. 12 UN member states have no official affiliation with the WTO.

The members of the WTO comprise both states and customs territories that conduct their own trade policies. States that were members of GATT 1947 on January 1, 1995, along with the EU, were eligible to become "original members" of the WTO. A state that did not qualify for admission as an original member must negotiate entry into the WTO on terms to be agreed on between it and the WTO and approved by the WTO Ministerial Conference by a two-thirds majority of the member states of the WTO.

Structure of the WTO – The WTO has five main organs: (1) a Ministerial Conference, (2) a General Council that also functions as the WTO's Dispute Settlement Body and Trade Policy Review Body, (3) a Council for Trade in Goods, (4) a Council for Trade in Services, and (5) a Council for Trade-Related Aspects of Intellectual Property Rights.

The composition of the Ministerial Conference and especially the General Council has been criticized on the grounds that "mass management does not lend itself to operational efficiency or serious policy discussion."

In addition to the main organs of the WTO, there is also a secretariat headed by a director-general, who is appointed by the Ministerial Conference. The staff of the GATT 1947 secretariat became the staff of the WTO secretariat on the latter's inauguration. The director-general of the WTO is responsible for supervising the administrative functions of the WTO. The director-general has little power over matters of policy, other than his/her ability to negotiate, mediate, and persuade.

Ministerial Conference

The Ministerial Conference generally meets at least every other year to oversee the operation of the WTO. Five standing committees deal with (1) trade and development; (2) balance-of-payments restrictions; (3) budget, finance, and administration; (4) trade and the environment; and (5) regional agreements.

General Council

The General Council carries on the functions of the Ministerial Conference in the intervals between the meetings of the Conference. The General Council convenes as appropriate to function as the WTO Dispute Settlement Body and the WTO Trade Policy Review Body. The Council for Trade in Goods, the Council for Trade in Services, and the Council for Trade-Related Aspects of Intellectual Property Rights function under the guidance of the General Council to oversee the implementation and administration of the three main WTO agreements. The General Council is also responsible for making arrangements for "effective cooperation" with other intergovernmental organizations.

Decision Making within the WTO – The WTO Agreement says that the WTO will "continue the practice of decision making by consensus followed under the GATT 1947." Consensus is the making of a decision by general agreement and in the absence of any voiced objection.

If consensus cannot be reached, decisions are made by a simple majority vote. At meetings of the Ministerial Conference and the General Council, each WTO member state has one vote, with the EU having a number of votes equal to the number of its member states that are members of the WTO.

Waivers – GATT 1947 was sometimes characterized as a system of loopholes held together by waivers. The WTO agreements dramatically changed this.

With one exception, the waivers of obligations in existence under GATT 1947 terminated no later than two years after the inauguration of the WTO.

The procedures for obtaining new or continuing waivers are more rigorous. Thus, an applying member state must (1) describe the measures that it proposes to take, (2) specify the policy objectives it seeks to obtain, and (3) explain why it cannot achieve those objectives without violating its obligations under GATT 1994.

Waivers must be approved by the Ministerial Conference, which has up to 90 days to do so by consensus. If a consensus cannot be reached in that period, waivers must then be approved by a three-quarters majority of the members. Waivers are reviewed annually thereafter.

Any dispute that arises in connection with a waiver, whether or not the waiver is being carried out in conformity with its terms and conditions, can be referred for settlement under the Dispute Settlement Understanding.

Dispute Settlement – The Understanding on Rules and Procedures Governing the Settlement of Disputes (the Dispute Settlement Understanding, or DSU) carries forward and improves on the dispute settlement procedures of GATT 1947. The DSU establishes a unified system for settling disputes that arise under the WTO Agreement and its annexes.

Trade Policy Review – Annex 3 of the WTO Agreement establishes a Trade Policy Review Mechanism. The Trade Policy Review Board (TPRB) that is meant to be the WTO's auditor or watchdog. It is responsible for promoting "improved adherence" by all WTO member states to the WTO Multilateral Trade Agreements and, for the member states that are signatories, the Plurilateral Trade Agreements.

The TPRB (1) carries out periodic reviews of the trade policies and practices of all member states and (2) prepares an annual overview of the international trading environment.

III. THE 1994 GENERAL AGREEMENT ON TARIFFS AND TRADE

The current General Agreement on Tariffs and Trade (GATT 1994) is made up essentially of the same set of rules as GATT 1947. The changes in the text of GATT 1994 amount mainly to changes in terminology (e.g., member replaces contracting party and references to the "contracting parties acting jointly" are taken to mean the WTO or its Ministerial Conference).

The significance of the two instruments being legally distinct is that (1) the WTO is not the "legal successor" to the old GATT organization and (2) the member states of GATT 1994 owe no legal obligations to the contracting parties of GATT 1947. Thus, the WTO is not bound to service GATT 1947, nor is it bound by any obligations made by the previous GATT organization except to the extent that it expressly assumes those responsibilities.

States that become member states of GATT 1994 without withdrawing from GATT 1947 will be bound by two different sets of commitments involving two different lists of states. Similarly, states that withdraw from GATT 1947 after becoming members of GATT 1994 will only continue to have GATT obligations under GATT 1994.

Some of the decisions of the past GATT council were modified at the time GATT 1994 came into force by a series of "Understandings" annexed to the new General Agreement.

Direct Effect – Some of the provisions of GATT 1994 are directly effective. That is, they may be relied upon by private persons to challenge the actions of a member state. Those provisions that prohibit a state from taking action contrary to the General Agreement are directly effective.

Those that require a contracting state to take some positive action may only be challenged by individuals if the state adopts implementing legislation authorizing such a challenge.

Case 7–1 Finance Ministry v. Manifattura Lane Marzotto, SpA

Italy, Court of Cassation (Joint Session), 1973.

Foro Italiano, vol. 1, p. 2443 (1973); Italian Yearbook of International Law, vol. 1976, p. 383 (1976); International Law Reports, vol. 77, p. 551 (1988).

Manifattura Lane Marzotto, SpA, an Italian manufacturer of woolen goods, sued the Italian Finance Ministry after being charged an "administrative services duty" on wool it imported from Australia, claiming that this duty violated the General Agreement on Tariffs and Trade. GATT 1947, Article III(1)(b), prohibits member states from charging duties in excess of those set out in the Agreement's annexes and schedules, or from increasing its duties after the time the member state accedes to the General Agreement. Because the law that first imposed the administrative services duty was enacted after Italy acceded to the General Agreement, Marzotto claimed that it was illegal. The Finance Ministry asked the court to dismiss the case, contending that Article III(1)(b) was not directly effective because parliament had not adopted implementing legislation. The trial court in Milan dismissed the suit, but the Court of Appeal reversed, ruling that the duty was illegal. The Finance Ministry appealed to the Court of Cassation.

JUDGMENT OF THE COURT:

Article III...of the General Agreement deals first with ordinary customs duties and provides that they are applicable to the products included in the schedules at a rate not higher than that indicated in those same lists. It then establishes that duties other than ordinary customs duties may not be higher than those in force on the date of the General Agreement. . . .

Law No. 295 of 5 April 1950, which implemented the GATT Agreement, provides in Article 2:
The aforementioned Agreements, Annexes and Protocols are fully and entirely implemented as from the time limits established by the Protocols. . . .

As Italy has fully integrated into its legal system the first part of the General Agreement—including the provision concerning customs duties—it remains to be seen whether this provision is merely a simple declaration of principle, deprived of any direct legal effect within the country. If that is so, the member states would only be obliged to each other to harmonize their laws, and there would be no immediate right for individuals to bring actionable claims. According to the Finance Ministry, Parliament is the only entity that can properly determine when and to what extent the existing customs laws should be modified, and no other person or entity should be allowed to do so.

This Court cannot agree. It seems clear to us that the provision of the General Agreement that we are examining is directly effective, giving rights both to the member states of the GATT and to individuals within those states, without any need for additional legislative implementation. The provision—which is essentially a prohibition against increasing duties above those in effect on the date a member state accedes to the General Agreement—is clearly one which imposes on the acceding state an obligation not to act. There is, therefore, no need for the state to make any additional legislation.

Accordingly, this prohibition is complete and directly effective not only between the member states but also between the member states and their nationals. . . .

Thus, in compliance with the law implementing the General Agreement, we hold that goods imported from one GATT member state to another are not subject to internal duties and charges of any kind which are higher than those that were in force on the date the General Agreement became effective. . . .

The judgment of the Court of Appeal was affirmed.

Case Brief for Case 7-1: *Finance Ministry v. Manifattura Lane Marz Otto, SpA*
Italy, Court of Cassation (Joint Session), 1973.

Facts: Italy imposed an "administrative services duty" on woolen goods that Manifattura Lane Marzotto (MLM) had imported from Australia. MLM then sued the government claiming that this duty violated

Article III(1)(b) of the GATT. The government moved to have the case dismissed, arguing that Article III(1)(b) is not directly effective and that the Italian Parliament had not adopted implementing legislation.

Issue: Is GATT Article III(1)(b) directly effective?

Holding: Yes.

Law: (1) GATT Article III establishes the maximum amounts of tariffs that contracting states can impose. (2) Italy's Law No. 295 of 5 April 1950, implementing the GATT in general, provided that the entire agreement was "fully and entirely implemented." (3) Treaty provisions that mandate that a state is not to act do not require the state to act to be fully implemented.

Explanation: The GATT is fully part of Italy's legal system. Because Article III is a prohibition requiring the state not to act, there is no need for specific implementing legislation. It is directly effective and may be invoked by private persons.

Order: The duty charged MLM is illegal.

Nondiscrimination – The most fundamental principle of GATT is that international trade should be conducted without discrimination. This principle is given concrete form in the most-favored-nation (MFN) and national treatment rules.

The MFN Rule

Article I of GATT requires each member to apply its tariff rules equally to all other members. The MFN rule does not apply to:
- The use of measures to counter dumping and subsidization.
- The creation of customs unions and free trade areas.
- Restrictions that protect public health, safety, welfare, and national security.

GATT provides for a special exception in the case of developing states. In order both to promote and protect the economies of developing states, GATT encourages the developed states not to demand reciprocity from them in trade negotiation, and it authorizes developed member states to adopt measures that give preferences to developing member states.

The contracting parties to GATT 1947 approved two preferential treatment schemes that are carried forward into GATT 1994. One, the Generalized System of Preferences (GSP), allows developing countries to export all (or nearly all) of their products to a participating developed country on a nonreciprocal basis. The other, the South-South Preferences (so called because most developing nations are located in the Southern Hemisphere), lets developing countries exchange tariff preferences among themselves without extending the same preferences to developed states.

The National Treatment Rule

The national treatment rule requires a country to treat products equally with its own domestic products once they are inside its borders. Article III, paragraph 4, of GATT provides: The products of the territory of any member state imported into the territory of any other member state shall be accorded treatment no less favorable than that accorded to like products of national origin in respect of all laws, regulations and requirements affecting their internal sale, offering for sale, purchase, transportation, distribution, or use.

Article III, paragraph 2, sets out the same nondiscriminatory requirement with respect to internal taxes.

Brief for Case 7-2: *Japan—Taxes on Alcoholic Beverages*
World Trade Organization, Dispute Settlement Panel, 1998.

Facts: Japan imposed higher taxes on imported vodka than it did on "shochu," a similar locally manufactured alcoholic beverage. Canada, the EU, and the United States claimed that this violated GATT Article III, paragraph 2, which requires that imported products be taxed the same as like domestic products. Japan and the U.S. argued that Article III:2 should be interpreted according to an "aim-and-effect" test. Japan also argued that vodka and shochu were not "like products" and that its taxes on alcoholic beverages did not violate Article III:2 because its tax/price ratio was "roughly constant."

Issues: (1) Are vodka and shochu like products? (2) Is a "roughly constant" tax/price ratio sufficient to meet the requirement of Article III:2?

Holdings: (1) Yes. (2) No.

Law: Article III:2 requires that WTO member states impose the same internal taxes on imported products as they impose on like domestic products. It also says that taxes must not be applied in violation of the principles of paragraph 1. Article III:1 says that taxes should not be imposed so as "to afford protection to domestic production. The meaning of the phrase "like products" must be determined on a case-by-case basis. With regard to Article III:2, the products need to share common end-users and have essentially the same physical characteristics.

Explanation: . (1) Vodka and shochu are consumed by the same end users and except for filtration have identical physical characteristics. They should be treated as like products. (2) "Roughly constant" provides for too much leeway. Article III:2 requires that taxes on imported products not exceed those of domestic products. The taxes on vodka exceed those on shochu by about 50 percent. Japan's "roughly constant" argument is inconsistent and it appears to have been made up as an after-the-fact justification, as it is not mentioned in Japan's legislation.

Order: Japan should bring its alcoholic beverages tax into compliance with Article III:2.

Case Summary: The WTO panel considered whether Japan's policy of taxing imported vodka (and whiskey, brandy, and other imported alcoholic beverages) at a higher rate than Japanese shochu was a violation of GATT Article III. This section of GATT requires that imported goods be accorded "national treatment"—that is, not subjected to higher internal taxes than similar domestic products. After comparing vodka and shochu, the panel decided that they were indeed "like" products. Since imported vodka was taxed at a higher rate, this practice constituted a violation of Japan's obligations under GATT-WTO rules.

Protection Only Through Tariffs – Each member state may protect its domestic industries only through the use of tariffs. Quotas and other quantitative restrictions that block the function of the price mechanism are forbidden by Article XI of GATT. To ensure that internal taxes are not disguised as tariffs, Article II requires that tariffs be collected "at the time or point of importation."

The following exceptions apply to the principle of protection through tariffs:

- The imposition of temporary export prohibitions or restrictions to prevent or relieve critical shortages of foodstuffs or other essential products.
- The use of import and export restrictions related to the application of standards or regulations for classifying, grading, or marking commodities.
- The use of quantitative restrictions on imports of agricultural and fisheries products to stabilize national agricultural markets.
- The use of quantitative restrictions to safeguard a state's balance of payments.
- The use of quantitative restrictions by a developing state to further its economic development.

GATT requires member states to work toward their "substantial reduction." Tariff reductions are negotiated among the member states and then recorded as Schedules of Concessions annexed to GATT. A bound tariff rate represents the highest rate that a member state may set on an item under the terms of GATT. Once such a rate is negotiated, the member state is required to extend it to all other GATT members by the MFN rule.

Transparency – Transparency is the requirement that governments disclose to the public and other governments the rules, regulations, and practices they follow in their domestic trade systems. Complementing this principle is the requirement that member states must strive to simplify their import and export formalities.

While negotiations were underway in Geneva in 1947 to set up the original GATT, discussions were also being held in Western Europe to establish a customs union. The participants agreed to take advantage of the accords that had been reached to establish a standardized system (or nomenclature) for classifying goods for the purpose of imposing customs duties. In 1950, the Convention on Nomenclature for the Classification of Goods in Customs Tariffs was signed, and the Customs Cooperation Council (CCC), an international organization based in Brussels, was established to administer it.

On January 1, 1989, the United States brought its tariff schedules into line with the CCC or "Harmonized" system. The Harmonized System (HS) is made up of a schedule of about 900 tariff headings, which are interpreted through explanatory notes and classification opinions published and regularly updated by the CCC.

Regional Integration – GATT seeks to promote international trade through regional economic integration. It accordingly encourages WTO member states to participate in free trade areas and customs unions.

A free trade area consists of a group of states that have reduced or eliminated tariffs among themselves but that maintain their own individual tariffs in dealing with other states. A customs union involves a group of states that have reduced or eliminated tariffs among themselves and have also established a common tariff for all other states.

WTO member states may participate in these regional groups only if the groups do not establish higher duties or more restrictive commercial regulations with respect to other WTO countries. The same prohibition also applies to interim agreements leading to the establishment of these groups.

Any member state seeking to participate in a free trade area or customs union is required to "promptly notify" the WTO of its intentions. The proposed agreement and a transition schedule are then reviewed by WTO working parties to ensure that they comply with GATT Article XXIV. The results of this review are reported to the WTO Ministerial Conference, which in turn approves the proposal or makes recommendations for modification. Recommendations are actually demands to make changes.

Once a free trade area or customs union is established, GATT rules apply to the area or union as a whole and not to its constituent states. A customs union or free trade area operates as a regional GATT, with its own tariff and nontariff codes.

Escape Clause – "Safeguards" Article XIX of GATT 1994—entitled "Emergency Action on Imports of Particular Products"—is an escape clause or safety valve that allows a member state to avoid, temporarily, its GATT obligations when there is a surge in the number of imports coming from other member states. The injured state can impose emergency restrictive trade measures known as safeguards. A state making use of the escape clause must notify the WTO and consult with the affected exporting state to arrange for compensation. If a notifying country fails to negotiate, the injured exporting countries are authorized to retaliate—that is, withhold "substantially equivalent concessions" in order to restore the previous balance of trade between the two states.

The procedures for engaging in consultations and for withholding concessions are incorporated in a Safeguards Agreement.

Exceptions – The drafters of GATT realized that states sometimes need to take certain measures as a matter of public policy that conflict with GATT's general goal of liberalizing trade. Article XX sets out "General Exceptions" and Article XXI "Security Exceptions."

The general exceptions excuse a member state from complying with its GATT obligations so long as this is not done as "a means of arbitrary or unjustifiable discrimination" or as "a disguised restriction on international trade." They allow a state to take measures contrary to GATT that:
- are necessary to protect public morals;
- are necessary to protect human, animal, or plant life or health;
- relate to the importation or exportation of gold or silver;
- are necessary to secure compliance with laws or regulations that are not inconsistent with GATT;
- relate to the products of prison labor;
- protect national treasures of artistic, historic, or archaeological value;
- relate to the conservation of exhaustible natural resources;
- are undertaken in accordance with an intergovernmental commodity agreement;
- involve restrictions on exports of domestic materials needed by a domestic processing industry during periods when the domestic price of those materials is held below world prices as part of a governmental stabilization plan; or
- are essential to acquiring products in short supply.

The security exceptions set out in Article XXI allow member states to avoid any obligations they may have under GATT that are contrary to their "essential security interests" or that conflict with their duties "under the United Nations Charter for the maintenance of international peace and security."

Export Controls – Member states commonly employ GATT exceptions to limit certain kinds of exports. Examples of export controls that relate to the security exceptions set out in Article XXI include export restrictions for national security reasons or in support of actions taken by the United Nations in maintaining peace.

IV. MULTILATERAL TRADE AGREEMENTS

In addition to GATT 1994, there are 13 other Agreements on Trade in Goods annexed to the WTO Agreement: Nine of these deal with regulatory matters; two are sectoral agreements that extend GATT to certain types of goods not covered under GATT 1947; one is a program to devise a new agreement; and one is a protocol.

The most significant aspect of these agreements is that they have to be acceded to by all WTO member states. Disputes between member states over their application are now uniformly governed by the WTO Dispute Settlement Understanding.

Preshipment Inspection – Developing states frequently engage private companies to verify price, quantity, quality, customs classifications, and other characteristics of goods before the goods are shipped from other states. This preshipment inspection (PSI) is meant to prevent over- and underinvoicing and fraud, and thus prevent the flight of capital and the evasion of customs duties. The Agreement on Preshipment Inspection authorizes developing states to make use of PSI, but it also tries to limit its harmful trade effects.

Central to the PSI process is the verification of prices. The PSI Agreement allows an entity engaged to carry out PSI activities to reject a contract price it believes wrong only if the entity follows certain guidelines.

The states in which PSI activities are carried out have certain obligations. These states must ensure that their laws and regulations relating to PSI activities are applied nondiscriminatorily and transparently. If requested, they also must offer to provide technical assistance to the states engaging in PSI activities within their territories.

Disputes between an exporter and an entity engaged to carry out PSI activities are to be resolved by mutual accord. If not, either party may refer the matter for review to an independent review body.

Technical Barriers to Trade – The Agreement on Technical Barriers to Trade (TBT Agreement) establishes rules governing the way WTO member states draft, adopt, and apply technical regulations and standards to ensure that they (1) provide an appropriate level of protection for the life and health of humans, animals, and plants, as well as for the environment; (2) prevent deceptive practices; and (3) do not create unnecessary obstacles to trade.

Technical regulations are mandatory laws and provisions specifying (1) the characteristics of products; (2) the processes and production methods for creating products; and (3) the terminology, symbols, packaging, marking, or labeling requirements for products, processes, or production methods.

Standards are voluntary guidelines that specify the same kind of requirements. Conformity assessment procedures include the sampling, testing, and inspecting of products; their evaluation, verification, and assurance of conformity; and their registration, accreditation, and approval.

All products, including agricultural and industrial products, are covered by the TBT Agreement, but purchasing specifications related to the production or consumption requirements of governmental bodies and sanitary and phytosanitary measures are not. The TBT Agreement applies to local governments and NGOs, and central governments are required to take "reasonable measures" to see that these bodies do so.

Sanitary and Phytosanitary Measures – The Agreement on the Application of Sanitary and Phytosanitary Measures (SPS Agreement) is meant to complement the Agreement on Technical Barriers to Trade by defining the measures that may be taken by WTO member states to protect human, animal, and plant life and health.

Member states may protect the life and health of living things, but they may not do so as a disguised means for restricting international trade, nor may they act arbitrarily to unjustifiably discriminate between states where identical or similar conditions exist. In addition, the measures taken must generally be justified by scientific evidence.

Trade-Related Investment Measures – The Agreement on Trade-Related Investment Measures (TRIMs Agreement) is aimed at facilitating foreign investment and eliminating some of the provisions commonly found in foreign investment laws that distort or reduce international trade. In particular, the agreement forbids provisions in investment laws that discriminate unfavorably against foreigners and that impose quantitative restrictions on the use of foreign products by foreign-owned local enterprises.

Import-Licensing Procedures – The Agreement on Import-Licensing Procedures seeks to ensure that import-licensing procedures are neutral in their application and administered in a fair and equitable manner.

Forms and procedures are to be as simple as possible and applicants should have to deal only with a single administrative body. Import licenses are not to be denied because of minor errors in completing the application; nor are imports to be barred because of minor deviations in the value, quantity, or weight designated on the license.

V.   ANTI-DUMPING, SUBSIDIES: REMEDIES AND COUNTERVAILING MEASURES

Anti-dumping – The Agreement on Implementation of Article VI of GATT 1994, or the Anti-dumping Code, replaces codes negotiated during the Tokyo and Kennedy Rounds. The current code defines dumping in the following way: "A product is to be considered dumped, i.e. introduced into the commerce of another country at less than its normal value, if the export price of the product exported from one country to another is less than the comparable price, in the ordinary course of trade, for the like product when destined for consumption in the exporting country."

Significantly, the Anti-dumping Code does not prohibit dumping. It recognizes instead that the dumping of imports may be countered through the application of anti-dumping duties, but only if an investigation determines that the dumped imports cause or threaten to cause material injury to, or materially retard the establishment of, a domestic industry within the importing country.

Provisional measures may be imposed after an investigation has been initiated, a preliminary determination has been made of dumping and consequential injury to a domestic industry, and the authorities concerned believe that such measures are necessary to prevent injury being caused during the course of the investigation.

Final anti-dumping duties may be imposed at the discretion of the authorities concerned upon the completion of an investigation and a final determination that dumping, injury, and a causal link between them exist.

Subsidies and Countervailing Measures – A subsidy is a financial contribution made by a government (or other public body) that confers a benefit on an enterprise, a group of enterprises, or an industry. Examples of subsidies are:

- direct transfers of funds (e.g., grants, loans, and equity infusions),
- potential direct transfers of funds (e.g., loan guarantees),
- the foregoing of revenues (e.g., tax credits),
- the providing of goods or services (other than general infrastructure), and
- the conferring of any form of income or price support.

The Agreement on Subsidies and Countervailing Measures, or SCM Agreement, replaces the 1979 Subsidies Code concluded at the Tokyo Round. The SCM Agreement clearly states that its "disciplines" apply only to "specific" subsidies; that is subsidies that target:
- a specific enterprise or industry,
- specific groups of enterprises or industries, or
- enterprises in a particular region.

The disciplines do not apply to (1) nonspecific subsidies, (2) certain specific subsidies defined in the agreement, and (3) agricultural subsidies (which are governed by the Agreement on Agriculture).

Categories of Specific Subsidies

Specific subsidies are divided into two categories: (1) prohibited subsidies (informally referred to as red subsidies), and (2) actionable subsidies (yellow). The agreement originally contained a third category: nonactionable subsidies. This category existed for five years, ending on December 31, 1999, and was not extended.

Prohibited subsidies (red subsidies) are subsidies that either (1) depend upon export performance or (2) are contingent upon the use of domestic instead of imported goods. Actionable subsidies (yellow subsidies) are subsidies that may or may not be trade distorting, depending on how they are applied. They are defined as specific subsidies that, in the way they are used, (1) injure a domestic industry of another member state, (2) nullify or impair benefits due another member state under GATT 1994, or (3) cause or threaten to cause "serious prejudice" to the interests of another member state.

Remedies and Countervailing Measures

A WTO member state that believes that its domestic industries have been injured by either prohibited subsidies or actionable subsidies is given four options: (1) do nothing, (2) request consultations, (3) seek a remedy from the WTO, or (4) independently impose countervailing duties.

If an injured member state chooses to do nothing, neither the WTO nor any other member state is entitled to intervene. To obtain a remedy from the WTO, a member state claiming an injury must first consult with the subsidizing member state. If the two states are unable to find a mutually acceptable solution, either one may refer the matter to the WTO's Dispute Settlement Body (DSB) for the latter to set up a Panel.

If the Panel concludes that there is a prohibited subsidy, it will recommend the subsidy's withdrawal; if it concludes that there is an actionable subsidy, it will recommend that the subsidizing member state either remove the subsidy's adverse effects or withdraw the subsidy. If neither party appeals to the DSB's Appellate Body, the DSB must promptly adopt the report (unless it rejects it by consensus). If there is an appeal, the Appellate Body's decision must be unconditionally observed.

For a look at how the WTO deals with allegations of subsidies, see below, Case 4-4: *United States— European Communities—Measures Affecting Trade in Large Civil Aircraft.* Here is a brief summary of that case.

Facts: The United States complained that the European Union was providing illegal subsidies to Airbus companies in violation of Articles 3, 5, and 6 of the SCM Agreement and Articles III:4, XVI:1, and XXIII:1 of GATT 1994. The measures at issue in this dispute are more than 300 separate instances of alleged subsidization, over a period of almost 40 years, by the European Communities and four of its member States, France, Germany, Spain and the United Kingdom, with respect to large civil aircraft ("LCA") developed, produced and sold by the company known today as Airbus SAS. The measures that are the subject of the U.S. complaint may be grouped into five general categories: (i) "Launch Aid" or "member State Financing" (LA/MSF); (ii) loans from the European Investment Bank; (iii) infrastructure and infrastructure-related grants; (iv) corporate restructuring measures; and (v) research and technological development funding. The United States claims that each of the challenged measures is a specific subsidy within the meaning of Articles 1 and 2 of the SCM Agreement, and that the European Communities and the four member States, through the use of these subsidies, cause adverse effects to the U.S. interests within the meaning of Articles 5 and 6 of the SCM Agreement. In addition, the United States claims that seven of the challenged LA/MSF measures are prohibited export subsidies within the meaning of Article 3 of the SCM Agreement.

Issue: Were the subsidies, which were provided by members of the European Union to Airbus companies, prohibited under the SCM Agreement and GATT 1994?

Holding: Yes.

Law / Explanation: The WTO panel considered whether subsidies provided by members of the European Union to Airbus companies constituted prohibited subsidies under the SCM Agreement and GATT 1994. Ultimately, the panel found that some of the subsidies brought to issue by the United States constituted "serious prejudice to the interests of the United States" within the meaning of Article 5(c) of the SCM Agreement. However, the panel also concluded that the United States failed to provide sufficient evidence that a number of specific subsidies provided by the European Communities and EC member states caused or threatened to cause injury to the U.S. domestic industry.

Order: The panel recommended the immediate withdrawal of all subsidies found to be prohibited.

If a member state does not comply with a DSB-adopted report or Appellate Body decision, the DSB will authorize (unless it agrees by consensus not to do so) a complaining member state to adopt countervailing measures. A countervailing measure is defined in the SCM Agreement simply as a duty specially levied to offset a subsidy.

A state may independently impose countervailing duties so long as it follows the procedures specified in the SCM Agreement.

VI.   DEVELOPING STATES, SAFEGUARDS, AND AGRICULTURE

Developing states are given special treatment in the SCM Agreement. The least developed states and developing states with a per capita income of less than U.S. $1,000 are allowed to use subsidies based on export performance and were given until the year 2003 to phase out subsidies based on domestic content. Other developing states were required to phase out both kinds of subsidies by the end of 1999.

Safeguards – Safeguards are emergency actions that a WTO member state may take to protect its domestic industries from serious injury from a sudden increase in the quantity of an imported product. Until the Agreement on Safeguards was adopted with the inauguration of WTO, the provisions of Article XIX (entitled "Emergency Actions on Imports of Particular Products") of GATT 1947 governed safeguards.

A WTO member state may apply safeguard measures against a product only after conducting an official investigation to determine that the product is being imported into its territory in such increased quantities and under such conditions as to cause or threaten to cause serious injury to the domestic industry that produces like or directly competitive products. The measures must then be applied to a product (1) regardless of its origin and (2) only for the time and to the extent necessary to prevent or remedy serious injury and to facilitate adjustment.

To encourage domestic industries to make adjustments, any safeguard measure that is to last longer than one year must be progressively liberalized at regular intervals over its lifetime. If it is to last for more than three years, a review must be made by its midterm to determine if the measure should be withdrawn or liberalized more quickly. The WTO Safeguards Committee meets twice a year to review all safeguard actions and notifications by member nations.

Agriculture – The Agreement on Agriculture establishes guidelines for "initiating a process of reform of trade in agriculture." Its ultimate goal is the establishment of a market-oriented system for trade in agricultural products that is free of restrictions and distortions.

To begin the process of reform, the agreement:
- specifies the agricultural products it governs;
- requires that nontariff barriers to agricultural imports be converted into customs tariffs;
- defines permissible forms of domestic supports;
- defines export subsidies;
- phases in initial reductions in tariffs, impermissible domestic support measures, and export subsidies during a six-year implementation period (developing countries are given a 10-year period); and
- progressively integrates international trade in agricultural products into the GATT system.

The agricultural products governed by the agreement include foodstuffs (except for fish and fish products), hides, skins, animal hairs, raw cotton, raw flax, raw hemp, raw silk, and certain related products. Domestic agricultural support measures and export subsidies for agricultural products can sometimes restrict or distort trade. The Agreement on Agriculture provides for the gradual phasing-in of member state obligations.

Textiles and Clothing – The Agreement on Textiles and Clothing is designed to eliminate the current system of special arrangements governing international trade in these products. Prior to its adoption, a series of collateral arrangements had been entered into by the states principally involved in the clothing and textiles trade that created an exception to the GATT principle of protection through tariffs. The Agreement on Textiles and Clothing provided for the complete elimination of the Multi-Fiber Arrangement at the end of a 10-year transition period.

Rules of Origin – Rules of origin are important in implementing such trade policy instruments as antidumping and countervailing duties, origin marking, and safeguard measures. The Agreement on Rules of Origin is essentially a program outlining procedures for bringing about an international system of harmonized rules of origin. Rules of origin are the laws, regulations, and administrative procedures used by states to determine the country of origin of goods.

According to the guidelines set out in the Agreement on Rules of Origin, the resulting rules of origin are to be:
- coherent;
- objective, understandable, and predictable;
- administered in a consistent, uniform, impartial, and reasonable manner;

- applied equally to each member state's nonpreferential commercial policy instruments; and
- based on a positive standard.

VII. MAINTENANCE OF NATIONAL SECURITY

Following World War II, export restrictions became a prominent feature of the West's Cold War with the East, and by 1949, the United States and its Western European allies had enacted legislation limiting exports to the Soviet Union and its Eastern European allies. In 1949, the United States and its allies formed the Coordinating Committee on Multilateral Export Controls (COCOM). In 1993, with the Cold War at an end, the COCOM member states agreed that its East–West focus was no longer an appropriate basis for establishing export controls, and they agreed to bring the committee to an end.

The Wassenaar Arrangement: In July 1996, 33 countries approved the Wassenaar Arrangement on Export Controls for Conventional Arms and Dual-Use Goods and Technologies. Its goals are to promote transparency, the exchange of views and information, and greater responsibility in transfers of conventional arms and dual-use goods and technologies.

Member countries are required to maintain export controls on a list of agreed-upon items. Additionally, they make semi-annual reports on the transfer of arms and controlled dual-use items.

Membership is open to all countries on a nondiscriminatory basis. A member must be a producer of arms or an exporter of industrial equipment; maintain nonproliferation policies and appropriate national policies, including adherence to relevant nonproliferation regimes and treaties; and maintain fully effective export controls.

Other Multilateral Export-Control Programs – The Australia Group is an informal multilateral group of states established to address concerns about the proliferation of chemical and biological warfare capabilities. Members meet annually to share information about proliferation dangers and to harmonize their national export controls in an effort to curb the transfer of materials or equipment that could be used in the creation of chemical or biological weapons.

The Zangger Committee was set up the year after the Treaty on Non-Proliferation of Nuclear Weapons came into force. It works to harmonize the member states' interpretations of the export-control provision of the treaty.

The Nuclear Suppliers Group (NSG) is a group of nuclear supplier countries—including members and nonmembers of the Treaty on Non-Proliferation of Nuclear Weapons—that seeks to contribute to the nonproliferation of nuclear weapons by maintaining control lists for nuclear exports and nuclear-related exports.

The Missile Technology Control Regime was established in 1987 to limit the proliferation of missiles "capable of delivering nuclear weapons." This is an informal group with no permanent organization; each member administers its missile-related export controls independently.

United Nations Action to Maintain International Peace

The United Nations Charter authorizes the UN Security Council to impose sanctions, including the adoption of bans on trade, on states whose actions threaten international peace, and on several occasions it has imposed such sanctions.

Case 4-3

UNITED STATES—IMPORT PROHIBITION OF CERTAIN SHRIMP AND SHRIMP PRODUCTS

World Trade Organization, Appellate Body, 1998.

Appellate Body Report WT/DS58/AB/R.[21]

I. INTRODUCTION: STATEMENT OF THE APPEAL

This is an appeal by the United States from certain issues of law and legal interpretations in the Panel Report, *United States—Import Prohibition of Certain Shrimp and Shrimp Products....*

***

The United States issued regulations in 1987 pursuant to the Endangered Species Act of 1973[22] requiring all United States shrimp trawl vessels to use approved Turtle Excluder Devices ("TEDs") or tow-time restrictions in specified areas where there was a significant mortality of sea turtles in shrimp harvesting.[23] These regulations, which became fully effective in 1990, were modified so as to require the use of approved TEDs at all times and in all areas where there is a likelihood that shrimp trawling will interact with sea turtles, with certain limited exceptions.

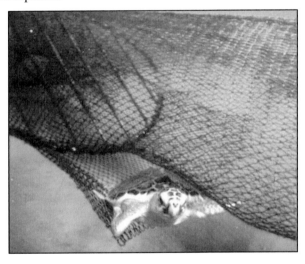

...Section 609(b)(1) imposed...an import ban on shrimp harvested with commercial fishing technology which may adversely affect sea turtles. Section 609(b)(2) provides that the import ban on shrimp will not apply to harvesting nations that are certified by the U.S. Department of State. To be certified a nation must either (a) not have any of the relevant species of turtles in its waters; (b) harvest shrimp exclusively by means that do not pose a threat to sea turtles, e.g., harvest shrimp exclusively by artisanal means; or (c) conduct its commercial shrimp trawling operations exclusively in waters subject to its jurisdiction in which sea turtles do not occur.

Second, certification shall be granted to harvesting nations that provide documentary evidence of the adoption of a regulatory program governing the incidental taking of sea turtles in the course of shrimp trawling that is comparable to the United States program and where the average rate of incidental taking of

---

[21] This report is posted at the WTO's Web site at http://www.wto.org/english/tratop_e/dispu_e/cases_e/ds58_e.htm.

[22] Public Law 93–205, *United States Code*, title 16, § 1531 et seq.

[23] United States Federal Regulation, title 52, para. 24244, June 29, 1987 (the "1987 Regulations"). Five species of sea turtles fell under the regulations: loggerhead (*Caretta caretta*), Kemp's ridley (*Lepidochelys kempi*), green (*Chelonia mydas*), leatherback (*Dermochelys coriacea*) and hawksbill (*Eretmochelys imbricata*).

sea turtles by their vessels is comparable to that of United States vessels.[24] According to the 1996 [*Administrative*] *Guidelines* [*for Implementing the Endangered Species Act*] the Department of State assesses the regulatory program of the harvesting nation and certification shall be made if the program includes: (i) the required use of TEDs that are "comparable in effectiveness to those used in the United States. Any exceptions to this requirement must be comparable to those of the United States program…"; and (ii) "a credible enforcement effort that includes monitoring for compliance and appropriate sanctions."…

***

    In the Panel Report, the WTO Panel reached the following conclusions:

> …[W]e conclude that the import ban on shrimp and shrimp products as applied by the United States on the basis of Section 609 of Public Law 101–162 is not consistent with article XI: 1 of GATT 1994, and cannot be justified under article XX of GATT 1994.

***

IV. ISSUES RAISED IN THIS APPEAL

In this appeal the United States raises several issues, including: whether the Panel erred in finding that the measure at issue constitutes unjustifiable discrimination between countries where the same conditions prevail and thus is not within the scope of measures permitted under article XX of the GATT 1994 ("Exceptions.")

    (b)

VI. APPRAISING SECTION 609 UNDER ARTICLE XX OF THE GATT 1994

***

A. [Introduction]

***

Article XX of the GATT 1994 reads, in its relevant parts:

> **ARTICLE XX GENERAL EXCEPTIONS**
>
> Subject to the requirement that such measures are not applied in a manner which would constitute a means of arbitrary or unjustifiable discrimination between countries where the same conditions prevail, or a disguised restriction on international trade, nothing in this agreement shall be construed to prevent the adoption or enforcement by any Member of measures:
>
> ***
>
> (g) relating to the conservation of exhaustible natural resources if such measures are made effective in conjunction with restrictions on domestic production or consumption;

***

    In *United States—[Standards for Reformulated and Conventional] Gasoline*,[25] we enunciated the appropriate method for applying article XX of the GATT 1994:

> In order that the justifying protection of article XX may be extended to it, the measure at issue must not only come under one or another of the particular exceptions—paragraphs (a) to (j)—listed under article XX; it must also satisfy the requirements imposed by the opening clauses

---

[24] Section 609(b) (2)(A) and (B).

[25] Appellate Body Report WT/DS2/AB/R, posted on the WTO's Web site at http://www.wto.org/english/tratope/envire/gas1e.htm

of article XX. *The analysis is, in other words, two-tiered: first, provisional justification by reason of characterization of the measure under XX(g); second, further appraisal of the same measure under the introductory clauses of article XX.* (emphasis added)

***

B. Article XX(g): Provisional Justification of Section 609

In claiming justification for its measure, the United States primarily invokes article XX(g)....

1. "Exhaustible Natural Resources" We begin with the threshold question of whether Section 609 of the U.S. law is a measure concerned with the conservation of "exhaustible natural resources" within the meaning of article XX(g)....The complainants' principal argument is rooted in the notion that "living" natural resources are "renewable" and therefore cannot be "exhaustible" natural resources. We do not believe that "exhaustible" natural resources and "renewable" natural resources are mutually exclusive. One lesson that modern biological sciences teach us is that living species, though in principle, capable of reproduction and, in that sense, "renewable," are in certain circumstances indeed susceptible of depletion, exhaustion and extinction, frequently because of human activities. Living resources are just as "finite" as petroleum, iron ore and other non-living resources.

***

We believe it is too late in the day to suppose that article XX(g) of the GATT 1994 may be read as referring only to the conservation of exhaustible mineral or other non-living natural resources. Moreover, two adopted GATT 1947 panel reports previously found fish to be an "exhaustible natural resource" within the meaning of article XX(g).[26] We hold that. . . measures to conserve exhaustible natural resources, whether living or non-living, may fall within article XX(g). Further, since all seven recognized species of sea turtle are today listed in the Convention on International Trade as "endangered species" we conclude that the sea turtles involved here do constitute "exhaustible natural resources" for the purpose of article XX(g) of the GATT 1993.

***

C. The Introductory Clauses of Article XX: Characterizing Section 609 Under the Chapeau's Standards

***

Although provisionally justified under article XX(g), , if it is ultimately to be justified as an exception under article XX, Section 609 must also satisfy the requirements of the introductory clauses—the "**chapeau**" [hat][27]—of article XX, which state, as quoted earlier, that:

> such measures are not to be *applied in a manner which would constitute a means of arbitrary or unjustifiable discrimination between countries where the same conditions prevail, or a disguised restriction on international trade* (emphasis added)

We turn, hence, to the task of appraising Section 609, and specifically the manner in which it is applied under the chapeau of article XX; that is, to the second part of the two-tier analysis required under article XX.

***

---

[26] United States—Prohibition of Imports of Tuna and Tuna Products from Canada, adopted 22 February 1982, BISD 29S/91, para. 4.9; Canada—Measures Affecting Exports of Unprocessed Herring and Salmon, adopted 22 March 1988, BISD 35S/98, para. 4.4.

[27] [French: "hat."]

In the previous case, *United States—Gasoline*, we stated that "the purpose and object of the introductory clauses of article XX is generally the prevention of 'abuse of the exceptions of [article XX].'" We went on to say that:

> …The **chapeau** is animated by the principle that while the exceptions of article XX may be invoked as a matter of legal right, they should not be so applied as to frustrate or defeat the legal obligations of the holder of the right under the substantive rules of the General Agreement. In other words, the exceptions must be applied reasonably, with due regard both to the legal duties of the party claiming the exception and the legal rights of the other parties concerned.

In drafting the preamble of the WTO Agreement, the draftersfollowed much of the language of the former GATT preamble but specifically did not include as one objective the phrase "full use of the resources of the world," apparently believing that this was no longer appropriate to the world trading system of the 1990's. Instead, they decided to qualify the original objectives of the GATT 1947 with the following words:

> …while allowing for the optimal use of the world's resources in accordance with the objective of sustainable development, seeking both to protect and preserve the environment and to enhance the means for doing so in a manner consistent with their respective needs and concerns at different levels of economic development.…

[T]his language demonstrates a recognition by WTO negotiators that optimal use of the world's resources should be made in accordance with the objective of sustainable development. As this preambular language reflects the intentions of negotiators of the WTO Agreement, we believe it must add color, texture and shading to our interpretation of the agreements annexed to the WTO Agreement, in this case, the GATT 1994.…

In our view, the language of the chapeau makes clear that each of the exceptions in paragraphs (a) to (j) of article XX is a limited and conditional exception from the substantive obligations contained in the other provisions of the GATT 1994, that is to say, the ultimate availability of the exception is subject to the compliance by the invoking Member with the requirements of the chapeau.…

***

2. "Unjustifiable Discrimination" We scrutinize first whether the U.S. regulations have been applied in a manner constituting "unjustifiable discrimination between countries where the same conditions prevail."…. Section 609, in its application, is, in effect, an economic embargo which requires *all other exporting Members*, if they wish to exercise their GATT rights, to adopt *essentially the same* policy… (together with an approved enforcement program) as that applied to, and enforced on, United States domestic shrimp trawlers. Viewed alone, Section 609(b)(2)(A) and (B) appears to permit a degree of discretion or flexibility in how the standards for determining comparability might be applied, in practice, to other countries. However, any flexibility that may have been intended by Congress when it enacted the statutory provision has been effectively eliminated in the implementation of that policy through the 1996 *Guidelines* promulgated by the Department of State and through the practice of the administrators in making certification determinations.

According to the 1996 *Guidelines*…any exceptions to the requirement of the use of TEDs must be comparable to those of the United States program.…[And] in practice, the competent government officials only look to see whether there is a regulatory program requiring the use of TEDs or one that comes within one of the extremely limited exceptions available to United States shrimp trawl vessels.

The actual *application* of the measure…*requires* other WTO Members to adopt a regulatory program that is not merely *comparable*, but rather *essentially the same*, as that applied to the United States shrimp trawl vessels. Thus, the effect of the application of Section 609 is to establish a rigid and unbending standard by which United States officials determine whether or not countries will be certified, thus granting or refusing other countries the right to export shrimp to the United States. Other specific policies and measures that an exporting country may have adopted for the protection and conservation of sea turtles are not taken into account, in practice, by the administrators making the comparability determination.

…It may be quite acceptable for a government…to adopt a single standard applicable to all its citizens throughout that country. However, it is <u>not acceptable</u>, in international trade relations, for one WTO Member to use an economic embargo to *require* other Members to adopt essentially the same comprehensive regulatory program … *without* taking into consideration different conditions which may occur in the territories of those other Members.

[Furthermore, the record shows that] *shrimp caught using methods identical to those employed in the United States* have been excluded from the United States market solely because they have been caught in waters of *countries that have not been certified by the United States*….This suggests to us that this measure, in its application, is more concerned with effectively influencing WTO Members to adopt essentially the same comprehensive regulatory regime as that applied by the United States to its domestic shrimp trawlers, even though many of those Members may be differently situated. We believe that discrimination results not only when countries in which the same conditions prevail are differently treated, but also when the application of the measure at issue does not allow for any inquiry into the appropriateness of the regulatory program for the conditions prevailing in those exporting countries.

***

3. "Arbitrary Discrimination" We next consider whether Section 609 has been applied in a manner constituting "arbitrary discrimination between countries where the same conditions prevail." We have already observed that Section 609, in its application, imposes a single, rigid and unbending requirement that countries applying for certification under Section 609(b)(2)(A) and (B) adopt a comprehensive regulatory program that is essentially the same as the U.S. program, without inquiring into the appropriateness of that program for the conditions prevailing in the exporting countries. Furthermore, there is little or no flexibility in how officials make the determination for certification pursuant to these provisions.[28] In our view, this rigidity and inflexibility also constitute "arbitrary discrimination" within the meaning of the chapeau.

***

…The certification processes under Section 609 consist principally of administrative *ex parte*[29] inquiry or verification by staff of the Office of Marine Conservation in the Department of State with staff of the United States National Marine Fisheries Service. With respect to both types of certification, there is no formal opportunity for an applicant country to be heard, or to respond to any arguments that may be made against it, in the course of the certification process before a decision to grant or to deny certification is made. There is no formal written, reasoned decision, whether of acceptance or rejection, rendered on applications and countries are not even notified of denial of their applications, but must await the publication of a list of approvals in the Federal Register. No procedure for review of, or appeal from, a denial of an application is provided.

***

We find, accordingly, that the United States measure is applied in a manner which amounts to a means not just of "unjustifiable discrimination," but also of "arbitrary discrimination" between countries where the

---

[28] In the oral hearing, the United States stated that "as a policy matter, the United States government believes that all governments should require the use of turtle excluder devices on all shrimp trawler boats that operate in areas where there is a likelihood of intercepting sea turtles" and that "when it comes to shrimp trawling, we know of only one way of effectively protecting sea turtles, and that is through TEDs."

[29] Latin: "from one party or side." An *ex parte* inquiry is one conducted without notice to the other party or parties adversely interested and without the latter being present or having the opportunity to contest the decision made there.

same conditions prevail, contrary to the requirements of the chapeau of article XX. The measure, therefore, is not entitled to the justifying protection of article XX of the GATT 1994....

In reaching these conclusions, we wish to underscore what we have *not* decided in this appeal. We <u>have not decided</u> that the protection and preservation of the environment is of no significance to the Members of the WTO. Clearly, it is. We <u>have not decided</u> that the sovereign nations that are Members of the WTO cannot adopt effective measures to protect endangered species, such as sea turtles. Clearly, they can and should. And we <u>have not decided</u> that sovereign states should not act together bilaterally, plurilaterally or multilaterally, either within the WTO or in other international fora,[30] to protect endangered species or to otherwise protect the environment. Clearly, they should and do.

<u>What we have decided</u> in this appeal is simply this: although the measure of the United States in dispute in this appeal serves an environmental objective that is recognized as legitimate under paragraph (g) of article XX of the GATT 1994, this measure has been applied by the United States in a manner which constitutes arbitrary and unjustifiable discrimination between Members of the WTO, contrary to the requirements of the chapeau of article XX....

***

The Appellate Body *recommends* that the DSB request the United States to bring its measure found to be inconsistent with article XI of the GATT 1994, and found in this Report to be not justified under article XX of the GATT 1994, into conformity with the obligations of the United States under that agreement.

Summary:

The WTO Appellate Body considered whether the U.S. ban on imported shrimp that were harvested in a manner not meeting U.S. environmental requirements violated GATT rules. Generally, WTO members must treat imported goods the same way as domestic goods and not subject them to additional requirements. There are some exceptions to these rules, including one that allows a nation to take action to protect "exhaustible natural resources." The United States had imposed strict rules on shrimp harvesting, in an effort to protect endangered sea turtles, and then required all other nations to essentially adopt the same rules in order for shrimp to be imported into the United States.

Case 4-4

UNITED STATES—EUROPEAN COMMUNITIES — MEASURES AFFECTING TRADE IN LARGE CIVIL AIRCRAFT

World Trade Organization, Appellate Body, 2011.

Appellate Body Report WT/DS316/AB/R.[31]

The United States complained that the European Union was providing illegal subsidies to Airbus companies in violation of Articles 3, 5, and 6 of the SCM Agreement and Articles III:4, XVI:1, and XXIII:1 of GATT 1994.

---

[30] Plural of "forum." A meeting place, such as a court or tribunal.

[31] This report is posted at the WTO's Web site at http://www.wto.org/english/tratop_e/dispu_e/cases_e/ds316_e.htm

Measures at Issue

The measures at issue in this dispute are more than 300 separate instances of alleged subsidization, over a period of almost forty years, by the European Communities and four of its member States, France, Germany, Spain and the United Kingdom, with respect to large civil aircraft ("LCA") developed, produced and sold by the company known today as Airbus SAS. The measures that are the subject of the US complaint may be grouped into five general categories: (i) "Launch Aid" or "member State Financing" (LA/MSF); (ii) loans from the European Investment Bank; (iii) infrastructure and infrastructure-related grants; (iv) corporate restructuring measures; and (v) research and technological development funding. The United States claims that each of the challenged measures is a specific subsidy within the meaning of Articles 1 and 2 of the SCM Agreement, and that the European Communities and the four member States, through the use of these subsidies, cause adverse effects to the US interests within the meaning of Articles 5 and 6 of the SCM Agreement. In addition, the United States claims that seven of the challenged LA/MSF measures are prohibited export subsidies within the meaning of Article 3 of the SCM Agreement.

"Specific Subsidies" under SCM Agreement Articles 1 and 2

Turning to the allegations of subsidization, the panel found that each of the challenged LA/MSF measures constitutes a specific subsidy. However, the panel found that the United States had failed to establish the existence, as of July 2005, of a commitment of LA/MSF for the A350 constituting a specific subsidy, and that the United States had failed to demonstrate the existence of a "LA/MSF Programme" as a distinct measure, separate from the individual grants of LA/MSF. Finally, the panel concluded that the United States had established that the German, Spanish and UK A380 LA/MSF measures are subsidies contingent in fact upon anticipated export performance, and therefore prohibited export subsidies, but that the four other measures challenge in this respect are not prohibited export subsidies, either in law or in fact.

The panel found that each of the 12 challenged loans provided by the European Investment Bank ("EIB") to various Airbus entities between 1988 and 2002 is a subsidy, but that none of these subsidies was specific, and therefore dismissed the US claims in respect of the EIB loans from further consideration.

… The panel also concluded that the challenged grants provided by national and regional authorities in Germany and Spain for the construction of manufacturing and assembly facilities in several locations in Germany and Spain are specific subsidies. However, the panel found that road improvements by French authorities related to the ZAC Aéroconstellation industrial site were measures of general infrastructure, and thus not subsidies, and that GBP 19.5 million provided to Airbus UK in respect of its operations in Broughton, Wales, and a grant provided by the government of Andalusia to Airbus in Puerto Santa Maria, were not specific subsidies.

"Adverse Effect" under SCM Agreement Articles 5(a) and (c)

Having determined which of the measures challenged by the United States are specific subsidies, the panel proceeded to evaluate whether these subsidies to Airbus cause adverse effects to the US interests within the meaning of Articles 5(a) and (c) of the SCM Agreement. Specifically, the panel considered whether, through the use of these subsidies, the European Communities, France, Germany, Spain and the United Kingdom cause or threaten to cause: (i) "injury" to the US industry producing LCA (Article 5(a)); and (ii) "serious prejudice" to US interests (Article 5(c)), in that the effect of the subsidies is (a) to displace or impede imports of US LCA into the EC market, (b) to displace or impede exports of US LCA from third country markets, and (c) significant price undercutting by EC LCA as compared with the price of US LCA in the same market, and significant price suppression, price depression and lost sales in the same market, within the meaning of Articles 6.3(a), (b) and (c) of the SCM Agreement.

The panel first concluded that it was appropriate to conduct the analysis of adverse effects on the basis of one subsidized product, all Airbus LCA, as proposed by the United States, and that there is a single US product that is "like" the subsidized product, namely all Boeing LCA. With respect to the appropriate "reference period" for the assessment of injury and serious prejudice, the panel rejected the US view that it was required to make the determination concerning adverse effects "as of" the date of establishment of the panel in July 2005. The panel concluded it is charged with making a determination of "present" adverse effects, taking into account all of the evidence before it, including the most recent information available, consistent with due process, that is relevant and reliable.

The panel addressed the claims with respect to serious prejudice following a "two-step" approach, considering first whether the evidence demonstrated that the particular market effects identified in Article 6.3(a), (b) and (c) of the SCM Agreement existed, and second whether any of the effects found to exist was caused by the specific subsidies it had found. The panel concluded that the United States had demonstrated the existence of displacement of imports and exports from the European and certain third country markets, as well as significant price depression, price suppression and lost sales, but had failed to demonstrate the existence of significant price undercutting.

With respect to causation, the panel concluded that LA/MSF shifts a significant portion of the risk of launching an aircraft from the manufacturer to the governments supplying funding, which was in all instances on non-commercial terms, and that Airbus' ability to launch, develop, and introduce to the market, each of its LCA models was dependent on subsidized LA/MSF. The panel found that all of the remaining specific subsidies at issue were sufficiently linked to the product and the particular market effects in question to make it appropriate to analyze the effects of the subsidies on an aggregated basis. The panel concluded that Airbus would have been unable to bring to the market the LCA that it launched as and when it did but for the specific subsidies it received from the European Communities and the governments of France, Germany, Spain and the United Kingdom. The panel did not conclude that Airbus necessarily would not exist at all but for the subsidies, but merely that it would, at a minimum, not have been able to launch and develop the LCA models it actually succeeded in bringing to the market. Thus, the panel considered that Airbus' market presence during the period 2001-2006, as reflected in its share of the EC and certain third country markets and the sales it won at Boeing's expense, was clearly an effect of the subsidies in this dispute. However, the panel rejected the US argument that the specific subsidies in this dispute provided Airbus with significant additional cash flow and other financial resources on non-market terms which allowed it to price its aircraft more aggressively than it would otherwise be able to without those subsidies, or that the effect of LA/MSF on cost of capital was such that it enabled Airbus to lower prices of LCA during the period 2001-2006. Therefore, the panel concluded that the United States had failed to demonstrate that an effect of the subsidies was the significant price depression or price suppression observed during that period.

Conclusions and Recommendations

Overall, the panel concluded that the United States had established that the effect of the specific subsidies found was (i) displacement of imports of US LCA into the European market; (ii) displacement of exports of US LCA from the markets of Australia, Brazil, China, Chinese Taipei, Korea, Mexico, and Singapore; (iii) likely displacement of exports of US LCA from the market of India; and (iv) significant lost sales in the same market, and that these effects constituted serious prejudice to the interests of the United States within the meaning of Article 5(c) of the SCM Agreement. However, the panel concluded that the United States had not established that the effect of the specific subsidies found was (i) significant price undercutting; (ii) significant price suppression; and (iii) significant price depression. In addition, the panel concluded that the United States had not established that, through the use of the subsidies, the European Communities and certain EC member States cause or threaten to cause injury to the US domestic industry.

126

***

Taking into account the nature of the prohibited subsidies it had found in this dispute, and in the light of Article 4.7 of the SCM Agreement, the panel recommended that the subsidizing Member granting each subsidy found to be prohibited withdraw it without delay, specifying that this be within 90 days. In light of its conclusions with respect to adverse effects, the panel recommended, pursuant to Article 7.8 of the SCM Agreement, that upon adoption of its report… the Member granting each subsidy found to have resulted in such adverse effects "take appropriate steps to remove the adverse effects or ... withdraw the subsidy". However, the panel declined to make any suggestions concerning steps that might be taken to implement its recommendations.

Summary:

The WTO panel considered whether subsidies provided by members of the European Union to Airbus companies constituted prohibited subsidies under the SCM Agreement and GATT 1994. Ultimately, the panel found that some of the subsidies brought to issue by the United States constituted "serious prejudice to the interests of the United States" within the meaning of Article 5(c) of the SCM Agreement. However, the panel also concluded that the United States failed to provide sufficient evidence that a number of specific subsidies provided by the European Communities and EC member states caused or threatened to cause injury to the U.S. domestic industry. Accordingly, the panel recommended the immediate withdrawal of all subsidies found to be prohibited.

Commentary on this case:

Both sides claimed victory after the WTO appellate decision was announced. The ruling upheld a panel decision that <u>Boeing</u> lost market share to its European rival, <u>Airbus</u>, as a result of billions of dollars in low-cost government loans, according to European and American officials. But the decision rejected claims by the United States that state financing for the Airbus A380 superjumbo jet was automatically prohibited under global trade rules.

The appellate body concurred with the earlier WTO panel finding that loans extended to Airbus over the course of four decades did constitute unfair subsidies that had caused Boeing to lose aircraft sales. But the ruling also rejected the most crucial American argument: namely, that the loans — known as launch aid — that Airbus received from Germany, Spain and Britain for the twin-deck A380 jets were expressly prohibited because governments expected a significant export market for the planes when they granted the support.

As we have discussed, the W.T.O. defines two broad categories of subsidies: those that are "prohibited" and those that are "actionable" — that is, subject to legal challenge or to countervailing measures like punitive tariffs. Prohibited subsidies are those that are specifically designed to promote exports or to encourage production using domestically made components.

Under W.T.O. rules, any "prohibited" subsidy must be withdrawn within 90 days of the adoption of a dispute panel's findings. "Actionable" subsidies are not prohibited automatically, but they can be challenged if the complaining country shows that the subsidy caused material injury — a loss of jobs, profit or production capacity — or "adverse effects" to its industry, like a loss of export market share or sales.

The appellate ruling did not find European "launch aid" loans for the A380 to be prohibited. But it did find many of them to be actionable, which will require European governments to propose some form of remedy in the coming months to offset the benefit of any outstanding subsidies, trade lawyers said.

Other nations also gave their opinions on this blockbuster decision of the WTO.

China noted that the Appellate Body report made a significant contribution to the interpretation of subsidies, including systemic issues related to the life of a subsidy, the infrastructure measures, the export subsidies and the determination of serious prejudice. China hoped that the EU would take appropriate steps to withdraw subsidies found inconsistent with the SCM Agreement, or remove the adverse effects caused by them to ensure that the industries of other WTO members would not suffer from such adverse effects any longer.

Brazil said that it continued to be concerned about distortive effects of subsidies of a particularly pernicious nature such as the launch aid measure that were at issue in this case. Brazil highlighted some of its concerns regarding the Appellate Body interpretation on export subsidies. Brazil believed that the panel and Appellate Body findings would help safe-guard the disciplines of the SCM Agreement in a way that contributed to ensuring a level playing field, where manufacturers can develop products and compete with each other on the basis of their own strength, and not on the basis of the leverage provided by national treasuries.

Australia said that export subsidies were prohibited because of their potential to directly distort international trade. Australia added that it was therefore imperative that members, when designing public programmes, were clearly aware of the rules that determined whether a particular programme would amount to an export subsidy. Australia added that the Appellate Body developed that test for determining export contingency and thus the test for determining whether a particular subsidy amounted to a prohibited export subsidy.

EU Wins Similar WTO Case Against Boeing and the United States

In response to the United States case against the European Union challenging the Airbus subsidies, the EU countered in 2004 by filing a similar case with the WTO against U.S. airplane manufacturer Boeing.[32] In this suit, Boeing was alleged to have received billions of dollars in illegal subsidies from the U.S. government, just as Airbus was alleged to have received from the EU in the case filed by the United States, in the case summarized above. In 2011, following the WTO's ruling against Airbus for having received over $18 billion in illegal subsidies from the EU, the WTO also ruled against Boeing for having received at least $5.3 billion in illegal subsidies from the U.S. government. As of July 2011, the standoff has yet to be resolved, as United States officials are expected to appeal the WTO's ruling against Boeing. In the next few years, the EU and United States will undoubtedly be trying to reach a settlement of these two cases.

The Tuna Dolphin Controversy

For many years, the U.S. tuna fishing industry employed purse seine netting to fish for tuna. This method had dramatically negative effects on dolphin populations in the eastern tropical Pacific. The following video explains how one person, Sam LaBudde, was able to provide visual evidence of the toll that purse seine netting was doing to dolphin populations.

https://youtu.be/OOg8TdPV_cA

---

[32] Clark, N. (2011, March 31). Retrieved July 6, 2011, from The New York Times: http://www.nytimes.com/2011/03/31/business/global/01trade.html?_r=1; see also IBTimes Staff Reporter. (2011, January 31). *Boeing received illegal subsidies: WTO*. Retrieved July 5, 2011, from International Business Times: http://www.ibtimes.com/articles/107115/20110131/boeing-received-illegal-subsidies-wto.htm

The controversy led to stronger U.S. legal sanctions against importing tuna caught in ways that harmed and killed dolphins. U.S. fishing boats began re-flagging under Mexican law, as well as a few other nations (like Vanuatu) to avoid the restrictions on imports. When those restrictions were expanded to cover non-U.S. owned fishing vessels, Mexico and Vanuatu challenged the U.S. restrictions, using what was then the GATT dispute mechanisms. A summary of those arguments follows.

INTRODUCTION

In 1991, the Mexican government brought a trade dispute to a provisional GATT tribunal alleging that U.S. restrictions on tuna imports violated free trade principles. The U.S. regulations, enforcing the Marine Mammal Protection Act of 1972, had evolved over time in response to fishing practices which had resulted in millions of dolphin deaths since the 1950s.

In the Eastern Tropical Pacific(ETP), boats with purse seine nets often seek out schools of dolphin as a means of locating and catching the yellowfin tuna that often swim below. Purse-seining is an extremely cost-effective method of tuna harvesting, but leads to high dolphin mortality. The dolphin schools are pursued with helicopters and speedboats and encircled with mile-long nets. The main vessel then "purses" the net by drawing in a cable at the top of the net to gather its contents. Most dolphins have time to leap over the net as it is pursed, but many become trapped and drown. As kills "incidental" to the harvesting of tuna, over six million dolphins have been drowned or fatally injured in the ETP since purse seining began.

The U.S. fishing fleet both invented and perfected the practice of purse seine netting on dolphin, and may have killed more than 300,000 dolphins annually during the early 1970s. These practices created enough public opposition that in 1972 Congress passed the Marine Mammal Protection Act. The MMPA's certification requirements for foreign vessels were not enforced, however, and by 1988, fishing boats from Mexico, Venezuela, Vanuatu and other nations were killing an estimated 50,000 - 100,000 dolphins each year.

As a result, the 1988 MMPA amendments tried to further restrict foreign fishing practices; they allowed the U.S. fishing fleet to keep killing dolphin up to a certain annual quota, but required that other countries' tuna fleets kill rates not significantly greater than the U.S .or risk a trade embargo. This embargo seemed potentially effective, since the U.S. market accounts for approximately half of the world's annual sales of canned tuna.

Mexico, which has by far the largest number of boats engaged in purse seine techniques, regarded this new provision as an unfair trade practice and took its dispute to a GATT panel. Mexico argued that the U.S. embargo was a unilateral and protectionist trade measure that violated GATT rules.

THE GATT: BASIC PRINCIPLES AND GOALS OF GLOBAL FREE TRADE

The foundation of global free trade is the General Agreement on Tariffs and Trade, better known as the GATT. It is the only multilateral agreement on terms of trade, and functions as a forum for the member nations to negotiate reductions in trade barriers and discuss trade distortions affecting the free flow of goods among member nations. Conceived to eliminate the kinds of protectionist legislation that contributed to the global depression in the 1930's, the GATT has evolved since 1948 in response to major changes in the world economic scene.

The major purpose of GATT is to "liberalize world trade" by means of three basic principles. First, international trade should be conducted on the basis of non-discrimination. Second, governmental restraints on the movement of goods should be kept to a minimum. Third, the conditions of trade should be agreed upon within a multilateral framework.

The principle of non-discrimination is furthered in Article I of the GATT, which requires that member states undertake to grant each other "most-favored-nation treatment," such that any bilateral tariff reduction between member countries is automatically extended to all other GATT members.

The second manifestation of GATT's nondiscrimination principle is the obligation of contracting parties, once an imported product has cleared customs, to treat both foreign and domestic "like products" equally. Article III states the "national treatment" principle, in which contracting parties agree to treat foreign and domestic products equally if they have met tariffs and other import requirements. As applied, Article III seems to prevent member nations from applying tariffs or other import restrictions "to protect the competitiveness of a domestic industry that internalizes environmental costs in its product cost."

The second principle - keeping governmental restraints to a minimum - has as a corollary the notion that governmental restraints should in general be reduced over time rather than increased. The tuna/dolphin panel decision, while not invoking this notion, embraces it as a generalized presumption against which domestic measures bear the burden of qualifying as a recognized policy exception under Article XX.

The third principle - multilateral trade action - has been realized in continuing negotiations under Article XXVIII. The GATT's tariff structure has developed through a series of negotiating rounds in which member countries lowered tariffs through reciprocal concessions. In the first twenty years of GATT, six general negotiation were held. The seventh round was formally initiated in 1973; the so-called "Tokyo Round" of Multilateral Trade Negotiations ended in 1979, and focused on the elimination of non-tariff barriers. This round produced a series of specialized codes dealing with subsidies and countervailing duties, discrimination against foreign goods in government procurement and product quality specifications that hindered the importation of foreign goods, and unified rules as to dumping.

In 1986, preparations were begun for a new round of multilateral trade negotiations which would address restraints on trade in services such as insurance, banking, and transportation. This new round has become known as the Uruguay Round. In each round of negotiations, reducing "protectionism" has been a concern, but issues of environmental protection have not. The Reagan and Bush administrations and most foreign countries have opposed the inclusion of environmental standards in trade agreements. In addition to the three basic principles described above, the GATT contains two more that bear directly on the tuna/dolphin controversy: (1) no prohibitions or restrictions other than tariffs are allowed, and (2) subsidies on exports, while not entirely prohibited, are disapproved and limited. This second subsidiary principle is in accordance with generally accepted economic theory that export subsidies may have "a distorting effect comparable to a tariff on the import side (Art. XVI)."

The first subsidiary principle means that quantitative restrictions such as quotas - or complete bans - are inconsistent with GATT; Article XI makes this prohibition plain. Quotas and bans - along with discriminatory tariffs - are seen as inconsistent with the free flow of goods, the operation of comparative advantage, and an efficient allocation of global goods.

Limited exceptions to GATT's basic and subsidiary principles are provided for in Article XX. Two of the exceptions, Articles XX(b) and XX(g), permit measures necessary to protect human animal or plant life or health, or to conserve exhaustible natural resources. Notably, the GATT nowhere mentions the word "environment," nor do its original provisions make any allowance for member countries to impose any tariffs on imports to ensure better conservation of a scarce natural resource or to compensate domestic industries for the imposition of costs for environmental protection.

Yet, increasingly, the United States is using or "threatening to use [certain] prohibitions in order to force foreign states to adopt the U.S. view of appropriate conservation measures concerning species, such as whales, dolphins, and sea turtles." In addition to the Marine Mammal Protection Act and the Endangered Species Act, certain international agreements, including the Montreal Protocol on Substances That Deplete the Ozone Layer, contemplate unilateral trade sanctions against imports from nations whose products or production methods may threaten the global environment. Finally, several legislative proposals from the 102nd Congress would require the United States to adopt measures in response to foreign governments' non-compliance with international environmental agreements.

Thus, the tuna/dolphin controversy provides a useful and current case study in the gathering conflict between global free trade and international environmental protection. The controversy itself is summarized in the next section, which describes dolphins, the practice of purse seine netting on dolphins to catch yellowfin tuna, and the protracted administrative, legislative and judicial actions taken in the U.S. to protect dolphins, actions largely driven by environmental advocates.

Dolphins have highly developed communication systems, remarkable creative capacities, and a larger brain to body size ratio (a factor many scientists consider to be an accurate measure of intelligence) than human beings. A linguistics study conducted by Dr. Louis M. Herman at the University of Hawaii, has shown that dolphins "can understand both the semantic and the syntactic features of imperative sentences given to them..." Indeed, it is theorized that dolphins possess communication skills far in advance of our own. "For years, the Navy has been attempting to emulate dolphins natural sonar capabilities..." The dolphin is "probably capable of directly transmitting imagery to another dolphin. It has the ability to communicate, in other words, in a manner that would be analogous to direct transmission of visual imagery from one human to another."

Intelligence and communicative capacities, however, are not the only characteristics of dolphins that allow us to relate to them so readily. They are extremely gregarious creatures, highly socialized, amongst both their own and human species. Sea lore is rich with fables, facts, and legends of dolphins rescuing humans. We attribute human traits to dolphins, and this willingness to anthropomorphize them has inspired us to grant them legal protection. Similar protection does not extend to non-mammalian species of the sea, such as tuna.

No one knows why, but spotted dolphins in the Eastern Tropical Pacific Ocean travel in affinity groups with the highly prized yellowfin tuna. On seeing a school of dolphins, a fleet will set out purse seine nets in a process known as "setting on dolphin," encircle the school, and trap the tuna by closing off the net from below. Most dolphin leap over the nets but many are caught below, and as air-breathing mammals, drown when they cannot reach the surface. Others escape the nets, only to return and drown while trying to rescue their mates or young.

In the early 1950's, the U.S. fishing fleet learned that yellowfin tuna will swim under dolphins, and in the late fifties major technological advances were made in purse seining fishing methods. The confluence of these two factors has resulted in the death of over six million dolphins over the past thirty years. The slaughter peaked in 1965 when over 365,000 dolphins died from "incidental takings." Dolphin deaths caused by U.S. vessels are now less than 1,000 annually, but foreign vessels are estimated to cause in excess of 50,000 deaths each year.

Setting on dolphin is only practiced by yellowfin fishermen, almost exclusively in the Eastern Tropical Pacific Ocean, and this species of tuna, sold as "light meat," accounts for 20% of retail tuna sales in the United States. Public concern over dolphin killing was a motivating factor persuading Congress to pass "one of the most progressive, far-reaching pieces of environmental legislation ever drafted," the Marine Mammal Protection Act (MMPA) of 1972.

The Marine Mammal Protection Act (MMPA)

The purpose of the MMPA was to protect marine mammals, recognizing that they have aesthetic and recreational value as well as economic value. To this end, the MMPA calls for maintenance of the optimum sustainable population (OSP) of each species or population stock of marine mammal, and imposes a complete moratorium when necessary on the taking and importation of marine mammals and marine mammal products. The MMPA further provides that "the incidental kill or incidental serious injury of marine mammals permitted in the course of commercial fishing operation be reduced to insignificant levels *approaching a zero mortality and serious injury rate*."

There are certain exceptions to this moratorium. One of them is the taking of marine mammals incidental to commercial fishing operations. The MMPA charges the Secretary of Commerce to protect dolphins and other marine mammals, but also provides discretionary authority for the Secretary to issues permits to groups or industries who qualify for exemptions from the moratorium. The National Marine Fisheries Service (NMFS), as part of the Commerce Department, was given jurisdiction over most permits and certificates.

The MMPA's prohibitions extended to all takings within waters under the jurisdiction of the United States, except as provided in an international treaty, convention or agreement to which the United States was a party prior to the effective date of the MMPA. The MMPA's prohibitions also extend to takings on the high seas by persons or vessels subject to the jurisdiction of the United States.

In *Committee for Humane Legislation v. Richardson,* a coalition of environmental organizations sued to challenge the authority of NMFS to grant permits and certificates of inclusion. The court permitted five organizations representing the United States tuna industry to intervene as defendants. The industry argued that the MMPA required a balancing of interests between the fishing industry and the marine mammals. But Judge Richey held that the interests of the fishing industry were to be considered only after protection of the marine mammals had been secured. The court held that the MMPA required the NMFS to issue permits and certificates only after adequate estimates of existing population levels had been published, along with the OSP of each species, and the estimated impact of the regulations on achieving an OSP for each species.

In addition, Judge Richey rejected a suggested alternative of imposing a quota, declaring as void the general permit issued by the NMFS to the American tunaboat Association (ATA) which allowed an unlimited number of dolphin to be taken between October 21, 1974 and December 31, 1975. Judge Richey reasoned that the ATA had not proven that the takings would not work to the disadvantage of the marine mammals, a proof required under the Act, and that the permit did not specify the number and kinds of animals authorized to be taken.

The decision was affirmed on appeal, but the Circuit Court immediately stayed the order at the request of the NMFS. While the stay of the court's orders to cease and desist from fishing practices violative of the MMPA was still in effect, the National Oceanic and Atmospheric Administration (NOAA), an arm of the NMFS, promulgated regulations to meet the concerns of the *Richardson* court, and these regulations went into effect in December, 1977. Among other things, the regulations provided for a listing of existing population levels of dolphins caught in fishing for yellowfin tuna and specified the technical criteria to be employed by NMFS in determining whether or not to grant a permit. The criteria involved determinations of whether the dolphins in question were at an OSP or were considered "depleted." Permits for incidental taking required that the dolphin species not be depleted.

But the NOAA's regulatory definitions of optimum sustainable levels and depletion were severely criticized. The Act was amended in 1981, with compromise language agreed upon by both commercial fishermen and environmentalists. Under the amendments, the NMFS clarified the meaning of OSP by declaring this to mean the range between the largest population "supportable within the ecosystem and the population level that results in maximum net productivity." The definition of "depletion" was also dealt with in the 1981 amendments, where it was determined that a stock of a species would be considered depleted when its number fell below the optimal sustainable population or when the stock was listed as endangered or threatened under the Endangered Species Act.

Based on these new definitions, the NMFS issued regulations and a five-year, industry-wide permit to yellowfin tuna fishermen in the Eastern Tropical Pacific, setting an annual "incidental taking" quota of 20,500 dolphins.

Environmental groups soon challenged the permit on the basis that the explicit language of the MMPA set a goal of incidental taking levels approaching "zero mortality and serious injury rate." In *Friends of the Animals v. Roe,* plaintiffs claimed that in implementing the quota the NMFS failed to the meet the MMPA's explicit requirements. The tuna industry's position, as represented by David Burney, Counsel for the U.S. Tuna Foundation, was that the industry "has met the mandate of the act and there are other components of the marine ecosystem which must be taken into account. *We are not going to reach zero.*" That position was reinforced by Nancy Foster, Director of the Office of Protected Resources at NMFS, who said, "[e]ven though we all say the objective is a zero take, you're sort of locked into this number . . . Once you put a number in print, it becomes the rule." In 1984, the original 1980 permit to allow 20,500 incidental dolphin takings in purse seine tuna fishing was extended indefinitely.

Through the use of various techniques, many of which have been mandated by regulations, the United States tuna fleet has drastically reduced its incidental taking of dolphins from the high levels of the late 1960s and early 1970s to an average annual taking of less than 20,000 dolphins in the years, 1983-1987. "During the 1987 season the U.S. fleet had the lowest take on record-10,700 as of the end of October." There is reason to believe that current levels are even lower.

Yet while the United States tuna fleet made progress in reducing the incidental kill of dolphins, many U.S. boats simply reflagged under foreign sails, avoiding the more stringent MMPA regulations. "The separation of the U.S. and foreign tuna industries is in fact a kind of myth. In the past ten years two thirds of the big U.S. seiners have reflagged with foreign fleets . . . American captains still skipper some of those boats, and available evidence suggests that new ownership is often nominal." These boats carried fewer observers, were under no national or international regulatory restrictions, and were not required to use the techniques that the U.S. had fought vigorously against.

By 1984, Congress recognized that foreign fleets from Ecuador, Mexico, Panama, Vanuatu, and Venezuela were responsible for most of the dolphin killing in the ETP, with their collective killing estimated at more than 100,000 per year. 1989 estimates claimed that the foreign fleet was killing five times as many dolphins as the United States' tuna fleet. Estimates of the number of dolphins killed yearly by Mexican fishing vessels vary from 50,000 to 100,000.

Since the inception of the MMPA, the United States "maintained the basic approach of banning imports, except when a foreign state can show that U.S. standards are being met." Yet the NMFS did not strictly apply the standards to foreign fishing interests, and in 1984, Congress tried to "strengthen the requirements of the [MMPA] with respect to documentation of compliance by foreign nations with the essential features of the MMPA." The MMPA was amended to require an embargo of tuna from any nation whose kill rates were more than twice the U.S. rate in 1989 and 1.25 times the U.S. rate in 1990. Since the United States market accounts for as much as half of the world's tuna consumption, the strategy seemed promising. Indeed, the amendment prompted several countries to tell their fleets to meet MMPA guidelines by following dolphin rescue procedures used by United States' fishing crews.

From 1984 to 1988, the Commerce Department did not make any findings or implement regulations to enforce the 1984 amendment, even though the agency had credible evidence that dolphin mortality rates on foreign tuna boats were two to four times higher than U.S. rates. In Senate hearings on the MMPA's reauthorization in 1988, Senator John Kerry of Massachusetts asked why the NMFS had not even formulated interim final regulations banning import of tuna from foreign nations that hadn't shown dolphin-saving programs similar to U.S. standards, as required under the MMPA. The answer, given by Charles Fullerton of the NMFS, provides some insight into Reagan-era regulation of the tuna industry. According to Fullerton,

> We developed some (regulations) over a year ago which were *not acceptable either to the tuna industry or to the foreign nations*. So we went back to the drawing board and developed a whole new set..."

A fair translation of this seems to be that the regulatees were unsatisfied with the original regulations, so the regulators dropped them. It took a combination of environmentalists, legislators, consumers, and the courts to finally force United States administrators to impose a ban on tuna from foreign nations whose standards for dolphin protection were not comparable to U.S. standards.

1988 Reauthorization of the MMPA

On November 23, 1988, the MMPA reauthorization, known as the Marine Mammal Protection Act Amendments of 1988, was passed by Congress. The 1988 amendments had three basic elements. First, Congress outlined the kind of regulatory program that a foreign country must adopt before the United States would allow imports of yellowfin tuna or tuna products. In so doing, the Commerce Department's discretion was eliminated and mandatory embargo language was inserted. Nations wishing to export tuna to the U.S. during the 1989 fishing season must not exceed two times the U.S. fleet rate of dolphin kill, and during 1990 and beyond, national fleets must not exceed 1.25 times the U.S. rate.

The second basic element of the 1988 amendments was a secondary embargo on yellowfin tuna or tuna products from intermediary nations that might have imported such products from nations who were not allowed under the amendments to export such products to the United States. The third basic element was a requirement that the Secretary of Commerce, within six months after imposition of an import ban on a country's yellowfin tuna or tuna products, certify such an imposition to the President. This certification process is significant, as it qualifies as a certification under the Pelly Amendment and could lead to an import ban on any or all fish and fish products.

Even though the 1988 amendments expressed a clear intent to modify the fishing practices of foreign vessels, the Secretary had not, by 1990, issued the required comparability findings to allow imports of tuna, and had not made efforts to ban such imports. Earth Island Institute, a nonprofit organization engaged in marine mammal protection, sued the Secretary to force the government to enforce provisions of the MMPA against foreign violators.

In *Earth Island Institute v. Mosbacher (Earth Island I)*, the Ninth Circuit affirmed a preliminary injunction against the Secretary of Commerce, enjoining the importation of yellowfin tuna from Mexico, due to the Secretary's failure to "make a positive finding, as required by the Act, that Mexico had met the applicable standards regarding the incidental killing of dolphins." The embargo was ordered by the district court on August 28, 1990, and went into effect on February 22, 1991.

On January 25, 1991, Mexico requested a dispute settlement panel under Article XXIII(2) of the GATT. A GATT dispute settlement panel hears complaints from one member country against another, reaches a conclusion and submits its report to the GATT Council. When the Council adopts the panel decision (and it has never failed to do so) the report has legal force, and the losing party must take steps to make its actions consistent with the report. On February 6, 1991, the GATT Council agreed to convene the panel as Mexico had requested. The panel held hearings in May and June of 1991; Australia, the European Community, Indonesia, Japan, Korea, the Philippines, Senegal, Thailand, Venezuela, and Norway all submitted statements supporting Mexico's position. The panel submitted a draft opinion on August 16, 1991 that the U.S. embargoes, both primary and secondary, violated GATT. On September 3, 1991, the panel issued its final opinion in the case.

In September of 1991, Earth Island Institute filed a lawsuit against the Secretary of Commerce, and in January of 1992 obtained an injunction to enforce the MMPA's secondary embargo provisions against imports from nations that fail to meet MMPA's certification and proof requirements (Earth Island II). The court's opinion, rendered in February of 1992, did not mention GATT or the tuna/dolphin dispute settlement panel. Were it not for passage of the International Dolphin Conservation Act of 1992 in October of 1992, the MMPA's impact on imports of tuna from Mexico would still be in effect.

THE GATT PANEL DECISION

Mexico asked the panel to find the embargo provisions inconsistent with GATT's prohibitions on quantitative restrictions under Article XI and invalid under the "like products" requirement of Article III and violative of the United States' obligations under Articles I and IX. The U.S. contended that Articles XX(b) and XX(g) provided applicable exceptions.

How should the panel rule, and why?

134

Chapter Questions for Discussion

1.   Several automobile manufacturers from Crazania are exporting large number of cars to Freedonia, taking over a large share of Freedonia's automobile market, and causing some layoffs in Freedonia's own auto companies. Crazania's government does not subsidize its auto companies, and the companies are not dumping their cars at below cost prices. Can Freedonia do anything to respond that is well within the rules of the GATT 1994?

2.   Tarzania and Livonia are both member states of the WTO. When it joined the WTO, Tarzania had long prohibited the importation of foreign grown rice. The prohibition has never been lifted. Presently, rice in Tarzania sells for about three times the world price. Livonia, as a large grower of rice seeking to increase its exports, wants access to Tarzania's markets. What can Livonia do to respond that is consistent with the GATT 1994?

3.   Recently the nation of Ebonia became concerned that its nationals are being poisoned by chemical growth stimulants fed to livestock to make them grow faster and heavier, so Ebonia enacts legislation that forbids its own livestock producers from using the stimulants. The legislation also prevents the importation or sale of any animals that have been given such stimulants, and prevents the sale or use of any such stimulants, and prevents the important of meat from animals that have been given such stimulants.

Because it is impossible to detect the growth of stimulant either live animals or their meat, the legislation requires importers to certify that the animals have never been fed a growth stimulant. A fairly elaborate certification system is set up by Ebonia, with strict testing protocols that livestock producers in Foldova cannot ever meet. The livestock producers in Foldova have been using these growth stimulants for years, and both they and Foldova's government believe them to be safe for the animals and that the animals are safe for human consumption. Foldova's government, on behalf of its livestock producers, asks the WTO to consult with Ebonia, but the consultations go nowhere. The WTO's Dispute Settlement Body appoints a panel, and you are on it: has Ebonia's legislation violated its obligations under GATT 1994?

4.   Canada is a major exporter of lumber products, especially plywood, to the United States. Canada's lumber companies are able to manufacture and sell their products in the U.S. inexpensively because the government of Canada charges only a very small fee for cutting lumber in its national forests. In the U.S., by contrast, the fee is more significant, adding 15% to the cost of the finished lumber product. One of the U.S. manufacturers of plywood, Wirehauser, has lost significant market share to Canadian companies, and has complained that Canada is unfairly subsidizing its lumber companies by charging such a low fee for cutting on national forest lands in Canada. Wirehauser wants the U.S. to impose a countervailing duty on imports of plywood from Canada. Both the U.S. and Canada are WTO members. You are in the Enforcement and Compliance unit within the International Trade Administration of the Department of Commerce, responsible for countervailing duty proceedings and determinations. What do you need to know and how do you think you should rule?

CHAPTER FIVE:

THE INTERNATIONAL SALE OF GOODS

INTRODUCTION

This chapter covers the UN Convention on contracts for the international sale of goods. Along with that, we will look at the phenomenon of documentary sales: most international transactions, a document — usually a bill of lading—identifies the goods that are being shipped and also represents those goods. The documentation of internationally transported goods is often companied by a letter of credit, which enables the seller to be paid on presentation of bill of lading and other key documents as the goods are being shipped.

This chapter includes several cases on the international sale of goods, and how the CIS G is interpreted in cases of disputes between buyer and seller. because so many goods travel by oceangoing container ships, we also look at the U.S. Carriage of Goods by Sea Act (COGSA) in the context of a dispute over A shipment of oranges from Morocco to the US that was damaged on route. That is the case of <u>Vimar Seguros v. Sky Reefer.</u>

I. UNITED NATIONS CONVENTION ON CONTRACTS FOR THE INTERNATIONAL SALE OF GOODS

The 1980 United Nations Convention on Contracts for the International Sale of Goods (CISG) came into force January 1, 1988, climaxing more than 50 years of negotiations. CISG is organized in four parts:
*   Part I (Articles 1–13) contains the convention's general provisions, including rules on the scope of its applications and rules of interpretation.
*   Part II (Articles 14–24) governs the formation of contracts.
*   Part III (Articles 25–88) governs the rights and obligations of buyers and sellers.
*   Part IV (Articles 89–101) contains provisions for the ratification and the entry into force of the Convention.

Transactions Covered in the CISG

CISG applies to contracts for the international sale of goods—that is, the buyer and seller must have their places of business in different states. In addition, either (1) both of the states must be contracting parties to the convention or (2) the rules of private international law must "lead to the application of the law of a contracting state."

CISG may apply even if the buyer's and seller's places of business are not in a contracting state. The final provisions of the convention allow a ratifying state, if it wishes, to declare that it will apply CISG only when the buyer and seller are both from contracting states.

<u>Opting In and Opting Out</u> – The parties to a contract may exclude or modify its application by a choice-of-law clause. Whether they can use that same clause to exclude a domestic law and adopt CISG in its place depends on the rules of the state where the case is heard.

Sales Defined – CISG does not directly define sales. Instead, it speaks of the seller's and buyer's obligations. The seller is to "deliver the goods, hand over any documents relating to them and transfer the property in the goods, as required by the contract and this Convention"; the buyer, in exchange, is to "pay the price." This is the same definition found in many domestic laws, including the U.S. Uniform Commercial Code, which describes a sale as the "passing of title from the seller to the buyer for a price."

Goods Defined – CISG also does not directly define goods. Instead, it defines those kinds of sales that are not governed by the convention. Six specific categories are excluded. Three are based on the nature of the transaction, three on the kinds of goods. The excluded transactions are (1) "goods bought for personal, family, or household use"; (2) auction sales; and (3) sales "on execution or otherwise by authority of law." The excluded goods are (1) stocks, shares, investment securities, negotiable instruments, or money; (2) ships, vessels, hovercraft, or aircraft; and (3) electricity.

Goods bought for personal, family, or household use are excluded for two reasons. First, a double standard could arise if different rules governed sales by local shopkeepers to foreigners. Second, many local laws protect consumers, and that protection would be lost if CISG applied. This exclusion does not apply "unless" the seller "knew or ought to have known" that the goods were bought for personal use or consumption.

Auction sales, sales on execution, and sales "otherwise by authority of law" are excluded because of the uniqueness of the transactions involved. Auction sales present problems in determining when the contract was formed. Executions and other kinds of forced sales do not involve the negotiation of terms by the parties. Transactions in stocks, shares, investment securities, negotiable instruments, and money are excluded because a wide variety of local rules govern them, and the drafters could not agree on how to harmonize the rules in this convention. Sales of ships, vessels, hovercraft, aircraft, and electricity were also excluded from CISG because most domestic legal systems have special rules that apply to them.

Mixed Sales – CISG looks upon mixed sales and services contracts as sales of goods, unless "the preponderant part of the obligations" of the seller "consists in the supply of labor or other services." Preponderant has its normal meaning of "more than half," but whether this is measured by the cost, the sale price, or some other basis is something the convention does not make clear.

Contracts for goods to be manufactured are treated by CISG as sales of goods unless the buyer "undertakes to supply a substantial part of the materials." Although substantial probably means less than half, how much less is unclear.

Contractual Issues Excluded from the Coverage of CISG

CISG only deals with (1) the formation of the contract and (2) the remedies available to the buyer and seller. It specifically excludes questions about (1) the legality of the contract, (2) the competency of the parties, (3) the rights of third parties, and (4) liability for death or personal injury.

Illegality and Incompetency – Domestic laws vary greatly in determining when a contract is illegal and when it is void or voidable because one or both of the parties are incompetent. The extent to which a contract can be avoided because it was fraudulently obtained varies greatly. Domestic rules on insanity, infancy, and other contractual disabilities are equally diverse.

The drafters of the convention recognized that legality and competency are sensitive issues that reflect the mores and social values of particular cultures. To avoid a disagreement that might have jeopardized the adoption of CISG, these questions were left for settlement by domestic law.

<u>Third-Party Claims and Personal Injuries</u> – Diverse domestic laws apply to the matters of third-party claims and the liability of a seller for death or personal injury. Again, to avoid the possibility of a deadlock in the drafting of the convention, the drafters left them out.

Preemption

To determine if CISG applies to a particular contractual issue, one must look to the convention itself, not to domestic law. If the convention does apply, domestic law is preempted. That is, the remedies provided in CISG are the only remedies available. This result is the consequence of the convention's basic function: to establish uniform rules for international sales contracts.

Preemption applies both in cases where domestic law calls the matter contractual and where it gives it some other name. Under CISG, a remedy is available if the goods failed to conform to the contract (Article 35) and damage resulted from the defect (Article 74). Despite the fact that local law may require a third proof element to establish product liability, this does not mean that a tort remedy is available. The only permissible remedy is the one provided by CISG.

Interpreting the CISG

The underlying goal of CISG is the creation of a uniform body of international commercial sales law. In deciding legal questions governed by the convention, Article 7(2) directs a court to look to the following sources, in the following order: (1) the convention itself, (2) the general principles on which the convention is based, and (3) the rules of private international law.

<u>The Convention</u> – When the words of CISG itself require interpretation, Article 7(1) directs a court to consider (1) the international character of the convention, (2) the need to promote uniformity in the convention's application, and (3) the observance of good faith.

On its face, CISG implies that a court may use only the plain meaning rule of the language in the convention. In many countries, the courts also look to a statute's legislative history—the *travaux préparatoires*—to determine its intent. In addition to *travaux préparatoires*, courts in most countries use case law to interpret statutes and treaties.

<u>General Principles</u> – CISG calls for courts to look to the general principles on which the convention is based when interpreting its provisions, but it gives no list of general principles. The following two have been suggested: (1) A party to a contract has the duty to communicate information needed by the other party, and (2) parties have the obligation to mitigate damages resulting from a breach. The CISG requires that the principles must be derived from particular sections of the convention and then extended, by analogy, to the case at hand.

<u>Rules of Private International Law</u> – The rules of private international law are the third and final source for interpreting the convention. They may be used, however, only when CISG itself does not directly settle a matter or when the matter cannot be resolved by the application of a general principle derived from the convention itself.

Private international law rules vary from country to country. Some states have enacted private international law codes, whereas others rely on case law. By allowing courts to turn to the rules of private international law, the convention avoids the possibility that courts will adopt interpretive aids on an entirely *ad hoc* basis.

Interpreting Sales Contracts

Article 8 of CISG establishes rules for interpreting the statements and conduct of the parties; Article 9 deals with usages and practices.

<u>Statements and Conduct of the Parties</u> – Varying approaches in domestic law:
- The subjective intent approach: A contract is sometimes said to be formed only when the parties have a "meeting of the minds" or a "common intent."
- The objective intent approach: A party's statements and other conduct "are to be interpreted according to the understanding that a reasonable person of the same kind as the other party would have had in the same circumstances."

The subjective intent of the parties is the best evidence for interpreting a contract—if it can be fairly ascertained—and CISG allows courts to turn to it first. Thus, courts are to use the subjective intent of a speaker, but only if "the other party knew or could not have been unaware" of the speaker's intent. When a speaker's intent is not clear, CISG directs the court to look at objective intent.

<u>Negotiations</u> – When a court is to determine intent, Article 8(3) of CISG directs that "due consideration" be given "to all relevant circumstances," including (1) the negotiations leading up to the contract, (2) the practices that the parties have established between themselves, and (3) the parties' conduct after they agree to the contract.

The purpose of Article 8(3) is to do away with the technical rules that domestic courts sometimes use to interpret contracts. One notable example is the common law's parol evidence rule. Article 6 allows the parties to "derogate from or vary the effect of" any of the provisions of the convention. Thus, if the parties include a contract term (often called an integration clause) that directs a court to ignore all prior or contemporaneous agreements, the court will have to give effect to that term.

CISG lets a court consider the parties' subsequent conduct. CISG, however, does reflect the most widely followed practice and, as is the case for parol evidence, the parties are free to insert a provision in their contract excluding its consideration.

<u>Practices and Usages</u> – Both Article 8(3) and Article 9(1) of CISG state that parties are bound by "any practices which they have established between themselves." Article 9(1) also allows a court to consider any usages that the parties agreed to, and Article 9(2) lets it consider "a usage of which the parties knew or ought to have known and which in international trade is widely known to, and regularly observed by parties to contracts of the type involved in the particular trade concerned."

Case brief 5-1: *Treibacher Industrie, A.G. v. Allegheny Technologies, Inc.*
United States Court of Appeals, Eleventh Circuit, 2006.

Facts: Treibacher, an Austrian seller of hard metal powders, agreed to sell specific quantities of tantalum carbide (TaC) to TDY Industries, Inc. for delivery to "consignment." After taking delivery of some TaC, TDY refused to take delivery of the balance specified in two contracts, and by letter stated it would not pay for any TaC that it did not use. TDY had bought the TaC it needed from another seller at lower prices, and Treibacher sold the TaC which TDY refused to take delivery of at lower prices to others. Treibacher sued for damages, and TDY and Treibacher disputed the meaning of the word "consignment" in the contracts at a bench trial. The trial judge ruled that under CISG, evidence of the parties' interpretation of the term in their course of dealings trumped evidence of the term's customary industry usage. Because the parties, in their course of dealings, understood the term to mean "that a sale had occurred, but that invoices would be delayed until the materials were withdrawn" from storage, the court awarded plaintiff $5.3 million in compensatory damages and interest.

Issue: Does CISG provide that the parties' interpretation of a term trumps the term's customary industry usage?

Holding: Yes.

Law: Plaintiff relies on CISG Article 9(1), while defendant relies on art. 9(2). Article 8(1) provides that a party's statements and conduct are interpreted according to that party's actual intent "where the other party knew … what that intent was." To determine a party's actual intent, we consider all the circumstances including "any practices which the parties have established between themselves, usages and any subsequent conduct of the parties," art. 8(3).

Explanation: Plaintiff's construction of CISG is correct. TDY segregated Treibacher's materials in a consignment store, published usage reports on withdrawals, and paid invoices on them as they came due. In every case, TDY withdrew and paid in full for the materials specified in each contract. The district court was not clearly erroneous in finding that the parties understood their contracts to require TDY to buy all the TaC specified, and Treibacher took reasonable measures to mitigate its losses.

Order: The judgment of the district court is affirmed.

Form – Most of the delegates involved in the drafting of CISG were of the opinion that a writing requirement is inconsistent with modern commercial practice, especially in market economies where speed and informality characterize so many transactions. The Soviet delegates, however, insisted that a writing requirement is important for protecting their country's longtime pattern of making foreign trade contracts. The result of this disagreement was a compromise:

- Article 11 of the convention states that a contract of sale need not be concluded in or evidenced by writing and is not subject to any other requirements as to form. It may be proved by any means, including witnesses.
- Article 96 authorizes a contracting state "whose legislation requires contracts of sale to be concluded in or evidenced by writing" to make a declaration at the time of ratification that Article 11 "does not apply where any party has his place of business in that state."

Formation of the Contract

A contract is formed, and the parties are bound by its provisions, when an offer to buy or sell a good is accepted.

The Offer – An offer is a proposal addressed to specific persons indicating an intention by the offeror to be bound to the sale or purchase of particular goods for a price. Should there be some doubt whether a communication is an offer or not, CISG directs a court to ascertain if the offeror communicated an intention to be bound. This can be determined from the general rules of interpretation in Article 8 of the convention— that is, by looking at the offeror's proposal within its full context, including any negotiations, any practices between the parties, any usages, and any subsequent conduct. It can also be determined from the subsidiary rules contained in Article 14.

Definiteness

According to Article 14, a "proposal is sufficiently definite if it indicates the goods and expressly or implicitly fixes or makes provision for determining the quantity and price." In other words, an offer must describe the goods with sufficient clarity that the parties know what is being offered for sale, and it must also state the quantity and price.

Article 55 provides: Where a contract has been validly concluded but does not expressly or implicitly fix or make provision for determining the price, the parties are considered in the absence of any indication to the contrary, to have impliedly made reference to the price generally charged at the time of the conclusion of the contract for such goods sold under comparable circumstances in the trade concerned.

Specific Offerees

For a proposal to be an offer, it must be addressed to "one or more specific persons." Proposals made to the public are ordinarily intended to be nothing more than invitations to negotiate. CISG, accordingly, adopts the rule that public offers are only invitations to negotiate "unless the contrary is clearly indicated."

Effectiveness of an Offer – An offer becomes effective only after it reaches the offeree. Thus, offers— including offers that promise that they are irrevocable—can be withdrawn before they reach the offeree.

Revocation

Offers that do not state that they are irrevocable can be revoked any time before the offeree dispatches an acceptance. This revocation rule is based on the famous English common law mailbox rule, which limits the ability of the offeror to cancel an offer where the offeree has reasonably relied on it.

Firm Offers

Most common law countries are allowing offerees to enforce firm offers made by merchants if they are made in writing, are signed by the offeror, and are effective for only a limited time period. The promise of irrevocability does not have to be signed, does not have to be in writing, and there is no time limitation. A firm offer is enforceable if the offeror makes the offer irrevocable or if the offeree can reasonably rely on conduct that implies that the offer is firm.

Acceptance – A contract comes into existence at the point in time an offer is accepted. Acceptance is a statement or conduct by the offeree indicating assent that is communicated to the offeror. The form or mode in which an offeree expresses assent is unlimited; however, the offeree must communicate his assent to the offeror.

Silence

Silence or inactivity does not, in and of itself, constitute acceptance. Where a party voluntarily assumes the duty to respond, silence will constitute acceptance.

Time of Acceptance

Acceptance must be received by the offeror within the time period specified in the offer. If no time period is given, acceptance must be received within a reasonable time. If the offer is oral, the acceptance must be made immediately, unless the circumstances indicate otherwise.

In devising the acceptance rule for CISG, the drafters opted for the receipt theory used in civil law countries. In common law countries, the dispatch or mailbox theory is used. The difference between the two relates to the allocation of risk when an acceptance is lost or delayed.

Assent by Performance of an Act

If the offeror asks for performance of an act rather than the indication of acceptance, the acceptance is effective at the moment the act is performed. However, the offer, a trade usage, or the practice of the parties must make it clear that the offeree is not required to notify the offeror.

Withdrawal

Because an acceptance is normally not effective until the offeror receives it, an offeree may withdraw his acceptance any time before or simultaneous with its receipt.

Rejection

A rejection becomes effective when it reaches the offeror. If an offeree were to dispatch both a rejection and an acceptance at the same time, the one that reached the offeror first would be the one given effect

Acceptance with Modifications – Battle of the Forms occurs when merchants use preprinted forms both to make offers and to send back acceptances. The typed-in descriptions commonly match up; it is the "fine print" on the back of the forms, however, that contains differences. Under CISG, if the inconsistencies are "material" the would-be acceptance is a counteroffer.

Article 19(3) states: Additional or different terms relating, among other things, to the price, payment, quality of the goods, place and time of delivery, extent of one party's liability to the other, or the settlement of disputes are considered to alter the terms of the offer materially.

Terms that are not material are considered to be proposals for addition that will become part of the contract unless the offeror promptly objects.

Case brief 5-2: *Filanto, SpA v. Chilewich International Corp.*

United States, District Court, Southern District of New York, 1992.

Facts: Chilewich (a U.S. export-import firm) had a contract to deliver footwear to Russia. This contract contained an arbitration provision that called for all disputes to be arbitrated in Moscow. Chilewich then engaged Filanto (an Italian corporation) to supply it with footwear that Chilewich had contracted to deliver to Russia. Chilewich's correspondence to Filanto said that the arbitration provision in the Russian contract was to be part of their contract as well. Filanto supposedly sent Chilewich a counteroffer rejecting the arbitration provision. Chilewich meanwhile proceeded to obtain a letter of credit benefiting Filanto and proceeded as if there was a contract. Filanto, however, signed a contract on August 7 that contained this provision, although it said in its cover letter that it was not bound by the provision. When a dispute arose and Filanto sued in a U.S. court, Chilewich invoked the arbitration provision and asked the court to dismiss Filanto's suit.

Issue: (1) Was the August 7 reply a counteroffer? (2) If it was, was there a contract anyway based on unobjected-to performance?

Holding: (1) Yes. (2) Yes.

Law: A reply that purports to be an acceptance but contains material (such as the rejection of an arbitration provision) additions, limitations, or modifications are a rejection of the offer and a counteroffer. If the offeree knows that the offeror has begun performance and fails to notify the offeror within a reasonable time that it objects to the terms of the contract, it will be deemed to have assented to those terms.

Explanation: (1) The objections to the arbitration provision in the August 7 cover letter were a material modification amounting to a rejection of the offer. (2) Because Chilewich went ahead with the contract (getting the letter of credit) and Filanto did not timely object, Filanto accepted the terms of Chilewich's proposed contract.

Order: Case dismissed; the matter must be arbitrated in Moscow.

General Standards of Performance

CISG imposes general standards of performance on both the buyer and seller. In general, both parties are entitled to get from their contract what they expect. A party that fails to perform accordingly is in breach of contract. When one party breaches, the other party may avoid the contract or make a demand for specific performance.

Fundamental Breach – Article 25 defines a fundamental breach thus: A breach of contract committed by one of the parties is fundamental if it results in such detriment to the other party as substantially to deprive him of what he is entitled to expect under the contract, unless the party in breach did not foresee and a reasonable person of the same kind in the same circumstances would not have foreseen such a result.

Avoidance – If there has been a fundamental breach, one remedy available to the injured party is avoidance. To be entitled to avoid a contract, the injured party must notify the other party and be able to return any goods he has already received.

When a party avoids, only the obligation to perform is affected. Avoidance does not cancel (1) any provision in the contract concerning the settlement of disputes or (2) any other provisions governing the rights and duties of the parties "consequent upon the avoidance of the contract."

Requests for Specific Performance – CISG authorizes an injured party to ask a court "to require performance" if the other party fails to carry out his obligations. A court is not obliged to grant this request, however, unless the court can do so under its own domestic rules. What constitutes specific performance varies from country to country, and the rule in CISG reflects the difficulties the drafters had in defining the concept.

Seller's Obligations

A seller is required to (1) deliver the goods, (2) hand over any documents relating to them, and (3) ensure that the goods conform with the contract.

Place for Delivery – The place for delivery is the place agreed to in the contract; otherwise, it is (1) the first carrier's place of business if the contract involves the carriage of goods or (2) the place where the parties knew the goods were located or were to be manufactured or produced.

The seller must, at the time he delivers the goods to a carrier, either (1) identify to the carrier both the goods and the buyer "by markings on the goods, by shipping documents or otherwise" or (2) "give the buyer notice of the consignment of the specifying goods."

Time for Delivery – The seller is to deliver the goods on the date fixed in the contract or, if no date is fixed, within a reasonable time after the conclusion of the contract. If a time period is provided, the seller may deliver at any time within that period, unless the contract expressly says that the buyer is to choose the time.

The Turning Over of Documents – At the time and place for delivery, the seller must turn over any documents relating to the goods that the contract requires. If he does so early, he has the right to "cure any lack of conformity in the documents," so long as this does not cause the buyer "unreasonable inconvenience or unreasonable expense."

Conformity of Goods – Article 35(1) of CISG states that the seller "must deliver goods which are of the quantity, quality, and description required by the contract and which are contained or packaged in the manner required by the contract." This provision is similar to many warranty provisions found in common law countries, with the notable exception that it does not use the terms warranty or guarantee. This is important, because the seller's obligation (and the buyer's right) arises—and can be waived—without the use of these terms.

Determining Conformity: The rules for determining whether the goods conform are set out in Article 35(2). Except where the parties have agreed otherwise, the goods do not conform with the contract unless they are:
- fit for the ordinary purposes of such goods.
- fit for the particular purposes that:
   ❖ were expressly or impliedly made known to the seller at the time of the conclusion of the contract, and
   ❖ the buyer reasonably relied upon the seller's skill and judgment.
- of the same quality as a sample or model provided by the seller.
- contained or packaged in the same manner that is:
   ❖ usual for such goods, or
   ❖ adequate to preserve and protect the goods.

Third-Party Claims: Goods also do not conform if they are subject to third-party claims. Third-party claims include assertions of ownership and rights in intellectual property such as patents, copyrights, and trademarks.

Waiver: Although the seller is obliged to produce goods that conform to the contract, the parties may (1) expressly excuse him/her from complying or (2) impliedly excuse him/her if the buyer knew or "could not have been unaware" that the goods were nonconforming. These rules are similar to the waiver provisions found in most common law countries, except there is no requirement to use any particular terms to make the waiver. Moreover, unlike the practice in many civil law countries, a waiver can be implied from the buyer's conduct.

Time for Examining Goods: The buyer has an obligation to examine the goods for defects "within as short a period as is practicable" after delivery. If the goods are shipped, the examination "may be deferred until after the goods have arrived at their destination" and, if the buyer has to redirect or redispatch the goods while they are in transit, the examination "may be deferred until after the goods have arrived at the new destination," so long as the seller "knew or ought to have known of the possibility of such redirection or redispatch."

Notice of Defect: In order for the buyer to avoid waiving his rights to require performance, he is obligated to inform the seller of any defects he discovers within a reasonable time after delivery. If the buyer discovers a defect at some later time, he must also promptly notify the seller in order to preserve his rights.

In any event, the seller will not be responsible for a defect that arises more than two years after delivery unless (1) the seller knew or ought to have known of a nonconformity and did not disclose it to the buyer or (2) the contract establishes a longer "period of guarantee." CISG does not describe specifically what the buyer has to do in notifying the seller of a defect, but the notice undoubtedly must be sufficient to inform the seller of the problem.

Curing Defects: If the seller delivers his goods early, he may correct or cure any defect up to the agreed-upon date for delivery, so long as this does not cause the buyer any unreasonable inconvenience or expense. Nevertheless, even if the seller does make a cure, the buyer retains the right to claim any damages that are provided for in CISG.

Buyer's Obligations

A buyer is required to (1) pay the price and (2) take delivery of the goods. CISG's rules apply only when a contract fails to describe how this is done.

Payment of the Price – The buyer is obliged to take whatever preliminary steps are necessary "under the contract or any laws or regulations to enable payment to be made." He is then to pay the price at the time and place designated in the contract. If no time is specified, the buyer is to pay when "the goods or the documents controlling their disposition" are delivered.

The buyer has to pay "without the need for any request or compliance with any formality on the part of the seller." However, unless the parties agree otherwise, the buyer does not have to pay until after he has had a chance to examine the goods.

If the parties have not agreed to a place for payment but have agreed to a place for the delivery of either the goods or their controlling documents, then payment will be made at that place. If they did not specify a place for delivery, then the buyer must pay at the seller's place of business.

Case brief 5-3: *The Natural Gas Case*
Austria, Supreme Court, 1996.

Facts: Buyer agreed to buy natural gas for itself and a third party. Seller agreed to ship gas from the U.S. Buyer agreed to obtain a letter of credit, but told seller that its bank needed to know the place of loading in order to issue the letter. Seller agreed to provide the place of loading, but never did so. Later, the seller told buyer that its U.S. supplier would not agree to export the gas to buyer in Belgium. The third party bought gas from another source for an additional $141,131. Buyer then sued seller to recover the $141,131 for the third party plus $15,000 in lost profits for itself. Seller asserted that it was not liable because the buyer had never obtained the letter of credit; if it was liable, that the buyer had avoided the contract and the damages should be calculated accordingly; and that the buyer was not entitled to lost profits and that the buyer/third party failed to mitigate damages.

Issues: (1) Had the buyer breached by not obtaining the letter of credit? (2) Had the seller breached? (3) Was the contract avoided? (4) Was the buyer entitled to lost profits? (5) Had the buyer failed to mitigate?

Holdings: (1) No. (2) Yes. (3) No. (4) Yes. (5) No.

Law: (1) A defendant cannot complain that a plaintiff failed to fulfill its obligations when the defendant's own failure to act caused the plaintiff's inaction. CISG Article 41 says that a seller must deliver goods free from any right or claim of third parties. (2) A non-breaching party's intention to avoid must be clear to the breaching party for there to be an avoidance. (3) A plaintiff is entitled to loss of profits only if the defendant was aware of an intended resale. (4) The defendant has the burden of proving that the plaintiff failed to mitigate.

Explanation: (1) The buyer did not breach, because the failure to provide a letter of credit was caused by the seller's failure to provide the place of loading. (2) The seller breached by failing to obtain clearance for the export of the gas and failing to deliver the gas. (3) The buyer never notified the seller that it was avoiding the contract. Notification of the amount of losses incurred is not a notification of avoidance. (4) When merchantable goods are sold to a merchant, resale is presumed. Indeed, seller knew that this was the case. Lost profits, therefore, are an appropriate measure of damages. (5) The seller failed to show how the buyer could have mitigated.

Order: Decision of the Court of Appeals was affirmed.

Taking Delivery – In connection with the taking of delivery, a buyer is obligated to cooperate with the seller to facilitate the transfer and to actually "take over the goods." A buyer who fails to cooperate will be responsible for any resulting costs, and one who fails to take delivery assumes the risk for any damage to the goods after that time.

The Passing of Risk

The loss of goods through fire, theft, or other means can occur at any time: prior to delivery, during transit or inspection, or after delivery. The legal concept of passage of risk determines who is responsible for the loss. In most cases, the loss will be covered by insurance.

Passage of risk is defined as the shifting of responsibility for loss or damage from the seller to the buyer. This means that once the risk passes, the buyer must pay the agreed-upon price for the goods involved. The buyer must then absorb the cost of the loss or lodge a claim against his insurer. Only if he can show that the loss or damage was due to an act or omission of the seller is he excused from paying the price.

CISG allocates risks by considering the agreement of the parties and the means of delivery. CISG's risk allocation is not affected by breach of contract.

Agreement of the Parties – CISG allows parties to allocate risk among themselves and to specify when the risk will pass between them. The parties most commonly do so through the use of trade terms, such as Free on Board (FOB) or Cost, Insurance, and Freight (CIF).

Case brief 5-4: *Chicago Prime Packers, Inc. v. Northam Food Trading Co.*
United States Court of Appeals, 7th Circuit, 2005.

Facts: Chicago Prime Packers, Inc., a seller of pork ribs, filed suit against Northam Food Trading Co., a purchaser of its ribs, in order to recover the purchase price of the product after Northam refused to pay for ribs that arrived in an "off condition." Chicago Prime, a Colorado corporation, and Northam, a partnership formed under the laws of Ontario, Canada, are both wholesalers of meat products.

Issues: (1) Is Chicago Prime responsible for the loss if the ribs were spoiled at the time Northam's agent, Brown, received them from Chicago Prime's agent, Brookfield? (2) Is Northam responsible if they did not become spoiled until after the transfer?
Holdings: (1) Yes. (2) Yes.

Law / Explanation: The CISG does not clearly state which party has the burden of proof in a case involving whether a product conforms to a purchase and sale contract. Therefore the U.S. Court of Appeals looked at a comparable law, the Uniform Commercial Code, which governs most contracts for the sale of goods in the United States, and closely parallels the CISG in many respects. Finding that the UCC puts the burden on the buyer, the Court upheld the lower court verdict that in this case the buyer had not proved conclusively (although there was much conflicting evidence) that the goods were spoiled when the risk of loss passed to the buyer. Generally an appellate court will not reverse a "finding of fact" by the lower court unless it can be shown that the decision was "clearly erroneous."

Order: Verdict affirmed in favor of Chicago Prime.

Means of Delivery – Goods may be transported by a carrier or delivered by the seller without being transported by a carrier.

Goods Transported by Carrier

CISG distinguishes between shipment, transshipment, in-transit, and destination contracts. No matter which of these contracts is used, the risk of loss will not pass until the goods are clearly "identified" to the contract by markings on the goods, shipping documents, notice given to the buyer, or otherwise.

Shipment Contracts: When a contract requires the seller to deliver the goods to a carrier for shipment and does not require the seller to deliver them to a particular place, the risk of loss passes when the goods are "handed over" to the first carrier.

Transshipment Contracts: If a contract requires the seller to deliver the goods to a carrier at a named place, who will then carry the goods to the buyer, the risk of loss passes to the buyer when the goods are handed over to the carrier at that place.

In-Transit Contracts: Sometimes goods are sold after they are already aboard a carrier. In such a case, the risk of loss passes to the buyer at the time the contract is concluded. However, if, at the time the contract was made, the seller knew or ought to have known that goods had been lost or damaged and he did not disclose this to the buyer, the risk will remain with the seller.

Destination Contracts: When a contract requires the seller to arrange transportation to a named place of destination, the risk of loss passes to the buyer when the goods are handed over or placed at his disposal at that place.

<u>Goods Delivered Without Being Transported</u>

When goods are not shipped to the buyer, the risk of loss passes when the goods are handed over by the seller or otherwise put at the buyer's disposal. The goods are not considered to be put at the buyer's disposal, however, until they are clearly identified to the contract.

<u>Breach of Contract</u> – The CISG rules on risk of loss are not concerned with breach of contract. That is, with the exception of in-transit contracts, the risk of loss passes to the buyer at the agreed-upon time and place of delivery.

Remedies

CISG provides for remedies that are (1) unique to the buyer, (2) unique to the seller, and (3) available to either party. Although the buyer's and seller's remedies relate to their specific needs, they are also interrelated.

　　　*Buyer's Remedies – The buyer's remedies are cumulative and immediate. CISG forbids a court or arbitral tribunal from granting the seller a period of grace (*délai de grâce*) in which to comply with a buyer's demand for a remedy.

The remedies that are unique to the buyer are to:
- compel specific performance,
- avoid the contract for fundamental breach or nondelivery,
- reduce the price,
- refuse early delivery, and
- refuse excess quantities.

<u>Specific Performance</u>

The availability of a decree of specific performance depends on the domestic rules applicable to the court hearing the suit. Assuming it is available, a buyer can ask that a seller either (1) deliver substitute goods or (2) make repairs.

In either case, the buyer must first notify the seller that the goods are nonconforming and, if he is asking for substitute goods, the nonconformity must amount to a fundamental breach. Also, the buyer cannot have avoided the contract or resorted to some other inconsistent remedy.

<u>Avoidance</u>

CISG's provisions for avoidance by a buyer are patterned after German law, especially in the convention's adoption of the German *Nachfrist* notice. Under CISG, a buyer may avoid a contract if either (1) the seller commits a fundamental breach or (2) the buyer gives the seller a *Nachfrist* notice and the seller rejects it or does not perform within the period it specifies.

A buyer's *Nachfrist* notice is the fixing of "an additional period of time of reasonable length for performance by the seller of his obligations." The period must be definite, and the obligation to perform within that period must be clear. Once the *Nachfrist* period has run, or once the fundamental breach becomes clear, the buyer has a reasonable time in which to avoid the contract.

During the *Nachfrist* period, the seller is entitled to correct (i.e., cure) the nonconformity at his own expense. Even if there has been a breach, the seller is entitled to make a cure, unless the circumstances—including the circumstance of the offer to make the cure—indicate that the breach is fundamental and the buyer chooses to avoid the contract.

Case brief 5-5 *The Shoe Seller's Case*
Germany, Court of Appeals, Frankfurt am Main, 1994.

Facts: The plaintiff delivered shoes to the defendant. Delivery was late and the shoes did not completely conform to the sample the plaintiff-seller had originally shown to the defendant-buyer. When the defendant-buyer refused to pay on two invoices, the plaintiff-seller brought suit. On appeal, the defendant argued that she was entitled to invoke the remedy of avoidance because of the plaintiff's late delivery and the nonconformity of the goods.

Issue: Is the remedy of avoidance available to the defendant?

Holding: No.

Law: (1) Avoidance is only allowed after a buyer gives the seller a *Nachfrist* notice and defines an additional fixed period in which the seller is to make delivery. (2) There is no nonconformity in cases where a buyer is able to use some of the goods.

Explanation: The buyer did not give the seller a *Nachfrist* notice. The buyer also was able to use some of the goods delivered.

Order: Decision in favor of the plaintiff is affirmed.

Reduction in Price

If a buyer is not entitled to damages when a seller delivers nonconforming goods, the buyer will be entitled to a reduction in price. This remedy has its origins in the Roman law remedy of *actio quanti minoris.*

The price reduction remedy is different from damages because it applies to a very special situation. First, the buyer must have accepted goods that are nonconforming. Second, the seller must not be responsible for the nonconformity.

The amount of the reduction is determined by a formula that considers the relative price of conforming and nonconforming goods at the time of delivery. That is, "the buyer may reduce the price in the same proportion as the value that the goods actually delivered had at the time of delivery bears to the value that conforming goods would have had at that time."

$$\text{Price Reduction} = [\text{Price}] - \left[\frac{\text{Price} \times \text{Value of goods as delivered}}{\text{Value of conforming goods at the time of delivery}} \right]$$

Refusing Early Delivery and Excess Quantity

If the seller delivers early, the buyer is under no obligation to take delivery. If the seller delivers more than the amount agreed upon, the buyer may also accept or reject the excess part. However, if the buyer does accept, he must pay for the excess goods at the contract rate.

The Effect of Nonconformity in a Part of the Goods

As to a defective part, CISG provides that the buyer may seek specific performance, obtain a price reduction, or avoid that part of the contract. In doing so, however, he must comply with CISG's rules for those particular remedies. As for avoiding the whole contract, a buyer may do so only if the partial delivery amounts to a fundamental breach of the whole.

*Seller's Remedies – The seller's remedies are both cumulative and immediate. That is, the right to recover damages is not lost if a seller exercises any other available remedy, and courts will not grant the buyer a grace period in which to perform.

The remedies that are unique to the seller are
- to compel specific performance,
- to avoid the contract for a fundamental breach or failure to cure a defect, and
- to obtain missing specifications.

Specific Performance

Assuming that a decree of specific performance is available under local law, a seller may require a buyer to (1) take delivery and pay the contract price or (2) perform any other obligation required by the contract. The availability of this remedy depends on the domestic rules applicable to the court hearing the suit.

Avoidance

The seller may avoid the contract only if there has been a fundamental breach or, following a *Nachfrist* notice, the buyer refuses to cure any defect in his performance.

Missing Specifications

The missing specifications remedy applies to a special problem that can face sellers: obtaining specifications for goods that the buyer fails to supply. If the buyer does not produce the measurements that the seller needs by the date specified in the contract or within a reasonable time after the seller asks for them, CISG allows the seller to ascertain them himself "in accordance with the requirements of the buyer that may be known to him."

The seller must then inform the buyer of what he has done and set a reasonable time period for the buyer to supply different specifications. However, if the buyer does not respond, the seller's specifications become "binding."

150

*Remedies Available to Both Buyers and Sellers – The remedies available to both buyers and sellers are (1) suspension of performance, (2) avoidance in anticipation of a fundamental breach, (3) avoidance of an installment contract, and (4) damages.

Suspension of Performance

CISG, Article 71, describes the remedy of suspension of performance as follows:
- Applying to threats of nonperformance: A party may stop performing.
- Applying to threats of nonpayment discovered after the goods are in transit: A party may prevent the handing over of the goods to the buyer even though the buyer holds a document which entitles him to obtain them. This relates only to the rights in the goods as between the buyer and the seller.
- A party suspending performance, whether before or after dispatch of the goods, must immediately give notice of the suspension to the other party and must continue with performance if the other party provides adequate assurance of his performance.

Anticipatory Avoidance

Anticipatory avoidance is different from the avoidance remedies that apply specifically to buyers and sellers. Those remedies apply only after an offending party has committed a fundamental breach. The remedy provided in Article 72 arises as soon as "it is clear" that the other party "will commit a fundamental breach."

Likely cases in which this remedy could be invoked include:
- the specific goods promised to the buyer are wrongfully sold to a third party;
- the seller's only employee capable of producing the goods dies or is fired; and
- the seller's manufacturing plant is sold.

If a party opts to anticipatorily avoid, CISG requires him, "if time allows," to notify the other party so that the latter can "provide adequate assurance of his performance."

Damages

Article 74 states: Damages for breach of contract by one party consist of a sum equal to the loss, including loss of profit, suffered by the other party as a consequence of the breach. Such damages may not exceed the loss which the party in breach foresaw or ought to have foreseen at the time of the conclusion of the contract, in the light of the facts and matters of which he then knew or ought to have known, as possible consequence of the breach of contract.

To calculate the damages, the convention uses two different rules. First, if an avoiding party has entered into a good-faith substitute transaction—the buyer obtaining substitute goods or the seller reselling the goods to another party—then damages are measured by the difference between the contract price and the price received in the substitute transaction.

Alternatively, if the avoiding party did not enter into a substitute transaction, then the damages are calculated by taking the difference between the contract price and the current price at the time of avoidance. The current price is defined as "the price prevailing at the place where delivery of the goods should have been made or, if there is not current price at that place, the price at such other places as serves as a reasonable substitute."

The party claiming damages is under an obligation to take reasonable measures "to mitigate the loss." If the claiming party fails to take such action, the other may seek a proportionate reduction in the damages.

Excuses for Nonperformance

Two excuses are provided in CISG for a party's failure to perform. One is *force majeure*; the other is dirty hands.

Force Majeure – A party is not liable for any damages resulting from his failure to perform if he can show that:
- his failure was "due to an impediment beyond his control,"
- the impediment was not something he could have reasonably taken into account at the time of contracting, and
- he remains unable to overcome the impediment or its consequences.

This excuse, commonly known as *force majeure*, applies to situations—such as natural disasters, war, embargoes, strikes, breakdowns, and the bankruptcy of a supplier—that frustrate both the party attempting to perform and the party expecting performance. Because neither party is really at fault, the breaching party is excused from paying damages. He is not, however, exempted from the application of any other appropriate remedy.

A party seeking to use CISG's excuse of *force majeure* is under some additional limitations:
- He/she has a duty to promptly notify the other party of "the impediment and its effect on his ability to perform."
- If his/her claim is based on the failure of a third person to perform (such as a supplier), the third party must itself be able to claim the excuse.
- The excuse may be used only as long as the underlying impediment continues in existence.

Dirty Hands – One party may not rely on a failure of the other party to perform, to the extent that such failure was caused by the first party's act or omission.

II. DOCUMENTARY SALES AND CARRIAGE OF GOODS BY SEA

Most goods and commodities sold globally are transported by container vessels. These vessels have become immense, and bring with them their own logistical and even ethical issues. At sea for weeks, the goods are represented by documents known as bills of lading. Each bill of lading represents three different things: a contract for the carriage of the goods, title to the goods, and the carrier's receipt for the goods to be transported. As evidence of title to goods in transit, the bill of lading is likely to be traded several times among buyers and sellers of certain goods and commodities.

And because the seller will be putting goods or commodities on board container ships, both bills of lading and letters of credit will enable the seller to be paid upon performance: the act of putting goods on board that comply with the contract. A clean" bill of lading will usually allow the seller to be paid when issued, if the bill of lading meets the specification of the letter of credit.

Most goods are transported by a common carrier — a carrier that carries goods for more than one party. Only a few shipments are large enough to require the shipper to hire an entire vessel. The contract to employ an entire vessel is known as a *charterparty*. We will first discuss common carriage, then the charterparty concept.

Common Carriage

Unlike private carriers, common carriers are the subject of extensive municipal legislation and international conventions.

The Bill of Lading

A bill of lading is an instrument issued by an ocean carrier to a shipper with whom the carrier has entered into a contract for the carriage of goods.[33] The domestic laws implementing these conventions are typically called Carriage of Goods by Sea acts. In the U.S., the Carriage of Goods by Sea Act can be found at Pub.L. 109-304, § 6(c), Oct. 6, 2006, 120 Stat. 1516.

A bill of lading serves three purposes: First, it is a carrier's receipt for goods. Second, it is evidence of a contract of carriage. Finally, it is a document of title; that is, the person rightfully in possession of the bill is entitled to possess, use, and dispose of the goods that the bill represents.

Receipt for Goods

A bill of lading describes the goods put on board a carrier, states the quantity, and describes their condition. The form itself is normally filled out in advance by the shipper; then, as the goods are loaded aboard the ship, the carrier's tally clerk will check to see that the goods loaded comply with the goods listed. The carrier, however, is responsible only to check for outward compliance—that is, that the labels comply and that the packages are not damaged. If all appears proper, the appropriate agent of the carrier will sign the bill and return it to the shipper. Bills certifying that the goods have been properly loaded on board are known as *on board bills of lading* or clean bills of lading.

Should there be a discrepancy between the goods loaded and the goods listed, the statement on the bill is considered *prima facie* evidence that the goods were received in the condition shown in any dispute between the shipper and the carrier. Nevertheless, the carrier can, if it is able, introduce evidence to rebut this evidence. However, once the bill is endorsed and negotiated to a third party, this is no longer the case. An endorsee's knowledge of the goods is limited to what is on the bill of lading. For this reason, the Hague and Hague-Visby Rules hold that the bill is conclusive evidence as to the goods loaded once the bill has been negotiated in good faith to a third party. The carrier is then barred from introducing evidence to contradict the bill of lading.

If, at the time the goods are being loaded, the carrier's tally clerk notes a discrepancy, a notation to this effect may be added to the bill of lading. Called a claused bill of lading, such bills are normally unacceptable to third parties, including a buyer of the goods under a CIF contract or a bank that has agreed to pay the seller under a documentary credit on receipt of the bill of lading and other documents. Such a notation, however, may be made on the bill only at the time the goods are loaded. Later notations will have no effect, and the bill will be treated as if it were "clean." The significance of clean and claused bills of lading is discussed in Case 5-2.

---

[33] The multilateral treaty governing bills of lading is the International Convention for the Unification of Certain Rules of Law Relating to Bills of Lading. This treaty is known both as the 1921 Hague Rules—because they were originally proposed by the International Law Association at a meeting at The Hague in 1921—and the Brussels Convention of 1924—because they were recommended for adoption at a diplomatic conference held in Brussels in 1924. The Hague Rules were extensively revised in 1968 by a Brussels Protocol, and the amended 1968 version is known as the Hague-Visby Rules. Most countries, including the United States, are parties to the 1921 Hague Rules. A few, including France and the United Kingdom, have adopted the Hague-Visby amendments.

Contract of Carriage Between the shipper and the carrier, the bill of lading is evidence of their contract of carriage. Either may rebut this by producing evidence of other terms. However, as is the case where the bill functions as a receipt, the bill becomes conclusive evidence of the terms of the contract of carriage once it is negotiated to a good-faith third party. Again, this is because the endorsee's knowledge of the terms of the contract of carriage is limited to what appears on the bill of lading.

Document of Title Two kinds of bills of lading need to be distinguished: the straight bill and the order bill. A straight bill is issued to a named consignee and is nonnegotiable. The transfer of a *straight bill* gives the transferee no greater rights than those of his transferor. An *order bill*, on the other hand, is negotiable and conveys greater rights. The holder of an order bill of lading, provided he has received it in good faith through due negotiation, has a claim to title and, by surrendering the bill, to delivery of the goods. In 1883, Lord Justice Bowen wrote what has become the time-honored definition of the order bill of lading:

> A cargo at sea while in the hands of the carrier is necessarily incapable of physical delivery. During this period of transit and voyage, the bill of lading by the law merchant is universally recognized as its symbol, and the endorsement and delivery of the bill of lading operates as a symbolical delivery of the cargo. Property in the goods passes by such endorsement and delivery of the bill of lading, whenever it is the intention of the parties that the property should pass, just as under similar circumstances the property would pass by an actual delivery of the goods. And for the purpose of passing such property in the goods and completing the title of the endorsee to full possession thereof, the bill of lading, until complete delivery of the cargo has been made on shore to someone rightfully claiming under it, remains in force as a symbol, and carries with it not only the full ownership of the goods, but also all rights created by the contract of carriage between the shipper and the shipowner. It is a key which in the hands of the rightful owner is intended to unlock the door of the warehouse, floating or fixed, in which the goods may chance to be.

Order bills, although they are negotiable instruments, should not be confused with bills of exchange (such as checks or trade acceptances). Maritime commercial practice is less developed than the law of commercial paper, and though both classes of instruments are related, they are also distinct.

Like bills of exchange, order bills of lading may be made out *to bearer* or *to the order* of a named party. Bearer instruments are transferred by delivery; order instruments by negotiation, that is, by endorsement and delivery. In practice, bills of lading are seldom made out to bearer, as they are documents of title that serve as the symbol or token of the goods described in the bill.

The negotiation of an order bill transfers title in the goods. This is what makes the bill valuable. Because the bill is *negotiable*, so too are the goods. This enables the person named on the bill to transfer the goods while a ship is in transit. In other words, possession of the order bill is in most respects the same as possession of the goods.

Unlike transferees of bills of exchange, a transferee who obtains an order bill of lading in good faith and for value paid is not a holder in due course who is entitled to claim the goods from the carrier *free of equities* or *free of personal defenses*. This is a significant difference. In practice, it means that should an order bill of lading be obtained by fraud and endorsed to a bona fide purchaser for value, the recipient will not acquire title to the goods described in the bill. On the other hand, if the same thing were to happen with a bill of exchange (such as a draft, check, or note) that was neither overdue nor dishonored, the recipient (who would be a holder in due course) would be entitled to the money or property described in that bill. Because of this difference, an order bill of lading is sometimes described as only a *quasi-negotiable* instrument.

The definitional basis for this difference between bills of exchange and order bills of lading can be found in Lord Justice Bowen's description, quoted earlier. Even when a bill of lading is properly endorsed and delivered, title to the goods will pass only when the bill of lading is negotiated with the intention of transferring the goods. For example, a seller may endorse a bill of lading to his agent in the port where the goods are to be discharged so that the agent can deal directly with a particular buyer. Because the seller did not intend to pass title to the agent by his endorsement, title would not pass. If the agent were to fraudulently sell the bill to a third party, the third party would also not have title. In such a circumstance, the seller could order the carrier to deliver the goods only to the intended buyer, or if delivery had already been made to the third party, the seller could sue that person for conversion. This is so because the transferee of an order bill of lading acquires both the rights and the liabilities of his transferor.

Bills of lading are also distinct from bills of exchange because they additionally represent a contract for carriage. Negotiation of an order bill of lading produces the unique result of a transfer of the right to enforce the underlying transportation agreement. For example, in the case of *The Albazero*, cargo was lost due to the alleged negligence of the carrier. The holders of the bill of lading were unable to sue because the statute of limitation set by the Hague Rules had run. Accordingly, the charterers, who were business affiliates of the holders, attempted to sue under the charterparty, which was not subject to the same statutory time limits. The British House of Lords held that the charterers could not sue. By endorsing the bill of lading, which also represented the contract of carriage, they had transferred all of their contractual rights to the transferee.

Carrier's Duties Under a Bill of Lading

A carrier transporting goods under a bill of lading is required by the Hague and Hague-Visby Rules to exercise "due diligence" in:
   (a) Making the ship seaworthy.
   (b) Properly manning, equipping, and supplying the ship.
   (c) Making the holds, refrigerating, and cool chambers, and all other parts of the ship in which goods are carried, fit and safe for their reception, carriage, and preservation.
   (d) Properly and carefully loading, handling, stowing, carrying, keeping, caring for, and discharging the goods carried.

Most courts strictly enforce this obligation. For example, in *Riverstone Meat Co. Pty., Ltd. v. Lancashire Shipping Co., Ltd.*, cargo was damaged by water due to the negligent work of a shipfitter employed by a ship repair company. The court held that the carrier had failed to use due diligence in making the ship seaworthy.

---

[39] All England Law Reports, vol. 1976, pt. 3, p. 129 (House of Lords, 1976).
[40] International Convention for the Unification of Certain Rules of Law Relating to Bills of Lading, Article 3 (1924) (the 1921 Hague Rules); Brussels Protocol, Article 3 (1968) (the Hague-Visby Rules).
[41] All England Law Reports, vol. 1961, pt. 1, p. 495 (1961).

Carrier's Immunities

Both the Hague and Hague-Visby Rules exempt carriers from liability from damages that arise from any

(a) Act, neglect, or default of the master, mariner, pilot, or the servants of the carrier in the navigation or in the management of the ship;
(b) Fire, unless caused by the actual fault or privity of the carrier;
(c) Perils, dangers, and accidents of the sea or other navigable water;
(d) Act of God;
(e) Act of war;
(f) Act of public enemies;
(g) Arrest or restraint of princes, rulers, or people, or seizure under legal process;
(h) Quarantine restrictions;
(i) Act or omission of the shipper or owner of the goods, or his agent or representative;
(j) Strikes or lockouts or stoppage or restraint of labor from whatever cause, whether partial or general; provided that nothing herein contained shall be construed to relieve a carrier from responsibility for the carrier's own acts;
(k) Riots and civil commotions;
(l) Saving or attempting to save life or property at sea;
(m) Wastage in bulk or weight or any other loss or damage arising from inherent defect, quality, or vice of the goods;
(n) Insufficiency of packing;
(o) Insufficiency or inadequacy of marks;
(p) Latent defects not discoverable by due diligence; and
(q) Any other cause arising without the actual fault and privity of the carrier and without the fault or negligence of the agents or servants of the carrier, but the burden of proof shall be on the person claiming the benefit of this exception to show that neither the actual fault or privity of the carrier nor the fault or neglect of the agents or servants of the carrier contributed to the loss or damage.

These immunities are narrowly construed. If cargo is injured and the injury falls within one of the exemptions, the carrier will nonetheless be responsible if the underlying cause was the result of the carrier's failure to exercise due diligence in carrying out its fundamental duties.

In the case at the end of this chapter, Vimar Seguros v. Sky Reefer, the question is not so much about the carrier's liability, but about the particular forum in which that liability will be assessed. The U.S. Supreme Court here enforces an agreement to arbitrate in Tokyo, even though it's not clear that the Carriage of Goods by Sea Act will be fairly applied to the facts of the case.

Finally, we should note that bills of lading for goods carried in container ships will usually have a letter of credit, as well. A letter of credit, when properly arranged, can assure a seller shipping to a distant nation's buyer that, on presentation of the proper documents, a bank in the seller's nation will pay if the documents are in good order and correspond to the contract.

Illustration

https://thescarbroughgroup.com/wp-content/uploads/2016/05/Letter-of-Credit.jpg

---

[42] International Convention for the Unification of Certain Rules of Law Relating to Bills of Lading, Article 4, (1924) (the 1921 Hague Rules); Brussels Protocol, Article 4, (1968) (the Hague-Visby Rules).

III.   CASES

Case 5-1

UNITED TECHNOLOGIES INTERNATIONAL, INC. v. MAGYAR LÉGI KÖZLEKEDÉSI VÁLLALAT

Hungary, Metropolitan Court of Budapest, 1992.

Case No. 3.G.50.289/1991/32.[43]

Magyar Légi Közlekedési Vállalat (Málev Hungarian Airlines) planned to buy wide-bodied jet aircraft either from Boeing Aircraft Co. of the United States or Airbus Industries of Europe. It planned to buy the engines for these aircraft separately. After completing negotiations for engines with the Pratt & Whitney division of United Technologies International, Málev Hungarian Airlines reneged on going forward with the purchase. United Technologies International thereupon sued in the Metropolitan Court of Budapest to obtain a declaratory judgment holding that a valid contract existed between Pratt & Whitney and Málev.

JUDGE PISKOLTI

***

The Offer

The plaintiff [Pratt & Whitney] delivered an offer to the defendant's [Málev Hungarian Airlines'] General Manager on December 14, 1990. This offer described Pratt & Whitney's financial assistance plans, product warranties, as well as the support services that it would provide for its PW4056 engine. The offer updated and amended an earlier offer made on November 9, 1990. It said that plaintiff was "pleased to submit this revised support services proposal in connection with Málev Hungarian Airlines' purchase of two 767-200ER aircraft, powered by Pratt & Whitney PW4056 engines (with an option to purchase a third such aircraft), and the purchase of one PW4056 spare engine (with an option to buy a second spare), all of which are scheduled to be delivered as stated in Attachment 1."... The plaintiff's offer also set out a complete technical description of the PW4000 series engines....

    Paragraph Y of the plaintiff's offer is entitled "Purchase Agreement." This states that the buyer agrees to buy, and the seller agrees to sell, four new PW4056 engines to be mounted on two 767-200ER aircraft according to the attached schedule. The buyer also is given an option to buy two more new PW4056 engines in the event that it exercises its option to buy an additional 767-200ER aircraft. Additionally, the buyer agrees to buy one PW4056 engine as a spare....The plaintiff's Purchase Agreement also establishes a deadline of December 21, 1990, for the buyer to accept the offer. If the buyer needs additional information or assistance, it is encouraged to contact the plaintiff's legal and accounting staff. In this regard, the plaintiff's offer notes that the buyer's acceptance is conditional on the agreement being approved by the governments of both Hungary and the United States.

***

Extension of the Offer

In a separate document, also delivered to the defendant on December 14, 1990, the plaintiff offered to sell to the defendant its PW4152 or PW4156/A engines. Again, this offer updated and amended an earlier offer

---

[43] Another English translation of this case is posted on the Internet at http://cisgw3.law.pace.edu/cases/920110h1.html.

made on November 9, 1990. It also described the assistance the plaintiff would provide the defendant with respect to defendant's purchase of two A310-300 aircraft (with an option to buy a third) that were to be equipped [with] either the two PW4152 or two PW4156/A engines (with the option to [buy] a third engine) according to the attached schedule….Additionally, paragraph W of this offer, which is entitled "Spare Engine Price," states that the base price of a new PW4152 is $5,552,675 and the base price of a new PW4156/A engine is $5,847,675. Finally, once again, December 21, 1990, is set as the date by which the buyer must accept the plaintiff's offer.

***

The parties have stipulated that their relationship is governed by the United Nations Convention on Contracts for the International Sale of Goods (CISG).[44] According to CISG, Article 14(1), "a contract addressed to one or more specific persons constitutes an offer if it is sufficiently definite and indicates the intention of the offeror to be bound in case of acceptance." Additionally, "[a] proposal is sufficiently definite if it indicates the goods and expressly or implicitly fixes or makes provision for determining the quantity and the price."

It is clear from the circumstances that the plaintiff's proposal was addressed to the defendant. What needs to be ascertained, first, is whether the offer sufficiently describes the goods involved. The first of the offers described above clearly states that the goods offered for sale are PW4056 and PW4060 engines and the second offer clearly states that goods offered are the PW4152 and PW4156/A engines….The fact that the defendant has the right to choose between the listed engines, depending on whether it elects to buy the Boeing 767-200ER aircraft (which requires either the PW4056 or the PW4060 engine) or the Airbus A310-300 (which requires the PW4152 or the PW4156/A engine) does not affect the description of the goods. The offer gives the buyer the right to choose between offered engines. Such a unilateral right is common in…commercial practice and it does not make the description of the goods uncertain, as the defendant has argued. Contrary to the defendant's argument, the plaintiff's proposals unambiguously describe the goods offered to the defendant.

Defendant also argues that the plaintiff's proposals could not be construed to be offers because they do not establish the quantity of the goods involved [because the defendant is allowed to choose between taking two or three engines]. This argument is also untenable. Again, the offer gives the unilateral right to the defendant to determine the quantity.

That is, the defendant is able to determine the quantity involved based on its choice as to the number of aircraft….As the plaintiff has pointed out in oral argument, the plaintiff's proposal clearly indicates that the defendant intended to purchase at least two aircraft, whether they were made by Boeing or Airbus, and that the defendant had an option to purchase a third aircraft. If the defendant does not choose to exercise its option to buy a third aircraft, the quantity specified in the plaintiff's proposal is for four engines and one spare engine. If the defendant does choose to exercise its option, then quantity would be six engines and one spare.

The defendant's argument that the plaintiff's offers fails to state a price is also unfounded. The plaintiff's written offers (described above) state that the price of a PW4056 engine is $5,552,675 and the price of the PW4152 and PW4156/A engine is $5,847,675….

Finally, the plaintiff's proposals include a schedule setting out the time for the delivery of the engines, so the defendant could not be uncertain as to this either.

---

[44] The convention is in force in Hungary. See Law Decree No. 20 of 1987. [The convention was also in force in the United States at the time of this dispute.]

In light of the above, it is clear that the plaintiff's proposal of December 14, 1990, is an offer. It clearly describes the goods, states the price and quantity, and sets out the time for delivery. Thus, the plaintiff's offer satisfies all of requirements of Article 14(1) of CISG.

The Acceptance

On December 21, 1990, the defendant sent a letter of acceptance to the plaintiff. This was within the deadline set by the plaintiff. In its letter of acceptance the defendant informed the plaintiff that it had chosen the PW4000 series engine for its fleet of wide-bodied aircraft. Moreover, it gave its reasons for doing so (namely, that its decision was based on a thorough technical and economic evaluation)….

The letter unambiguously states it accepts all of the terms and conditions set out in the plaintiff's proposal of December 14, 1990. It only asks that the letter be kept confidential until the parties can make a joint public announcement….

… According to Article 18(1) of CISG, an acceptance is "[a] statement made by, or other conduct of, the offeree indicating assent to an offer is an acceptance." It is clear that the defendant's letter of acceptance is just that.

Article 19(1) of CISG adds that "[a] reply to an offer which purports to be an acceptance but contains additions, limitations, or other modifications is a rejection of the offer and constitutes a counter-offer." The request made by the defendant at the end of its letter of acceptance [to keep the letter confidential until a joint announcement could be made] cannot be construed as an addition, limitation, or other modification. It is not a counter-offer. This being so, the defendant's letter of acceptance is an acceptance. That being so, it had the effect of creating a contract between the plaintiff and defendant.

***

CISG, Article 23, provides that "[a] contract is concluded at the moment when an acceptance of an offer becomes effective in accordance with the provisions of this Convention." Accordingly, the present contract came into effect when the plaintiff received the defendant's letter of acceptance. In other words, the effect of the defendant's letter of acceptance agreeing to all of the terms of the plaintiff's offer was to create a contract between them.

***

[The Condition Requiring Government Approval]

… Section 215(1) of the Hungarian *Civil Code* states, that, if the conclusion of a contract requires the approval of a third person, or official approval, the contract will not come into force until the approval is obtained….Section 228(1) of the *Civil Code* states that, if the parties agree to terms that makes a contract's entry into force dependent on an the occurrence of an uncertain future event (a condition precedent), the agreement will not come into force until the event occurs. And Section 228(2) provides that, if the parties provide for the termination of a contract upon the occurrence an uncertain future event (a condition subsequent), the contract will terminate upon the occurrence of that event.

Notably, there are no provisions of this sort to be found in the CISG. Accordingly, these provisions cannot be used in ascertaining the validity of the contract under consideration….

While there are no provisions in CISG describing the effect of a condition, there is also nothing in the CISG that forbids the parties from agreeing to a condition. Thus, the provision in the plaintiff's offer that "Málev Hungarian Airlines' acceptance of this offer is conditional on the agreement being approved by the governments of both Hungary and the United States" is not ineffective. However, the exact nature of the provision's effect has to be determined in light of the CISG's directive that a contract comes into existence at the time that an acceptance is received by the offeror. The parties may not ignore this mandate, even though they are otherwise free to set the terms and conditions of their contract.

During the course of the oral hearings in this case, it became evident to the court that the plaintiff viewed the condition that it had included in the contract as a device for avoiding governmental interference…and not as a condition precedent to the creation of a contract.…

***

[Only after the plaintiff received the defendant's acceptance] did it become clear to the plaintiff that the defendant, although owned by the State, was an independent company that did not require the State's approval to make decisions. The Hungarian Ministry of Transportation, Communication, and Construction eventually did make a declaration in connection with the contract at hand, but this was to assure the plaintiff that the defendant had the right to act on its own.

As for the approval required from the U.S. government, the plaintiff was only thinking in terms of obtaining the appropriate export license.…

In sum, the plaintiff intended, and the defendant agreed to, a condition subsequent. That is, to a condition that would terminate the contract. They did not agree to a condition precedent; a condition that must be fulfilled before a contract can come into effect.

Considering all of the above, it is the opinion of this court that the parties entered into a valid and enforceable contract.

SUMMARY: The legal issue before the court in this case was whether an offer had been made and accepted under the CISG and international rules. After reviewing the correspondence and actions of the parties, the court found that it was clear that an offer and acceptance had been made, and a binding contract had come into existence. The term requiring *government approval* was not a condition precedent to a valid contract, but was only a condition subsequent, which, if it occurred, might suspend the parties' obligations. Thus, there was an enforceable contract between the parties.

Case 5-2
M. GOLODETZ & CO., INC. v. CZARNIKOW-RIONDA CO., INC. (THE GALITIA)

England, Queen Bench's Division (1978).

All England Law Reports, vol. 1979, pt. 2, p. 726 (1979)

The sellers contracted to sell to the buyers between 12,000 and 13,200 tons of sugar, C & F Bandarshapur, Iran. The contract provided, among other things, that payment was to be made against a complete set of clean "on board" bills of lading evidencing that freight had been paid. After part of the consignment of sugar had been loaded, a fire broke out on the ship, as a result of which 200 tons of sugar were damaged and had to be discharged. The remainder of the consignment was loaded and carried to its destination. The sellers tendered two bills of lading to the buyers. The first was in respect to the 200 tons of sugar that had been lost and the second was in respect to the balance of the consignment. The first bill in its printed clauses acknowledged shipment of the goods in apparent good order and condition. In addition, however, it bore a typewritten note stating that the cargo covered by the bill had been discharged because it had been damaged by fire and/or water. The second bill was taken up and paid for by the buyers, but the first bill was rejected by them on the ground that it was not a clean bill of lading. The sellers claimed that the typewritten note did

---

[45] Affirmed by the Court of Appeal, Civil Division, All England Law Reports, vol. 1980, pt. 1, p. 501 (1980). The statement of facts is from the appellate report.

not prevent it from being a clean bill of lading and that they were entitled to be paid the price of the 200 tons of sugar that had been lost.

Judge Donaldson

The parties to this dispute are household names in the world trade in sugar. Both are based in New York. The sugar concerned was to be shipped from Kandla in India to Iran. The reason why the matter comes to the English Commercial Court is that the contract incorporated the rule of the Refined Sugar Association and provided for arbitration in London.

….The question at issue is, of course, who is to stand the loss in respect of the 200 tons of sugar which was destroyed by or as a consequence of the fire? The board of appeal of the Refined Sugar Association has held that the loss must fall on the sellers. The sellers now appeal.

***

The Sellers' Claim to the Price

Under the terms of the contract, the sellers are entitled to be paid the price on tender of "clean 'On Board' bills of lading evidencing freight having been paid." Counsel for the sellers submitted that this bill of lading qualified for this description, notwithstanding the notation recording that the sugar had been discharged fire damaged.…In his submission, the sellers, having tendered this bill of lading, were entitled to be paid the price. Alternatively, the sugar was at the risk of the buyers when it was destroyed and, that being so, the sellers were entitled to be paid the price whether or not they tendered this or any other bill of lading.

Counsel for the buyers challenged these submissions root and branch. In his submission, there were no less than eight reasons why the sellers were not entitled to be paid the price. It is, of course, for the sellers to make out their case, but in all the circumstances, it is convenient to consider whether they have done so in the context of counsel's objections.

(a) That the Bill of Lading Was Not "Clean"

(i) The Practical Test

Counsel for the buyers submits that there are two possible tests to be applied, the practical and the legal. The practical test is whether a bill of lading in this form is acceptable to banks generally as being a "clean" bill of lading. Since 1962, virtually all banks have accepted the international rules set out in a document issued by the International Chamber of Commerce entitled *Uniform Customs and Practices for Documentary Credits* ("UCP Rules"). Rule 16 provides as follows:

> A clean shipping document is one which bears no superimposed clause or notation which expressly declares a defective condition of the goods and/or the packaging. Banks will refuse documents bearing such clauses or notations unless the credit expressly states clauses or notations which may be accepted.

This definition fails to specify the time with respect to which the notation speaks. The bill of lading and any notation speak at the date of issue, but they may speak about a state of affairs which then exist or about an earlier state of affairs or both. If the rule refers to notations about the state of affairs at the time of the issue of the bill of lading or, indeed, at any time after shipment of the 200 tons was completed, the bill of lading is not "clean" within the meaning of that word in the rule, for the notation clearly draws attention to the cargo being damaged. If, however, it refers to notations about the state of affairs on completion of shipment, the bill of lading is equally clearly clean for it shows that the goods were in apparent good order and condition on shipment and suggests only that they were damaged after shipment.

Counsel for the buyers draws attention to the fact that this bill of lading was rejected by two different banks. The first rejection was by the sellers' own bank when the bill of lading was tendered by the shippers under the FOB supply contract. The second rejection was by the buyers' subpurchasers bank when it was tendered to them by the buyers without prejudice to the rights of the parties as between sellers and buyers. On these facts, counsel for the buyers invites me to hold that this bill of lading is not a "clean" bill in commercial or practical terms.

Let me consider this "practical" test. The information as to what prompted the banks' action is somewhat sparse….

….There is no contemporary note of why the banks refused to accept the documents, but there is a letter dated March 24, 1976, reading:

> Your draft and documents valued $183,732.00, payment for which was not effected because Bills of Lading showing the following clause Quote "Cargo covered by this Bill of Lading has been discharged at Kandla View damaged by fire and/or water used to extinguish fire for which general average declared" Unquote, whereas credit class of clean (unclaused) Bills of Lading.

It is not uninteresting that it was not the buyers' bank which rejected the documents, but the buyers themselves (by a letter of April 22nd, 1975, referred to in the [arbitration] award). Furthermore, although they gave as a reason the fact that the clause prejudiced their ability to negotiate the documents with their buyers, the letter of 24th March 1976 set out above suggests that the documents were only rejected by the subbuyers' bank some weeks later on May 13th, 1975. However, there may have been more than one rejection.

It is clear that the subbuyers' bank thought that a letter of credit incorporating the UCP rules and calling for "clean" bills of lading was only satisfied if the bills were wholly unclaused. This goes further than the UCP rules justify since they appear to take exception only to a "superimposed clause or notation which expressly declares a defective condition of the goods and/or the packaging," whatever that may mean.

There is, I think, more than one answer to this "practical test" objection. First, the contract…does not provide that the documents shall be such as to satisfy the UCP rules as to "clean" bills of lading.…Furthermore, if there is ambiguity as to the meaning of those rules, that ambiguity should, if possible, be resolved in a way which will result in the rules reflecting the position under general maritime and commercial law. So construed they add nothing to the legal test which I consider hereafter.

Second, the evidence does not disclose that banks generally would reject such a bill of lading as that relating to the 200 tons as not being a "clean" bill of lading or that, if they would do so, it would be for any better reason than that they were applying what they though the UCP rules required.

Third, I am not satisfied that it is right to apply a practical test.…What is really being said here is that the very fact that the buyers and two banks rejected these documents proves that they are not "clean." This is a proposition which I decline to accept.

(ii) The Legal Test

I, therefore, proceed to apply the legal test. As Judge Salmon remarked in *British Imex Industries, Ltd., v. Midland Bank, Ltd.*, a "clean bill of lading" has never been exhaustively defined. I have been referred to a number of textbooks and authorities which support the proposition that a "clean" bill of lading is one in which there is nothing to qualify the admission that the goods were in apparent good order and condition and that the seller has no claim against the goods except in relation to freight. Some clearly regard the relevant time as being that of shipment. Some are silent as to what is the relevant time. None refers expressly to any time subsequent to shipment.

As between the shipowner and the shipper (including those claiming through the shippers as holders of the bill of lading) the crucial time is shipment. The shipowner's prime obligation is to deliver the goods at the contractual destination in the like good order and condition as when shipped. The cleanliness of the bill of lading may give rise to an estoppel and the terms of the bill of lading contract may exempt the shipowner from a breach of this obligation, but everything stems from the state of the goods as shipped. As between seller and CIF or C&F buyer, the property and risk normally pass on the negotiation of the bill of lading, but do so as from shipment. Thus, the fact that the ship and goods have been lost after shipment or that a liability to contribute in general average or salvage has arisen is no reason for refusing to take up and pay for the documents.

In these circumstances, it is not surprising that there appears to be no case in which the courts or the textbook writers have had to consider a bill of lading which records the fate of the goods subsequent to shipment and, indeed, I have never seen or heard of a bill of lading like that in the present case. Nor is it surprising that some of the judgments and textbooks do not in terms say that when reference is made to the condition of the goods what is meant is their condition on shipment.

However, I have no doubt that this is the position. The bill of lading with which I am concerned casts no doubt whatsoever on the condition of the goods at that time and does not assert that at that time the shipowner had any claim whatsoever against the goods. It follows that in my judgment this bill of lading, unusual though it is, passes the legal test of cleanliness.

(b) The Bill of Lading Was Rightly Rejected as Being Unmerchantable

Counsel for the buyers submits that documents tendered under a C & F contract must be merchantable and that, in the context of a bill of lading, this may be a factor of cleanliness or an independent quality which is required. He seeks to support this proposition by reference to *Hansson v. Hamel & Horley, Ltd.* in which Lord Sumner said:

> When documents are to be taken up the buyer is entitled to documents which substantially confer protective rights throughout. He is not buying a litigation, as Lord Trevethin (then Judge A. T. Lawrence) says in the *General Trade Co.'s Case*. These documents have to be handled by banks, they have to be taken up or rejected promptly and without any opportunity for prolonged inquiry, they have to be such as can be re-tendered to subpurchasers, and it is essential that they should so conform to the accustomed shipping documents as to be reasonable and readily fit to pass current in commerce.

I need hardly say that I accept this proposition unreservedly. A tender of documents which, properly read and understood, calls for further enquiry or are such as to invite litigation is clearly a bad tender. But the operative words are "properly read and understood." I fully accept that the clause on this bill of lading makes it unusual, but properly read and understood it calls for no inquiry and it casts no doubt at all on the fact that the goods were shipped in apparent good order and condition or on the protection which anyone is entitled to expect when taking up such a document whether as a purchaser or as a lender on the security of the bill....

The only ground for holding that the bill of lading was not "reasonably and readily fit to pass current in commerce" is that the form is unusual and that two banks and the buyers rejected it. If the buyers wanted bills of lading which were not only "clean," but also in "usual form," they should have contracted accordingly. They did not do so and I am not prepared to hold that the bill was unmerchantable....

Conclusion

For the reasons which I have sought to express, I consider that this was a "clean" bill of lading and that the buyers should have accepted it and paid the price. In reaching this conclusion, I have, regretfully, to disagree with the decision of the board of appeal [of the Refined Sugar Association]. That decision seems to me to have been based solely on considerations of law. Had it been a conclusion based on trade practice and included, for example, a finding that a bill in this form was not acceptable in the trade, my decision would, of course, have been different.

....Accordingly, for the reasons which I have expressed, I answer the questions of law in favor of the sellers.

Order accordingly. Leave to appeal to the Court of Appeal.

Summary: The decision turned on whether the bill of lading here was clean and merchantable. The goods were apparently delivered to the ship in good condition, and then 200 tons of the sugar were destroyed by fire and water. Two bills of lading were then issued, one covering the 200 tons, which noted that this portion of the goods was destroyed, and a second bill of lading covering the balance of the shipment. The second bill of lading was paid without problem, but the buyers refused to pay the first. The court thoroughly examined both a "practical test" and a "legal test" and concluded that the key point of time was when the goods were "shipped" by the seller (loaded on the ship). Since the bill of lading did not note any problems with the goods "when shipped," the document was therefore clean under applicable law, despite the notation.

CHAPTER SIX:

INTELLECTUAL PROPERTY AND GLOBAL COMMERCE

INTRODUCTION

Intellectual property is useful information or knowledge. It is divided into two principal branches: artistic property and industrial property.

Artistic property encompasses artistic, literary, and musical works. These are protected, in most countries, by copyrights and neighboring rights. Industrial property is itself divided into two categories: inventions and trademarks. Inventions include both useful products and useful manufacturing processes. They are mostly protected by patents, petty patents, and inventors' certificates. Trademarks include "true" trademarks, trade names, service marks, collective marks, and certification marks. All of these are markings that identify the ownership rights of manufacturers, merchants, and service establishments. They are protected by trademark laws.

Intellectual property is a creature of national law. International law sets down guidelines for its uniform definition and protection, and it sets up ways that make it easier for owners to acquire rights in different countries. National law—and sometimes regional law—is also important in establishing the rules for assigning and licensing intellectual property.

The realm of information that can be owned, assigned, and licensed can involve either statutory or nonstatutory rights. Statutory rights include copyrights, patents, and trademarks. The latter include know-how, which is also often termed "trade secrets."

I. COPYRIGHTS

A copyright is title to certain pecuniary rights and certain moral rights for a specified period of time. These rights belong to the authors of any work that can be fixed in a tangible medium for the purpose of communication, such as literary, dramatic, musical, or artistic works; sound recordings; films; radio and television broadcasts; and computer programs. A copyright does not give its owner the right to prevent others from using the idea or the knowledge contained in the copyrighted work; it only restricts the use of the work itself.

Pecuniary Rights

Economic or pecuniary rights are legislative or judicial grants of authority that entitle an author to exploit a work for economic gain. Pecuniary rights include the right of reproduction, the right of distribution, and the right of performance.

Right of reproduction is one of the oldest and most common of the copyright rights. The German statute defines it as the "right to make copies of a work, irrespective of the method or number"; the British Copyright Act refers to "reproducing the work in any material form"; the French Copyright Law defines a work reproduction as "the material fixation of a work by any method that permits indirect communication to the public"; and the U.S. Copyright Act refers merely to the making of "copies."

In socialist countries, although a copyright does include the right of reproduction, the right can be exercised effectively only by state agencies. As a consequence, copyright holders have to assign their rights to an agency—commonly their employer—and hope that the agency will promote their copyrighted work.

Distribution rights are neither consistently defined nor consistently granted by one country to another. To understand distribution rights, one has to consider two questions: (1) What is meant by distribution? and (2) When are distribution rights exhausted?

The German Copyright Law defines distribution as "the right to offer to the public, or to place in circulation, the original work or copies of the work." In most countries, once a particular copy of a work has been sold to a public transferee, the author's right to control any subsequent transfers of that particular copy ends. This is known as the "first sale doctrine," or sometimes as the "doctrine of exhaustion."

There are three important limitations to the doctrine of exhaustion:
- The first is that the right only applies to sales. An author who transfers an original or a copy by lending, leasing, or as part of an exhibition retains his/her distribution right as to any subsequent transfer.
- The second limitation is that the doctrine only applies to the right of distribution of that copy. The right to reproduce the original work, as well as other rights (such as performance rights and moral rights), is not affected.
- The third limitation has to do with the author's right to limit rentals of distributed original works and copies. By a widely subscribed-to international agreement, authors are entitled (at least with regard to computer programs and motion pictures) to prohibit commercial rentals of their copyrighted works.

Copyright owners also have a pecuniary right of performance. There are basically two approaches to the granting of this right. One is to grant a general right of performance (*droit de représentation*). The right of performance is the right "to communicate the work to the public by any means whatsoever, including public recitation, lyrical performance, public presentation, public projection, and telecommunication." The second approach is to create several subsidiary rights—in particular, the right to recite a literary work, the right to perform a musical work, the right to make a remote presentation over loudspeakers or similar devices, the right to make a projected image, the right to communicate by visual or sound records, and the right to make radio and television broadcasts.

Regardless of the approach, the right of performance applies only to public performances. Private performances—that is, performances limited to a small group of people "inter-connected personally by mutual relations or by a relationship to the organizer"—do not infringe the copyright. Performance of a play by members of a ladies' club to other members of the same club and playing music in the lobby of a hotel, in a television showroom, in a record shop, over loudspeakers to workers in a factory, and to members of a dance club denote public performances. A private performance would be a reading of a book to one's family or to a small group of close friends.

Case brief 6-1: *Performing Right Society, Limited v. Hickey*

Zambia, High Court at Lusaka, 1978.

Facts: Hickey (H) was an owner of a restaurant where he played music on a record player for the enjoyment of his customers, especially at weekly dances. Chipumza (C), an agent of the Performing Right Society (PRS), visited the restaurant and determined that some of the recordings that H was playing were songs in which PRS owned the copyright. C wrote H informing him of the copyright and demanded payment of a royalty. H, unaware that a copyright could exist in music, thought the letters were some sort of moneymaking racket. After contacting his lawyer, however, H stopped playing the copyrighted music. PRS nevertheless sued, contending it had lost royalties from H's intentional refusal and/or negligence in playing the music. H answered that his playing of the records was done innocently, and that if PRS is entitled to damages, the damages should be limited to the single date stated in PRS's complaint.

Issues: (1) Is lack of knowledge of the existence of a copyright an excuse for infringing a copyright? (2) What is the measure of damages for an innocent infringement?

Holdings: (1) Yes. (2) The profits earned from the infringement.

Law: Where infringement is admitted, but the defendant "was not aware, and had no reasonable grounds for suspecting, that copyright subsisted in the work," a plaintiff is only entitled to the profits earned from the infringement.

Explanation: It is clear that the infringement was done innocently. That being so, PRS is only entitled to the profits earned by H in connection with the infringement.

Order: The parties are to meet with the judge in chambers to determine the amount of profits due PRS.

Moral Rights
============

The personal rights of authors to prohibit others from tampering with their works are called moral rights. These rights are independent of the author's pecuniary rights, and in most states that grant moral rights, they continue to exist in the author even after the pecuniary rights have been transferred—that is, when someone else owns the copyright to the work.

The 1886 Belgian Copyright Law recognized what today are considered the three basic moral rights: (1) the right to object to distortion, mutilation, or modification (*droit de respect*); (2) the right to be recognized as the author (*droit à la paternité*); and (3) the right to control public access to the work (*droit de divulgation*). France and Germany have subsequently added a fourth moral right—the right to correct or retract a work (*droit de repentir, Rückrufsrecht*)—but it is not as universally recognized as the other three.

Moral rights are not recognized in the copyright laws of the United Kingdom, the United States, and most countries that have inherited their law from England. Member states of the Berne Convention are obliged to protect the moral rights of authors. The United Kingdom complies with its international obligations, at least arguably, by claiming that an author can bring an action for libel to complain of distortion, mutilation, or modification and an action for passing off to protect the author's rights of paternity. It also has argued that the right to control public access is inseparable from the economic right of reproduction and therefore is similarly protected. American courts and legal writers have often denied the existence of moral rights in the United States.

The Agreement on Trade-Related Aspects of Intellectual Property Rights (TRIPS Agreement), which is an annex to the Agreement Establishing the World Trade Organization, requires WTO member states to comply with provisions of the Berne Convention (whether or not they are parties to that convention) with one significant exception: Member states are not required to grant moral rights to authors.

Case brief 6-2: *Amar Nath Sehgal v. Union of India*
30 PTC 253 (2005).

Facts: In 1959, the Indian Government commissioned sculptor Mr. Sehgal to design a mural for the walls at Vigyan Bhawan, New Delhi. Completed in 1962 and molded from tons of solid bronze, the mural was 40 feet high and 140 feet long. In 1979, as part of other renovations, the mural was removed in pieces and put in storage. In May 1992, Sehgal was granted an interim injunction restraining defendants from causing further damage to the artwork. He also claims violation of his moral rights, including the mutilation of his work, prejudice to his artistic reputation, and violation of his right to claim authorship by destroying his name from the work.

Issue: Does assigning the copyright and ownership in a work to the government end the artist's moral rights in the work?

Holding: No.

Law: Section 57 of the Indian Copyright Act (1957), based on the Berne Convention Article 6bis, "codifies the concept of moral rights, by protecting an author's right, independent of his copyright, to claim to authorship of his work, and to restrain any distortion, mutilation or modification of the work which could be prejudicial to his honor or reputation."

Explanation: The Delhi High Court awarded rights to the mural to Mr. Sehgal, ordered the mural returned to him, and assessed U.S. $12,000 in damages on the government. The government appealed, but finally settled the matter.

Order: Mr. Sehgal waived his damages claim against the government in exchange for the return of the mural to him.

Works Covered

The object of copyright protection is a work, that is, an intellectual creation in the field of art, literature, music, or science. A work must also be original; that is, an author must infuse creativity into it. Originality, however, should not be confused with the patent law requirements of novelty or merit. The originality must be such that the work is capable of being "fixed in any tangible medium of expression, now known or later developed."

What is protected is not the idea or knowledge contained in the work, but the expression of the work. That is, copyrights do not apply to "ideas, procedures, methods of operations, or mathematical concepts as such." Anyone may use the information or knowledge in the work; they are limited only in the way they may use the original or a particular copy.

Neighboring Rights

Copyright laws generally apply to most works of an artistic, literary, musical, or scientific nature. Technology, however, has a habit of producing new kinds of works that fall outside of existing definitions. Legislatures respond to such changes in different ways. Sometimes they make amendments to existing copyright laws to incorporate these new works. Sometimes, however, new laws, parallel to but separate from the existing copyright statutes, are enacted. The rights created by such laws are often called neighboring rights (from the French *droits voison*) because they are neighbors to, but not part of, an author's copyright.

Formalities

Prior to March 1989, the United States was the only country that required authors to observe certain formalities to obtain a copyright. In particular, all publicly distributed copies of a work had to include a copyright notice consisting of the symbol © or the word "Copyright" or the abbreviation "Copr."; the year the work was first published; and the name of the copyright owner. In addition, two copies of certain kinds of works had to be deposited with the Copyright Office of the U.S. Library of Congress. This is no longer the case in the United States as now a copyright exists at the moment a copyrightable work is produced in a "tangible medium of expression."

Scope

A copyright applies only within the territory of the state granting it. A state will not prevent the making of copies of copyrighted material outside its territory. However, most states will keep unauthorized copies of copyrighted works from being imported into their territory.

Duration

The common rule for the duration of a copyright is that it lasts for 50 years *post mortem auctoris* (i.e., for 50 years following the author's death). Many nations, including the United States, have extended the duration to 70 years following the author's death.

Exceptions to Copyright Protection

Virtually every copyright law describes certain uses of works that do not constitute an infringement of the author's copyright. Copyrighted material can be used lawfully in at least some countries:
- in a court or administrative proceeding or by the police should the material (such as a portrait) be needed to maintain public safety;
- for instructional purposes in schools; in the U.S., "fair use" is allowed.
- for purely private use (except that computer programs may not be copied, regardless of the use involved);
- in brief quotations in scholarly or literary works or in reviews; and
- in extended quotations of newsworthy speeches or political commentaries.

II. PATENTS

A patent is "a statutory privilege granted by the government to inventors, and to others deriving their rights from the inventor, for a fixed period of years, to exclude other persons from manufacturing, using, or selling a patented product or from utilizing a patented method or process." The idea that patents should be granted to reward inventors for advancing the public interest was incorporated in the U.S. Constitution of 1789, where Congress is given the task of promoting "To promote the Progress of Science and useful Arts, by securing for limited Times to Authors and Inventors the exclusive Right to their respective Writings and Discoveries." (from Article I, Sec. 8)

Although a patent is commonly referred to as a monopoly, it is not truly so. The owner of a patent may be prevented from exploiting the grant by other laws (such as national security laws or unfair competition laws) or by contractual agreement. What a patent grants, rather, is the protection of a monopoly for a limited period of time.

Two reasons have been given to justify the granting of patents. Those reasons are (1) that patents are a confirmation of the private property rights of the inventor and (2) that a patent is a grant of a special monopoly to encourage invention and industrial development. Students of business ethics will recognize that a trade-off is deliberately set up by patent grants: the greatest good will result if people and firms are given incentives to innovate by getting a temporary monopoly on a product.

Today, both the private rights of inventors and the public's interest in promoting development continue to be the primary justifications given both in patent acts and by legal writers for the granting of inventors' privileges. In some respects, however, a patent is now viewed as a device for reconciling these two competing interests.

Patents and Other Inventor's Grants

The primary method of protecting and rewarding inventors is the patent. A patent is an exclusive privilege granted to an inventor, for a fixed term, to manufacture, use, and sell a product or to employ a method or a process. Most countries, accordingly, grant three basic kinds of patents:
- Design patents – granted to protect new and original designs of an article of manufacture.
- Plant patents – granted for the creation or discovery of a new and distinct variety of a plant.
- Utility patents – granted for the invention of a new and useful process, machine, article of manufacture, or composition of matter.

Several variations on these basic patents include:
- Confirmation patents – issued for inventions already patented in another country.
- Patents of addition – cover improvements on already patented inventions.
- Precautionary patents – issued for short periods of time to an inventor who has not completely perfected an invention so that he/she will be notified when any other inventors apply for a patent on the same invention and so that he/she will have the opportunity to object to their applications.

A few countries provide protection for lesser inventions, i.e., technical improvements of a minor nature. Developed in Germany and Japan and adopted in Spain and a few other countries, this form of protection is known as a petty patent or an inventor's right in a utility model.

Inventions That Qualify for Patent Protection

An invention:
- is new if no other inventor has obtained a patent for the same invention;
- it involves an inventive step if the "subject matter" of the invention was not "obvious at the time the invention was made to a person having ordinary skill in the art to which said subject matter pertains"; and
- it is capable of industrial application if the product or process is one that can be used in industry or commerce.

Case brief 6-3: *Monsanto Co. v. Coramandal Indag Products, (P) Ltd.*
India, Supreme Court, 1986.

Facts: Monsanto (M) sued Coramandal Indag Products (CIP) for patent infringement. On February 20, 1970, M had patented in India a weed killer that contained "Butachlor" in an emulsifier. Butachlor is the common name for the herbicide 2-Chloro-2, 6-Diethyl-N-(Butoxy-Methyl)-Acetanilide, or CP 53619. Because CIP was marketing a weed killer containing Butachlor, M claimed that its patent was being infringed. CIP countersued to have M's patent revoked on the grounds that M had not invented Butachlor, and that its formula was in the public domain. The facts showed that Dr. John Olin invented Butachlor in 1966 or 1967, and that it was part of the public domain. M also argued that its patent applied to the process of emulsifying Butachlor so that it could be conveniently used as a weed killer. The emulsifying agent, however, was a common product produced in India.

Issue: Had Monsanto invented its weed killer?

Holding: No.

Law: The Patents Act states that a patent may be revoked if the invention is obvious or does not involve any inventive step having regard to what was publicly known or publicly used in India or was published in India before the priority date of the claim. With respect to being publicly known, the only requirement is that a process or product be known to persons in pursuit of such processes or products, either as persons of science or commerce.

Explanation: The International Rice Institute had described Butachlor in its annual report for 1968, and that report had circulated in India. Thus, Butachlor was publicly known before M applied for its patent. The process of emulsification is well known and thus obvious. So, neither Butachlor nor the emulsification process qualifies for patent protection.

Order: Monsanto's patent is revoked.

Determining Qualifications

Questions about the existence or nonexistence of newness, inventive steps, and industrial application may arise during the initial review of an application, during the appeal of a denial, during a revocation or cancellation hearing, or in suits for infringement where the person charged with infringement disputes the validity of the patent.

With regard to the review of an application by a patent office, procedures range from a simple review of the application form to an extensive search of domestic and foreign materials to determine if the product or process is both novel and inventive. In completing an application form, an inventor is uniformly required to disclose sufficient information about the product or process "in such full, clear, concise, and exact terms as to enable any person skilled in the art to which it pertains, or with which it is most clearly connected, to make and use the same."

Inventions Excluded from Patent Protection

Patents may be denied to inventions that do not meet the basic definition of patentability. They may also be denied to inventions that violate basic social policies. The Agreement on Trade-Related Aspects of Intellectual Property Rights allows a WTO member state to deny a patent to an inventor in order "to protect public order or morality" so long as the state also forbids the commercial exploitation of the invention. The TRIPS Agreement also allows WTO member states to deny patents for certain inventions that involve:

- diagnostic, therapeutic, and surgical methods for the treatment of humans and animals;
- plants and animals other than microorganisms (except that member states must provide patent protection or its equivalent for plant varieties); and
- essentially biological processes for the production of plants or animals.

Duration of Patents

The World Trade Organization's Agreement on Trade-Related Aspects of Intellectual Property Rights requires that the term of a patent be no less than 20 years.

Scope of Patents

A patent is valid only within the territory of the state granting it; hence, states cannot prevent the use of patented technology outside their territory. States will, however, stop the importation of goods from countries that infringe a patent.

III.   TRADEMARKS

Merchants and others use five marks to identify themselves and their products:

- A true trademark is "any word, name, symbol, or device or any combination thereof adopted and used by a manufacturer or merchant to identify his goods and distinguish them from those manufactured or sold by others."
- A trade name is the name of the manufacturer rather than the manufacturer's products.
- A service mark is a "mark used in the sale or advertising of services to identify the services of one person and distinguish them from the services of another."
- When trademarks or service marks are used by members of an association, collective, or cooperative organization to identify their products or services to members, they are called collective marks.
- A certification mark is a mark used exclusively by a licensee or franchisee to indicate that a product meets certain standards.

From the perspective of an owner, a trademark is the right to put a product protected by the mark into circulation for the first time. From the viewpoint of a consumer, a trademark serves to:

- designate the origin or source of a product or service,
- indicate a particular standard of quality,
- represent the goodwill of the manufacturer, and
- protect the consumer from confusion.

Acquiring Trademarks

Trademarks are acquired in two ways: (1) by use and (2) by registration. In a few countries, registration is not available. In Canada and the Philippines, a trademark can be registered only if it has already been put into use.

The fact that a trademark cannot be registered does not mean that its owner is without rights. In countries like Panama and Taiwan, a foreign owner of a famous unregistered trademark can oppose registration but cannot sue a local company for infringement. In other countries, only a locally registered owner can protest either registration or infringing use.

In any of the countries that allow an unregistered foreign trademark holder to challenge either a competing registration or an infringing use, the trademark in question must be well known. In addition to the objections that can be raised by famous trademark holders, most countries allow a local user of a mark to object to its registration by another individual—even if the mark is not famous—so long as the opponent's local use began before that of the applicant.

A few states will register a trademark to the first person to apply for it, regardless. Thus, prior users are denied the right to challenge the application or to later seek cancellation of the registration.

Registration

One registers a trademark to publicly notify other potential users of one's claim to a mark. The registration process commonly begins with an examination done by an official in the Trademark Office to determine a mark's suitability for registration.

Registration Criteria

The common statutory definitional criterion that appears in all trademark laws is distinctiveness. This means that a mark must possess a unique design that functions to distinguish the product on which it is used from other similar products. To be registered, a trademark must (1) not infringe on another mark and (2) be distinctive.

Case brief 6-4: *Experience Hendrix, L.L.C. v. Hammerton*
World Intellectual Property Organization Arbitration and Mediation Center, 2000.

Facts: Hammerton is a domain name speculator who registered the domain name jimihendrix.com. He advertised to sell the name for $1 million. Experience Hendrix (EH) is the owner of all of the music, name, image, and recording rights associated with the deceased Jimi Hendrix, including the domain name jimi-hendrix.com and several trademarks and service marks using the name Jimi Hendrix. It seeks to have Hammerton's registration revoked.

Issue: Should Hammerton's registration of the domain name jimihendrix.com be revoked?

Holding: Yes.

Law: The Domain Name Registration Policy, which all registrants agree to observe, provides that a domain name registrant must submit to an administrative proceeding to determine ownership if a complainant can show (1) the domain name holder's domain name is identical or confusingly similar to a trademark or service mark in which the complainant has rights; (2) the domain name holder has no rights or legitimate interests in respect of the domain name; and (3) the domain name of the domain name holder has been registered and is being used in bad faith.

Explanation: (1) The name is identical to EH's registered trademark and service names. (2) Hammerton registered the name primarily with the expectation of reselling it. (3) Hammerton did so in bad faith, having registered many other names of well known artists (e.g., Elvis Presley, Mick Jagger, etc.).

Order: Registration revoked.

Refusing Registration

The statutory grounds for refusing a trademark vary from country to country. For example, a mark or name will be denied in the United States if it:

- does not function as a trademark to identify the goods or services as coming from a particular source (for example, the matter applied for is merely ornamentation);
- is immoral, deceptive, or scandalous;
- may disparage or falsely suggest a connection with persons, institutions, beliefs, or national symbols, or bring them into contempt or disrepute;
- consists of or simulates the flag or coat of arms or other insignia of the United States, or a state or municipality, or any foreign nation;
- is the name, portrait, or signature of a particular living individual, unless he has given written consent; or is the name, signature, or portrait of a deceased President of the United States during the lifetime of his widow, unless she has given her consent;
- so resembles a mark already registered in the Patent and Trademark Office as to be likely, when applied to the goods of the applicant, to cause confusion, or to cause mistake, or to deceive;
- is merely deceptive or deceptively misdescriptive of the goods or services;
- is primarily geographically descriptive or deceptively misdescriptive of the goods or services of the applicant; or
- is primarily merely a surname.

Registration Review

Once a Trademark Office official determines that a mark is suitable for registration, the mark will be published in the office's official gazette. Opponents to the registration then have a period of time—typically 30 to 90 days—in which to oppose the registration or to ask for an extension to do so. An opposition hearing is then held before a review board of the Trademark Office. If no opposition is filed or if the review board rules in favor of the applicant, a registration will issue.

The Term of Registered Trademarks

The Agreement on Trade-Related Aspects of Intellectual Property Rights (TRIPS) requires WTO member states to protect trademarks for a term of at least seven years. Additionally, it provides that trademarks are to be indefinitely renewable.

Usage Requirements

After a trademark is registered, many countries require the holder to present proof, upon the renewal of registration, that the mark was actually used within the country during the prior term. A few countries require the trademark owner to present interim proof of use before the term expires.

In addition to requiring the user to prove use at the time of renewal, many countries allow third parties to bring actions to cancel the trademark if it has not been used for some specified period of time. The TRIPS Agreement now sets this period of time at no less than three years. Challenges for nonuse are uncommon. Many trademark owners have a policy of never initiating a nonuse action against others for fear of retaliatory actions against their own unused marks. Similarly, challenges against new registrants attempting to file marks that are similar or identical to marks already in use are equally uncommon.

Not all countries have a user requirement. A few, such as Canada and the United States, make it difficult for challengers to establish nonuse by additionally requiring them to prove that the owner intentionally abandoned the use of a trademark.

IV.   KNOW-HOW

Know-how is practical expertise acquired from study, training, and experience. It has been defined as factual knowledge, not capable of separate description but that, when used in an accumulated form, after being acquired as a result of trial and error, gives to the one acquiring it an ability to produce something that he/she otherwise would not have known to produce with the same accuracy or precision found necessary for commercial success.

Unlike other forms of intellectual property, know-how is generally not protected by specific statutory enactments. It is protected, rather, by contract, tort, and other basic legal principles. When specific information or know-how is kept secret, it is often called trade secrets and protected in some countries by trade secrecy laws.

The TRIPS Agreement requires WTO member states to protect what the agreement calls "undisclosed information." Natural and legal persons must be given the legal means to prevent information from being disclosed to, acquired by, or used by others without their consent in a manner contrary to honest commercial practice.

The owner of know-how may prevent an assignee, licensee, or employee from disclosing secret know-how to third parties and may require these same people to pay for the training or assistance or use of the know-how they acquire from the owner.

V.   INTERNATIONAL INTELLECTUAL PROPERTY ORGANIZATIONS

Two main international organizations take an active role in defining and protecting international intellectual property rights: the World Intellectual Property Organization (WIPO) and the Council for Trade-Related Aspects of Intellectual Property Rights (TRIPS Council) of the World Trade Organization.

World Intellectual Property Organization (WIPO)

WIPO is responsible for administering the Paris and Berne Conventions and, generally, promoting intellectual property rights. WIPO is also a specialized agency of the United Nations.

WIPO's promotional activities include the sponsoring and hosting of conferences for the development of new intellectual property rights agreements. One of WIPO's more important tasks is to facilitate the transfer of technology, especially to and among developing countries. Another responsibility taken on by WIPO is that of resolving Internet domain disputes.

Since 1994, the WIPO Arbitration and Mediation Center has offered Alternative Dispute Resolution (ADR) options for the resolution of international commercial disputes between private parties. Developed by leading experts in cross-border dispute settlement, the procedures offered by the center are widely used to resolve disputes involving technology, entertainment, and other intellectual property issues.

Council for Trade-Related Aspects of Intellectual Property Rights –

The council is charged with overseeing the operation of the Agreement on Trade-Related Aspects of Intellectual Property Rights. The council is also responsible for monitoring WTO member state compliance with the Agreement on TRIPS, for helping members consult with each other on trade-related aspects of intellectual property rights, and for assisting members in settling disputes. The council consults with WIPO and cooperates with WIPO's constituent bodies.

VI.   INTELLECTUAL PROPERTY TREATIES

Intellectual property rights are protected and regulated internationally by both bilateral treaties and multilateral conventions. Bilateral treaties were the original means of preventing illegal copying, and they were once quite commonplace. Today, most bilateral intellectual property treaties are used by states that are not parties to the multilateral conventions.

Multilateral treaties nowadays regulate most matters relating to intellectual property rights. These treaties generally cover industrial property or artistic property, but not both together. Moreover, patents, petty patents, and trademarks are commonly dealt with in a single treaty, while copyrights are dealt with separately.

Comprehensive Agreements – The principal comprehensive agreement establishing general intellectual property obligations for most of the world's states is the Agreement on Trade-Related Aspects of Intellectual Property Rights.

Agreement on Trade-Related Aspects of Intellectual Property Rights (TRIPS Agreement)

The purpose of the TRIPS Agreement is to create a multilateral and comprehensive set of rights and obligations governing the international trade in intellectual property. As a consequence, the agreement establishes a common minimum of protection for intellectual property rights applicable within all the WTO member states. It does this in five ways:
- It requires WTO members to observe the substantive provisions of the most important existing multilateral intellectual property treaties: Paris Convention, Berne Convention, Rome Convention, and the IPIC Treaty.
- The substantive provisions of the TRIPS Agreement create obligations that are meant to "fill in the gaps" in the other international intellectual property conventions.
- The TRIPS Agreement establishes criteria for the effective and appropriate enforcement of intellectual property rights and for the prevention and settlement of disputes between the governments of the WTO member states.
- To encourage the widest possible adoption and application of the common rules and obligations set out in the TRIPS Agreement, the agreement establishes transitional arrangements that give more time to developing member states and to member states in transition from a centrally planned economy to a free market economy to comply, and even more time to those that are the least developed.
- The TRIPS Agreement extends the basic principles of the General Agreement on Tariffs and Trade (GATT) to the field of international intellectual property rights. The national treatment principle requires each member state to extend to nationals of other members treatment no less favorable than that which it gives its own nationals regarding protection of intellectual property. The transparency principle requires member states to publish and notify the Council for TRIPS of all relevant laws, regulations, and the like and to respond to requests from other members for information.

The TRIPS Agreement includes a provision requiring most-favored-nation treatment, under which, "any advantage, favor, privilege, or immunity granted by a member to the nationals of any other country [whether or not it is a WTO member] shall be accorded immediately and unconditionally to the nationals of all other members."

Artistic Property Agreements – The main international agreements dealing with artistic property are the Berne Convention for the Protection of Literary and Artistic Works; the International Convention for the Protection of Performers, Producers of Phonograms, and Broadcasting Organizations; the Patent Cooperation Treaty; the Satellite Transmission Convention; and the WIPO Copyright Treaty.

Berne Convention

Adopted in Paris in 1886, the Berne Convention for the Protection of Literary and Artistic Works (Berne Convention) establishes a "union" of states that is responsible for protecting artistic rights. Four basic principles underlie the members' obligations:
- The principle of national treatment requires each member state to extend to nationals of other member states treatment no less favorable than that which it gives its own nationals.
- Nonconditional protection is the requirement that member states must provide protection without any formalities.
- The principle of protection independent of protection in the country of origin allows authors who are nationals of nonmember states to obtain protection within the Berne Union by publishing their works in a member state.
- The principle of common rules establishes minimum standards for granting copyrights common to all member states.

Rome Convention

The International Convention for the Protection of Performers, Producers of Phonograms, and Broadcasting Organizations (Rome Convention) protects artists from the unauthorized recording of their original performances and from the use of authorized recordings for a purpose other than that to which the artist consented. Producers of phonograms are protected from the direct or indirect reproduction of their works.

Broadcasters are protected from the unauthorized recording, rebroadcasting, and use of their broadcasts. The Rome Convention also provides that a broadcaster making a public communication or broadcast of an authorized phonogram is required to pay the producer or the artist, or both, a single equitable payment.

Phonogram Piracy Convention

The Convention for the Protection of Producers of Phonograms Against Unauthorized Duplication of Their Phonograms provides that member states must protect producers of phonograms from the unauthorized reproduction and importation of their works for a period of not less than 20 years.

Satellite Transmission Convention

The Convention Relating to the Distribution of Program-Carrying Signals Transmitted by Satellite requires member states to take "adequate measures" to prevent the unauthorized distribution in or from their territory of any program-carrying signal transmitted by satellite.

WIPO Copyright Treaty

The World Intellectual Property Organization Copyright Treaty was adopted for the purpose of extending the provisions of the Berne Convention to computer programs and databases and protecting copyright ownership information embedded in programs and databases.

Industrial Property Agreements –

The principal international conventions concerned with industrial property are the International Convention for the Protection of Industrial Property, the Treaty on Intellectual Property in Respect of Integrated Circuits, the Madrid Agreement for the Repression of False or Deceptive Indications of Sources of Goods, the Patent Cooperation Treaty, and the Trademark Law Treaty.

Paris Convention

Drafted in 1880, the International Convention for the Protection of Industrial Property (Paris Convention) establishes a "union" of states responsible for protecting industrial property rights. Among the members' duties is the obligation to participate in regular revisions. Three basic principles are incorporated in the Paris Convention:
- National treatment is the requirement that each member state must grant the same protection to the nationals of other states that it grants to its own nationals.
- Right of priority gives an applicant who has filed for protection in one member country a grace period of 12 months in which to file in another member state, which then must treat the application as if it were filed on the same day as the original application.
- The principle of common rules sets minimum standards for the creation of intellectual property rights.

Patent Cooperation Treaty

The Patent Cooperation Treaty establishes a mechanism for making an international application whose effect in each member state is the same as the filing for a national patent. The goal of the treaty is the elimination of unnecessary repetition by both patent offices and applicants.

Agreement on Sources of Goods

The Madrid Agreement for the Repression of False or Deceptive Indications of Sources of Goods requires its members to either deny importation to or confiscate at the time of importation any goods bearing false or deceptive indications about their source.

Trademark Law Treaty

The Trademark Law Treaty is meant to simplify both national and regional trademark registration systems by establishing common minimum rules.

VII. THE INTERNATIONAL TRANSFER OF INTELLECTUAL PROPERTY

There are five ways in which intellectual property rights are transferred from one country to another:
- the owner may work the property rights abroad,
- the owner may transfer or assign the rights to another,
- the owner may license another to work them,

- the owner may establish a franchise, or
- a government may grant a compulsory license so that a third party may exploit them.

A license is a nonexclusive revocable privilege that allows a licensee to use a licensor's property. A license is created by contract, and standard contractual rules are used to interpret it. A license allows a licensee to use a property for the licensee's own purposes. Depending on the licensing agreement, the licensee may use the property as a component in its own products, it may sell the property or the products derived from it under the licensor's name, or it may do the same thing under its own name. Sometimes the licensee may even sell the property, or the products derived from it, in direct competition with the licensor.

A franchise is a specialized license that requires a franchisee to work the property under the supervision and control of a franchisor. A franchisee has more limited rights. It is regarded as a unit or element of the franchisor's business. A distributorship franchise exists when a manufacturer licenses a dealer to sell its products. A chain-style business franchise is an arrangement in which a franchisee operates under a franchisor's trade name and is identified as part of the franchisor's business chain. A manufacturing or processing plant franchise comes about when a franchisor provides the franchisee with the formula or the essential ingredients to make a particular product. The franchisee then wholesales or retails the product according to the standards established by the franchisor.

If the owner of intellectual property (in particular, patents or copyrights) refuses to work the property in the country within a certain period of time, a third party may apply for a compulsory license. The government issues such a license without the consent of the owner, so it is not subject to the same rules that apply to licensing and franchising.

Licensing Regulations

Grants of patents, trademarks, and copyrights create monopolies. In free-market countries, these grants run contrary to unfair competition laws. In centrally planned economies, they run contrary to the notion of state ownership of the means of production. To balance the interests of consumers in free-market countries and the interests of the state in planned-economy countries with the rights of intellectual property owners, most countries treat intellectual property rights as special exceptions to their general laws prohibiting monopolies. As such, the rights held by patent, trademark, and copyright owners are strictly construed and limited to the narrow confines of the grant.

Licensing arrangements involving statutory grants must, accordingly, be limited to the rights contained in the grant. Any attempt to go beyond the scope of the grant is a misuse of the grant and is either without effect or illegal.

Nonstatutory grants do not qualify for the special exceptions granted to patents, trademarks, and copyrights. As such, any licensing of these rights has to comply with the appropriate unfair competition laws.

The propriety of states adopting rules to regulate the anticompetitive aspects of intellectual property licenses is now specifically recognized in international law. In developing countries, anticompetition rules are commonly found in transfer-of-technology codes. In the developed free-market countries they are found in long-standing antimonopoly legislation. The U.S. Sherman Antitrust Act provides:
- Every contract, combination in the form of trust or otherwise, or conspiracy, in restraint of trade or commerce among the several states, or with foreign nations, is hereby declared to be illegal.
- Every person who shall monopolize, or attempt to monopolize, or combine or conspire with any other person or persons, to monopolize any part of the trade or commerce among the several states, or with foreign nations, shall be deemed guilty of a felony.

Court-developed "rule of reason" establishes limits to the prohibitions. It requires courts to consider the overall impact of the particular agreement on competition within the relevant market. Courts, accordingly, must identify the precompetitive effects of the agreement and then weigh them against its anticompetitive effects.

The EC Treaty provisions contain an express exemption (Article 81(3)) that allows the European Commission to authorize arrangements that would otherwise violate the general prohibitions, either through block grants or on a case-by-case basis. The commission may do so when the overall effect of a challenged activity is one that "contributes to improving the production or distribution of goods, or to promoting technical or economic progress, while allowing consumers a fair share of the resulting benefit."

Territorial Restrictions – In most countries, a restriction on the territorial scope granted in the license of a statutory right is treated as a normal incidence of that right. Such restrictions, however, apply only to the immediate licensee. Attempts to limit the territory in which an article can be traded after it has left the hands of the licensee are universally condemned. The rationale underlying this is a doctrine known as exhaustion of rights.

Although the exhaustion-of-rights doctrine first appeared as a court-made rule in the United States and Germany, the European Court of Justice has given the doctrine its broadest application and its most careful analysis. This is because the EU is confronted with the problem of rationalizing the separate intellectual property laws of its member states with its own express goal of establishing the free movement of goods among those states.

The European Court of Justice has devised another doctrine, related to the doctrine of exhaustion of rights, to promote the free movement of goods at the expense of trademark owners. This is the common origin doctrine. Although there is some authority for the proposition that the EU's common origin doctrine may apply to other forms of intellectual property, there are several good arguments for believing that it applies only to trademarks.

It is important to note that both the exhaustion-of-rights doctrine and the common origin doctrine apply only in cases involving the movement of goods between the member states of the EU. When protected products are manufactured outside the EU, they may not be imported into the EU without the express consent of the EU intellectual property owner.

U.S. courts have faced the problem of parallel imports of protected products that have been lawfully manufactured outside the United States—a problem known in the United States as gray marketing.

Case brief 9-5: *L'Oréal v. eBay*

Court of Justice of the European Union, July 2011.

Facts: The plaintiff, L'Oréal, is suing the defendant eBay, seeking to hold it partially responsible for trademark infringement by the users of eBay's online marketplace. The defendant eBay is the operator of an online marketplace that facilitates the exchange of goods on the Internet by individuals through a search engine and a secure payment system, covering a widespread geographical area. The plaintiff is a global producer with a large product range, considerable trademark protection, and a worldwide reputation for some of its trademarked cosmetics, perfume, and other products. The plaintiff alleges that counterfeit L'Oréal products have been sold on the defendant's marketplace. Furthermore, the plaintiff has claimed that some of the products exchanged on the marketplace were licensed for sale only in North America and were not meant for sale in the European Economic Area (EEA). The plaintiff is seeking court orders against the defendant in order to stop individual sellers on the electronic marketplace from distributing trademarked products and to better protect its trademarks in the future.

Issue: When protected products are manufactured outside the EU, may they be imported into the EU without the express consent of the EU intellectual property owner?

Holding: No.

Law / Explanation: The decision of the European Union Court of Justice in this case will affect not only the defendant, eBay, but all other online auction sites. eBay and other online auction sites can be held liable for advertisements by users of their sites if the ads do not clearly show that the offered goods do not originate from the trademark owner. An online provider will also need to put better monitoring systems in place regarding the products sold on its site, as well as the geographical location of individual buyers and sellers, and remove trademarked keywords from their advertising, or face severe legal consequences. This court decision will not only tighten restrictions of online marketplaces within the European Union, but all over the world.

Order: Left the determination to national courts after further facts have been presented and developed.

Export Restrictions – Export restrictions limit, partially or entirely, the rights of a licensee to export goods from the territory where the licensee or its production facilities are located.

In some countries, restrictions will be tolerated if they limit exports to a country where (1) the licensor owns intellectual property rights and (2) the local laws allow the licensor to restrict foreign imports. In other countries, export restrictions will be tolerated if the limitation applies to a territory where (1) the licensor is manufacturing or distributing the restricted goods or (2) the licensor has granted an exclusive license to a third party to manufacture or distribute the goods.

In the United States, export restriction agreements between competitors (so-called horizontal competition agreements) have been held to be *per se* violations of the Sherman Antitrust Act. On the other hand, agreements between a seller and a buyer (vertical competition agreements) are not bad per se and will be tested by a rule of reason.

In the EU, export restriction agreements that affect the movement of goods between EU member states violate the Union's European Community Treaty's unfair competition article (Article 81), whether they are reasonable or not. Restrictions on exports to countries outside the EU are prohibited only if they can be shown to have a direct effect on the member states.

Cartels – A cartel is an agreement between several business enterprises that is designed, among other things, to allocate markets, to fix prices, to promote the exchange of knowledge resulting from technical and scientific research, to exchange patent rights, or to standardize products.

A cross-licensing agreement is an arrangement between two parties to exchange licenses; that is, each party is both a licensor and a licensee. A patent pool is an agreement among several owners of related technology to "pool" their patents and other related technology. A multiple licensing agreement involves the licensing of technology to a number of recipients by a single licensor.

The EU forbids cartel-type arrangements when they have as their purpose or effect the prevention, restriction, or distortion of competition between EU member states. Such arrangements may include agreements to allocate markets between competitors, horizontal price fixing, and patent pools.

Agreements to cross-license improvements and new applications are valid for up to seven years so long as licensees are not precluded from using their own improvements or licensing them to third parties. On the other hand, cross-licensing agreements that involve any territorial restraint with respect to the manufacture, use, or marketing of goods are invalid.

In the United States, cross-licensing and patent pooling are not unlawful unless they are used to divide up territories among competitors, exclude others from competing, or otherwise restrain trade. Moreover, a rule known as the bottleneck principle may require the participants in an industry-wide patent exchange to grant reasonable access to any firm wishing to compete so that no firm will be disadvantaged and competition will not be impaired. Price-fixing and division of markets between competitors, however, are held illegal *per se* in both the United States and the EU. Japan provides much broader exemptions to its basic prohibition against cartels. Likewise, manufacturers' rationalization cartels aimed at improving technology, productivity, product quality, cost reduction, or any similar entrepreneurial rationalization scheme are also legal.

Exclusive Licenses – Laws in several countries expressly state that the grant of a patent, trademark, or copyright gives the owner the right to confer either an exclusive license or a nonexclusive license. In most other countries, both the government and the courts have held that such arrangements are implicitly proper.

A licensee may receive sole rights (to the exclusion of all others, including the licensor), exclusive rights (preventing everyone except the licensor from competing), or nonexclusive rights (which allow the licensor to grant other licenses).

Sales and Distribution Arrangements – A sales or distribution arrangement limits a licensee's freedom to organize its distribution system independently of the licensor. There are three basic approaches to the regulation of these agreements. One group of developing countries prohibits any interference by the licensor in the licensee's distribution system. A second group of developing and developed countries prohibits only those provisions that give the licensor exclusive distribution rights. Finally, a third group of generally developed countries only prohibit those exclusive sales arrangements that tend to allocate or monopolize markets.

Price-Fixing – A price-fixing clause requires a licensee to sell products at a price specified by the licensor. It may specify either maximum or minimum prices. It may be restricted to the technology or goods being licensed, or it may cover other products as well. It may apply only to the price charged by the licensee, or it may extend to the prices charged by retailers who purchase the goods from a wholesaler-licensee. Price-fixing also arises in the context of cartels, particularly cross-licensing and patent pools. Most developed and developing countries prohibit all forms of price-fixing.

Noncompetition Clauses – Noncompetition clauses forbid a licensee from entering into agreements to acquire or distribute technologies or products that compete with ones furnished or designated by the licensor. In general, noncompetition clauses are prohibited in all countries.

Direct prohibitions may include an understanding that the licensee is not to manufacture or sell competing technologies, or that the licensee is to terminate the use of particular technologies or terminate the manufacture and distribution of particular products. Indirect prohibitions may require the licensee not to cooperate with a competing business or not to pay higher royalties for competing products.

Challenges to Validity – No-challenge clauses forbid a licensee from challenging the validity of the statutory right granted by the licensor. The purpose of these clauses is to ensure that a licensee will comply with the agreed-to restrictions and payment obligations. Only a few countries permit no-challenge clauses generally. Most consider such a clause in a patent or copyright license to be a restrictive trade practice. No-challenge clauses in trademark licenses are regarded in the same negative way by developing and some developed countries. The United States, however, does not regard a no-contest clause in a trademark license as violating either its trademark laws or its anti-trust laws.

Tying Clauses – A tying clause is a provision that requires a licensee to acquire or use, separately from the technology wanted, additional goods (such as raw materials, intermediate products, machines, or additional technology) or designated personnel either from the licensor or from a source named by the licensor. In other words, the acquisition of these additional goods or services is a prerequisite to obtaining the technology license. In general, tying clauses are illegal in virtually every country. Most countries, however, provide for exemptions in varying degrees.

Quantity and Field-of-Use Restrictions – Countries regulate licensing arrangements with quantity and field-of-use restrictions in three ways.
- Developing countries generally regard limitations on the quantity of goods that may or must be produced, or limits on the fields in which goods may be used or sold, as illegal.
- A second group of countries, including Japan, the European Community, the United States, and most countries in the developed world, regard quantity and field-of-use restrictions as implicit elements in the statutory rights of a licensor.
- A third approach to quantity and field-of-use restrictions is found in Germany. There, restrictions on both statutory and nonstatutory rights—including limitations on the use of know-how and trade secrets—are expressly allowed.

Restrictions on Research and Development – Restrictions on research and development may relate to two different kinds of activities: (1) the research, adaptation, and improvement of the transferred technology or (2) the research and development of competing technologies. Both of these are condemned in almost all countries.

Quality Controls – Requirements that a licensor meet certain quality standards or comply with certain quality controls imposed by the licensor are almost uniformly accepted in all countries. Quality control clauses are justified where the trademark of the licensor is being applied to a product manufactured and/or distributed by the licensee. They are also justified when they are imposed for the purpose of avoiding product liability.

Quality control clauses are prohibited where they are used as a means of improperly tying in other products or services, where they seek to make the licensee dependent on the licensor, or where they seek to allocate trade territories.

Grant-Back Provisions – A grant-back provision requires a technology recipient to transfer back to the supplier any improvements, inventions, or special know-how that it acquires while using the technology. Such a provision may be unilateral or reciprocal, exclusive or nonexclusive.

A unilateral grant-back provision requires one of the parties—usually the licensee—to transfer back new knowledge, whereas a reciprocal provision requires both to do so. Sometimes a reciprocity agreement will require both parties to exchange their developments but at other times only one party will be required to transfer new knowledge, while the other will be required merely to pay adequate compensation. An exclusive grant-back provision requires one of the parties—usually the licensee—to transfer any rights in the new development to the other party. A nonexclusive provision allows the parties to share these rights.

Most countries prohibit grant-back provisions that unilaterally require the licensee to transfer exclusive rights to the licensor. In contrast, most countries do not prohibit grant-back provisions that are reciprocal and nonexclusive.

Restrictions That Apply After the Expiration of Intellectual Property Rights – Countries generally hold that payment obligations or restrictions based on statutory intellectual property rights must terminate when the statutory right expires. The principal problem that arises in connection with the expiration of statutory rights involves package licenses. Package licensing is the transfer of multiple statutory rights under a single license.

Generally, if the licensing agreement was entered into voluntarily by both sides and the payment obligations do not extend beyond that of the last-to-expire statutory right, these agreements will be enforceable. On the other hand, if the licensee was at an economic disadvantage and given only the option of taking or leaving the arrangement, it will commonly be found to be illegal as a form of statutory misuse.

Concerning restrictions and payment obligations in connection with nonstatutory rights, in particular trade secrets and other secret know-how, there are several different approaches. In Germany, a licensor may not enforce payment obligations or other restrictions once the know-how has lost its secret character or becomes economically worthless or technically outdated. In some developing countries, national legislation prohibits any restriction on the free use of know-how once a reasonable period has lapsed following the transfer of the technology.

In other developing countries, the obligation to pay for the use of secret know-how will cease when it "becomes public knowledge otherwise than through the fault of the licensee." By contrast, in the United States, a licensee's agreement to pay for the use of secret know-how will remain in effect even after the secret becomes public knowledge, so long as the licensee's contractual obligation was "freely undertaken in arm's length negotiations."

Restrictions That Apply After the Expiration of the Licensing Agreement – Licensing agreements may impose obligations on the licensee that continue even after the expiration of the license.

The national regulations that apply to these kinds of arrangements can be categorized into three groups. One group of countries allows licensors to impose most types of reasonable restrictions. The second group of countries generally takes the same approach as the countries in the first group, except that they hold that a former licensee has a right to continue to use any acquired know-how so long as the licensee pays reasonable compensation. The third group of countries holds that a former licensee is free to use or dispose of the statutory property rights or secret know-how once the licensing agreement terminates.

VIII.   COMPULSORY LICENSES

Compulsory licenses arise when the owner of intellectual property refuses or is unable to work the property in a particular country within a certain period of time. In such a case, a third party may apply for a compulsory license, which will be issued by the government without the consent of the owner.

Patents – The International Convention for the Protection of Industrial Property (the Paris Convention) recognizes the right of countries to "grant compulsory licenses to prevent abuses of the exclusive rights conferred by the patent."

The WTO's Agreement on Trade-Related Aspects of Intellectual Property Rights (TRIPS) similarly allows its member countries to grant "use of the subject matter of a patent without the authorization of the right holder," provided that
- a proposed user is unable to enter into a licensing arrangement with the patent holder on commercially reasonable terms or there is a national emergency or other circumstance of extreme urgency.
- the license is non-exclusive.
- the license is non-assignable.
- the use is primarily in the domestic market.
- the patent owner is paid adequate remuneration.

Copyrights – Two types of compulsory licensing apply to copyrights. A statutory copyright license authorizes third parties to use a copyrighted work in exchange for a fee, which is fixed either in the legislation itself or by a public or private agency authorized to fix, collect, and distribute license fees.

A compulsory copyright license compels a copyright owner to grant a license, but it allows the owner to negotiate the terms of the license. The Berne Convention for the Protection of Literary and Artistic Works recognizes the right of countries to impose compulsory licenses for broadcasting and recording.

The Congressional Research Service published a useful document in 2015 that discusses Intellectual Property and International Trade.

https://crsreports.congress.gov/product/pdf/RL/RL34292/20

Case 6 – 1

Patagonia, Inc. and Patagonia Provisions, Inc. v. Anheuser Busch (2020)
U.S. Federal District Court, Middle District of California
2020 U.S. Dist. LEXIS 250122

Background

This action arises out of a trademark dispute between Patagonia and Anheuser-Busch regarding use of the PATAGONIA mark. Plaintiffs allege that their PATAGONIA brand and P-6 logo have become among the most identifiable brands in the world. In 2012, Plaintiff Patagonia Provisions, Inc., a related company, began developing, marketing and selling socially and environmentally responsible food items under the PATAGONIA PROVISIONS® mark (Registration No. 4,168,329), including beer, buffalo jerky, salmon, fruit and almond bars, and soup mixes.

Defendant Anheuser-Busch (AB) is a global producer of beer and other products and services under a multitude of brands. Among its brands is Anheuser-Busch's PATAGONIA beer, which it sells under the business name Patagonia Brewing Company. Anheuser-Busch purports to own the registered trademark PATAGONIA (Registration No. 4,226,102) for use in connection with beer (having purchased the rights to Patagonia beer from Warsteiner Importers Agency, Inc. in 2012).

Plaintiffs allege that Anheuser-Busch, in launching its PATAGONIA beer, has deliberately misappropriated the goodwill that Plaintiffs have cultivated in their PATAGONIA brand. Plaintiffs allege that Anheuser-Busch has created a logo that is strikingly similar to Patagonia, Inc.'s P-6 logo. Plaintiffs further allege that Anheuser-Busch's environmental conservation initiative is a clear attempt to copy Plaintiffs' famous brand identity.

Each party now moves for partial summary judgment.

A.   Undisputed Facts

Patagonia, Inc. designs and sells outdoor apparel, sportswear, and related products. Patagonia Provisions, Inc. is a related company founded in 2012 that offers various food items, such as buffalo jerky and soups. Patagonia, Inc. was named after the famous Patagonia region in South America that inspired its founders. Patagonia, Inc.'s label is inspired by a silhouette of the peaks of the Mt. Fitz Roy skyline, located in the Patagonia region in South America.

Intent to Use (ITU) and Assignment of Mark

Warsteiner Importers Agency, Inc. filed an intent-to-use application to Register PATAGONIA for beer on June 8, 2006, based on its plan to sell beer in the United States imported from its brewery in Argentina. In 2007, the United States Patent and Trademark Office ("PTO") issued a Notice which said that Warsteiner's mark was entitled to registration, and published the mark in "the Official Gazette" to see if anyone would oppose registration of the mark. Plaintiffs did not file an opposition to the PATAGONIA application.

Some time after the ITU application, Warsteiner indicated to the PTO that it did not plan to import and sell beer in the U.S. using the Patagonia trademark. Accordingly, it filed several extensions with the US PTO in connection with its 2006 application. Warsteiner filed its final request for an extension of time on January 5, 2012, setting the deadline on July 21, 2012. AB and Warsteiner entered into a Purchase Agreement effective March 16, 2012, relating to the PATAGONIA mark for beer in the U.S.

A statement of use (SOU) was then filed by AB on July 17, 2012, stating that "The mark was first used by the applicant, or the applicant's related company, licensee, or predecessor in interest at least as early as 07/16/2012, and first used in commerce at least as early as 07/16/2012, and is now in use in such commerce."

On October 16, 2012, the PTO issued the trademark registration for PATAGONIA for beer in Warsteiner's name. Warsteiner then assigned the trademark to AB.

Continuous Use

Between 2012 and 2015, AB made sporadic sales of PATAGONIA beer to retailers in Hawaii . . . The parties do not dispute that between March 20, 2015, and June 19, 2015, AB sold 10 cases of PATAGONIA beer to retailers in Hawaii.

Between May 2016, after the World Beer Cup, and December 31, 2016, there is no evidence of sales by AB of PATAGONIA beer. Between January 1, 2018, and September 5, 2018, there is no evidence of sales by AB of PATAGONIA beer.

On October 5, 2018, Mr. Davidovits submitted a declaration to the PTO swearing on AB's behalf that the PATAGONIA "mark has been continuously used in commerce for five (5) consecutive years after the date of registration . . . and is still in use in commerce on or in connection with all goods/all services . . . listed in the existing registration . . ." Prior to October 5, 2018, the PTO website showed that AB had not filed its declaration of use of PATAGONIA for beer.

On or about November 12, 2013, Patagonia, Inc. launched a beer called "California Route" in partnership with New Belgium. In connection with the launch of California Route, Patagonia, Inc.'s spokesperson made clear that it was "not getting into the beer business in a permanent way." Plaintiffs admit that they considered using and "likely refrained from using its PATAGONIA branding on beer products themselves at that time as a result of AB's ostensible claim to own those rights." Plaintiffs did not challenge AB's PATAGONIA registration in 2013 or at any time before it filed this Action. Indeed, the parties do not dispute that, during this time period, Patagonia appeared to believe that AB owned the rights to the PATAGONIA mark for beer, and considered trying to purchase the rights.

B.   Disputed Facts

The parties offer competing explanations for why Warsteiner initially signed the assignment on April 16, 2012, and only later changed it to December 20, 2012. They further dispute whether the original April 16, 2012, date was consistent with the terms of the Purchase Agreement. The parties also dispute whether the Patagonia beer in Argentina features a substantially similar label and background, and same shaped bespoke bottle as that used in the U.S. They further dispute whether AB distributed PATAGONIA branded merchandise, such as fleece jackets and other items Patagonia sells, to promote the launch of their new beer. Indeed, Patagonia argues that "AB put PATAGONIA on jackets, scarves and winter hats, and distributed the apparel to employees and those serving its beer to customers in connection with the launch and that, in connection with the launch of its PATAGONIA beer, AB served the beer to consumers at ski slopes, with its employees and representatives wearing PATAGONIA apparel." AB argues that in September 2018, AB merely "communicated by email . . . about creating a limited number of promotional items with its Cerveza Patagonia brand, including T-shirts and fleeces."

AB argues that the sustainability element of the U.S. brand stems from the Argentinian brand's commitment to the environment, a contention Patagonia disputes.

DISCUSSION

Under the Lanham Act, federal courts have the authority to cancel an invalid trademark registration. In this action, both parties claim the rights to the PATAGONIA mark, and both parties move for summary judgment on certain trademark cancellation and other claims.

Patagonia also argues that, even if the mark had been assigned properly (to AB), it would not be incontestable because AB failed to meet the use requirement. Under the Lanham Act, "[a] mark attains incontestable status in a category if the registrant continuously uses the mark for five consecutive years after registering it in that category[.]" 15 U.S.C. § 10652; A district court may "rectify the register with respect to the registrations of any party to the action." According to Patagonia, "AB never used the mark continuously for five years and its claimed mark thus is not incontestable." Patagonia moves for "summary judgment on Patagonia's rectification claim" and asks this Court to "strip AB's registration of incontestability status."

Continuous Use Claim

The parties dispute whether AB used the mark continuously for five years. AB argues that its "beer [was] sold on a limited basis in test markets before a wider launch." Yet AB does not state that its beer was seasonal, or that it was sold with any regularity. Furthermore, as discussed below, AB has failed to raise genuine factual issues in response to Patagonia's evidence of AB's inconsistent use of the PATAGONIA mark.

Patagonia argues that AB has not used the PATAGONIA mark continuously for five years, stating that "there is no evidence of sales of PATAGONIA beer by AB in the United States between August 24, 2012 and March 19, 2015." AB has failed to provide specific records of sales from this period. "In its responses to 'Patagonia's discovery requests, "AB state[d] that 'it has not yet located any records of its sale to an outside distributor of PATAGONIA beer' in 2013 or 2014.'" Patagonia argues further that "AB made no sales at all of PATAGONIA beer . . . from May 2016 to December 2016." AB attempts to dispute this by stating that "[i]n May 2016, PATAGONIA beer also participated in the World Beer Cup, an international beer tasting competition held in the U.S." Nevertheless, even accepting this as true, AB still has failed to produce any sales records indicating any use of the PATAGONIA label between June and December 2016. Once more, AB argues that there may exist records that document sales during that time period, but has not produced such records.

It is well established that mere assertions, unsupported by evidence, are insufficient to create a genuine issue of material fact. The Court accordingly concludes that AB did not use the PATAGONIA mark continuously for five years and grants Patagonia's Motion for Summary Judgment on its Ninth Claim.

Misrepresentation of Source claim, 15 U.S.C. § 1064(3)

AB moves for summary judgment on Patagonia's claim under 15 U.S.C. § 1064(3), fraud in obtaining a trademark registration. 15 U.S.C. § 1064(3) provides that "[a] petition to cancel a registration of a mark. . . may . . . be filed . . . by any person who believes that he is or will be damaged, including as a result of a likelihood of dilution by blurring or dilution by tarnishment under section 1125 (c) of this title, by the registration of [that] mark . . . if the registered mark is being used by, or with the permission of, the registrant so as to misrepresent the source of the goods or services on or in connection with which the mark is used." Both parties refer to this as a "passing off" claim.

"Passing off . . . occurs when a producer misrepresents his own goods or services as someone else's." To succeed on a "passing off" claim, a party must show "blatant misuse of the subject mark by [registrant] in a manner calculated to trade on the goodwill and reputation of [the other party]." Patagonia has raised triable issues of fact regarding this claim.

To the extent AB is arguing that, because Patagonia does not produce a beer named "Patagonia," AB could not have "passed off" its own PATAGONIA beer as a Patagonia product, such a contention lacks merit. Patagonia has provided evidence showing that its Patagonia logo and AB's PATAGONIA logo are highly— and perhaps intentionally—similar; that AB's own employees or contractors were confused about the difference between Patagonia's Long Root Ale beer and AB's PATAGONIA beer; and that customers actually were confused about whether the PATAGONIA beer was affiliated with Patagonia. Patagonia has further provided evidence supporting its argument that AB intentionally coopted Patagonia's image and identity. Patagonia has provided evidence suggesting, for example, that "AB created documents for AB's PATAGONIA brand development and launch that explicitly reference Patagonia, Inc.'s Patagonia brand, and define advertising strategies that target customers of 'Patagonia (clothing).'" Such evidence is sufficient to raise a factual dispute regarding whether AB intentionally tried to pass off its own beer as a Patagonia product. The Court accordingly DENIES AB's Motion for Summary Judgment as to Patagonia's Seventh Claim.

CONCLUSION

The Court granted Patagonia's Motion for Partial Summary Judgment on trademark cancellation and blurring or tarnishment ("passing off").

IT IS SO ORDERED.   Dated: 9/3/2

Case 6 – 2

SAMSUNG ELECTRONICS CO. v. APPLE INC.

Supreme Court of the United States

Sotomayor, J., delivered the opinion for a unanimous Court.

Section 289 of the Patent Act provides a damages rem- edy specific to design patent infringement. A person who manufactures or sells "any article of manufacture to which [a patented] design or colorable imitation has been applied shall be liable to the owner to the extent of his total profit." 35 U. S. C. §289. In the case of a design for a single-component product, such as a dinner plate, the product is the "article of manufacture" to which the design has been applied. In the case of a design for a multicomponent product, such as a kitchen oven, identifying the "article of manufacture" to which the design has been applied is a more difficult task.

This case involves the infringement of designs for smartphones. The United States Court of Appeals for the Federal Circuit identified the entire smartphone as the only permissible "article of manufacture" for the purpose of calculating §289 damages because consumers could not separately purchase components of the smartphones. The question before us is whether that reading is consistent with §289. We hold that it is not.

I. A

The federal patent laws have long permitted those who invent designs for manufactured articles to patent their designs. See Patent Act of 1842, §3, 5 Stat. 543–544. Patent protection is available for a "new, original and ornamental design for an article of manufacture." 35 U. S. C. §171(a). A patentable design "gives a peculiar or distinctive appearance to the manufacture, or article to which it may be applied, or to which it gives form." *Gorham Co.* v. *White*, 14 Wall. 511, 525 (1872). This Court has explained that a design patent is infringed "if, in the eye of an ordinary observer, giving such attention as a purchaser usually gives, two designs are substantially the same." *Id.,* at 528.

In 1885, this Court limited the damages available for design patent infringement. The statute in effect at the time allowed a holder of a design patent to recover "the actual damages sustained" from infringement. Rev. Stat. §4919. In *Dobson* v. *Hartford Carpet Co.*, 114 U. S. 439 (1885), the lower courts had awarded the holders of design patents on carpets damages in the amount of "the entire profit to the [patent holders], per

189

yard, in the manufacture and sale of carpets of the patented designs, and not merely the value which the designs contributed to the carpets." *Id.,* at 443. This Court reversed the damages award and construed the statute to require proof that the profits were "due to" the design rather than other aspects of the carpets. *Id.,* at 444; see also *Dobson* v. *Dornan,* 118 U. S. 10, 17 (1886) ("The plaintiff must show what profits or damages are attributable to the use of the infringing design").

In 1887, in response to the *Dobson* cases, Congress enacted a specific damages remedy for design patent infringement. See S. Rep. No. 206, 49th Cong., 1st Sess., 1–2 (1886); H. R. Rep. No. 1966, 49th Cong., 1st Sess., 1–2 (1886). The new provision made it unlawful to manufacture or sell an article of manufacture to which a patented design or a colorable imitation thereof had been applied. An act to amend the law relating to patents, trademarks, and copyright, §1, 24 Stat. 387. It went on to make a design patent infringer "liable in the amount of" $250 or "the total profit made by him from the manufacture or sale . . . of the article or articles to which the design, or color- able imitation thereof, has been applied." *Ibid.*

The Patent Act of 1952 codified this provision in §289. 66 Stat. 813. That codified language now reads, in relevant part:

"Whoever during the term of a patent for a design, without license of the owner, (1) applies the patented design, or any colorable imitation thereof, to any article of manufacture for the purpose of sale, or (2) sells or exposes for sale any article of manufacture to which such design or colorable imitation has been applied shall be liable to the owner to the extent of his total profit, but not less than $250 . . . ." 35 U. S. C. §289.

1.B

Apple Inc. released its first-generation iPhone in 2007. The iPhone is a smartphone, a "cell phone with a broad range of other functions based on advanced computing capability, large storage capacity, and Internet connectivity." *Riley* v. *California,* 573 U. S. ___, ___ (2014) (slip op., at 2). Apple secured many design patents in connection with the release. Among those patents were the D618,677 patent, covering a black rectangular front face with rounded corners, the D593,087 patent, covering a rectangular front face with rounded corners and a raised rim, and the D604,305 patent, covering a grid of 16 colorful icons on a black screen. App. 530–578.

Samsung Electronics Co., Samsung Electronics America, Inc., and Samsung Telecommunications America, LLC (Samsung), also manufacture smartphones. After Apple released its iPhone, Samsung released a series of smartphones that resembled the iPhone. *Id.,* at 357–358.

Apple sued Samsung in 2011, alleging, as relevant here, that various Samsung smartphones infringed Apple's D593,087, D618,677, and D604,305 design patents. A jury found that several Samsung smartphones did infringe those patents. See *id.,* at 273–276. All told, Apple was awarded $399 million in damages for Samsung's design patent infringement, the entire profit Samsung made from its sales of the infringing smartphones. See *id.,* at 277–280, 348–350.

The Federal Circuit affirmed the design patent infringement damages award.[1] In doing so, it rejected Samsung's argument "that the profits awarded should have been limited to the infringing 'article of manufacture' "—for example, the screen or case of the smartphone—"not the entire infringing product"—the smartphone. 786 F. 3d 983, 1002 (2015). It reasoned that "limit[ing] the dam- ages" award was not required because the "innards of Samsung's smartphones were not sold separately from their shells as distinct articles of manufacture to ordinary purchasers." *Ibid.*

We granted certiorari, 577 U. S. ___ (2016), and now reverse and remand.

II

Section 289 allows a patent holder to recover the total profit an infringer makes from the infringement. It does so by first prohibiting the unlicensed "appli[cation]" of a "patented design, or any colorable imitation thereof, to any article of manufacture for the purpose of sale" or the unlicensed sale or exposure to sale of "any article of manufacture to which [a patented] design or colorable imitation has been applied." 35 U. S. C. §289. It then makes a person who violates that prohibition "liable to the owner to the extent of his total profit, but not less than $250." *Ibid.* "Total," of course, means all. See American Heritage Dictionary 1836 (5th ed. 2011) ("[t]he whole amount of something; the entirety"). The "total profit" for which §289 makes an infringer liable is thus all of the profit made from the prohibited conduct, that is, from the manufacture or sale of the "article of manufacture to which [the patented] design or colorable imitation has been applied."

Arriving at a damages award under §289 thus involves two steps. First, identify the "article of manufacture" to which the infringed design has been applied. Second, calculate the infringer's total profit made on that article of manufacture.

This case requires us to address a threshold matter: the scope of the term "article of manufacture." The only question we resolve today is whether, in the case of a multicomponent product, the relevant "article of manufacture" must always be the end product sold to the consumer or whether it can also be a component of that product. Under the former interpretation, a patent holder will always be entitled to the infringer's total profit from the end product. Under the latter interpretation, a patent holder will sometimes be entitled to the infringer's total profit from a component of the end product.

II.A

The text resolves this case. The term "article of manufacture," as used in §289, encompasses both a product sold to a consumer and a component of that product.

"Article of manufacture" has a broad meaning. An "article" is just "a particular thing." J. Stormonth, A Dictionary of the English Language 53 (1885) (Stormonth); see also American Heritage Dictionary, at 101 ("[a]n individual thing or element of a class; a particular object or item"). And "manufacture" means "the conversion of raw materials by the hand, or by machinery, into articles suitable for the use of man" and "the articles so made." Stormonth 589; see also American Heritage Dictionary, at 1070 ("[t]he act, craft, or process of manufacturing products, especially on a large scale" or "[a] product that is manufactured"). An article of manufacture, then, is sim- ply a thing made by hand or machine.

So understood, the term "article of manufacture" is broad enough to encompass both a product sold to a consumer as well as a component of that product. A component of a product, no less than the product itself, is a thing made by hand or machine. That a component may be integrated into a larger product, in other words, does not put it outside the category of articles of manufacture.

This reading of article of manufacture in §289 is consistent with 35 U. S. C. §171(a), which makes "new, original and ornamental design[s] for an article of manufacture" eligible for design patent protection.[3] The Patent Office and the courts have understood §171 to permit a design patent for a design extending to only a component of a multicomponent product. See, *e.g., Ex parte Adams*, 84 Off. Gaz. Pat. Office 311 (1898) ("The several articles of manufacture of peculiar shape which when combined produce a machine or structure having movable parts may each separately be patented as a design . . . "); *Application of Zahn*, 617 F. 2d 261, 268 (CCPA 1980) ("Section 171 authorizes patents on ornamental designs for articles of manufacture. While the design must be *embodied* in some articles, the statute is not limited to designs for complete articles, or 'discrete' articles, and certainly not to articles separately sold . . . ").

This reading is also consistent with 35 U. S. C. §101, which makes "any new and useful . . . manufacture . . . or any new and useful improvement thereof" eligible for utility patent protection. Cf. 8 D. Chisum, Patents §23.03[2], pp. 23–12 to 23–13 (2014) (noting that "article of manufacture" in §171 includes "what would be considered a 'manufacture' within the meaning of Section 101"). "[T]his Court has read the term 'manufacture' in §101 . . . to mean 'the production of articles for use from raw or prepared materials by giving to these materials new forms, qualities, properties, or combinations, whether by hand-labor or by machinery.' " *Diamond* v. *Chakrabarty*, 447 U. S. 303, 308 (1980) (quoting *American Fruit Growers, Inc.* v. *Brogdex Co.*, 283 U. S. 1, 11 (1931)). The broad term includes "the parts of a machine considered separately from the machine itself." 1 W. Robinson, The Law of Patents for Useful Inventions §183, p. 270 (1890).

II.B

The Federal Circuit's narrower reading of "article of manufacture" cannot be squared with the text of §289. The Federal Circuit found that components of the infringing smartphones could not be the relevant article of manu facture because consumers could not purchase those components separately from the smartphones. See 786 F. 3d, at 1002 (declining to limit a §289 award to a component of the smartphone because "[t]he innards of Samsung's smartphones were not sold separately from their shells as distinct articles of manufacture to ordinary purchasers"); see also *Nordock, Inc.* v. *Systems Inc.*, 803 F. 3d 1344, 1355 (CA Fed. 2015) (declining to limit a §289 award to a design for a " 'lip and hinge plate' " because it was "welded together" with a leveler and "there was no evidence" it was sold "separate[ly] from the leveler as a complete unit"). But, for the reasons given above, the term "article of manufacture" is broad enough to embrace both a product sold to a consumer and a component of that product, whether sold separately or not. Thus, reading "article of manufacture" in §289 to cover only an end product sold to a consumer gives too narrow a meaning to the phrase.

The parties ask us to go further and resolve whether, for each of the design patents at issue here, the relevant article of manufacture is the smartphone, or a particular smartphone component. Doing so would require us to set out a test for identifying the relevant article of manufacture at the first step of the §289 damages inquiry and to parse the record to apply that test in this case. The United States as *amicus curiae* suggested a test, see Brief for United States as *Amicus Curiae* 27–29, but Samsung and Apple did not brief the issue. We decline to lay out a test for the first step of the §289 damages inquiry in the absence of adequate briefing by the parties. Doing so is not necessary to resolve the question presented in this case, and the Federal Circuit may address any remaining issues on remand.

III

The judgment of the United States Court of Appeals for the Federal Circuit is therefore reversed, and the case is remanded for further proceedings consistent with this opinion.

It is so ordered

Case 6 – 3
Judgment in Case C-610/15
Stichting Brein v Ziggo BV, XS4ALL Internet BV

COURT of Justice of the European Union

PRESS RELEASE No 64/17

Luxembourg, 14 June 2017

Making available and managing an online platform for sharing copyright-protected works, such as 'The Pirate Bay', may constitute an infringement of copyright

Even if the works in question are placed online by the users of the online sharing platform, the operators of that platform play an essential role in making those works available.

Ziggo and XS4ALL are internet access providers. A significant number of their subscribers use the online sharing platform 'The Pirate Bay'. This platform allows users to share and upload, in segments ('torrents'), works present on their computers[1] . The files in question are, for the most part, copyright-protected works in respect of which the rightholders have not given the operators or users of that platform consent to share those works.

Stichting Brein, a Netherlands foundation which safeguards the interests of copyright holders, has brought proceedings before the courts in the Netherlands seeking an order that would require Ziggo and XS4ALL to block the domain names and IP addresses of 'The Pirate Bay'.

The Hoge Raad der Nederlanden (Supreme Court of the Netherlands), before which the dispute has been brought, has decided to refer questions to the Court of Justice on the interpretation of the EU Copyright Directive[2] . The Hoge Raad wishes, in essence, to ascertain whether a sharing platform such as 'The Pirate Bay' is making a 'communication to the public' within the meaning of the directive and may therefore be infringing copyright.

In today's judgment, the Court holds that **the making available and management of an online sharing platform must be considered to be an act of communication for the purposes of the directive**.

The Court first draws attention to its previous case-law from which it can be inferred that, as a rule, any act by which a user, with full knowledge of the relevant facts, provides its clients with access to protected works is liable to constitute an 'act of communication' for the purposes of the directive.

In the present case it is common ground that copyright-protected works are, through 'The Pirate Bay', made available to the users of that platform in such a way that they may access those works from wherever and whenever they individually choose. Whilst it accepts that the works in question are placed online by the users, the Court highlights the fact that the operators of the platform play an essential role in making those works available.

In that context, the Court notes that the operators of the platform index the torrent files so that the works to which those files refer can be easily located and downloaded by users. 'The Pirate Bay' also offers — in addition to a search engine — categories based on the type of the works, their genre or 1 BitTorrent is a protocol through which users can share files. The files to be shared are divided into segments, which reduces the burden on individual servers during the sharing process. In order to be able to share files, users must first download specific software which allows the creation of torrent files. Torrent files refer to a central server which identifies the users available to share a particular torrent file as well as the underlying media file. Those torrent files are uploaded to the online sharing platform, which then proceeds to index them so that they can be located by users of the online sharing platform and the works to which those torrent files refer can be downloaded onto the users' computers. 2

Article 3(1) of Directive 2001/29/EC of the European Parliament and of the Council of 22 May 2001 on the harmonisation of certain aspects of copyright and related rights in the information society (OJ 2001 L 167, p. 10). www.curia.europa.eu their popularity.

Furthermore, the operators delete obsolete or faulty torrent files and actively filter some content.

The Court also highlights that the protected works in question are in fact communicated to a public.

Indeed, a large number of Ziggo's and XS4ALL's subscribers have downloaded media files using 'The Pirate Bay'. It is also clear from the observations submitted to the Court that the platform is used by a significant number of persons (reference is made on the online sharing platform to several tens of millions of users).

Moreover, the operators of 'The Pirate Bay' have been informed that their platform provides access to copyright-protected works published without the authorisation of the rightholders. In addition, the same operators expressly display, on blogs and forums accessible on that platform, their intention of making protected works available to users, and encourage the latter to make copies of those works. In any event, it is clear from the Hoge Raad's decision that the operators of 'The Pirate Bay' cannot be unaware that this platform provides access to works published without the consent of the rightholders.

Lastly, the making available and management of an online sharing platform, such as 'The Pirate Bay', is carried out with the purpose of obtaining a profit, it being clear from the observations submitted to the Court that that platform generates considerable advertising revenues.

Short Cases for Consideration: Intellectual Property (Week 6)

1. Alvin, Callie, Mukesh, and Pedro are friends who enroll in a university course to study international business law. The textbook required for the course costs $50, which the five friends agree is expensive. They agree to chip in $10 each and buy one copy from a bookstore. They then take the copy to the local Discount Copy Store and make five copies of the complete book for $15 a copy. Then they return the book to the bookstore and get a refund of their original purchase price. Have the five friends done anything wrong? If so, what? Explain.

2. Elvira is an abstract painter of incredible talent, but of little notoriety. One of her paintings, entitled "Blue Lady 13," is a piece of intense power and sensuality. In 1990, she sold it to Mega Company for display in the main public entrance of the business's new headquarters building. Several art critics attending the opening of the building mistook the painting for a long lost work of Pablo Picasso. The critics wrote about the painting in their newspaper columns as though they had made a great discovery. When people began flooding into the Mega Building to see "Blue Lady 13," the directors of Mega were delighted. They even went so far as to put up a sign that said: "This painting, entitled 'La Dama Azul,' was probably painted by Pablo Picasso during his blue period, ca. 1913." Is there anything that Elvira can do? Explain.

3. The First-to-Market Computer Software Company owns the copyright to a highly successful spreadsheet program—Blossom 3-2-1—which has dominated the worldwide market for several years. Recently, Clone Software Co. devised a look-alike program that does everything that the Blossom 3-2-1 program does, except that the Clone sells for only one-tenth the price of the original. First-to-Market has sued Clone for copyright infringement. Clone defends itself by saying that the coding of its program is entirely different from that of Blossom 3-2-1 and that the only similarity between the programs is that the images that appear on the computer screen and the key sequences used to operate the program are identical. Has Clone infringed First-to-Market's copyright? Explain.

4.   Jacques Pierre, Paris France, manufactures and sells a line of perfume—Le Peux—in distinctively shaped containers that are instantly recognizable. May Jacques Pierre register the shape of the containers as a trademark? Explain. If not, how else might Jacques Pierre keep competitors in other nations from selling their perfumes in similar containers?

5.   A Japanese firm, Omega Company, manufactures cassette tapes with the trademark TXX. Omega licensed Alpha Company to distribute and sell the tapes in Australia and Sigma Company to do the same in South Africa. The license with Sigma expired after three years, and Omega refused to renew the license. Sigma then began buying cassettes from Alpha in Australia in bulk quantities and importing them into South Africa. These tapes had no individual wrappers or labels and Sigma affixed both wrappers and labels with the TXX trademark on the cassettes, which it then sold throughout South Africa. Omega, which owns the TXX trademark in South Africa, has brought suit to enjoin Sigma from importing the cassettes into South Africa. Will Omega succeed? Would it make any difference if Omega's license with Alpha forbade Alpha from selling tapes for export to South Africa? Explain.

CHAPTER SEVEN:

EMPLOYMENT LAW, DOMESTICALLY AND GLOBALLY

INTRODUCTION — EMPLOYMENT LAW AND WORKERS' RIGHTS

"Industrialization" has brought considerable wealth to the industrialized democracies, including the U.S. But industrialization, combined with globalization, clearly has its downsides. Of all the debates surrounding globalization, one of the most contentious involves trade and workers' rights.

How does U.S. employment law compare with that of other nations? Those who push for "workers' rights" argue that nations active in global trade should hold themselves to certain standards. The moral argument is that "human rights" — freedom of association, the right to collectively bargain, the right to be free from forced labor or indentured servitude (slavery) — requires that all trading nations should avoid supporting such violations of human rights. But we will see in <u>Doe v. Nestle</u>, for example, that global trade in some of our favorite foods (chocolate, in this case) is entwined with very questionable labor practices. Proponents of global workers' rights would say that nations that wish to be granted access to the U.S. and E.U. markets should observe labor rights.

I. U.S. EMPLOYMENT LAW BASICS

At common law, "freedom" was the operative concept in employment law: employees were free to seek work anywhere, without requiring notice to the employer. But conversely, employers were free to fire anyone for any reason at any time period this was known as employment at will. Gradually this was modified by judges who would allow wrongful discharge cases at common law where (1) employers were firing employees for testifying truthfully at trials, (2) employers were firing employees for not getting out of jury duty, and (3) Employers not abiding by their own employee handbook guidelines. More dramatically, States and the federal government began imposing certain moral concepts opponent employers' "freedoms." In 1964, In the Civil Rights Act, Title VII, employers were prohibited from discriminating against employees or prospective employees on the basis of race, color, sex, religion, or national origin. As We will see below, the Supreme Court assumed that Congress did not mean to apply Title VII outside of US boundaries. But Congress did amend the Civil Rights Act to allow complaints by U.S. citizens against US employers for overseas discrimination.

Other federal statutes came to protect right so pregnant women, those with disabilities, and those being discriminated against based on their age. All along, the states had also begun to provide protection against employer discrimination, changing the common law rule of "employement at will." For example, in Michigan, workers are protected from being fired just for being "over weight," as long as they can get the job done. The Elliott-Larsen Civil Rights Act, MCL 37.2202, says it is illegal for an employer to "fail or refuse to hire or recruit, discharge, or otherwise discriminate against an individual with respect to employment compensation because of religion, race, color, national origin, age, sex, height, weight, or marital status."

II U.S. MULTINATIONALS AND LABOR RIGHTS

But with a case like <u>Doe v. Nestle</u>, at the end of this chapter, and the materials in Chapter Eight on International Business Ethics, we see that it's not just "nations" that should pay attention to labor rights and human rights generally, but corporations, as well. "Outsourcing" is so common now that we take it for granted, but not too long ago, many companies struggled with high labor costs in the U.S. and determined to lower those costs by outsourcing, sometimes to nations that allowed horrific labor conditions, conditions similar to the years when Britain had its "dark, Satanic mills." (A phrase from the great English poet, William Blake). In the U.S., "sweatshops" abounded as well. We hear about disasters like the Rana Plaza collapse in Bangladesh.

https://www.youtube.com/watch?v=3MSL2WUGYuo

But we also have the U.S. example of the Triangle Shirtwaist Fire.

https://www.history.com/topics/early-20th-century-us/triangle-shirtwaist-fire

In a good legal/political system, such events would ordinarily result in greater protections for workers. This did happen in the U.S., as the video makes clear.

In China, we now have the equivalent of Blake's "dark, Satanic mills."

https://www.youtubc.com/watch?v=F4dnAdO8its

It remains to be seen what legal protections China will offer to workers, and those citizens shown in the video that are adversely affected by the "negative externalities" of pollution from industrialization. U.S. multinationals rely heavily on Chinese labor, including companies like Apple, Inc. For example, not long ago, Apple was criticized for using Foxconn's facilities in Chengdu, where overworked employees began killing themselves. This is discussed in greater detail in Chapter Eight.

Note: Negative externalities are costs borne by those who are not part of the financial transaction; e.g. the people shown in the video that can no longer use the water are not customers of the factories that are spoiling the water, but are "third parties" experiencing losses they have not bargained for or consented to.

Starting in the 1990s, the iconic American company Levi Strauss, had to decide how much to maintain its U.S. labor force or outsource overseas. Levi Strauss made its first pair of jeans in 1873 after the California gold rush. The company decided to close a manufacturing facility in San Antonio, Texas in early 1990. (Stanford Business School offers a case that follows then-vice president of operations Pete Thigpen and his team as they wrestle with the economic and human capital impact of closing the U.S.-based plant and outsourcing the manufacture of the company's Dockers line to a contractor in Costa Rica.)[46]

In 2014, the company decided to ship a number of jobs, including customer service, to the subcontinent and other far-flung locations. Simply put, in a global market, with price and quality being far and away the most important factor in consumer purchasing decisions, the company had little choice if it wanted to survive, much less maximize profits.

Labor Rights and the WTO

We've looked at the WTO and GATT trading rules. One key question that arises is whether a market like the U.S. (or the E.U.) could add tariffs for the import of textiles or other goods where (1) the working conditions in the country of export to the U.S. are dangerous (like Rana Plaza), are based on forced labor (as in Uiyghur labor in China), or indentured servitude (as in Doe v. Nestle and the cocoa trade, a case featured below in this chapter.). We have already seen that, for the WTO, a "tuna is a tuna," a "shrimp is a shrimp,"

---

[46] https://www.gsb.stanford.edu/faculty-research/case-studies/levi-strauss-co-b

and that the unsafe, unhealthy, or unsustainable conditions under which something is manufactured or "taken" from the land or oceans is not something that the U.S. government can tax via tariffs. If the U.S. government could do so under the WTO rules, the financial benefits of corporate outsourcing would be fewer, and, arguably, there would be less outsourcing. But the WTO rules would regard this as "protectionist" legislation. As long as the U.S. remains a member of the WTO, it cannot pass such legislation without being challenged in the WTO dispute resolution process.

The second key question is whether, even if the WTO were to allow such tariffs, would the U.S. Congress (and President) want to impose such taxes? Would the U.S. Chamber of Commerce support such a move, or, politically, would such a proposal be "dead on arrival"? (My own sense is that the Chamber of Commerce favors "free trade" and "globalization," and would hesitate to support such measures.)

So, under the WTO system now, a trading partner that fails to enforce basic protections for its workers can gain an unfair trade advantage, boosting its market competitiveness against countries with stronger labor safeguards. So, with NAFTA and its replacement, the USMCA, are there labor standards in the trade deal that protect workers' rights?

The U.S. Department of Labor provides the following information:

https://www.dol.gov/agencies/ilab/our-work/trade/labor-rights-usmca

If the U.S. government should pursue trade agreements with labor rights in mind, there are some pivotal questions: First, what labor standards are most important to U.S. trade and foreign policy? Second, how can labor standards, once negotiated, be enforced? Finally, does it make sense to insist that our trade partners adhere to a common set of core labor standards? and if so, which standards?

While the so-called "international community" mostly agrees on the need to respect labor standards, that agreement does not extend to what those standards should be. Forced labor and slavery are almost universally regarded as repugnant, but other labor safeguards thought vital in the world's richest countries are not widely observed elsewhere.

The ILO

The International Labor Organization, created by the Treaty of Versailles after World War I, has published labor standards in dozens of areas, but it has identified eight essential core standards, most of which refer to basic human rights. Of the 175 ILO member countries, overwhelming majorities have ratified most of the eight standards. More than 150 have ratified the four treating forced labor and discrimination in employment and wages. Washington has ratified just two standards, one abolishing forced labor and the other eliminating the worst forms of child labor, placing the United States in the company of only eight other ILO member countries, including China, Myanmar, and Oman.

Many proponents of labor standards would expand the core list of ILO protections to cover workplace safety, working conditions, and wages. The U.S. Trade Act of 1974 defines "internationally recognized worker rights" to include "acceptable conditions of work with respect to minimum wages, hours of work, and occupational safety and health." The University of Michigan, for example, obliges producers of goods bearing its insignia to respect the core ILO standards and also requires them to pay minimum wages and to offer a "safe and healthy working environment." (Who supplies your university's athetic apparel and other "swag," and under what conditions are such items produced? Does it even matter, given the many consumer decisions we have to make every day?)

The ILO reports regularly and periodically on the steps each nation takes to implement the standards it has ratified. If complaints are lodged, the ILO investigates the alleged violation and publicizes its findings. Even if a member nation has not ratified the freedom-of-association conventions, the ILO may investigate alleged violations of those conventions. The ILO cannot, however, authorize retaliatory trade measures or sanctions. Rather, it provides technical assistance to member countries to bring their labor laws and enforcement procedures into compliance.

Many observers are skeptical that it can protect workers using its existing enforcement tools since the ILO can do little besides give non-compliant nations and companies bad publicity.

Putting Teeth into Standards Enforcement

At the 1996 WTO ministerial meeting, developing countries strongly resisted efforts to allow the WTO to enforce labor standards, and the meeting concluded by affirming the ILO's role in determining and dealing with labor standards. Similarly, when President Clinton and some EU leaders tried to bring workers' rights into the next round of multilateral trade negotiations at the 1999 WTO ministerial meeting in Seattle, developing countries rejected the initiative.

In a recent free trade pact, Jordan and the United States agreed to protect core ILO workers' rights. They also spelled out how to resolve disputes over labor standards: if one country weakens its labor laws or fails to bring its laws or enforcement into compliance with the ILO core standards, the other may take appropriate measures, including withdrawal of trade benefits.

The AFL-CIO has endorsed the labor provisions of the Jordan trade pact, while the U.S. Chamber of Commerce has denounced them. The Chamber favors free trade agreements, and it fears that most countries will resist including enforceable labor standards in any new agreement. This view is almost certainly correct, at least in the developing world.

Practical Difficulties

Some Americans may fear that including enforceable labor standards in trade agreements will open the United States to charges that it fails to enforce ILO core standards, exposing it to possible trade penalties. But U.S. civil rights and labor laws already contain the fundamental protections demanded by the ILO conventions.

Citizens in developing countries might be less confident that their laws and enforcement procedures will meet the tests implied by the ILO conventions, especially as construed by observers from affluent countries. Interpretations devised in the drawing rooms of Paris or the recreation rooms of suburban Washington might seem out of touch with conditions in countries where half or more of the population lives on less than $2 a day.

Two of the most troublesome ILO standards involve child labor. Rich countries—very sensibly—restrict children's participation in the job market so that youngsters can attend school and prepare to become workers. But in poor countries, where children's earnings are a crucial family resource and schooling may be unavailable, the restrictions may not be appropriate. Of course, children in poor countries deserve protection and education too, but the standard of protection and the resources available for schooling will be far below those in a wealthy country.

A standard of protection that is appropriate in rich countries can impose excessive burdens on poor ones. Third-world leaders fear, understandably, that including enforceable labor standards in trade treaties will expose their countries to constant challenge in the WTO—and that the standards will be used mainly to protect workers and businesses in developed countries from competition from third-world workers.

AFL-CIO President John Sweeney denies that enforcing labor standards can have a protectionist impact. The ILO standards, he notes, are designed to protect the interests of workers in low-income as well as high-income countries. The WTO and United States strongly defend intellectual property (IP) rights and enforce trade penalties when developing countries violate those rights. Extending the same protections to workers' rights, he reasons, cannot be protectionist.

While it is easy to sympathize with Sweeney's view, there is a big difference between worker rights in another country and the IP rights of a country's own citizens. If Burma denies its workers the right to organize independent unions, its actions are deplorable but do not directly injure me. If Burma allows publishers and recording companies to reproduce my copyrighted books and songs without compensating me, the theft of my creative efforts injures me directly. It is hardly surprising that U.S. voters would insist on remedies for injuries to themselves before fixing the problems of workers overseas. Sweeney may object that the injury to Burmese workers from human rights abuses is much more serious than the monetary losses from copyright infringement suffered by a handful of artists, inventors, and U.S. corporations. And he may well be right. But American artists, inventors, and corporate shareholders can vote in U.S. elections; Burmese workers cannot.

How to Assess WTO Penalties

If the WTO is to be used to assess penalties against countries violating international labor norms, its member countries must devise a new way to assign penalties for violations. Under current procedures, a country found to have a valid trade complaint may retaliate against the offending country by withholding a trade benefit roughly equivalent to the benefit denied it by the offender as a result of the violation of WTO rules. It is not obvious how to calculate the penalty when the violation involves a labor standard. There the injury has been suffered by workers in the offending country, and residents of the complaining country may have enjoyed a net benefit.

Suppose, for example, the United States accuses another country of employing underage children in its apparel industry. The violation increases the offending country's supply of low-wage workers, thus reducing producers' wage costs and the prices charged to domestic and overseas consumers. The adult workers in the offending country have clearly suffered injury, as have the children if their work has deprived them of schooling that was otherwise available.

How did the violation affect Americans? U.S. apparel workers probably lost wages and jobs. But their losses are counterbalanced by gains to U.S. consumers, who bought clothing more cheaply because of child labor in the offending country. Since all American workers, including those in the apparel industry, are themselves consumers, it is not clear whether the violation injured U.S. workers as a class. Last year apparel imports into the United States exceeded exports by about $55 billion. If the use of child labor overseas cut the cost of imports, Americans spent less for clothing than they otherwise would have. While most Americans deplore child labor, at home or abroad, it is hard to see how an overseas violation of the child labor standard has injured them. Nor is the United States likely to weaken its own child labor laws because it has benefited from the availability of cheaper imported clothes.

Private Sanctions

As a final option for enforcing labor standards, American consumers can apply their own private sanctions. Anyone who finds child labor or forced labor reprehensible can refuse to buy products made in countries that tolerate those practices. The ILO could push consumers into action by publishing information about offending countries and their violations. It could also publicize any country's refusal to cooperate with ILO investigations. If voters want more information about imported goods and services from countries that comply with ILO standards, their own national governments can provide it. Washington can help American consumers increase pressure on offending countries by requiring sellers to label products with the country of origin. It could also encourage or require sellers to identify goods and services produced in countries that fully comply with ILO's core labor standards.

Should Uncle Sam Enforce Labor Standards?

The case for requiring U.S. trade partners to respect international labor standards is least compelling when it involves the terms and conditions of employment. If a country respects ILO core standards, then workers will be able to negotiate for the best combination of pay, fringe benefits, work hours, and workplace amenities that their level of productivity allows. If we insist that the resulting compensation package meet minimum international standards, we are substituting our own judgment for that of the affected workers and their employers.

But the weak bargaining position of workers in poor countries makes it unlikely that their negotiations with employers will secure decent compensation and safe working conditions. Their weak bargaining position is linked to their low productivity and skills. Today U.S. and European labor standards are much higher, and labor regulation enforced more rigorously, than they were 50 years ago. The improvement is closely associated with workers' increased skill and productivity; better-off countries are more likely than the poorest to conform to ILO labor standards. In countries with per capita income of $500 a year or less, 30—60 percent of children between the ages of 10 and 14 work. In countries with per capita income of $500—1,000, just 10—30 percent of youngsters work. As productivity improves, so too will the bargaining position and wages of industrial workers. If history is any guide, national labor standards will improve as well.

The most reliable way to improve the condition of third-world workers is to boost their average productivity. Concerned voters in rich countries can help make this happen by pressing to open up their own markets to third-world products. Many low-income countries have a comparative advantage in manufacturing apparel, textiles, and footwear and in producing staple foods, fruits, and vegetables. Rich countries often impose high tariffs or quotas on these products, and nearly all provide generous subsidies to their farmers—thus denying third-world producers and farmers access to a huge potential market. The World Bank estimates that tariff and nontariff barriers, together with subsidies lavished on U.S. and European farmers, cost third-world countries more in lost trade than they get in foreign aid.

If we insist that developing countries meet immediately the labor standards that the richest countries achieved only gradually, we will keep some of them out of the world's best markets. The poor countries that agree to abide by ILO standards will occasionally be challenged—sometimes by representatives of rich countries more intent on protecting their own workers from "unfair" overseas competition than on improving the lot of third-world workers. While the moral case for requiring our trading partners to respect labor rights is compelling, the case for removing trade barriers that limit the product markets and incomes of the world's poorest workers is just as powerful.

II. EMPLOYMENT LAWS ABROAD

As suggested above, nations have different customs and laws regarding employment. For a long time, an employer in Saudi Arabia could not hire a woman (Saudi or otherwise) if the job duties included driving.

Business ethicists have also found that in places as diverse as South Korea, Mexico, or India that "nepotism" is perfectly legal, and even customarily expected. Standards of safety for construction workers also vary from nation to nation.

Astute business managers will strive to understand the "rule of the road" while hiring, retaining, or promoting employees beyond U.S. borders. Even "host country" employers may not always appreciate the customs and rules of their own country. In the following case, a Japanese radio station was surprised when it could not legally fire an employee who had failed to show up as scheduled on several occasions.

Kochi Hoso (Broadcasting Company)

Supreme Court of Japan Rokelsoku No. 937 (1977)

Japanese firms are required to maintain rules of employment that specify the terms for discharging an employee. Kochi Hoso, a radio broadcasting Company, made it clear to all employees that tardiness for a broadcast was sufficient cause for dismissal. The plaintiff was a radio announcer who it failed twice to arrive at the studio on time for a news broadcast. After the second offense the company discharged the plaintiff. The plaintiff sued for reinstatement, arguing that while the discharge was within the company rules, it was nevertheless unreasonable or contrary to public policy.

The Supreme Court of Japan ruled that even when employees conduct is cause for termination, the employer may not discharge and employee if the discharge is significantly unreasonable under the specific situation. The "socially accepted view" would be that such a discharge was an abusive exercise of the employers power to discharge. The Supreme Court ordered that the radio announcer be reinstated in his job.

If you were US company establishing an office in Japan, how would you go about determining what was socially accepted? How would integrating social contracts theory apply here?

III. TITLE VII AND THE "EXTRA-TERRITORIALITY" QUESTION

As noted earlier, after two decades of Title VII, the Supreme Court was not sure that Congress meant to apply Title VII outside of US territory. Under the concept of nationality jurisdiction become the United states can make and enforce law with respect to its citizens for actions beyond US borders. This is known as extraterritorial jurisdiction based on "nationality." A citizen of the U.S. is a U.S. "national," so an American oil company operating in Saudi Arabia would be subject to U.S. law only insofar as it applied to U.S. nationals working there. Just such a case was heard by the Supreme Court in 1991. In Boureslan v. Aramco, however, the Supreme Court declined to apply Title VII, saying that Congress should be explicit in its intention any time it wished to extend a U.S. law's reach beyond U.S. borders.

EEOC v. Arabian American Oil Co.

Supreme Court of the United States

January 16, 1991, Argued; March 26, 1991, [*] Decided

Opinion by: REHNQUIST, Chief Justice

[1A]

These cases present the issue whether Title VII applies extraterritorially to regulate the employment practices of United States employers who employ United States citizens abroad. The United States Court of Appeals for the Fifth Circuit held that it does not, and we agree with that conclusion.

Petitioner Boureslan is a naturalized United States citizen who was born in Lebanon. The respondents are two Delaware corporations, Arabian American Oil Company (Aramco), and its subsidiary, Aramco Service Company (ASC). Aramco's principal place of business is Dhahran, Saudi Arabia, and it is licensed to do business in Texas. ASC's principal place of business is Houston, Texas.

In 1979, Boureslan was hired by ASC as a cost engineer in Houston. A year later he was transferred, at his request, to work for Aramco in Saudi Arabia. Boureslan remained with Aramco in Saudi Arabia until he was discharged in 1984. After filing a charge of discrimination with the Equal Employment Opportunity Commission (EEOC or Commission), he instituted this suit in the United States District Court for the Southern District of Texas against Aramco and ASC. He sought relief under both state law and Title VII of the Civil Rights Act of 1964, on the ground that he was harassed and ultimately discharged by respondents on account of his race, religion, and national origin.

Respondents filed a motion for summary judgment on the ground that the District Court lacked subject-matter jurisdiction over Boureslan's claim because the protections of Title VII do not extend to United States citizens employed abroad by American employers. The District Court agreed and dismissed Boureslan's Title VII claim. . . .Both Boureslan and the EEOC petitioned for certiorari. We granted both petitions for certiorari to resolve this important issue of statutory interpretation.

[2] Both parties concede, as they must, that Congress has the authority to enforce its laws beyond the territorial boundaries of the United States. Whether Congress has in fact exercised that authority in this case is a matter of statutory construction. It is our task to determine whether Congress intended the protections of Title VII to apply to United States citizens employed by American employers outside of the United States.

[3] It is a longstanding principle of American law "that legislation of Congress, unless a contrary intent appears, is meant to apply only within the territorial jurisdiction of the United States.
In applying this rule of construction, we look to see whether "language in the [relevant Act] gives any indication of a congressional purpose to extend its coverage beyond places over which the United States has sovereignty or has some measure of legislative control." (citation Foley Bros., Inc. v. Filardo, 336 U.S. 281, 1949).

We assume that Congress legislates against the backdrop of the presumption against extraterritoriality. Therefore, unless there is "the affirmative intention of the Congress clearly expressed," we must presume it "is primarily concerned with domestic conditions." (citing Foley Bros. case)

[1B] Boureslan and the EEOC contend that the language of Title VII evinces a clearly expressed intent on behalf of Congress to legislate extraterritorially. They rely principally on two provisions of the statute. First, petitioners argue that the statute's definitions of the jurisdictional terms "employer" and "commerce" are sufficiently broad to include United States firms that employ American citizens overseas. Second, they maintain that the statute's "alien exemption" clause, 42 U.S.C. §20001e-1, necessarily implies that Congress intended to protect American citizens from employment discrimination abroad. Petitioners also contend that we should defer to the EEOC's consistently held position that Title VII applies abroad. We conclude that petitioners' evidence . . .falls short of demonstrating the affirmative congressional intent required to extend the protections of Title VII beyond our territorial borders.

Title VII prohibits various discriminatory employment practices based on an individual's race, color, religion, sex, or national origin. An employer is subject to Title VII if it has employed 15 or more employees for a specified period and is "engaged in an industry affecting commerce." An industry affecting commerce is "any activity, business, or industry in commerce or in which a labor dispute would hinder or obstruct commerce or the free flow of commerce and includes any activity or industry 'affecting commerce' within the meaning of the Labor-Management Reporting and Disclosure Act of 1959 [(LMRDA)] 29 U.S.C.401 et. Seq. §2000e(h). "Commerce," in turn, is defined as "trade, traffic, commerce, transportation, transmission, or communication among the several States; or between a State and any place outside thereof; or within the District of Columbia, or a possession of the United States; or between points in the same State but through a point outside thereof." §2000e(g).

Petitioners argue that by its plain language, Title VII's "broad jurisdictional language" reveals Congress's intent to extent the statute's protections to employment discrimination anywhere in the world by a United States employer who affects trade "between a State and any place outside thereof." More precisely, they assert that since Title VII defines "States" to include States, the District of Columbia, and specified territories, the clause "between a State and any place outside thereof" must be referring to areas beyond the territorial limit of the United States. Reply Brief for EEOC at page 3.

Respondents Aramco et al. offer several alternative explanations for the statute's expansive language. They contend that the "or between a State and any place outside thereof" clause "provides the jurisdictional nexus required to regulate commerce that is not wholly within a single state, presumably as it affects both interstate and foreign commerce" but not to "regulate conduct exclusively within a foreign country." Brief for Respondents p. 21, n. 14. They also argue that since the definitions of the terms "employer," "commerce," and "industry affecting commerce" make no mention of "commerce with foreign nations," Congress cannot be said to have intended that the statute apply overseas. In support of this argument, petitioners point to Title II of the Civil Rights Act of 1964, governing public accommodation, which specifically defines commerce as it applies to foreign nations. . . .

[1C] [4] We need not choose between these competing interpretations as we would be required to do in the absence of the presumption against extraterritorial application discussed above. Each is plausible, but no more persuasive than that. The language relied upon by petitioners -- and it is they who must make the affirmative showing -- is ambiguous, and does not speak directly to the question presented here. The intent of Congress as to the extraterritorial application of this statute must be deduced by inference from boilerplate language which can be found in any number of congressional Acts, none of which have ever been held to apply overseas. See, e. g., Consumer Product Safety Act, 15 U.S.C. §2052 (a)(12) Federal Food, Drug, and Cosmetic Act, 21 U. S. C. § 321(b); Transportation Safety Act of 1974, 49 U. S. C. App. § 1802(1); Labor-Management Reporting and Disclosure Act of 1959; Americans with Disabilities Act of 1990.

[1D] Petitioners' reliance on Title VII's jurisdictional provisions also finds no support in our case law; we have repeatedly held that even statutes that contain broad language in their definitions of "commerce" that expressly refer to "foreign commerce" do not apply abroad. For example, in N.Y. Central Railroad v Chisolm, 268 U.S. 29 (1925), we addressed the extraterritorial application of the Federal Employers' Liability Act (FELA), 45 U.S.C. §51 et seq. FELA provides that common carriers by railroad while engaging in "interstate or foreign commerce" or commerce between "any of the States or territories and any foreign nation or nations" shall be liable in damages to its employees who suffer injuries resulting from their employment. §51. Despite this broad jurisdictional language, we found that the Act "contains no words which definitely disclose an intention to give it extraterritorial effect," and therefore there was no jurisdiction under FELA for a damages action by a United States citizen employed on a United States railroad who suffered fatal injuries at a point 30 miles north of the United States border into Canada.

. . . .

Thus petitioner's argument based on the jurisdictional language of Title VII fails both as a matter of statutory language and of our previous case law. Many Acts of Congress are based on the authority of that body to regulate commerce among the several States, and the parts of these Acts setting forth the basis for legislative jurisdiction will obviously refer to such commerce in one way or another. If we were to permit possible, or even plausible, interpretations of language such as that involved here to override the presumption against extraterritorial application, there would be little left of the presumption.

Petitioners argue that Title VII's "alien exemption provision," 42 U.S.C. §2000e-"clearly manifests an intention" by Congress to protect United States citizens with respect to their employment outside of the United States. The alien-exemption provision says that the statute "shall not apply to an employer with respect to the employment of aliens outside any State." Petitioners contend that from this language a negative inference should be drawn that Congress intended Title VII to cover United States citizens working abroad for United States employers. There is "no other plausible explanation [that] the alien exemption exists," they argue, because "if Congress believed that the statute did not apply extraterritorially, it would have had no reason to include an exemption for a certain category of individuals employed outside the United States." Brief for Petitioner in No. 89-1838, pp. 12-13. Since "the statute's jurisdictional provisions cannot possibly be read to confer coverage only upon aliens employed outside the United States," petitioners conclude that "Congress could not rationally have enacted an exemption for the employment of aliens abroad if it intended to foreclose all potential extraterritorial applications of the statute." Id., at 13.

Respondents resist petitioners' interpretation of the alien-exemption provision and assert two alternative reasons for that language. First, they contend that since aliens are included in the statute's definition of employee, * and the definition of commerce includes possessions as well as "States," the purpose of the exemption is to provide that employers of aliens in the possessions of the United States are not covered by the statute. Thus, the "outside any State" clause means outside any State, but within the control of the United States. Respondents argue that "this reading of the alien exemption provision is consistent with and supported by the historical development of the provision" because Congress' inclusion of the provision was a direct response to this Court's interpretation of the term "possessions" in the Fair Labor Standards Act in Vermilya-Brown Co. v. Connell, 335 U.S. 377 (1948), to include leased bases in foreign nations that were within the control of the United States. Brief for Respondents 27. They conclude that the alien-

---

* Title VII defines "employee" as:
"An individual employed by an employer, except that the term 'employee' shall not include any person elected to public office in any State or political subdivision of any State by the qualified voters thereof, or any person chosen by such officer to be on such officer's personal staff, or an appointee on the policy making level or an immediate adviser with respect to the exercise of the constitutional or legal powers of the office. The exemption set forth in the preceding sentence shall not include employees subject to the civil service laws of a State government, governmental agency or political subdivision."

exemption provision was included "to limit the impact of Vermilya-Brown by excluding from coverage employers of aliens in areas under U.S. control that" were not encompassed within Title VII's definition of the term "State." Id., at 29.

Second, respondents assert that by negative implication, the exemption "confirms the coverage of aliens in the United States." Id., at 26. They contend that this interpretation is consistent with our conclusion in Espinoze v Farah Mfg. Co, 414 U.S. 86 (1973) that aliens within the United States are protected from discrimination both because Title VII uses the term "individual" rather than "citizen," and because of the alien-exemption provision.

If petitioners are correct that the alien-exemption clause means that the statute applies to employers overseas, we see no way of distinguishing in its application between United States employers and foreign employers. Thus, a French employer of a United States citizen in France would be subject to Title VII -- a result at which even petitioners balk. The EEOC assures us that in its view the term "employer" means only "American employer," but there is no such distinction in this statute and no indication that the EEOC in the normal course of its administration had produced a reasoned basis for such a distinction. Without clearer evidence of congressional intent to do so than is contained in the alien-exemption clause, we are unwilling to ascribe to that body a policy which would raise difficult issues of international law by imposing this country's employment-discrimination regime upon foreign corporations operating in foreign commerce.

. . .

Similarly, Congress failed to provide any mechanisms for overseas enforcement of Title VII. For instance, the statute's venue provisions, §2000e-5(f)(3) are ill-suited for extraterritorial application as they provide for venue only in a judicial district in the State where certain matters related to the employer occurred or were located. And the limited investigative authority provided for the EEOC, permitting the Commission only to issue subpoenas for witnesses and documents from "any place in the United States or any Territory or possession thereof," 29 U.S.C. §161, incorporated by reference into 42 U.S.C. §2000e-9 suggests that Congress did not intend for the statute to apply abroad.

It is also reasonable to conclude that had Congress intended Title VII to apply overseas, it would have addressed the subject of conflicts with foreign laws and procedures. In amending the Age Discrimination in Employment Act of 1967 (ADEA), 81 Stat. 602, as amended, 29 U.S.C. §621 et seq., to apply abroad, Congress specifically addressed potential conflicts with foreign law by providing that it is not unlawful for an employer to take any action prohibited by the ADEA "where such practices involve an employee in a workplace in a foreign country, and compliance with [the ADEA] would cause such employer . . . to violate the laws of the country in which such workplace is located." §623(f)(1). Title VII, by contrast, fails to address conflicts with the laws of other nations.

. . .

[1E] Petitioners have failed to present sufficient affirmative evidence that Congress intended Title VII to apply abroad. Accordingly, the judgment of the Court of Appeals is

Affirmed

The following year, Congress would amend the Civil Rights Act of 1964 to explicitly make its application "extra-territorial." This means that a U.S. company operating abroad must abide by Title VII's non-discrimination mandate for any U.S. citizens working there. This could pose "HR" problems, since then the U.S. company would have to treat U.S. citizens differently from host country employees. This was the fictional employers' dilemma in the "Sara Strong" case, below, where the Mexican branch of a U.S. bank sought to have one of its female employees "fit in" to Mexican culture by dressing more provocatively and pretending not to have any decision making authority at the Mexico City bank. This, according to the fictional branch manager, was to make sure that "customer preferences" were honored.

A U.S. company, operating abroad under Title VII's non-discrimination mandates, is still free to obey the mandates of the host country. In the following case, decided prior to Bourelsan, the federal district court assumed that Title VII applied, but that Saudi Arabia's laws created a "BFOQ" relative to religion. The plaintiff, or his estate, argued that as a Christian, he had a cause of action against the firm for requiring that he convert to Islam.

Kern v. Dynalectron Corp.,

577 F. Supp. 1196 (N.D. Tex. 1983)

U.S. District Court for the Northern District of Texas

Wade Kern filed this religious-discrimination suit pursuant to Title VII of the Civil Rights Act of 1964, 42 U.S.C. § 2000e-2000e-17 (1976) against Dynalectron Corporation. Since filing, Wade Kern died and his wife Mildred Kern was properly substituted as Plaintiff by an Order signed on September 25, 1980.

42 U.S.C. § 2000e-5 (Title VII), 28 U.S.C. § 1331 (federal question), and 28 U.S.C. § 1343 (civil rights actions) all confer jurisdiction upon this Court over the subject matter involved herein. Plaintiff is a resident of Fort Worth, Texas and Defendant is a Delaware corporation. Thus, this Court has jurisdiction over the persons involved pursuant to 28 U.S.C. § 1332, diversity of jurisdiction. The parties stipulate that Defendant is an employer within the definition of Title VII, 42 U.S.C. § 2000e(b).

The case was tried before the Court without a jury. Having heard and considered all the evidence presented at trial and the arguments and briefs of the parties, the Court now enters its opinion and judgment.

On August 17, 1978, Wade Kern entered into a written contract of employment with the Defendant, Dynalectron Corporation, to perform duties as a helicopter pilot. Defendant was under a subcontract with Kawasaki Heavy Industries, Limited, to provide pilots to work in Saudi Arabia. The work to be performed in Saudi Arabia consisted of flying helicopters over crowds of Moslems making their pilgrimage along Muhammad's path to Mecca. The purpose of these flights was twofold: to protect against any violent outbreaks and to help fight fires. Apparently, while en route to Mecca, the marchers lived in tents. Frequently, fires would erupt as a result of cooking over fires which were started too close to the tents.

Three bases were established for Dynalectron's pilots: at Jeddah, Dhahran, and Riyadh. Those pilots who were stationed at Jeddah would be required to fly into the holy area, Mecca. Saudi Arabian law, based upon the tenets of the Islamic religion, prohibits the entry of non-Moslems into the holy area, Mecca, under penalty of death. Thus, Dynalectron, in accordance with its contract with Kawasaki, requires all pilots stationed at Jeddah to be (or become) Moslem. Had Wade Kern continued to work for Dynalectron, he would have been based in

Jeddah and, therefore, his conversion from Baptist to Moslem would have been required.

Such a conversion was not unusual for pilots flying for Dynalectron. In fact, the Defendant regularly sent pilots to indoctrination courses where they were taught the basic formulation of the Islamic faith, converted thereto, and received a certificate manifesting said conversion. Wade Kern went through such a course which was taught in Tokyo, Japan, chose his new Islamic name, signed his certificate of conversion and then changed his mind about his conversion. At that point Kern returned to Fort Worth at his own expense and told Defendant of his decision. Defendant later offered Kern a job as a member of the air crew, a position not requiring his conversion. However, Kern declined to take that job.

Within one hundred eighty days after Kern left the Defendant's employ on September 4, 1978, Kern filed a sworn complaint with the Equal Employment Opportunity Commission alleging that he was denied an employment opportunity with Defendant due to its discrimination against him because of his religious beliefs. On July 6, 1979, the Equal Employment Opportunity Commission issued Kern a right to sue letter and Kern properly filed suit in this Court within the following ninety-day period.

To establish a prima facie case of discrimination based on Title VII, Plaintiff Kern has the initial burden of pleading and proving: (1) Wade Kern's bona fide belief that conversion to Islam is contrary to his religious faith; (2) that he informed his employer of his beliefs; and (3) he was discharged because of his refusal to convert. Although Kern was not actually fired from his job, both Kern and Dynalectron understood that the job required Kern's conversion. Kern refused to continue working for Dynalectron because he did not want to be a Moslem. Had he not quit, however, Dynalectron would have fired him from this job since it required his conversion. Therefore, this Court holds that Kern was constructively discharged. . . . Plaintiff here has established a prima facie case.

After the Plaintiff in a case such as this has proved his prima facie case by a preponderance of the evidence, the burden shifts to the Defendant. The United States Supreme Court, in a case vacating a Fifth Circuit opinion which misconstrued the defendant's burden, stated:

The burden that shifts to the defendant, therefore, is to rebut the presumption of discrimination by producing evidence that the plaintiff was rejected, or someone else was preferred, for a legitimate, nondiscriminatory reason. The defendant need not persuade the court that it was actually motivated by the proffered reasons. It is sufficient if the defendant's evidence raises a genuine issue of fact as to whether it discriminated against the plaintiff. To accomplish this, the defendant must clearly set forth, through the introduction of admissible evidence, the reasons for the plaintiff's rejection. The explanation provided must be legally sufficient to justify a judgment for the defendant.... We have stated consistently that the employee's prima facie case of discrimination will be rebutted if the employer articulates lawful reasons for the action; that is, to satisfy this intermediate burden, the employer need only produce admissible evidence which would allow the trier of fact rationally to conclude that the employment decision had not been motivated by discriminatory animus.

Texas Department of Community Affairs v. Burdine, 450 U.S. 248, 254 and 257, 101 S. Ct. 1089, 1094 and 1095-1096, 67 L. Ed. 2d 207 (1981) (footnotes omitted). Thus, the burden that shifts to the defendant after the plaintiff has proven the prima facie case is one of production, not persuasion. The burden of persuasion never leaves the plaintiff regardless of the intermediate shifts in the burden of production.

One of the several ways in which the defendant can carry this secondary burden is by establishing that the discrimination was not unlawful since religion may be a bona fide occupational qualification (B.F. O.Q.).

The B.F.O.Q. defense is set forth in § 703(a) of Title VII:

"Notwithstanding any other provision of this title ... it shall *not* be an unlawful employment practice for an employer to hire and employ employees ... on the basis of religion, sex, or national origin in those certain instances where religion, sex, or national origin is a bona fide occupational qualification reasonably necessary to the normal operation of that particular business or enterprise."

This defense has properly been construed by the cases as a narrow exception in order to avoid the situation where the exception swallows the rule.

. . .

In *Diaz v. Pan American World Airways,* 442 F.2d 385 (5th Cir.1971), the Court looked to the primary function of the employer's business to judge whether or not the B.F.O.Q. defense could properly be utilized. "The use of the word 'necessary' in section 703(e) requires that we apply a business *necessity* test, not a business *convenience* test. That is to say, discrimination based on sex is valid only when the *essence* of the business operation would be undermined by not hiring members of one sex exclusively." 442 F.2d at 388 (emphasis in original). The Fifth Circuit held that the primary function of an airline is the safe transportation of passengers and, thus, hiring females exclusively as stewardesses could not properly fit into the B.F.O.Q. exception. That is, hiring male stewards would in no way undermine the essence of providing safe air transportation.

. . .

Two cases have upheld the use of the B.F.O.Q. exception in instances where the safety of third parties might be risked if the exception were not used. That is, the discriminatory acts were allowed to stand since preventing the discrimination in these cases would result in the diminished safety of third parties. Both of these cases involved the Age Discrimination in Employment Act of 1967, 29 U.S.C. § 621-634 (1967) which contains a B.F.O.Q. exception that is identical to the one in Title VII.

. . .

The case presently in issue is unique in several respects: it concerns the possible application of the B.F.O.Q. exception to a *religious* discrimination case and it involves the safety of the employee only, not that of third parties. Clearly, Title VII makes the B.F.O.Q. exception applicable to religious discrimination cases. However, the instances where the exception is actually applied to such a case are few indeed.

In the instant case, discrimination exists: only pilots who either already are Moslem, or those who convert thereto, can be hired to fly from the Jeddah base into the holy area. Since all pilots stationed at Jeddah would be required to fly into Mecca, all of them must be Moslem. This Court as a factfinder holds that regardless of the exact moment Wade Kern found out about the requirement that he convert, he continued to perform his duties under the contract by travelling to Japan solely for the purpose of attending the indoctrination sessions and completing his conversion to the Islamic faith. Further, when Wade Kern changed his mind about the conversion and returned to Fort Worth, he knew he could no longer keep his job flying out of Jeddah since he was not a Moslem. Plaintiff, upon his return to Texas, informed his supervisor, Mr. Zedikee that he could not convert to the Islamic faith in good conscience. As a non-Moslem, he could no longer hold the job that he had with Dynalectron. Dynalectron offered him a different job which started some months in the future which Kern declined to accept. Thus, the elements of Kern's prima facie case are established.

The Defendant's burden of producing a legitimate reason for the existing discrimination is properly sustained through the application of the B.F.O.Q. exception to Kern's case. By applying the standard set forth in *Weeks,* this Court holds that Dynalectron has proven a factual basis for believing that *all* non-Moslems would be unable to perform this job safely. Specifically, non-Moslems flying into Mecca are, if caught, beheaded.

In the language used in *Diaz,* the essence of Dynalectron's business is to provide helicopter pilots. In this instance, under a subcontract with Kawasaki Heavy Industries, the Defendant had to provide Moslem pilots for the Jeddah base. Specifically, the subcontract dated August 28, 1977, required that Moslem pilots and mechanics be provided as necessary for operations in the holy area of Saudi Arabia. Thus, the essence of Dynalectron's business would be undermined by the beheading of all the non-Moslem pilots based in Jeddah.

As to the second unique aspect of this case, the fact that the safety of the employee is in jeopardy instead of the safety of third parties as was the case in *Greyhound,* this application of the B.F.O.Q. may be new, but it is certainly not without some precedent.

209

The specific facts of this case, *e.g.* where the safety of the employee requires the existence of religious discrimination, can be analogized to the often discussed situation involving discrimination against women of child-bearing age in order to protect the safety of their unborn children. The latter situation is a much harder one in which to apply the B.F.O.Q. exception since proof that a toxic environment directly harms women in this age group and not male workers who might father children is lacking. Thus, the discrimination against women hired to work in a toxic environment in favor of men would be hard to justify without a showing that men working in that environment are less apt than women to produce abnormal children. See: Comment, *Employment Rights of Women in the Toxic Workplace,* 65 Calif.L.Rev. 113 (1977). However, no such problem exists in applying the B.F.O.Q. exception to the instant case.

There can be no question but that non-Moslem pilots stationed in Jeddah are not safe as compared to Moslem pilots. Therefore, Dynalectron's discrimination against non-Moslems in general, and Wade Kern specifically, is not unlawful since to hire Moslems exclusively for this job "is a bona fide occupational qualification reasonably necessary to the normal operation of that particular business," § 703(a) of Title VII. Notwithstanding the religious discrimination in this case, the Court holds and finds that the B.F.O.Q. exception is properly applicable.

There are cases which hold that mere stereotypic impressions of male and female roles or customer preferences of one gender over the other are not enough to justify discrimination as a B.F.O.Q., *City of Los Angeles Dept. of Water v. Manhart,* 435 U.S. 702, 707, 98 S. Ct. 1370, 1374, 55 L. Ed. 2d 657 (1978); *Diaz v. Pan American World Airways, Inc.,* 442 F.2d 385, 389 (5th Cir.1971), *cert. den.,* 404 U.S. 950, 92 S. Ct. 275, 30 L. Ed. 2d 267 (1971). It is also true that the same maxims are equally applicable to religious discrimination. That is, mere customer preference of one religion over another is not enough to raise religious discrimination to the level of B.F. O.Q. However, as is more fully explicated below, the case at bar is distinguishable from the customer preference cases.

. . .

. . .it is clear from the evidence adduced at trial that being Moslem was linked to job performance. In fact, as has been stated before, an absolute prerequisite to doing this job (flying helicopters into Mecca) is that one be a Moslem.

As to the statement contained in *Fernandez* that no foreign nation can compel the non-enforcement of Title VII here, this too is inapplicable to the present case. Title VII was written with a B.F.O.Q. exception which was clearly applicable to religious discrimination. Merely by using this exception and applying it to the instant facts, this Court is not engaging in the non-enforcement of Title VII. It clearly is applying Title VII's B.F.O.Q. exception as it was intended to be applied (*i.e.* in those limited instances where one must tolerate religious discrimination where it is a necessity, in fact, a prerequisite for the performance of a job). Thus, this Court is in no way allowing a foreign nation, here Saudi Arabia, to compel the non-enforcement of Title VII in this country.

The second count in Kern's complaint is one against Dynalectron for breach of its employment contract. Plaintiff asserts that the contract does not specifically require the employee to be a Moslem and, thus, because Dynalectron failed to keep him on as an employee after he decided not to convert, it breached its contract with him.

However, based upon the facts that Kern was fully aware of the requirement that he convert and that he started to perform under the contract by attending the indoctrination sessions in Japan, this Court holds that he is now estopped from denying that he either knew or assented to the requirement that he convert to the Islamic faith in order to get the job. Moreover, it was Kern who failed to meet the known requirement that he convert; thus, Dynalectron in no way breached its contract with him.

Therefore, this Court concludes that Dynalectron did not breach its contract with Wade Kern.

FINDINGS OF FACT

1. Plaintiff, Mildred M. Kern, is a female citizen of the United States and a resident of Fort Worth, Tarrant County, Texas.

2. Defendant, Dynalectron Corporation, is a corporation incorporated under the laws of the

State of Delaware, and is doing business in Fort Worth, Tarrant County, Texas.

3. Plaintiff has taken the necessary steps to confer jurisdiction upon this Court. Plaintiff, Mildred M. Kern, was duly appointed Executrix of the Last Will of Wade C. Kern and as the qualified Executrix of Mr. Kern's Last Will was duly substituted as Plaintiff in place of Wade C. Kern on September 25, 1980, by order of this Court.

4. Wade C. Kern (hereinafter "Kern") on or about August 7, 1978, entered into a written contract of employment with Defendant Dynalectron Corporation.

5. Pursuant to the employment contract with the Defendant Corporation, Kern commenced duty as a helicopter pilot and began training under the direction of the Defendant.

6. Kern was to perform duties as a helicopter pilot in the country of Saudi Arabia.

7. Defendant informed Kern prior to his departure for Tokyo, Japan, that a portion *1203 of Saudi Arabia was within the Holy Area surrounding Mecca, located within Saudi Arabia and that it was required by the laws of Saudi Arabia that any person entering the Holy Area be of the Islamic faith.

8. The employment contract of August 7, 1978, specifically refers to compliance with the laws and regulations of the country where services were to be performed.

9. Kern was aware of the religious laws of Saudi Arabia and that he would be required to perform some duties within the Holy Area.

10. The Contract of Agreement Heli-1 between the Minister of Interior, General Civil Defense Administration, the Kingdom of Saudi Arabia and Kawasaki Heavy Industries, Limited, required that Moslem pilots and mechanics be provided as necessary for operations in the Holy Area of Saudi Arabia.

11. Defendant is a subcontractor of Kawasaki Heavy Industries, the primary contractor with the government of Saudi Arabia, for the maintenance and operation of helicopters within Saudi Arabia. Defendant's subcontract specifically requires:

"Moslem pilots and mechanics shall be provided as necessary for operations in the Holy Area."

Kern was well-aware of this requirement.

12. Following his Islamic conversion in Tokyo, about noon on September 3, 1978, Kern changed his mind at about midnight that same day and returned to Fort Worth, Texas, and advised Defendant that he had changed his mind about employment in a pilot's position for Saudi Arabia.

13. Kern inquired with Defendant about other openings for air crews. He was advised by Defendant that he could be employed in January, 1979, in an air crew position not requiring the Moslem faith. Kern demanded that he be kept on the payroll of Defendant until such time, which action Defendant declined to take.

CONCLUSIONS OF LAW

1. To the extent that any of the foregoing Findings of Fact constitute Conclusions of Law, the same are adopted and are incorporated by reference herein.

2. The Court has jurisdiction over the subject matter of the suit by virtue of 42 U.S.C. § 2000e-5 and by 28 U.S.C. §§ 1331 and 1343.

3. Defendant corporation operates and maintains a business and is an employer within the meaning of 42 U.S.C. § 2000e(b) in that the company is engaged in an industry effecting commerce and employs at least fifteen persons.

4. Defendant requires for employment that an individual be a Moslem to perform the duties of helicopter pilot in certain portions of Saudi Arabia.

5. The requirement that an individual be a Moslem to perform the duties of a helicopter pilot in certain portions of Saudi Arabia is a bona fide occupational qualification within the meaning of 42 U.S.C. § 2000e-2(e).

6. Kern voluntarily and unilaterally rescinded his agreement to work for Defendant and thus breached his obligation under the contract.

Judgment will be entered in accordance with this Memorandum Opinion.

Unlike Kern's case, the fictional case of Sara Strong in Mexico City does not require the bank to treat her differently on the basis of sex/gender. Customer preference, as the Kern case indicates, is not a sufficient reason to discrimination against an employee on the basis of sex. Title VII would apply, and the case raises ethical issues more than legal ones.

Sara Strong in Mexico

Sara Strong, a 2014 graduate of Daniels College of Business, and a native of Castle Rock, Colorado, begins her career with Wells Fargo, but after four years in commercial loans takes a junior management position with the North American Bancorp, based in Chicago, with operations in Canada, Mexico, Central America, Colombia, Venezuela, and the United States. Over the next two years, she rises in the ranks, until she is considered for a "plum" foreign assignment in Mexico City. She is 28, a "quick study," very energetic, and has a winning personality. She considers herself a prime candidate for making a top management job at North American Bank sometime in her early 30's.

All 'fast track' employees heading for top management have foreign assignments, and, preferring sun and Spanish, Sara relishes the chance to have her foreign assignment in Mexico. She has a brief interview there with her soon-to-be-boss, William Vitam, who seems knowledgeable and fair, and is highly regarded at Chicago headquarters.

When she moves to Mexico City in June of 2020 and begins working with Vitam, she begins to see some things that bother her. For one thing, all the men (both Mexican and U.S. citizens) take a rather 'patronizing' attitude toward the women, whether the women are receptionists, tellers, or work in other positions in the bank. The Mexican bank clients expect that their accounts will be handled by men, and Vitam does nothing to promote Sara in their eyes, as someone with actual decision-making power in NAB. As she writes her long-time friend, Christina Markkula, "I feel like I'm being paraded around as something 'decorative.' I'm not allowed to meet with any client without my 'male handler' around, and Vitam is encouraging me to 'look and act more feminine.' He even gave me a thousand dollar bonus to go shopping for 'sexier' clothes so that 'our Mexican friends will be suitably impressed.' This place is driving me loco en la cabeza! Vamonos! I don't know how much longer I can take this!"

In October of 2020, she shares her concerns with Vitam in his office. He explains (patiently, he thinks) that he personally had a hand in seeing that she came to Mexico City, that she had tremendous potential to attract some of the top corporate customers in Mexico City, and that she just needed to "relax" and use her "feminine charms" to "beguile and bewitch" the CFOs and CEOs of major companies. He again encourages her to attend social events with them, to make herself "available" without doing anything she couldn't "write home to Sterling Heights about." He tells her, "Most of these guys are married; they just want the chance to be seen with an attractive American lady."

During this meeting, Vitam did tell her (as he had told her before on several occasions) that her mind and her analyses were still very important to the branch in Mexico City. She would still have decision-making authority, only it would not be visible to the Mexican clients. They would continue to think that men-only were making the decisions. He also assures her that, years hence, when there is equality among the sexes in Mexico, professional life at the branch will change as well. "But for now, when in Mexico, do as the Mexicans do."

All of this is so discouraging to Sara that her performance begins to suffer. She is not given the opportunities to appear professional that her male counterparts from the U.S. are given. After one year, her review from Vitam notes "the beginnings of a negative attitude that may reduce her effectiveness as an executive at the bank." Over Christmas vacation in 2020, she contacts Comerica again, and agrees to take a position with less prestige and pay than the one she will be leaving at NAB. She gives notice to Vitam in January of 2021, and shortly thereafter returns to Chicago.

One of her classmates from DU is now an attorney with a top firm in Chicago, and tells her that she has a valid Title VII cause of action against NAB. She promptly goes to the EEOC regional office, and the EEOC does an investigation. None of her allegations are disputed, but NAB stands firm on the notion that she was only "asked to do what was reasonably necessary in the business climate of Mexico City." The EEOC determines that she was discriminated against on the basis of her sex, and gives her a right to sue letter. Her attorney friend files a lawsuit against NAB alleging that the bank violated Title VII in its actions toward her in Mexico, and asking for damages based on the loss of income from that job versus her current job.

Assume that Mexico has passed laws regarding equal opportunity based on gender and race, but there is relatively little enforcement. There is no agency monitoring equal opportunities in employment, and few cases have gone to court. Most people doing business "just go along" with a patriarchal culture where women are to be seen and not heard. You may also assume that both NAB and Sara Strong are U.S. citizens and that Title VII does apply to this situation.

What are the ethical issues in this situation? That is: What should Vitam do? What should Sara do? What should the bank do? Explain.

IV.   CORPORATE AND GOVERNMENTAL LABOR ABUSES

The chase for profits can lead corporations to overlook abuses in its supply chain; the case of Doe v. Nestle and other U.S. companies trading in Ivory Coast chocolate confirms this. In the following case, the Supreme Court as of 2021 decides to leave it up to Congress to create protections for overseas workers in slave-like conditions, although it is highly unlikely that U.S. politicians from either major party will lean on U.S. corporations to curb reliance on overseas suppliers using slave labor.

NESTLE USA, INC., Petitioner) v. JOHN DOE I, et al.;
CARGILL, INC., Petitioner v. JOHN DOE I, et al.

Supreme Court of the United States (2021) JUSTICE **THOMAS** announced the judgment of the Court and delivered the opinion of the Court with respect to Parts I and] II, and an opinion with respect to Part III, in which JUSTICE **GORSUCH** and JUSTICE **KAVANAUGH** join.

The Alien Tort Statute (ATS) gives federal courts jurisdiction to hear certain civil actions filed by aliens.28U.S.C. § 1350. Although this jurisdictional statute does not create a cause of action, our precedents have stated that courts may exercise common-law authority under this statute to create private rights of action in very limited circumstances. See, *e.g.*, Sosa v. Alvarez-Machain, 542 U.S. 692 (2004). Respondents here seek a judicially created cause of action to recover damages from American corporations that allegedly aided and abetted slavery abroad. Although respondents' injuries occurred entirely overseas, the Ninth Circuit held that respondents could sue in federal court because the defendant corporations allegedly made "major operational decisions" in the United States. The Ninth Circuit erred by allowing this suit to proceed.

I

According to the operative complaint, Ivory Coast—a West-African country also known as Côte d'Ivoire—is responsible for the majority of the global cocoa supply. Respondents are six individuals from Mali who allege that they were trafficked into Ivory Coast as child slaves to produce cocoa.

Petitioners Nestlé USA and Cargill are U. S.-based companies that purchase, process, and sell cocoa. They did not own or operate farms in Ivory Coast. But they did buy cocoa from farms located there. They also provided those farms with technical and financial resources—such as training, fertilizer, tools, and cash—in exchange for the exclusive right to purchase cocoa. Respondents allege that they were enslaved on some of those farms.

Respondents sued Nestlé, Cargill, and other entities, contending that this arrangement aided and abetted child slavery. Respondents argue that petitioners "knew or should have known" that the farms were exploiting enslaved children yet continued to provide those farms with resources. App. 319. They further contend that petitioners had economic leverage over the farms but failed to exercise it to eliminate child slavery. And although the resource distribution and respondents' injuries occurred outside the United States, respondents contend that they can sue in federal court because petitioners allegedly made all major operational decisions from within the United States.

The District Court dismissed this suit after we held that the ATS does not apply extraterritorially. Kiobel v. Royal DutchPetroleum, 569 U.S. 108 (2013). It reasoned that respondents sought to apply the ATS extraterritorially because the only domestic conduct alleged was general corporate activity. While this suit was on appeal, we held that courts cannot create new causes of action against foreign corporations under the ATS. Jesner v. Arab Bank, PLC, 584 U.S. ___ (2018). The Ninth Circuit then reversed the District Court in part. Although the Ninth Circuit determined that *Jesner* compelled dismissal of all foreign corporate defendants, it concluded that the opinion did not foreclose judicial creation of causes of action against domestic corporations. The Ninth Circuit also held that respondents had pleaded a domestic application of the ATS, as required by *Kiobel*, because the "financing decisions . . . originated" in the United States Doe v. Netle, SA. 906 F.3d 1120, 1124-26 (2018). We granted certiorari, 591 U. S. ___, 141 S. Ct. 188, 207 L. Ed. 2d 1114 (2020), and now reverse.

II

Petitioners and the United States argue that respondents improperly seek extraterritorial application of the ATS. We agree.

Our precedents "reflect a two-step framework for analyzing extraterritoriality issues. First, we presume that a statute applies only domestically, and we ask "whether the statute gives a clear, affirmative indication" that rebuts this presumption. For the ATS, *Kiobel* answered that question in the negative. Although we have interpreted its purely jurisdictional text to implicitly enable courts to create causes of action, the ATS does not expressly "regulate conduct" at all, much less "evince a 'clear indication of extraterritoriality.'" Courts thus cannot give "extraterritorial reach" to any cause of action judicially created under the ATSSecond, where the statute, as here, does not apply extraterritorially, plaintiffs must establish that "the conduct relevant to the statute's focus occurred in the United States." RJR Nabisco, 579 U.S. at 337. "[T]hen the case involves a permissible domestic application even if other conduct occurred abroad." *Ibid.*

The parties dispute what conduct is relevant to the "focus" of the ATS. Respondents seek a judicially created cause of action to sue petitioners for aiding and abetting forced labor overseas. Arguing that aiding and abetting is not even a tort, but merely secondary liability for a tort, petitioners and the United States contend that "the conduct relevant to the [ATS's] focus" is the conduct that directly caused the injury. All of *that* alleged conduct occurred overseas in this suit. The United States also argues that the "focus" inquiry is beside the point; courts should not create an aiding-and-abetting cause of action under the ATS at all. . . . For their part, respondents argue that aiding and abetting is a freestanding tort and that courts may create a private right of action to enforce it under the ATS. They also contend that the "focus" of the ATS is conduct that violates international law, that aiding and abetting forced labor is a violation of international law, and that domestic conduct can aid and abet an injury that occurs overseas.

Even if we resolved all these disputes in respondents' favor, their complaint would impermissibly seek extraterritorial application of the ATS. Nearly all the conduct that they say aided and abetted forced labor—providing training, fertilizer, tools, and cash to overseas farms—occurred in Ivory Coast. The Ninth Circuit nonetheless let this suit proceed because respondents pleaded as a general matter that "every major operational decision by both companies is made in or approved in the U. S." But allegations of general corporate activity—like decisionmaking—cannot alone establish domestic application of the ATS.

As we made clear in *Kiobel*, a plaintiff does not plead facts sufficient to support domestic application of the ATS simply by alleging "mere corporate presence" of a defendant. Pleading general corporate activity is no better. Because making "operational decisions" is an activity common to most corporations, generic allegations of this sort do not draw a sufficient connection between the cause of action respondents seek—aiding and abetting forced labor overseas—and domestic conduct. "[T]he presumption against extraterritorial application would be a craven watchdog indeed if it retreated to its kennel whenever *some* domestic activity is involved in the case." Morrison v. Nat'l Austl. Bank Ltd., 561 U.S. 247 (2010). To plead facts sufficient to support a domestic application of the ATS, plaintiffs must allege more domestic conduct than general corporate activity. The Ninth Circuit erred when it held otherwise.

III

Respondents' suit fails for another reason, which does not require parsing allegations about where conduct occurred: We cannot create a cause of action that would let them sue petitioners. That job belongs to Congress, not the Federal Judiciary. *Sosa* indicated that courts may exercise common-law authority under the ATS to create private rights of action in very limited circumstances. *Sosa* suggested, for example, that courts could recognize causes of action for three historical violations of international law: "violation of safe conducts, infringement of the rights of ambassadors, and piracy." *Ibid.* But our precedents since *Sosa* have clarified that courts must refrain from creating a cause of action whenever there is even a single sound reason to defer to Congress. . . .. Tellingly, we have never created a cause of action under the ATS. Even without reexamining *Sosa*, our existing precedents prohibit us from creating a cause of action here.

215

A

Originally passed as part of the Judiciary Act of 1789, the ATS provides jurisdiction to hear claims brought "by an alien for a tort only, committed in violation of the law of nations or a treaty of the United States." 28 U.S.C. §1350. If, for example, a treaty adopted by the United States creates a tort-related duty, federal district courts have jurisdiction to hear claims by aliens for breach of that duty.

But the statute on its own does not empower aliens to sue. We have been clear that "the ATS is a jurisdictional statute creating no new causes of action." Aliens harmed by a violation of international law must rely on legislative and executive remedies, not judicial remedies, unless provided with an independent cause of action. In more than 200 years, Congress has established just one: the Torture Victim Protection Act of 1991. That Act creates a private right of action for victims of torture and extrajudicial killings in violation of international law.

Because that cause of action does not apply here, respondents ask us to create a new one. They suggest that a plaintiff is entitled to a judicially created cause of action absent compelling reasons to withhold one. But our precedents demand precisely the opposite rule.

In *Sosa*, we "assume[d]" that the First Congress, which enacted the ATS, believed that federal courts, under general common law, "would recognize private causes of action for certain torts in violation of the law of nations." Although our decision in Erie Railroad v. Tompkins, 1939, we noted, for example, that courts in certain circumstances likely could recognize causes of action for violations of three historical torts: "violation of safe conducts, infringement of the rights of ambassadors, and piracy.

At the same time, we stressed that this authority was narrow. We noted that there was "no basis to suspect Congress had any examples in mind beyond those [three] torts." *Ibid.* And we suggested that future "development" of law might "preclud[e] federal courts from recognizing" new causes of action

To guide our reasoning in the future, we described a two-step test that plaintiffs must satisfy before a court can create a cause of action under the ATS. First, the plaintiff must establish that the defendant violated "'a norm that is specific, universal, and obligatory'" under international law. . . .That norm must be "defined with a specificity comparable to" the three international torts known in 1789. Second, the plaintiff must show that courts should exercise "judicial discretion" to create a cause of action rather than defer to Congress.

. . . .

We recently identified a sound reason to think Congress might doubt a judicial decision to create a cause of action that would enforce torts beyond those three: Creating a cause of action under the ATS "inherent[ly]" raises "foreign-policy concerns." (Citing to the Jesner case) This suit illustrates the point, for the allegations here implicate a partnership (the Harkin-Engel Protocol and subsequent agreements) between the Department of Labor, petitioners, and the Government of Ivory Coast. Under that partnership, petitioners provide material resources and training to cocoa farmers in Ivory Coast—the same kinds of activity that respondents contend make petitioners liable for violations of international law. Companies or individuals may be less likely to engage in intergovernmental efforts if they fear those activities will subject them to private suits.

Although specific foreign-policy concerns may vary from case to case, our precedents are clear that creating a cause of action to enforce international law beyond three historical torts invariably gives rise to foreign-policy concerns. ("foreign-policy . . . concerns [are] inherent in ATS litigation"). Because "[t]he political branches, not the Judiciary, have the responsibility and institutional capacity to weigh foreign-policy concerns," there will always be a sound reason for courts not to create a cause of action for violations of international law—other than perhaps for those three torts that were well established in 1789.

***

The judgment of the Court of Appeals is reversed, and the cases are remanded for further proceedings.

It is so ordered.

1. Did this case ever go to trial?

2. Why would the majority describe the activities of US corporations as "ordinary"?

3. Would Congress ever consider amending the alien tort statute to allow for claims like these?

4. If the U.S. were to pledge to the United Nations that it would commit to fighting slavery and other practices considered illegal under international law, should it make U.S. corporations like these accountable in U.S. courts?

Arguably, if corporations put money above all other considerations, political rulers put power above other considerations. The efforts to hold governments accountable has been a long historical struggle. Originally, the immunity of foreign sovereign states to judicial process was absolute. There are historical reasons for this: English and European sovereigns typically disallowed their courts from entertaining lawsuits from its citizens that could result in judgments that would tap into the public treasury. But what if a plaintiff in France were to sue the King of England and win a judgment? The King of England would instruct his judges not to make payment, and also instruct his judges not to entertain lawsuits against the government of France. That way, alliances and cooperative relations could be strengthened among sovereigns. Thus, baked into international customary law in the 18th and 19th centuries was the concept that foreign sovereigns were immune from being sued in any nation's court system.

In the 20th century, however, newly formed communist nations engaged in global trade through state owned enterprises. When sued, the sovereign defendants would always claim sovereign immunity. Gradually, courts in the U.S. and England began yeah considering whether the activities of these sovereigns were commercial in nature, and, if so, courts were allowed to proceed with Judgments against the foreign sovereign. Often, the judgment could be satisfied by attaching assets in the US or England or elsewhere. This new, "restrictive" notion of sovereign immunity took hold; in 1976, the US passed the foreign sovereign immunities act, allowing for legal actions against foreign sovereigns where the cause of action was directly related to the commercial activities of the foreign sovereign.

28 U.S. Code § 1605 - General exceptions to the jurisdictional immunity of a foreign state

(a) A foreign state shall not be immune from the jurisdiction of courts of the United States or of the States in any case—
(1)
in which the foreign state has waived its immunity either explicitly or by implication, notwithstanding any withdrawal of the waiver which the foreign state may purport to effect except in accordance with the terms of the waiver;

(2)

in which the action is based upon a commercial activity carried on in the United States by the foreign state; or upon an act performed in the United States the in connection with a commercial activity of the foreign state elsewhere; or upon an act outside the territory of the United States in connection with a commercial activity of the foreign state elsewhere and that act causes a direct effect in the United States;

(3)

in which rights in property taken in violation of international law are in issue and that property or any property exchanged for such property is present in the United States in connection with a commercial activity carried on in the United States by the foreign state; or that property or any property exchanged for such property is owned or operated by an agency or instrumentality of the foreign state and that agency or instrumentality is engaged in a commercial activity in the United States;

(4)

in which rights in property in the United States the acquired by succession or gift or rights in immovable property situated in the United States are in issue;

(5)

not otherwise encompassed in paragraph (2) above, in which money damages are sought against a foreign state for personal injury or death, or damage to or loss of property, occurring in the United States and caused by the tortious act or omission of that foreign state or of any official or employee of that foreign state while acting within the scope of his office or employment; except this paragraph shall not apply to—

(A)

any claim based upon the exercise or performance or the failure to exercise or perform a discretionary function regardless of whether the discretion be abused, or

(B)

any claim arising out of malicious prosecution, abuse of process, libel, slander, misrepresentation, deceit, or interference with contract rights; or

(6)

in which the action is brought, either to enforce an agreement made by the foreign state with or for the benefit of a private party to submit to arbitration all or any differences which have arisen or which may arise between the parties with respect to a defined legal relationship, whether contractual or not, concerning a subject matter capable of settlement by arbitration under the laws of the United States the or to confirm an award made pursuant to such an agreement to arbitrate, if (A) the arbitration takes place or is intended to take place in the United States the (B) the agreement or award is or may be governed by a treaty or other international agreement in force for the United States calling for the recognition and enforcement of arbitral awards, (C) the underlying claim, save for the agreement to arbitrate, could have been brought in a United States court under this section or section 1607, or (D) paragraph (1) of this subsection is otherwise applicable.

In the following case, <u>Saudi Arabia v. Nelson</u>, the U.S. plaintiff (Nelson) was recruited in the U.S. to work for a government owned hospital in Saudi Arabia. After insisting on reporting a number of potential safety hazards, which was his job, he was arrested and jailed and tortured. On returning to the U.S. he sued Saudi Arabia, attempting to use the restrictive theory of sovereign immunity, saying that his action was based on Saudi Arabia's commercial activity, and therefore actionable in U.S. courts. The Supreme Court did not accept his legal theories, but the dissent provides an interesting counterpoint to the majority opinion. Of course, Congress could amend the Foreign Sovereign Immunities Act to make claims like Nelson's more clearly actionable, but it is unlikely that will happen.

Saudi Arabia v. Nelson (1993)

JUSTICE SOUTER delivered the opinion of the Court.

The Foreign Sovereign Immunities Act of 1976 entitles foreign states to immunity from the jurisdiction of courts in the United States, 28 U.S.C. 1604, subject to certain enumerated exceptions. 1605. One is that a foreign state shall not be immune in any case "in which the action is based upon a commercial activity carried on in the United States by the foreign state." 1605(a)(2). We hold that respondents' action alleging personal injury resulting from unlawful detention and torture by the Saudi Government is not "based upon a commercial activity" within the meaning of the Act, which consequently confers no jurisdiction over respondents' suit.

I

Because this case comes to us on a motion to dismiss the complaint, we assume that we have truthful factual allegations before us, see United States v. Gaubert, 499 U.S. 315, 327 (1991), though many of those allegations are subject to dispute. Petitioner Kingdom of Saudi Arabia owns and operates petitioner King Faisal Specialist Hospital in Riyadh, as well as petitioner Royspec Purchasing Services, the hospital's corporate purchasing agent in the United States. App. 91. The Hospital Corporation of America, Ltd. (HCA), an independent corporation existing under the laws of the Cayman Islands, recruits Americans for employment at the hospital under an agreement signed with Saudi Arabia in 1973.

In its recruitment effort, HCA placed an advertisement in a trade periodical seeking applications for a position as a monitoring systems engineer at the hospital. The advertisement drew the attention of respondent Scott Nelson in September, 1983, while Nelson was in the United States. After interviewing for the position in Saudi Arabia, Nelson returned to the United States, where he signed an employment contract with the hospital, id., at 4, satisfied personnel processing requirements, and attended an orientation session that HCA conducted for hospital employees. In the course of that program, HCA identified Royspec as the point of contact in the United States for family members who might wish to reach Nelson in an emergency.

In December, 1983, Nelson went to Saudi Arabia and began work at the hospital, monitoring all "facilities, equipment, utilities and maintenance systems to insure the safety of patients, hospital staff, and others." He did his job without significant incident until March, 1984, when he discovered safety defects in the hospital's oxygen and nitrous oxide lines that posed fire hazards and otherwise endangered patients' lives. Over a period of several months, Nelson repeatedly advised hospital officials of the safety defects and reported the defects to a Saudi Government commission as well. Hospital officials instructed Nelson to ignore the problems.

The hospital's response to Nelson's reports changed, however, on September 27, 1984, when certain hospital employees summoned him to the hospital's security office where agents of the Saudi Government arrested him. The agents transported Nelson to a jail cell, in which they "shackled, tortured and bea[t]" him, and kept him four days without food. Although Nelson did not understand Arabic, government agents forced him to sign a statement written in that language, the content of which he did not know; a hospital employee who was supposed to act as Nelson's interpreter advised him to sign "anything" the agents gave him to avoid further beatings. *Ibid.* Two days later, government agents transferred Nelson to the Al Sijan Prison "to await trial on unknown charges." *Ibid.*

At the prison, Nelson was confined in an overcrowded cell area infested with rats, where he had to fight other prisoners for food and from which he was taken only once a week for fresh air and exercise. Ibid. Although police interrogators repeatedly questioned him in Arabic, Nelson did not learn the nature of the charges, if any, against him. For several days, the Saudi Government failed to advise Nelson's family of his whereabouts, though a Saudi official eventually told Nelson's wife, respondent Vivian Nelson, that he could arrange for her husband's release if she provided sexual favors. *Ibid.*

Although officials from the United States Embassy visited Nelson twice during his detention, they concluded that his allegations of Saudi mistreatment were "not credible," and made no protest to Saudi authorities. It was only at the personal request of a United States Senator that the Saudi Government released Nelson, 39 days after his arrest, on November 5, 1984. Seven days later, after failing to convince him to return to work at the hospital, the Saudi Government allowed Nelson to leave the country.

In 1988, Nelson and his wife filed this action against petitioners in the United States District Court for the Southern District of Florida seeking damages for personal injury. The Nelsons' complaint sets out 16 causes of action, which fall into three categories. Counts II through VII and counts X, XI, XIV, and XV allege that petitioners committed various intentional torts, including battery, unlawful detainment, wrongful arrest and imprisonment, false imprisonment, inhuman torture, disruption of normal family life, and infliction of mental anguish. Counts I, IX, and XIII charge petitioners with negligently failing to warn Nelson of otherwise undisclosed dangers of his employment, namely, that, if he attempted to report safety hazards, the hospital would likely retaliate against him and the Saudi Government might detain and physically abuse him without legal cause. Finally, counts VIII, XII, and XVI allege that Vivian Nelson sustained derivative injury resulting from petitioners' actions. Presumably because the employment contract provided that Saudi courts would have exclusive jurisdiction over claims for breach of contract, the Nelsons raised no such matters.

The District Court dismissed for lack of subject matter jurisdiction under the Foreign Sovereign Immunities Act of 1976, 28 U.S.C. 1330, 1602 et seq. It rejected the Nelsons' argument that jurisdiction existed, under the first clause of 1605(a)(2), because the action was one "based upon a commercial activity" that petitioners had "carried on in the United States." Although HCA's recruitment of Nelson in the United States might properly be attributed to Saudi Arabia and the hospital, the District Court reasoned, it did not amount to commercial activity "carried on in the United States" for purposes of the Act. The court explained that there was no sufficient "nexus" between Nelson's recruitment and the injuries alleged. "Although [the Nelsons] argu[e] that, but for [Scott Nelson's] recruitment in the United States, he would not have taken the job, been arrested, and suffered the personal injuries, the court said, "this `connection' [is] far too tenuous to support jurisdiction" under the Act. Likewise, the court concluded that Royspec's commercial activity in the United States, purchasing supplies and equipment for the hospital, had no nexus with the personal injuries alleged in the complaint; Royspec had simply provided a way for Nelson's family to reach him in an emergency.

The Court of Appeals reversed. 923 F.2d 1528 (CA11 1991). It concluded that Nelson's recruitment and hiring were commercial activities of Saudi Arabia and the hospital, carried on in the United States for purposes of the Act, id., at 1533, and that the Nelsons' action was "based upon" these activities within the meaning of the statute, *id.*, at 1533-1536. There was, the court reasoned, a sufficient nexus between those commercial activities and the wrongful acts that had allegedly injured the Nelsons: "the detention and torture of Nelson are so intertwined with his employment at the Hospital," the court explained, "that they are `based upon' his recruitment and hiring" in the United States. The court also found jurisdiction to hear the claims against Royspec. After the Court of Appeals denied petitioners' suggestion for rehearing en banc, , we granted certiorari, 504 U.S. 972 (1992). We now reverse.

II

The Foreign Sovereign Immunities Act "provides the sole basis for obtaining jurisdiction over a foreign state in the courts of this country." Argentine Republic v. Amerada Hess Shipping Corp., 488 U.S. 528, 443 (1989). Under the Act, a foreign state is presumptively immune from the jurisdiction of United States courts; unless a specified exception applies, a federal court lacks subject matter jurisdiction over a claim against a foreign state. Verlinden B.V. v. Central Bank of Nigeria, 461 U.S. 480, 488-89 (1983). . .

Only one such exception is said to apply here. The first clause of 1605(a)(2) of the Act provides that a foreign state shall not be immune from the jurisdiction of United States courts in any case "in which the action is based upon a commercial activity carried on in the United States by the foreign state." The Act defines such activity as "commercial activity carried on by such state and having substantial contact with the United States," 1603(e), and provides that a commercial activity may be "either a regular course of commercial conduct or a particular commercial transaction or act," the "commercial character of [which] shall be determined by reference to" its "nature," rather than its "purpose," 1603(d).

There is no dispute here that Saudi Arabia, the hospital, and Royspec all qualify as "foreign state[s]" within the meaning of the Act (see 28 U.S.C. 1603(a), (b) (term "`foreign state'" includes "`an agency or instrumentality of a foreign state'"). For there to be jurisdiction in this case, therefore, the Nelsons' action must be "based upon" some "commercial activity" by petitioners that had "substantial contact" with the United States within the meaning of the Act. Because we conclude that the suit is not based upon any commercial activity by petitioners, we need not reach the issue of substantial contact with the United States.

We begin our analysis by identifying the particular conduct on which the Nelsons' action is "based" for purposes of the Act. . . . .Although the Act contains no definition of the phrase "based upon," and the relatively sparse legislative history offers no assistance, guidance is hardly necessary. In denoting conduct that forms the "basis," or "foundation," for a claim, see Black's Law Dictionary 151 (6th ed. 1990) (defining "base"); Random House Dictionary 172 (2d ed. 1987) (same); Webster's Third New International Dictionary 180, 181 (1976) (defining "base" and "based"), the phrase is read most naturally to mean those elements of a claim that, if proven, would entitle a plaintiff to relief under his theory of the case. . . .

What the natural meaning of the phrase "based upon" suggests, the context confirms. Earlier, we noted that 1605(a)(2) contains two clauses following the one at issue here. The second allows for jurisdiction where a suit "is based . . . upon an act performed in the United States in connection with a commercial activity of the foreign state elsewhere," and the third speaks in like terms, allowing for jurisdiction where an action "is based . . . upon an act outside the territory of the United States in connection with a commercial activity of the foreign state elsewhere and that act causes a direct effect in the United States." Distinctions among descriptions juxtaposed against each other are naturally understood to be significant, and Congress manifestly understood there to be a difference between a suit "based upon" commercial activity and one "based upon" acts performed "in connection with" such activity. The only reasonable reading of the former term calls for something more than a mere connection with, or relation to, commercial activity.

In this case, the Nelsons have alleged that petitioners recruited Scott Nelson for work at the hospital, signed an employment contract with him, and subsequently employed him. While these activities led to the conduct that eventually injured the Nelsons, they are not the basis for the Nelsons' suit. Even taking each of the Nelsons' allegations about Scott Nelson's recruitment and employment as true, those facts alone entitle the Nelsons to nothing under their theory of the case. The Nelsons have not, after all, alleged breach of contract, see supra, at 354, but personal injuries caused by petitioners' intentional wrongs and by petitioners' negligent failure to warn Scott Nelson that they might commit those wrongs. Those torts, and not the arguably commercial activities that preceded their commission, form the basis for the Nelsons' suit.

Petitioners' tortious conduct itself fails to qualify as "commercial activity" within the meaning of the Act, although the Act is too "`obtuse'" to be of much help in reaching that conclusion. We have seen already that the Act defines "commercial activity" as "either a regular course of commercial conduct or a particular commercial transaction or act," and provides that "[t]he commercial character of an activity shall be determined by reference to the nature of the course of conduct or particular transaction or act, rather than by reference to its purpose." 28 U.S.C. 1603(d). If this is a definition, it is one distinguished only by its diffidence; as we observed in our most recent case on the subject, it "leaves the critical term 'commercial' largely undefined." Republic of Argentina v. Weltover, Inc., 504 U.S. 607, 612 (1992). We do not, however, have the option to throw up our hands. The term has to be given some interpretation, and congressional diffidence necessarily results in judicial responsibility to determine what a "commercial activity" is for purposes of the Act.

We took up the task just last Term in Weltover, which involved Argentina's unilateral refinancing of bonds it had issued under a plan to stabilize its currency. Bondholders sued Argentina in federal court, asserting jurisdiction under the third clause of 1605(a)(2). In the course of holding the refinancing to be a commercial activity for purposes of the Act, we observed that the statute "largely codifies the so-called `restrictive' theory of foreign sovereign immunity first endorsed by the State Department in 1952." 504 U.S. at 612. We accordingly held that the meaning of "commercial" for purposes of the Act must be the meaning Congress understood the restrictive theory to require at the time it passed the statute. See id., at 612-613.

Under the restrictive, as opposed to the "absolute," theory of foreign sovereign immunity, a state is immune from the jurisdiction of foreign courts as to its sovereign or public acts (jure imperii), but not as to those that are private or commercial in character (jure gestionis). . . . .We explained in Weltover, supra, at 614, that a state engages in commercial activity under the restrictive theory where it exercises "`only those powers that can also be exercised by private citizens,'" as distinct from those "`powers peculiar to sovereigns.'" Put differently, a foreign state engages in commercial activity for purposes of the restrictive theory only where it acts "in the manner of a private player within" the market. Weltover, 504 U.S., at 614. See Restatement (Third) of the Foreign Relations Law of the United States 451 (1987) ("Under international law, a state or state instrumentality is immune from the jurisdiction of the courts of another state, except with respect to claims arising out of activities of the kind that may be carried on by private persons").

We emphasized in Weltover that whether a state acts "in the manner of" a private party is a question of behavior, not motivation:

"[B]ecause the Act provides that the commercial character of an act is to be determined by reference to its `nature,' rather than its `purpose,' the question is not whether the foreign government is acting with a profit motive or instead with the aim of fulfilling uniquely sovereign objectives. Rather, the issue is whether the particular actions that the foreign state performs (whatever the motive behind them) are the type of actions by which a private party engages in `trade and traffic or commerce.'" Weltover, supra, at 614.

We did not ignore the difficulty of distinguishing "`purpose' (i.e., the reason why the foreign state engages in the activity) from `nature' (i.e., the outward form of the conduct that the foreign state performs or agrees to perform)," but recognized that the Act "unmistakably commands" us to observe the distinction. Because Argentina had merely dealt in the bond market in the manner of a private player, we held, its refinancing of the bonds qualified as a commercial activity for purposes of the Act despite the apparent governmental motivation. (cite to Weltover).

Unlike Argentina's activities that we considered in Weltover, the intentional conduct alleged here (the Saudi Government' wrongful arrest, imprisonment, and torture of Nelson) could not qualify as commercial under the restrictive theory. The conduct boils down to abuse of the power of its police by the Saudi Government, and however monstrous such abuse undoubtedly may be, a foreign state's exercise of the power of its police has long been understood for purposes of the restrictive theory as peculiarly sovereign in nature. . . .

The Nelsons and their *amici* urge us to give significance to their assertion that the Saudi Government subjected Nelson to the abuse alleged as retaliation for his persistence in reporting hospital safety violations, and argue that the character of the mistreatment was consequently commercial. One amicus, indeed, goes so far as to suggest that the Saudi Government "often uses detention and torture to resolve commercial disputes." (Brief for Human Rights Watch as Amicus Curiae, at 6.) But this argument does not alter the fact that the powers allegedly abused were those of police and penal officers. In any event, the argument is off the point, for it goes to purpose, the very fact the Act renders irrelevant to the question of an activity's commercial character. Whatever may have been the Saudi Government's motivation for its allegedly abusive treatment of Nelson, it remains the case that the Nelsons' action is based upon a sovereign activity immune from the subject matter jurisdiction of United States courts under the Act.

In addition to the intentionally tortious conduct, the Nelsons claim a separate basis for recovery in petitioners' failure to warn Scott Nelson of the hidden dangers associated with his employment. The Nelsons allege that, at the time petitioners recruited Scott Nelson and thereafter, they failed to warn him of the possibility of severe retaliatory action if he attempted to disclose any safety hazards he might discover on the job. See supra, at 354. In other words, petitioners bore a duty to warn of their own propensity for tortious conduct. But this is merely a semantic ploy. For aught we can see, a plaintiff could recast virtually any claim of intentional tort committed by sovereign act as a claim of failure to warn, simply by charging the defendant with an obligation to announce its own tortious propensity before indulging it. To give jurisdictional significance to this feint of language would effectively thwart the Act's manifest purpose to codify the restrictive theory of foreign sovereign immunity. Cf. United States v. Shearer, 473 U.S. 52, 54 -55 (1985) (opinion of Burger, C.J.).

III

The Nelsons' action is not "based upon a commercial activity" within the meaning of the first clause of 1605(a)(2) of the Act, and the judgment of the Court of Appeals is accordingly reversed.

It is so ordered.

JUSTICE KENNEDY, joined by JUSTICE BLACKMUN and JUSTICE STEVENS, concurred in part, but also dissented in part. That opinion is here omitted.

JUSTICE STEVENS, dissenting.

Under the Foreign Sovereign Immunities Act of 1976 (FSIA), a foreign state is subject to the jurisdiction of American courts if two conditions are met: the action must be "based upon a commercial activity" and that activity must have a "substantial contact with the United States." These two conditions should be separately analyzed, because they serve two different purposes. The former excludes commercial activity from the scope of the foreign sovereign's immunity from suit; the second identifies the contacts with the United States that support the assertion of jurisdiction over the defendant.

In this case, as JUSTICE WHITE has demonstrated, petitioner kingdom of Saudi Arabia's operation of the hospital and its employment practices and disciplinary procedures are "commercial activities" within the meaning of the statute, and respondent Scott Nelson's claim that he was punished for acts performed in the course of his employment was unquestionably "based upon" those activities. Thus, the first statutory condition is satisfied; petitioner is not entitled to immunity from the claims asserted by respondent.

Unlike JUSTICE WHITE, however, I am also convinced that petitioner's commercial activities - whether defined as the regular course of conduct of operating a hospital or, more specifically, as the commercial transaction of engaging respondent "as an employee with specific responsibilities in that enterprise," Brief for Respondents 25 - have sufficient contact with the United States to justify the exercise of federal jurisdiction. Petitioner Royspec maintains an office in Maryland and purchases hospital supplies and equipment in this country. For nearly two decades, the hospital's American agent has maintained an office in the United States and regularly engaged in the recruitment of personnel in this country. Respondent himself was recruited in the United States and entered into his employment contract with the hospital in the United States. Before traveling to Saudi Arabia to assume his position at the hospital, respondent attended an orientation program in Tennessee. The position for which respondent was recruited and ultimately hired was that of a monitoring systems manager, a troubleshooter, and, taking respondent's allegations as true, it was precisely respondent's performance of those responsibilities that led to the hospital's retaliatory actions against him.

Whether the first clause of 1605(a)(2) broadly authorizes "general" jurisdiction over foreign entities that engage in substantial commercial activity in this country, or, more narrowly, authorizes only "specific" jurisdiction over particular commercial claims that have a substantial contact with the United States, petitioners' contacts with the United States in this case are, in my view, plainly sufficient to subject petitioners to suit in this country on a claim arising out of its nonimmune commercial activity relating to respondent. If the same activities had been performed by a private business, I have no doubt jurisdiction would be upheld. And that, of course, should be a touchstone of our inquiry; for as JUSTICE WHITE explains, ante, at 366, n. 2, 6, and when a foreign nation sheds its uniquely sovereign status and seeks out the benefits of the private marketplace, it must, like any private party, bear the burdens and responsibilities imposed by that marketplace. I would therefore affirm the judgment of the Court of Appeals.

Case Questions:

1. Did in this case ever go to trial?
2. Is the dissent convincing to you? why or why not?
3. If Congress were to change the FSIA, what would the "right" wording be, in your mind?
4. Why Is Congress unlikely to change the FSIA? Looking back at Chapter Three, what I think the executive branch would say about having the U.S. create greater liability for foreign sovereigns?
5. Saudi Arabia has long been considered an ally of the United states in the Middle East. Would either Congress or the President favor a U.S. judiciary that was more aggressive in finding Liability for foreign sovereigns?
6. If torture is illegal under international law, should the U.S. do more to hold torturers accountable?
7. Even if Nelson won in the Supreme Court, could he actually collect on a judgment against Saudi Arabia?

Chapter Eight:

International Business Ethics

The basic problem confronting any company doing business across national boundaries is that the rules and regulations are different from nation to nation, and the moral values tend to be different as well. Students will find a rich literature about customs and practices in different countries, and how astute businesspeople will embrace those different customs and practices. For example, after World War II, U.S. businesspeople gradually got used to the different customs of gift giving in Japan, for example, or how to bow and use both hands when presenting a business card there. The perennial question for international business ethics is to what extent a company should import its own values and practices into a different culture. The viewpoint of "moral relativism" — "when in Rome, do as the Romans do"— can be attractive at times, but those who have though long and hard about global values and standards insist that there are some practices that an ethical company would not engage in, regardless of whether it seems acceptable or widely practiced in the host country.

This chapter will address both the legal and ethical differences between doing business in the U.S. and doing business in foreign countries. We will address a number of issues in this chapter, including the following:

I.   Differing labor and environmental standards
II. Bribery and corruption
III. Industrial espionage and cyber-hacking
IV. Business and human rights
V.   Outsourcing
VI. Offshoring and multinational tax avoidance

I.   DIFFERING LABOR AND ENVIRONMENTAL STANDARDS

A.   Labor Standards and Supply Chains

There are numerous books and articles about US and European companies taking advantage of cheap labor abroad. in the US, jobs held by union workers in the 1950s and 1960s it became outsourced to other nations. Consumers may have benefited from cheaper prices, but many workers in the U.S. lost ground. The textile industry, for example, had seen US factory is moving from northern states to southern ones where so-called right to work laws made it more difficult for workers to form unions, but eventually even the textile industry in the southern U.S. states shuttered factories to use overseas labor. In some instances, labor forces overseas were underage, worked in so-called "sweatshop" conditions, and usually for wages considerably lower than U.S. wages.

Apple Inc. is often cited as a very successful U.S. company. Its founder and famous CEO, Steve Jobs, once told President Obama that Apple's outsourced jobs were never coming back to America. Apple, like many other notable U.S. companies, faced criticism for its outsourcing; for Apple, using the services of Foxconn in China was especially problematic. The following video highlights some of the working conditions where iPads and other Apple products are made.

https://www.youtube.com/watch?v=zgRrvPUOJ0Y

The textile industry now depends on outsourced labor from places like Bangladesh. In particular, the "fast fashion" industry uses cheap labor (and cheap materials) to create clothing that may only be worn once or twice. Those consumers who are (arguably) addicted to fast fashion are often inadvertently supporting the use of underage, overworked labor force, working in conditions that are hazardous. For example, the Rana Plaza disaster in 2013 revealed poor working conditions and very low wages, where U.S. companies were making use of that labor and making significant profits.

https://cleanclothes.org/campaigns/past/rana-plaza

We should also note that the fast fashion industry creates a lot of environmental damage as well, and uses key resources such as water that could better be devoted to basic human needs.

Why is Fast Fashion So Bad?

"According to Business Insider, fashion production comprises 10% of total global carbon emissions, as much as the European Union. It dries up water sources and pollutes rivers and streams, while 85% of all textiles go to dumps each year. Even washing clothes releases 500 000 tons of microfibres into the ocean each year, the equivalent of 50 billion plastic bottles."

https://earth.org/fast-fashions-detrimental-effect-on-the-environment/

U.S. consumers occasionally become aware of the hidden labor and environmental costs of their favorite products, and some boycotts and protests are not uncommon. In the 1990s, Nike, Inc. experienced considerable pushback from consumers and labor activists for its use of overseas labor, and even faced lawsuits for making false claims about its overseas practices.

See, e.g., Nike v. Kasky, 539 U.S.654 (2003), and also an excellent website from Middle Tennessee State University:

https://mtsu.edu/first-amendment/article/261/nike-v-kasky

In 2021, according to the National Review, Nike issued a statement "tepidly expressing concern" about forced labor in China's Xinjiang region earlier this year. Nike's statement was partly a response to the growing amount of evidence that led the U.S. government, in addition to the parliaments of almost ten Western countries, to "call the Chinese Communist Party's conduct there — a sweeping campaign to eradicate Uyghurs through arbitrary mass detention, population-control policies, and other horrors — genocide and crimes against humanity."

https://www.nationalreview.com/corner/nike-of-china-and-for-china/

B.   The Overlap Between Labor and the Environment

Labor and environmental issues often overlap. Asbestos, for example, creates environmental harms, especially to those who have to work with it. In an excellent article about different regulatory and cultural-ethical standards, Tom Donaldson points out how the consortium seeking to rehabilitate the S.S. United States found that labor and environmental standards in the U.S. made the project cost prohibitive. But the group found that sending the ship to Sevastopol, Ukraine for stripping out the asbestos would be considerably cheaper, but also expose the workers to serious environmental harms. As Donaldson notes:

A few years ago, for example, a group of investors became interested in restoring the SS *United States*, once a luxurious ocean liner. Before the actual restoration could begin, the ship had to be stripped of its asbestos lining. A bid from a U.S. company, based on U.S. standards for asbestos removal, priced the job at more than $100 million. A company in the Ukrainian city of Sevastopol offered to do the work for less than $2 million. In October 1993, the ship was towed to Sevastopol.

A cultural relativist would have no problem with that outcome, but I do. A country has the right to establish its own health and safety regulations, but in the case described above, the standards and the terms of the contract could not possibly have protected workers in Sevastopol from known health risks. Even if the contract met Ukrainian standards, ethical businesspeople must object. Cultural relativism is morally blind. There are fundamental values that cross cultures, and companies must uphold them."

Donaldson goes on to note that in many areas, nations and regions and communities within those nations have "moral free space" to create rules and expectations that people generally agree to, such as the practice of giving preference to hiring relatives of current workers (i.e., nepotism), rather than having a lengthy search based on "merit." Donaldson also cites the gift giving practices in Japan as not contradicting "fundamental values that cross cultures."

https://hbr.org/1996/09/values-in-tension-ethics-away-from-home

For the textile industry and low wage outsourced labor, Donaldson points out that many countries are in a formative stage of economic development and that it doesn't make a lot of sense to compare wages and working conditions in The United states or Europe with places like Bangladesh. In the video about Foxconn, above, we see that, despite the harsh conditions, many in China are ready willing and able to take those jobs. I believe that Donaldson would draw the line at working conditions that are clearly hazardous to the workers' health, such as his example of the S.S. United States in Sevastopol. In terms of the issues that arose in Doe v. Nestle (see Chapter Seven), the direct or indirect use of slave labor would be wrong, anywhere and everywhere. Yet at least five global companies make use of child/slave labor from the Ivory Coast.

https://www.theodysseyonline.com/5-major-chocolate-companies-child-labor

So, the basic ethical question for companies doing business globally is to identify those fundamental values that cross cultures — i.e. to identify values that are more universal, where the differing practices of nations and communities within those nations are actually antagonistic to those fundamental values. Below, we offer a brief explanation of now Donaldson and his colleague Thomas Dunfee, analyzed how to blend local cultural values and practices that are worthy of respect and compliance, with more fundamental, universal values that they call hyper norms.

C.   An Explanation of Integrative Social Contracts Theory

Tom Donaldson and Tom Dunfee wrote Ties that Bind (Harvard Business Press, 1999), a very influential book in the field of international business ethics offering a normative framework called Integrative Social Contracts Theory (ISCT). This is a summary of their process for determining the morality of any corporate act or policy in both a domestic and an international context. The authors, Donaldson and Dunfee, were colleagues at Wharton before Tom Dunfee's untimely death nine years ago.

227

There is arguably moral worth in the prevailing standards of a culture or community. That "everyone is doing it" may actually give us certain clues as to what is morally correct. ISCT offers a framework for analyzing business decision-making by discovering and articulating commonly shared assumptions, known in ISCT as *authentic norms*. Authentic norms are understood to be standards supported by a majority of some particular community. A *community* is a "self-defined, self-circumscribed group of people who interact in the context of shared tasks, values, or goals and who are capable of establishing norms of ethical behavior for themselves."[47] Accordingly, this broad concept embraces everything from nation-states to a group of professionals on a project.[48]

The relevant concept is that "local economic communities" can and do "generate ethical norms" for voluntary members of the group "through micro-social contracts."[49] Authentic norms might shift over time or might differ among business communities, but they offer a benchmark for measuring appropriate business behavior.

A close reading of *Ties that Bind* reveals that there is no clear test for evaluating the existence of particular authentic norms, although a requirement is that they are grounded in assumptions of consent and the right of exit for any member who disagrees. Further, ISCT suggests that authentic norms can emerge and be identified within *moral free space.* This space may be likened to a set of parameters or principles that provide a certain amount of breathing room in which various individuals and communities may establish differing values and norms.[50] But the diversity of norms has its limit; acting as a boundary to "moral free space" are various *hypernorms*, or "principles so fundamental that, be definition, they serve to evaluate lower order ethical norms."[51] This framework offers a way to assess whether otherwise authentic norms are fully legitimate (i.e., are consistent with hypernorms). Legitimacy assures that the authentic norms formed in moral free space can be claimed as ethical.

Briefly explained, a hypernorm provides a limit to the discretionary behavior of business, offering a strong standard that limits communal authentic norms and restricts the moral free space within which many business decisions are made. ICST divides hypernorms into procedural, structural and substantive, offering examples of each and admitting that others might still be discovered and articulated.

According to ISCT, procedural hypernorms "specify the rights of exit and voice" that are fundamental to supporting societal relations and communal decision-making.[52] Structural hypernorms are grounded in macro social contracts and are understood to "establish and support essential background institutions in society" such as the right to property and fair legal processes.[53] Substantive hypernorms " specify fundamental conceptions of the right and the good."[54] We will look at those first, then return later to a key structural hypernorm — the necessary social efficiency hypernorm.

---

[47] *Ties that Bind* (1999), at 39.

[48] Id. at 40-41

[49] Id. at 41

[50] Id. at 41-42

[51] Id. at 44

[52] Id. at 51

[53] Id. at 51-52, chart 53

[54] Id. at 52, chart 53

The Role of Hypernorms in ISCT

If all you have are micro-social contracts (with consent and right to exit), there would be many diverse standards, and very few general global standards for individual and corporate conduct. This is cultural relativism in full bloom.

Is this a problem? The authors think it is. Why? A thorough-going cultural relativism can easily become an agnostic, anything goes kind of moral relativism. If one nation's culture and practices (foot binding, female genital mutilation, violent suppression of dissent by businesspersons and others) are as morally valid as any other, there can be no general, global guidance for corporate behavior in matters of community, employees, human health and safety, and human rights generally.

"Convergence could occur around a set of twisted moral norms." (Ties, p. 57) That is, something can be ethically repugnant even if a majority of people around the world do not explicitly recognize it as such, and engage in practices such as:
- Indiscriminate lying
- Murder
- Theft
- Large scale bribery

Thus, there is a need for more general norms (standards) by which to evaluate micro social contracts. "Hypernorms constitute principles so fundamental that, by definition, they serve as second order norms by which lower order norms are to be judged."

Nature and Sources of Substantive Hypernorms

"Convergence" of religious, political, and philosophical thought.
- Rawls (A Theory of Justice)
- Aristotle (Nichomachean Ethics)
- Zagat (Mulsim concept)
- Action-less action (Hindu conception)

Also, where there are moral principles common to many cultures, and/or common methods of moral reasoning across diverse cultures.

Once it is clear that a decision involves ethical issues, those making a decision must make a preliminary determination whether there are hypernorms prohibiting, affirming, or circumscribing potential courses of action.

Yet in many parts of the world, there are such majority practices that you have to wonder if hypernorms could exist or be agreed upon. For example, gender discrimination (oppression against women), or continued tolerance of bribery, or authoritarian governments and cultures that do not encourage freedom of speech or religion.

Foundations for Substantive Hypernorms

Sources (philosophical, and collective agreement)
Sample of particular norms
       General: customary practices
       Global Legal Arrangements (treaties and conventions)
              Environment
              Social
              Economic

The Necessary Social Efficiency Hypernorm

This provides 'the basic underpinnings for liberty and opportunities for exchange' that are 'essential to enable individuals to achieve these necessary goods.' Necessary goods = justice and aggregate economic welfare. [This means that no group of human beings would set out to create a society in which injustice was the norm, or where economic welfare accrued only to a small percentage of participants. Of course, someone who is born privileged may wish to maintain material advantage, but the authors here are philosophizing: they posit, like Rawls, a "thought experiment" in which groups of people are brought together to create/imagine a society in which they would participate, but where their own place in that society is not known in advance.] Societies, in short, will almost always "want" justice and overall economic welfare.

Necessary goods "require a range of collective institutions," which in turn use a "range of institutional strategies." [e.g., property rights and enforcement of promises – both of which require public institutions for support].

Economic systems vary, and these systems impose certain obligations if the system is to work efficiently. If a society "chooses" a system to promote aggregate welfare, members of that society "should" play "their part" in maintaining the "underlying efficiency" of that system.[55]

[Not all economic systems qualify as legitimate, however; totalitarian or coercive environments may systematically violate procedural hypernorms or substantive hypernorm.]

How can efficiency be a moral norm? Isn't it just morally neutral, depending on the "end" to which the efficient means are applied? The authors think that *if* necessary social/public goods exist – justice and aggregate welfare – <u>then</u> efficiency in pursuing those goods is necessarily "good" in a moral sense. A judicial system that costs twice as much as an alternative system but delivers only the same amount of justice is "ripe for reform."[56]

Thus, they would exhort us to "discharge role duties stemming from the economizing parameters of Efficiency Strategies in which you participate." [57]

I would put it more simply: in a free market system, act consistently with the fundamental principles of that system [i.e., do nothing to undermine it]. If the system requires laws, institutions, and other public goods to support it, then do so; do not seek special exemptions, subsidies, impose externalities, hide information, subvert reasonable laws and regulations for the public good, etc.

---

[55] Id. at 119.
[56] Id. at 119-121.
[57] Id. at 130.

Rawls' duty of civility is translated here to mean a consistent honoring of the standards of cooperation. I like this sentence in particular:

"The duty, then, is to go beyond self-interest and in doing so to refuse to exploit the regrettable but inevitable ways in which institutions fail automatically to align self-interests with broader interests."[58]

To accept this proposition, we have to first reject the idea that "pursuing self-interest" at all times – both individually, corporately, and nationally – will actually result in overall justice and aggregate social welfare. Adam Smith's Wealth of Nations and his 'invisible hand' have often been misread to mean that all we need to do is to pursue self-interest and "the market" will take care of optimizing resources and, ultimately, general welfare. See generally Patricia Werhane, Adam Smith and his Legacy for Modern Capitalism, 1999. TD2 sum it up at page 138 of Ties that Bind, saying, "[a]s Adam Smith and other have noted, economic systems require the ethical cooperation of their participants. The efficiency hypernorm serves as a moral pathfinder, guiding business transactions where microsocial norms are obscure or inconsistent."

I would offer this thought: without the social and legal institutions and customs that Donaldson and Dunfee are speaking of – and that ethicist Richard DeGeorge mentions as 'background institutions' – there is no "market" that works in the way that neoclassical economists would espouse as champions of free market economics or free market capitalism. Without some allegiance or compliance with the principles of 'the system' – an allegiance commanded by the hypernorm of necessary social efficiency — the efforts of individuals to pursue their self-interest can actually be a system's undoing. If I champion my right to property but not yours, or champion your promise-keeping but not mine, the hypernorm of necessary social efficiency at the heart of our free market system is violated, and the system becomes inefficient in delivering justice and aggregate welfare.

Donaldson and Dunfee explicitly refer to the assumptions of a perfectly competitive market.[59] We should recall from economics and our many readings at Daniels that, in a perfectly competitive market, profit margins are razor-thin to zero; no one gets a monopoly, a government subsidy or preferential regulatory treatment, has a major information advantage over their counter-party, or a lucrative, non-competitive contract based on who you know in government. So, naturally enough, business people want advantages in order to make money, the more the better. So, they would seek monopolies, subsidies, special favors, etc. In a competitive free market capitalism, the institutions would be arranged to discourage such things. In crony capitalism, they happen all the time.

Digression on crony capitalism. You might be interested in Luigi Zingales' argument that the U.S. is becoming more like his home country, Italy, in failing to consistently reward competition and market excellence; instead, the U.S. has declined to where who you know (especially politicians) is more important than what you can provide to the market. A short article Zingales penned for the Wall Street Journal notes,

> "Traditionally, the U.S. has enjoyed a relatively honest democracy and transparent form of capitalism, which encouraged robust economic growth and contained the hunger for entitlements. This is less and less true. The U.S. tax code is filled with loopholes and special exemptions. Political connections increasingly count more than innovative ideas; young entrepreneurs often learn to lobby before they learn how to run a business."

---

[58] Id. at 134.
[59] Id. at 135.

"Seven out of the 10 richest counties in the U.S. are in the suburbs of Washington, D.C., which produces little except rules and regulations. Even worse, the slow growth and decreased social mobility of the last decade have damaged the free market's reputation as a creator of prosperity. The hundreds of millions of dollars awarded for disastrous economic performance—from Robert Rubin's salary as chairman of almost-bankrupt Citigroup to government loans for the actually bankrupt solar company Solyndra—have in turn weakened public belief in the system's fairness."

From *Crony Capitalism and the Crisis of the West*
Wall St. Journal, 2012.

On bribery

For various reasons, Donaldson and Dunfee agreed that bribery was an ethical offense anywhere and everywhere, even if widely practiced in various communities and nations. In Values in Tension, Donaldson notes:

"Bribery is widespread and insidious. Managers in transnational companies routinely confront bribery even though most countries have laws against it. The fact is that officials in many developing countries wink at the practice, and the salaries of local bureaucrats are so low that many consider bribes a form of remuneration. The U.S. Foreign Corrupt Practices Act defines allowable limits on petty bribery in the form of routine payments required to move goods through customs. But demands for bribes often exceed those limits, and there is seldom a good solution.
Bribery disrupts distribution channels when goods languish on docks until local handlers are paid off, and it destroys incentives to compete on quality and cost when purchasing decisions are based on who pays what under the table. Refusing to acquiesce is often tantamount to giving business to unscrupulous companies.

I believe that even routine bribery is intolerable. Bribery undermines market efficiency and predictability, thus ultimately denying people their right to a minimal standard of living. Some degree of ethical commitment—some sense that everyone will play by the rules—is necessary for a sound economy."

We can also relate this back to the hyper norm of necessary social efficiency. In a competitive market economy, we need to uphold the principles of competition, free and fair competition, to ensure aggregate social welfare. Because bribery undermines that, anywhere and everywhere, local bribing customs cannot be truly authentic — they violate the hypernorm of necessary social efficiency —and should not be followed.

II.   BRIBERY AND CORRUPTION

A.   Free Markets, The Commons, and Bribery

Markets, Free or Regulated?

A common misconception is that we could have a functioning market system with no regulations whatsoever. Put slightly differently, the misconception is that everyone (including people and firms) could, solely by pursing their self-interest, effectively contribute to making the best possible society. The truth is that without some form of regulation, slackers and cheaters would bring down the economy because people don't want to feel like "suckers." Let's explain this.

A sound "free market" requires voluntary exchanges in good faith and without fraud or deception. People and firms often break promises when it's in their self-interest to do so. They will also sometimes tell less than the truth, the whole truth, and nothing but the truth in marketing their goods. What happens when they do? After centuries of market exchanges, most nations have set rules for correcting exchanges that aren't truly voluntary and mutually beneficial — where people are tricked, lied to, manipulated, and so on. Without a legal system that enforces promises and guards against fraud and deception, there would be less trust in each other, and in the market system. Without enforced rules in place, the system would de-generate into a kind of anarchy where trust is minimal and markets are dysfunctional.

There's another reason for law and regulation, and that's about preserving trust and social capital, where cheating through bribery can become systemic without legal guardrails. We'll talk more about that below, but should also mention how trust and social capital are in many ways "public goods," part of a "commons" that we all share. Some of the best analogies for this come by looking to our environment, which is the "container" for all other economic activity: without clean air, clean water, sufficient natural resources, and a livable environment, our economy and lives suffer. But much of what we need in our environment is in what we call "the commons."

The Tragedy of the Commons & Public Goods

Although private property is at the core of capitalism and free markets (you can't sell what you don't own), not everything in the world can be assigned an owner. This is obviously true when it comes to the atmosphere, the oceans, migratory species like bluefin tuna or salmon, and major lakes and rivers. A pond can be owned, and there are riparian rights for landowners adjacent to rivers and streams, but it's impossible to assign ownership to much of Earth's air and water, and the living creatures that inhabit those spaces. Because we can't practically assign ownership to these spaces, they are considered "the commons."

We'll come to Garrett Hardin's famous "Tragedy of the Commons" in a moment. But first, we describe "the commons," where clean air and clean water are "public goods," because we cannot exclude anyone from using them. (They are, as economists would say, "non-excludable.) Also, and importantly, the enjoyment of clean air is "non-rivalrous" — that is, one person's use of enjoyment of the good does not use it up or preclude another's use or enjoyment of it. This is not, however, true of those species that fly through the air or edible life in the oceans. Bluefin tuna, for example, are fished to near-extinction because they are migratory and don't stay in any "owned" places on earth; they are "goods," and public in the sense of non-excludable, but rivalry is very much present. The human tendency is to use as much as possible from the commons, until the resources in the commons are exhausted, and exist no more.

On St. George's bank, for example, part of the oceanic commons that is closest to the U.S. and Canada's east coast, cod were once so abundant that cod fishermen were able to fish sustainably for many years. But advances in technology, including much larger boats, enabled commercial fishing crews to take more and more from the commons, until the species failed to reproduce in sufficient numbers to make fishing profitable.

If there had been an effective agreement on how to share the resource, many New England fishermen who are now unable to make a living by catching cod —as their parents and grandparents did— would still be doing that ancestral work. The problem is our human nature, which is illustrated by the public goods game. The game explains to us why unpunished "cheaters" threaten not only the efficiency of an economy, but also

233

its fairness to one and all. Because most of us hate to be "suckers," so we will withdraw our cooperativeness when one or more people start to defect from the agreement.

This relates to what is often called "the prisoner's dilemma," where police have captured two men who were conspiring to commit a crime and had promised not to "rat out" the other. In separate cells, each prisoner does not know what the other is telling the police investigators. If they both keep their promise to each other, according to game theorists, they are likely to go free or get minimal sentences for lack of confessional evidence from either. But if one defects (and this does reflect the reality of police investigatory tactics) by "flipping" or "cooperating" he can gain favored treatment at the expense of his partner. If both defect, according to game theory, the result is the worst possible for the two prisoners. Four possible outcomes are mapped out here: (1) keep promises, (2) A defects at the expense of B, (3) B defects at the expense of A, and (4) both defect. These are described as (1) mutual cooperation, (2) A as free rider, (3) A as "sucker", and (4) mutual defection.

No one wants to be the "sucker," maintaining cooperation while the other defects (and "wins"). Thus, where mutual coercion, mutually agreed upon rules exist, but there is no authority to keep the parties to their agreement, defections are likely. Likewise, we see the natural antipathy to being the "sucker" in the public goods game.

Here's how the public goods game goes:

Picture a group of ten people, you among them, and each person is given $10 in one dollar bills by an experimenter—one of many who now research human group behavior. The experimenter says that the group can put as much money as they want to in a community "pot," and the experimenter will then double that pot, and that amount will then be divided by 10 and redistributed, and the game goes on as long as everyone wants to play.

The best result is for everyone to put in ten dollars—the experimenter has provided a free resource, much like the abundant cod in the sea. But suppose group members are cautious, and try out the agreement in the first round by putting in two dollars. The pot is then $20, doubled to $40, and redistributed so that each member in the group now has $10 plus four dollars. In a rational, enlightened self-interested group, the game could go on and on, efficiently and fairly, so that in each round, everyone's trust increases and their money multiplies. To maximize income, once trust is established, group members could put in their entire portions; if trust were immediate, each would put in $10 to make a pot of $100, doubled to $200, and then each member of the group would have $20 to put in the collective pot. Round two would see $400 divided by 10, so that in round three, the potential maximum "take" of all members would be a pot of $800 divided by 10, or $80. And so it would go, if all members could abide by the agreement to maximize both individual and collective wealth.

But this is not what experimenters find. Inevitably, at least one member realizes that here she can put in little or nothing and start making more money than everyone else. Suppose that this is your realization: you decide to not put anything, in and everyone else puts it in two dollars. The pot would be $18, which gets doubled to $36, and everyone then gets $3.60 by the experimenter. This includes you, who put in nothing at all, so for zero investment you now have $13.60. This decision is very "efficient" for you, and everyone else is still gaining, so it's not all that unfair. But in experiments where this game is played so that everyone knows who is putting in a fair share and who is not, the pot will grow for a while and then start to shrink as other people start withholding funds from the collective pot. This behavior spreads, because no one wants to be a sucker, and eventually the game comes to a halt. Thus, the initial "cheaters" affect the other players in the game, who inevitably withdraw cooperative behavior. The same is true in any economy where individuals and firms temporarily gain by not contributing. Who can guarantee enforcement of the agreed upon rules? The punishment of "cheaters" is appropriately a public function, for government—usually this is state government enforcing promises made under contract law. In short, government is needed to maintain the "rules of the game" against free riders that don't put in their fair share.

In this link, Harvard psychologist Joshua Greene explains the Public Goods Game, and how its outcomes vary across cultures. (Optional for you to view.)

https://www.youtube.com/watch?v=4IIQrgplLu4

Garrett Hardin's Tragedy of the Commons is a bit different, but is very much the same in terms of how human nature works: we will tend to take as much as possible from the commons without contributing to it, until the commons no longer has the resources to keep the game going. Hardin asks us to image a set of "herdsmen" who raise cattle around a common area of grassy pasture, not owned by any of the herdsmen; each herdsmen uses not only his own property, but also lets his cattle graze on the commons that is not owned by anyone. It is to each herdsman's advantage to keep adding "just one more" cattle to the commons, but since this is typical of all herdsmen—and all humans, for that matter—the commons will eventually be overgrazed, and ultimately destroyed. Whether it eventually regenerates is a question of fact and science, but there is no assurance that it will regenerate. There are many overgrazed parts of this Earth that have become lifeless deserts.

Coming back to Hardin's commons for the cattle, we see most of all (1) a lack of systems thinking (how will my actions affect the entire system?), (2) short-term thinking (I'll do this now as I can see the immediate advantage of doing so), and (3) a tendency to look around and do what others are doing: someone who sees all the others adding cattle to the commons will usually conclude that they might as well do the same." But as masters of our own herds, if we could all think in our collective long-term self interest by comprehending and reminding ourselves about the entire system that sustains our herd, we would come to agreements on "best practices" for one and all. But we can't. It's particularly hard in the U.S. where "individualism" holds sway — no one else is going to tell us what to do!

But Hardin reminds us that we need "mutual coercion, mutually agreed upon" to make optimal use of the commons. Once upon a time, the cod on George's Bank were so plentiful that generations of fishing families from New England could make a good living.

Optional reading, but quite interesting: https://www.amnh.org/explore/videos/biodiversity/will-the-fish-return/the-sorry-story-of-georges-bank)

But after World War II, when fishing vessels from Russia, Canada, and the U.S. were all taking cod "unsustainably" from the George's Bank, we needed binding, coercive international agreements. Such agreements are very hard come by, with each nation pressing its own commercial advantages.

The lack of "mutual coercion mutually agreed upon" will often result in the degradation or complete loss of a given resource. This is happening in the case up bluefin tuna, where there are international agreements but the agreements are not strictly enforced. The same is true of rhino horns and elephant tusks. It is also true with regard to international agreements on money laundering, bribery, greenhouse gas emissions and climate change, and resources to fight the COVID-19 pandemic.

Let's go back to the prevailing "free market paradigm" and the invisible hand; in effect, that paradigm gives us permission to believe that we should act with maximum freedom or liberty, and that it will somehow "all work out" for the best socially and economically. If each individual "goes for it" and each company works to "maximize profits," the invisible hand will somehow optimize social and economic results. But Adam

Smith never claimed that for "the invisible hand." (See Werhane, Adam Smith and His Legacy for Modern Capitalism.) The myth of the invisible hand means that individuals and corporations feel justified acting selfishly, without thinking long term and without either comprehending the entire system and what would be "best practices" for the system as a whole. In short, because of the myth that "the free market" via the invisible hand optimizes social and economic outcomes they can feel intellectually and morally justified to do what the free riders in the public game do: think short-term and non-systematically.

Bribery and the Tragedy of the Commons

In Detroit, where I lived for 17 years, many companies wanted to sell to General Motors, who had buyers that had been influenced by "gifts" from these suppliers: hot tickets to Red Wings hockey games at the Joe Louis arena, and much more. GM cracked down on this, and eventually set a $30 limit on what "gifts" a buyer for GM could accept. Why crack down on something like that? Because GM wanted to make sure that its buyers were not influenced by factors other than quality and price. If a GM buyer were to choose a supplier based on the expectation of more "goodies" from the supplier's salesperson, that buyer's "self-serving bias" could easily yield a sub-par set of parts for GM's vehicles, or have GM paying more than it should in a free and fair market with buyers only looking out for GM's best interests.

In public contracting for the U.S. government, rules are also in place to insure that the U.S. taxpayer does not pay the wrong contractor, based on "gifts" or "bribes." That way, the government gets the best quality and price for the taxpayer's money.

But in many countries, there is so much corruption that almost any contract from the government can be influenced by a bribe. And, if you want to do business in that country, and all public officials are asking for bribes, your company is effectively locked out of that market unless you go along with what everyone else is doing: offering bribes or responding to requests for bribes.

So, again, what should you do if everyone is cheating? You may have had the experience of being in a classroom where a great majority of students appear to be cheating and getting away with it. How solid is your personal integrity to avoid joining them? Many cannot resist the temptation to cheat, but let's go back to the public goods game or to Garret Hardin: where all or most of the other people are doing X, and gaining advantages, and there are no rules preventing cheating, or if there are, no one is enforcing those rules.

Hobbes talks about the "state of nature" — but we have something similar going on here and now: the "state of self-nurture," where the herdsman near the commons or the player in a public goods game, realizing that they are getting less because of the actions of others, will soon join the others until "the commons" is seriously degraded. In the case of bribery of public officials, the "commons" would be a general and mutual agreement that public officials should not take bribes to contract on behalf of the government, and that laws would support that agreement. But such an agreement, even where that agreement is made into "law," can be undermined when enough people defect from agreement. Imagine that "the law" is to "drive 55" on most highways, but everyone drives 63-65 mph. More, you start to notice that no one ever gets pulled over from defecting from the general agreement, even where those defections are not just 63 mph, but 70 or 75 mph. Pretty soon, everyone is going 70 – 75. In general, once a few people (or firms) defect, then others will do likewise — and this suggests that Hardin is right, and that people follow the patterns of people playing the public goods game.

In short, if bribery is going on in a certain place, here in the U.S. or overseas, there will always be a temptation to join in. Even where bribery is contrary to law and prevailing morals, the temptation to gain advantage over others can be significant. See, for example, WalMart in Mexico. Where individuals and subunits in a company are being rewarded for economic gains, they will be even more tempted to break the law and/or break prevailing customs.

In a given country, bribery may be against the law, but if the law is not enforced, and lots of people and firms are doing it, it's almost inevitable that more and more people and firms will ignore the law, and where it's not a law but is still part of a social convention, more and more people will come to just go along because "everyone is doing it." When there are immediate short-term payoffs for joining in the bribery game, such as "maximizing shareholder value," defection from the law and from generally agreed upon norms is assured. The socially responsible company operating in places where bribery is common has a tough choice; the responsible choice is clear, but difficult — give up short term tangible advantage to "do the right thing."

That may ask too much, though. But this is where good law can come in. We see the FCPA, and note that the UK also has a serious fraud office monitoring British companies that might engage in corrupt practices.

B.   Foreign Corruption and U.S. Companies

The U.S. went first with the FCPA in 1976. Many U.S. companies complained that we were "shooting ourselves in the foot" in not being able to "compete" via bribery. Donald Trump has a similar view even now, which fits with his worldview that everyone and everything is corrupt, so just accept it and "compete." (Good firms believe they can compete on price and quality and refuse to engage in bribery.)

https://www.washingtonpost.com/business/2020/01/31/trump-fcpa/

Finally, the Organization for Economic Cooperation and Development (OECD) has a convention on bribery that 44 nations have ratified. See https://www.oecd.org/corruption/oecdantibriberyconvention.htm (please do look at this link).

This is mutual coercion, mutually agreed upon. We don't have time to dig into all the prosecutions, which continue; but evidently, many people and firms don't really think they'll be "pulled over" for exceeding the socially accepted limits around bribery.

Bottom line: without mutual coercion, mutually agreed upon, by all trading nations, and enforced vigorously, bribery will of course flourish, whether most people like it or not. Where bribery is "endemic" (regularly found among particular people or in a certain area), it does not mean that people actually like that it's inescapable, or that it's really just part of the "culture." It's up to U.S. businesses, and our government, to stand behind the FCPA and the OECD convention as something that represents the right direction for international law.

C.   Wal Mart in Mexico

The important Wal*Mart de Mexico bribery case is written about in detail in the NY Times, but there is a paywall.

Here is a brief summary from The Week magazine.

https://theweek.com/articles/476206/walmarts-explosive-mexican-bribery-scandal-concise-guide

In this summary, Tim Worstall makes the familiar argument that it's the FCPA that's the problem, not bribery.

"(While) it looks as if there's something at least worth investigating under the FCPA" in Walmart's Mexico fiasco, "I would argue that that is a problem with the FCPA," not Walmex's practices. We may not like bribery, and we shouldn't accept it in the U.S., but corruption is the price of doing business in Mexico and many other countries. "This really is just the way of the world," and we either tolerate it or put our companies at a competitive disadvantage.

In his Forbes article, Worstall says:

"[Bribery] really is just the way of the world. Some places do things differently from either the way we do or the way that we think things ought to be done. I tend to think that domestic laws which fail to recognise this fact are doomed to eventual failure. For those different ways are going to carry on even if we or our companies can no longer operate there because of our own domestic laws. My argument is simply that such laws as the FCPA and the Bribery Act shouldn't exist."

Elizabeth Spahn, who helped create the FCPA blog (free subscription) answers Tim Worstall this way:

"Bribery destroys rational markets, resulting in serious harm. The economists demonstrate case after case where the wrong project, wrong competitor, lack of quality or safety controls result in waste, inefficiency and in some cases massive deaths or environmental disasters. In addition, the economic studies show bribery used as an anti-competitive cartel device, increasing regulations to restrict market entry and harass competitors."

"In extreme cases, as Worstall recounts from his sad and terrifying personal experiences in Russia, unchecked bribery results in what economists term "state capture", or bi-lateral monopolies of bribe givers and takers. The people of Mexico, where Walmart is having some problems, are also struggling quite literally for their lives against corrupt cartels attempting to capture their country."

See Spahn, https://fcpablog.com/2012/4/23/so-what-bribes-destroy-market-capitalism-thats-what/

While Worstall complaints about the Foreign Corrupt Practices act and Spahn embraces it, we should take a look at one international bribery case it came to the Supreme Court in 1990.

D.   The FCPA and the "Act of State" Doctrine

The act of state doctrine basically is a separation of powers concept. The U.S. judiciary thinks of itself as secondary to the executive and legislative branches when it comes to foreign affairs. Thus, it hesitates to make any finding of fact or conclusion of law that might complicate U.S. foreign relations.

The act of state doctrine requires U.S courts to refrain from determining that acts carried out by a foreign state on its own territory are contrary to law. One exception might be determining violations of international norms that have broad consensus, such as cases of slavery, torture, or genocide.
The doctrine is not a legal obligation required by international law, but is a common law principle developed mainly by Anglo-Saxon jurisdictions on the basis of considerations of international comity, respect for the principles of sovereign equality and non-intervention in the internal affairs of other states, and separation of powers.

But U.S. courts will only dismiss a case where it is the official, public act of a foreign sovereign that is at issue. In the following case, the Court determined that the acceptance of a bribe by Nigerian public official was not an official public act, and that the case could proceed under the Foreign Corrupt Practices Act.

Kirkpatrick & Co. v. Environmental Tectonics,
493 U.S. 400 (1990)

Justice SCALIA delivered the opinion of the Court.

In this case, we must decide whether the act of state doctrine bars a court in the United States from entertaining a cause of action that does not rest upon the asserted invalidity of an official act of a foreign sovereign, but that does require imputing to foreign officials an unlawful motivation (the obtaining of bribes) in the performance of such an official act.

I

The facts as alleged in respondent's complaint are as follows: In 1981, Harry Carpenter, who was then Chairman of the Board and Chief Executive Officer of petitioner W.S. Kirkpatrick & Co., Inc. (Kirkpatrick), learned that the Republic of Nigeria was interested in contracting for the construction and equipment of an aeromedical center at Kaduna Air Force Base in Nigeria. He made arrangements with Benson "Tunde" Akindele, a Nigerian citizen, whereby Akindele would endeavor to secure the contract for Kirkpatrick. It was agreed that, in the event the contract was awarded to Kirkpatrick, Kirkpatrick would pay to two Panamanian entities controlled by Akindele a "commission" equal to 20% of the contract price, which would in turn be given as a bribe to officials of the Nigerian Government. In accordance with this plan, the contract was awarded to petitioner W.S. Kirkpatrick & Co., International (Kirkpatrick International), a wholly owned subsidiary of Kirkpatrick; Kirkpatrick paid the promised "commission" to the appointed Panamanian entities; and those funds were disbursed as bribes. All parties agree that Nigerian law prohibits both the payment and the receipt of bribes in connection with the award of a government contract.

Respondent Environmental Tectonics Corporation, International, an unsuccessful bidder for the Kaduna contract, learned of the 20% "commission" and brought the matter to the attention of the Nigerian Air Force and the United States Embassy in Lagos. Following an investigation by the Federal Bureau of Investigation, the United States Attorney for the District of New Jersey brought charges against both Kirkpatrick and Carpenter for violations of the Foreign Corrupt Practices Act of 1977, 91 Stat. 1495, *as amended,* 15 U.S.C. § 78dd-1 *et seq.,* and both pleaded guilty.

Respondent then brought this civil action in the United States District Court for the District of New Jersey against Carpenter, Akindele, petitioners, and others, seeking damages under the Racketeer Influenced and Corrupt Organizations Act, 18 U.S.C. § 1961 et seq., the Robinson-Patman Act, 49 Stat. 1526, 15 U.S.C. § 13 *et seq.,* and the New Jersey Anti-Racketeering Act, N.J.Stat.Ann. § 2C:41-2 *et seq.* (West 1982). The defendants moved to dismiss the complaint under Rule 12(b)(6) of the Federal Rules of Civil Procedure on the ground that the action was barred by the act of state doctrine.

The District Court, having requested and received a letter expressing the views of the legal advisor to the United States Department of State as to the applicability of the act of state doctrine, treated the motion as one for summary judgment under Rule 56 of the Federal Rules of Civil Procedure, and granted the motion. *Environmental Tectonics Corp., International v. W.S. Kirkpatrick & Co., Inc.,* 659 F. Supp. 1381 (1987). The District Court concluded that the act of state doctrine applies "if the inquiry presented for judicial determination includes the motivation of a sovereign act which would result in embarrassment to the sovereign or constitute interference in the conduct of foreign policy of the United States."

Id., at 1392-1393. Applying that principle to the facts at hand, the court held that respondent's suit had to be dismissed because, in order to prevail, respondents would have to show that

"the defendants or certain of them intended to wrongfully influence the decision to award the Nigerian Contract by payment of a bribe, that the Government of Nigeria, its officials, or other representatives knew of the offered consideration for awarding the Nigerian Contract to Kirkpatrick, that the bribe was actually received or anticipated and that, 'but for' the payment or anticipation of the payment of the bribe, ETC would have been awarded the Nigerian Contract." 659 F. Supp. at 1393.

The Court of Appeals for the Third Circuit reversed. 847 F.2d 1052 (1988). Although agreeing with the District Court that "the award of a military procurement contract can be, in certain circumstances, a sufficiently formal expression of a government's public interests to trigger application" of the act of state doctrine, *id.* at 1058, it found application of the doctrine unwarranted on the facts of this case. The Court of Appeals found particularly persuasive the letter to the District Court from the legal advisor to the Department of State, which had stated that, in the opinion of the Department, judicial inquiry into the purpose behind the act of a foreign sovereign would not produce the "unique embarrassment, and the particular interference with the conduct of foreign affairs, that may result from the judicial determination that a foreign sovereign's acts are invalid." *Id.* at 1061. The Court of Appeals acknowledged that "the Department's legal conclusions as to the reach of the act of state doctrine are not controlling on the courts," but concluded that "the Department's factual assessment of whether fulfillment of its responsibilities will be prejudiced by the course of civil litigation is entitled to substantial respect." *Id.* at 1062. In light of the Department's view that the interests of the Executive Branch would not be harmed by prosecution of the action, the Court of Appeals held that Kirkpatrick had not met its burden of showing that the case should not go forward; accordingly, it reversed the judgment of the District Court and remanded the case for trial. *Id.* at 1067. We granted certiorari, 492 U. S. 9 (1989).

II

This Court's description of the jurisprudential foundation for the act of state doctrine has undergone some evolution over the years. We once viewed the doctrine as an expression of international law, resting upon "the highest considerations of international comity and expediency," *Oetjen v. Central Leather Co.,* 246 U. S. 297, 246 U. S. 303-304 (1918). We have more recently described it, however, as a consequence of domestic separation of powers, reflecting "the strong sense of the Judicial Branch that its engagement in the task of passing on the validity of foreign acts of state may hinder" the conduct of foreign affairs, *Banco Nacional de Cuba v. Sabbatino,* 376 U. S. 398, 376 U. S. 423 (1964). Some Justices have suggested possible exceptions to application of the doctrine, where one or both of the foregoing policies would seemingly not be served: an exception, for example, for acts of state that consist of commercial transactions, since neither modern international comity nor the current position of our Executive Branch accorded sovereign immunity to such acts, *see Alfred Dunhill of London, Inc. v. Republic of Cuba,* 425 U. S. 682, 425 U. S. 695-706 (1976) (opinion of WHITE, J.); or an exception for cases in which the Executive Branch has represented that it has no objection to denying validity to the foreign sovereign act, since then the courts would be impeding no foreign policy goals, *see First National City Bank v. Banco Nacional de Cuba,* 406 U. S. 759, 406 U. S. 768-770 (1972) (opinion of REHNQUIST, J.).

The parties have argued at length about the applicability of these possible exceptions, and, more generally, about whether the purpose of the act of state doctrine would be furthered by its application in this case. We find it unnecessary however, to pursue those inquiries, since the factual predicate for application of the act of state doctrine does not exist. Nothing in the present suit requires the court to declare invalid, and thus ineffective as "a rule of decision for the courts of this country," *Ricaud v. American Metal Co.,* 246 U. S. 304, 246 U. S. 310 (1918), the official act of a foreign sovereign.

In every case in which we have held the act of state doctrine applicable, the relief sought or the defense interposed would have required a court in the United States to declare invalid the official act of a foreign sovereign performed within its own territory. In *Underhill v. Hernandez,* 168 U. S. 250, 168 U. S. 254 (1897), holding the defendant's detention of the plaintiff to be tortious would have required denying legal effect to "acts of a military commander representing the authority of the revolutionary party as government, which afterwards succeeded and was recognized by the United States."

In *Oetjen v. Central Leather Co., supra,* and in *Ricaud v. American Metal Co., supra,* denying title to the party who claimed through purchase from Mexico would have required declaring that government's prior seizure of the property, within its own territory, legally ineffective. *See Oetjen, supra,* 246 U.S. at 246 U. S. 304; *Ricaud, supra,* 246 U.S. at 246 U. S. 310. In *Sabbatino,* upholding the defendant's claim to the funds would have required a holding that Cuba's expropriation of goods located in Havana was null and void. In the present case, by contrast, neither the claim nor any asserted defense requires a determination that Nigeria's contract with Kirkpatrick International was, or was not, effective.

Petitioners point out, however, that the facts necessary to establish respondent's claim will also establish that the contract was unlawful. Specifically, they note that, in order to prevail, respondent must prove that petitioner Kirkpatrick made, and Nigerian officials received, payments that violate Nigerian law, which would, they assert, support a finding that the contract is invalid under Nigerian law. Assuming that to be true, it still does not suffice. The act of state doctrine is not some vague doctrine of abstention, but a "*principle of decision* binding on federal and state courts alike." *Sabbatino, supra,* 376 U.S. at 376 U. S. 427 (emphasis added). As we said in *Ricaud,* "the act within its own boundaries of one sovereign State . . . becomes . . . a rule of decision for the courts of this country." 246 U.S. at 246 U. S. 310. Act of state issues only arise when a court *must decide* -- that is, when the outcome of the case turns upon -- the effect of official action by a foreign sovereign. When that question is not in the case, neither is the act of state doctrine. That is the situation here. Regardless of what the court's factual findings may suggest as to the legality of the Nigerian contract, its legality is simply not a question to be decided in the present suit, and there is thus no occasion to apply the rule of decision that the act of state doctrine requires. *Cf. Sharon v. Time, Inc.,* 599 F. Supp. 538, 546 (SDNY 1984) ("The issue in this litigation is not whether [the alleged] acts are valid, but whether they occurred").

In support of their position that the act of state doctrine bars any factual findings that may cast doubt upon the validity of foreign sovereign acts, petitioners cite Justice Holmes' opinion for the Court in *American Banana Co. v. United Fruit Co.,* 213 U. S. 347 (1909). That was a suit under the United States antitrust laws, alleging that Costa Rica's seizure of the plaintiff's property had been induced by an unlawful conspiracy. In the course of a lengthy opinion Justice Holmes observed, citing *Underhill,* that "a seizure by a state is not a thing that can be complained of elsewhere in the courts." *Id.* at 213 U. S. 357-358. The statement is concededly puzzling. *Underhill* does indeed stand for the proposition that a seizure by a state cannot be complained of elsewhere -- in the sense of being sought to be declared *ineffective* elsewhere. The plaintiff in *American Banana,* however, like the plaintiff here, was not trying to undo or disregard the governmental action, but only to obtain damages from private parties who had procured it. Arguably, then, the statement did imply that suit would not lie if a foreign state's actions would be, though not invalidated, impugned.

Whatever Justice Holmes may have had in mind, his statement lends inadequate support to petitioners' position here, for two reasons. First, it was a brief aside, entirely unnecessary to the decision. *American*

Banana was squarely decided on the ground (later substantially overruled, *see Continental Ore Co. v. Union Carbide & Carbon Corp.,* 370 U. S. 690, 370 U. S. 704-705 (1962)) that the antitrust laws had no extraterritorial application, so that "what the defendant did in Panama or Costa Rica is not within the scope of the statute." 213 U.S. at 213 U. S. 357. Second, whatever support the dictum might provide for petitioners' position is more than overcome by our later holding in *United States v. Sisal Sales Corp.,* 274 U. S. 268 (1927). There we held that, *American Banana* notwithstanding, the defendant's actions in obtaining Mexico's enactment of "discriminating legislation" could form part of the basis for suit under the United States antitrust laws. 274 U.S. at 274 U. S. 276. Simply put, *American Banana* was notan act of state case, and whatever it said by way of dictum that might be relevant to the present case has not survived Sisal Sales.

Petitioners insist, however, that the policies underlying our act of state cases -- international comity, respect for the sovereignty of foreign nations on their own territory, and the avoidance of embarrassment to the Executive Branch in its conduct of foreign relations -- are implicated in the present case because, as the District Court found, a determination that Nigerian officials demanded and accepted a bribe "would impugn or question the nobility of a foreign nation's motivations," and would "result in embarrassment to the sovereign or constitute interference in the conduct of foreign policy of the United States." 659 F. Supp. at 1392-1393.

. . .

The United States as friend of the court in its amicus curiae brief suggests that we should resolve this case on the narrowest possible ground, *viz.,* that the letter from the legal advisor to the District Court gives sufficient indication that, "in the setting of this case," the act of state doctrine poses no bar to adjudication.

. . . .

The short of the matter is this: Courts in the United States have the power, and ordinarily the obligation, to decide cases and controversies properly presented to them. The act of state doctrine does not establish an exception for cases and controversies that may embarrass foreign governments, but merely requires that, in the process of deciding, the acts of foreign sovereigns taken within their own jurisdictions shall be deemed valid. That doctrine has no application to the present case, because the validity of no foreign sovereign act is at issue.

The judgment of the Court of Appeals for the Third Circuit is affirmed.

It is so ordered.

Case Questions:

1. For purposes of the act of state doctrine in the U.S. why does the court distinguish between official public acts and acts of a public official?
2. If Nigerian law prohibits bribery and a public official in Nigeria commits bribery, and finding a fact to that effect is made by U.S. court, could relations between Nigeria and the U.S. be adversely affected?
3. In general, do you think that corporations should be free to bribe public officials in other nations in order to make more money?
4. The court was unanimous in this case. Can you see any reason to dissent? What would your argument be?

III. INDUSTRIAL ESPIONAGE AND CYBER-HACKING

"Cyberespionage is a massive threat to critical industries such as manufacturing, pharmaceuticals, and chemicals. A company that has its trade secrets stolen could find itself unable to compete against a competitor that delivers a cheaper product to the world market. Modern ICS/SCADA security solutions that continuously monitor your OT network for vulnerabilities and anomalous behavior are essential to reducing this risk."

From: Industrial Espionage is a major threat to the Manufacturing Sector:

https://iiot-world.com/ics-security/cybersecurity/industrial-espionage-is-a-major-threat-to-the-manufacturing-sector/

- Manufacturing is the #1 industry targeted by cyberespionage.
- Cyberespionage is by far the most predominant attack vector in the manufacturing sector.
- Trade secrets are the #1 data type breached in manufacturing companies.

Verizon writes that the criminals' goal is to "infiltrate the network, find out where secrets are kept, and then slowly siphon off the nectar for as long as they can." Attacks typically begin with a phishing exploit allowing them to install malware that eventually enables IP theft.

The ethical issue here is similar to the situation where one employee offers his services to a competitor, taking client lists or other trade secrets with him. Short term, such an offer may be tempting, Although it's obvious that the competitor firm will be getting an unethical employee. In the realm of global cybertheft, it's clear that the law has some catching up to do, but also that a company engaging in cyberespionage would be violating an ISCT hypernorm: there are no national legal systems that do not discourage theft, and while global cyberespionage may not specifically be sanctioned in treaties, the company that engages in or uses information taken by espionage it is clearly violating ethical norms that are universal in nature.

IV. BUSINESS AND HUMAN RIGHTS

The subject of human rights is complex. What are "human rights," and Why do we usually exclude the rights of other mammals and other species when we talk about "rights." Where do rights come from? In the Declaration of Independence, the "founding fathers" noted "unalienable" rights, and President Lincoln came to embrace equality and dignity for every human being, as seen by the Declaration's phrase, "All men are created equal," as well as "life, liberty, and the pursuit of happiness."

After World War II, From many nations not only created the United nations but declared a universal statement of human rights. The Universal Declaration of Human Rights can be found here:

https://www.un.org/en/about-us/universal-declaration-of-human-rights

This document can be seen as largely aspirational as opposed to operational. That is, the manifestation of these rights is far from universal in the United states or beyond. In short we have a long way to go. But the UN was not done in 1948. Under its auspices, a code for multinationals was created in the 1980s, but later abandoned.

Resurrection of ethical goals for nations and corporations was revived in 2011 with the report sponsored by the U.N. on business and human rights.

The "Ruggie Report" can be found at:

https://digitallibrary.un.org/record/705860

The Report is briefly summarized as follows:

As the UN"s "special representative" on human rights and multinational corporations, John Ruggie reported to the UN's Human Rights Council on June 3, 2008.

Ruggie and his team of experts saw that "globalization" had produced a divide between business-related activities and the legal and institutional capabilities to govern those activities. These "governance gaps" allowd business-related human rights abuses can occur with relative impunity.

The Ruggie Report asserted that "there are few if any internationally recognized rights business cannot impact," and, therefore, any list of specific rights will be highly controversial while also being incomplete. The Report sets forth a framework based on the three core principles in its title —protect, respect and remedy. Second, it seeks to provide a foundation and an "authoritative focal point" to facilitate diverse efforts by various stakeholders pursuing common goals. Third, it provides a useful map to help identify where and how business affects human rights.

The Framework

The Report's framework "rests on differentiated but complimentary responsibilities," which include:
- the state duty to protect against human rights abuses by third parties, including business entities;
- the corporate responsibility to respect human rights; and
- the need for more effective access to remedies.

The State Duty to Protect Against Abuses by Non-State Actors

The Report adopts a classical view of human rights in which States form the cornerstones around which the human rights regime is constructed. Particularly relevant here is the duty of States to protect against human rights abuses by non-State actors, including national and foreign-based business entities. This duty requires that States "take all necessary steps to protect against such abuse, including to prevent, investigate, and punish the abuse, and to provide access to redress." The Report acknowledges the growing pressure for, and availability of, duties and avenues for redress in the home States of foreign investors.

Beyond this relatively non-expansive view of State duties in relation to business and human rights, the Report devotes significant attention to additional legal or policy actions States might take to fulfill their duty, including an "urgent policy priority" to "foster a corporate culture respectful of human rights." States can encourage a rights-respecting corporate culture by, for example, requiring sustainability reporting, as is currently required by a growing number of financial regulations. Similarly, States may facilitate the possibility of making corporate culture--a company's "policies, rules and practices"—relevant in claims of corporate criminal accountability and punishment.

The Report also addresses:

- The need for greater coherence between State's initiatives, policies, and institutions relevant to business and those focused on human rights, in order to reduce State activity that encourages and facilitates human rights abuses by business actors;
- The steps States can and should take to facilitate greater international coordination and understanding of the business and human rights problem; and
- Particular attention States should give to the human rights problems businesses can cause or exacerbate in conflict zones.

The Baseline Corporate Responsibility to Respect Human Rights

In addition to breaking from existing efforts to enumerate rights for which businesses should bear responsibility for violating, the Report asserts that the responsibilities of corporations "cannot and should not mirror the duties of States." Instead, the Report addresses "the more difficult question" of defining what responsibilities companies have. Corporations bear the responsibility to respect human rights. Where States have laws enforcing this responsibility, companies are occasionally charged in "actual courts." More commonly, companies deviate from societal expectations in respect to human rights, leading to adverse consequences in the "courts of public opinion."

The Report focuses the corporate responsibility to respect human rights on corporate due diligence regarding the full international bill of rights and the core conventions of the International Labor Organization. In order to demonstrate due diligence, companies would take into account the human rights contexts in the locations of their operations, the human rights impacts specific to those operations, and whether and how their operations contribute to human rights abuses.

The due diligence process for a company would include adopting a detailed human rights policy, conducting impact assessments of business operations, crafting plans to avoid negative human rights impacts, integrating human rights concerns into company operations, and developing monitoring and auditing processes.

The Ruggie Report references the OECD Guidelines for Multinationals. The OECD is the Organization for Economic Cooperation and Development. 38 nations are member-states of the OECD.

https://www.oecd.org/

The OECD guidelines number 95 pages.

https://www.oecd.org/daf/inv/mne/48004323.pdf

With regard to human rights, it should be clear that the profit-making priorities of a business usually come before consideration of human rights. The situation described in Doe v. Nestle (Chapter _____) shows that U.S. companies that market chocolate will unflinchingly make use of slave labor in the Ivory Coast.

Immanuel Kant, the great German "deontologist," sought to find some useful universalizable rules — he called them maxims, or "imperatives" — that all humans could follow. His second categorical imperative cautioned us to not use others for our own ends; every human being has value, and that value must be respected. Its first categorical imperative advised humans to only do those acts that could be universalized. Looking back at cybertheft, we could apply his imperatives to say that if everyone stole (if property rights were not respected), then property rights would no longer exist. Looking at slavery, if we were to will slavery as a universal condition, we would immediately confront the logical conundrum that if everyone had the right to own a slave, there could be no slaves — only "masters." The second categorical imperative is here even easier to apply, and strongly advises people (and companies) not to exploit others for their own ends. Slavery is, at the very least, exploitation by the more powerful against the more vulnerable among us. But where "winning in the marketplace" and making consistent profits matters most, Kant's ethical guidelines tend to be ignored.

John Ruggie, after finishing his work for the U.N., also published a book in 2013, "Just Business: Multinational Corporations and Human Rights."

The Amazon site where his book is sold says this:

"*Just Business* tells the powerful story of how these landmark "Ruggie Rules" came to exist. Ruggie demonstrates how, to solve a seemingly unsolvable problem, he had to abandon many widespread and long-held understandings about the relationships between businesses, governments, rights, and law, and develop fresh ways of viewing the issues. He also takes us through the journey of assembling the right type of team, of witnessing the severity of the problem firsthand, and of pressing through the many obstacles such a daunting endeavor faced."

Another exceedingly useful resource, the Business and Human Rights Resource Center can be found at: https://www.business-humanrights.org/en/

The Business and Human Rights Resource Center describes itself as 13 trustees and 70 plus colleagues dedicated to advancing human rights in business and eradicating abuse.

V.   OUTSOURCING

From the 1980s on, U.S. businesses took advantage of the movement towards globalization; they did so primarily by extending supply chains overseas, abandoning many U.S. manufacturing operations. For many in the U.S., this was controversial; jobs were lost to Mexico with NAFTA, and factory workers in the U.S. Midwest either lost their jobs or lost significant pay. Factory owners who stayed in the U.S. —such as Aaron Feuerstein — were applauded by business ethics writers, but the movement toward outsourcing could not be stopped.

Optional reading: Aaron Feuerstein, hero to his employees and business ethics commentators, rebuilds Malden Mills in Massachusetts rather than relocate to cheaper labor overseas. Ultimately, though, the company has to declare bankruptcy.

https://www.haaretz.com/jewish/2015-12-11/ty-article/.premium/1995-malden-mills-burns-down/0000017f-f0fe-d223-a97f-fdff406d0000

Global supply chains were aided tremendously by container shipping, and sourcing from Mexico or from Asia —especially China — became a go-to strategy for many companies. That only began to shift somewhat during the COVID-19 pandemic of 2020/2021/2022, when the usual supply chains became unreliable, and container ships from Asia were backed up in U.S. ports for days, and even weeks. "Re-shoring" might happen, but as of 2022 that is far from clear. It has become clear, however, that reliance on China as a trading partner may have drawbacks, especially as global alliances began to re-align after Russia's invasion of Ukraine in 2022.

VI.   Offshoring and multinational tax avoidance

Generally, companies will do what is legal and profitable. The international legal system is shot through with gaps and inconsistencies that promote legal yet less than stellar behaviors, whether by national leaders, multinational corporations, or individuals who use the complexity of the international legal system to evade accountability for dastardly acts. (As this is written, WNBA star Britney Griner is being held by Russian authorities, who reportedly would like to use her as a pawn to reclaim the "merchant of death" Victor Bout, notorious arms dealer to terrorist and authoritarian rulers, who escaped justice for many years before being set up by FBI agents for an illegal Colombian arms deal.)

Many U.S. companies have taken advantage of porous international system to park earnings abroad, to incorporate certain divisions in low-tax nations, using many of the same techniques used by illegal arms dealers (like Bout), narcotics smugglers, and terrorist organizations. (See, for example, Raymond Chandler's brilliant book, Capitalism's Achilles Heel: Dirty Money and How to Renew the Capitalist System.)[60]

Several "leading" U.S. companies have taken advantage of the international legal system to pay no taxes to the U.S. government, despite enjoying the benefits of having a principal place of business in the U.S.

The average American family making between $36,000 and $69,500 paid $15,748 in taxes to federal, state, and local governments in 2018. That's an effective tax rate of 22.7%, for those making $69,500.
In 2020, Nike earned $2 billion—and paid nothing in taxes.

Tax-avoiding corporations run the gamut of industry and receive billions in tax rebates, according to the Institute on Taxation and Economic Policy, a non-profit, non-partisan tax policy organization.

The statutory federal tax rate for corporate profits is 21%, according to ITEP, and 55 corporations pulled in nearly $40.5 billion in U.S. pretax income in 2020. Instead of paying a collective total of $8.5 billion for the year (21%) they received *3.5 billion* in tax rebates. That's an effective tax rate of -8.6%.
MSN lists 30 profitable companies that avoided all federal taxes in 2020, listed in order of highest pre-tax income, according to ITEP. Topping the list are Nike, Charter Communications, Salesforce.com, and American Electric Power.

https://www.msn.com/en-us/money/markets/30-biggest-companies-that-paid-zero-taxes/ss-AATmv2K#image=1

ITEP has an interesting fact sheet on Apple. They say: "Apple is also particularly adept at avoiding U.S. taxes on these gargantuan profits. The major strategy Apple uses to reduce its U.S. tax bill is to artificially shift large amounts of its domestic profits into tax havens. This allows Apple to avoid paying U.S. taxes on these profits while also paying very little in foreign taxes. This is possible due to a loophole in the tax code called "deferral" that allows U.S. multinational corporations to forego taxes on profits of their foreign subsidiaries until they are paid as dividends to the U.S. parent company. Like many other multinationals, Apple exploits this loophole by using accounting maneuvers to shift its U.S. profits overseas (often only on paper) and then indefinitely deferring U.S. taxes on them."[61]

---

[60] https://www.amazon.com/Capitalisms-Achilles-Heel-Free-Market-System/dp/1119086612
[61] https://itep.org/fact-sheet-apple-and-tax-avoidance/

Optional reading: Attorney Jan Weir, who also teaches law in Toronto, has written about the tools and techniques that Apple, Starbuck, Amazon, and other companies have used to avoid and evade taxes.

https://rantt.com/high-level-tax-avoidance-how-apple-amazon-and-starbucks-do-it

VII. DEALING WITH OTHER LEGAL/POLITICAL SYSTEMS

Trust and a commonality of values are important, not only in your personal friendships, but also for doing good business with other companies and within other nations. While making money may seem to be the most important "value" in business, some businesses have discovered that the price of doing business with some political regimes is far too high. One of the earliest examples of public pressure on companies to withdraw from its presence in other nations was the boycott of companies doing business in apartheid South Africa.

Led by Philadelphia pastor Leon Sullivan, the public pressure on U.S. corporations to "divest" from doing business in South Africa was ultimately quite effective.

"The Global Sullivan Principles, launched in 1977 by Philadelphia civil rights leader Leon H. Sullivan (1922-2001), represent one of the twentieth century's most powerful attempts to effect social justice through economic leverage. More a sustained movement than a static document, the principles sought to bring the power of American investment in South Africa to bear on the cruel injustice of the apartheid state by establishing baseline commitments to fairness and empowerment as conditions for operating in the country."

https://philadelphiaencyclopedia.org/essays/sullivan-principles/

"Divestment" movements today are more typically focused on banks and other institutions investing in fossil fuel companies, rather than entire nations. But in 2021 and 2022, more and more businesses realized the moral and practical difficulties of doing business in Russia and doing business in China.

As noted by Seth Kaplan in the Harvard Business Review in January of 2022:

"For decades, companies have poured into China to take advantage of the country's manufacturing prowess and to serve its enormous market. While firms were largely aware of potential business risks, like intellectual property theft and the need to navigate corruption, executives have been less concerned about risks to their firms' ethics and reputation. But in recent years the situation has changed dramatically, and companies such as Google, Disney, and the NBA have to steer through a much more perilous, and in some cases impassable, ethical landscape." Kaplan goes on to note that the Communist Party has grown increasingly repressive, and has failed to be a "responsible member of the liberal international order."

https://hbr.org/2022/01/how-to-navigate-the-ethical-risks-of-doing-business-in-china

Companies with business interests in Russia were also subject to legal and ethical constraints after the invasion of Ukraine in 2022.

https://theconversation.com/why-apple-disney-ikea-and-hundreds-of-other-western-companies-are-abandoning-russia-with-barely-a-shrug-178516

As noted in the article linked above, there are three factors that drive a company to withdraw from doing business in a particular nation.

"More specifically, research has identified three major factors that typically drive a company's decision to pursue corporate activism: employee beliefs, consumer pressure and the CEO's personal involvement or conviction. It's not always clear what is driving corporate decisions to suspend operations in Russia, but it seems as if all three factors are at play."

Given the strong bipartisan agreement in the U.S. that the Russian invasion was unjustified and horribly wrong, companies were likely "more worried about the risks to their reputation" if they did nothing. With so many companies pulling out, say the authors, it probably seemed better to explain to shareholders and customers back home why they are leaving rather than why they are staying.

Just as companies must decide where to do business, and with whom, nations have to make hard ethical decisions too. European nations faced giving up supplies of natural gas from Russia in order to sanction that nation's invasion of Ukraine, a sacrifice that some have predicted cannot be maintained. But, as long as it's consistent with WTO rules, each nation's legal system can impose sanctions or boycotts of nations where political and ethical differences are strong. The U.S. has refused to allow normal business relations with Cuba, for example, or with Iran, or North Korea, or (now) Russia. U.S. politicians, and courts, make judgments all the time as to what nation's legal rulings and judicial systems are worthy of respect and recognition. In the case of Chrysler v. Gonzalez, below, we see where the U.S. Court of Appeals decided it was not "ethical" to judge Mexican legal system as inadequate, but ethical to allow a U.S. company to avoid legal accountability in the U.S. for a defective product that killed a child.

Jorge Luis Machuca Gonazalez; Martha Patricia Lopez Guererero, individually and as Heirs and Representatives of the Estate of Luis Pablo Machuca Lopez, Deceased. v. Chrysler Corporation, TRW Vehicle Safety Systems, Inc. and Morton International, Inc.

U.S. Court of Appeals for the Fifth Circuit

301 F.3d 377 (2002)

Note: Although the court's opinion was appealed to the Supreme Court, no writ of certiorari was issued, so the following decision stands.

OPINION BY: E. GRADY JOLLY

In this forum non conveniens case, we first consider whether the cap imposed by Mexican law on the recovery of tort damages renders Mexico an inadequate forum for resolving a tort suit by a Mexican citizen against an American manufacturer and an American designer of an air bag. Holding that Mexico -- despite its cap on damages -- represents an adequate alternative forum, we next consider whether the district court committed reversible error when it concluded that the private and public interest factors so strongly pointed to Mexico that Mexico, instead of Texas, was the appropriate forum in which to try this case. Finding no reversible error, we affirm the district court's judgment dismissing this case on the ground of forum non conveniens.

In 1995, while in Houston, the plaintiff, Jorge Luis Machuca Gonzalez ("Gonzalez") n1 saw several magazine and television advertisements for the Chrysler LHS. The advertisements sparked his interest. So, Gonzalez decided to visit a couple of Houston car dealerships. Convinced by these visits that the Chrysler LHS was a high quality and safe car, Gonzalez purchased a Chrysler LHS upon returning to Mexico.

On May 21, 1996, the wife of the plaintiff was involved in a collision with another moving vehicle while driving the Chrysler LHS in Atizapan de Zaragoza, Mexico. The accident triggered the passenger-side air bag. The force of the air bag's deployment instantaneously killed Gonzalez's three-year-old son, Pablo.

Seeking redress, Gonzalez brought suit in Texas district court against (1) Chrysler, as the manufacturer of the automobile; (2) TRW, Inc. and TRW Vehicle Safety Systems, Inc., as the designers of the front sensor for the air bag; and (3) Morton International, Inc., as designer of the air bag module. Gonzalez asserted claims based on products liability, negligence, gross negligence, and breach of warranty. As noted, Gonzalez chose to file his suit in Texas. Texas, however, has a tenuous connection to the underlying dispute. Neither the car nor the air bag module was designed or manufactured in Texas. The accident took place in Mexico, involved Mexican citizens, and only Mexican citizens witnessed the accident. Moreover, Gonzalez purchased the Chrysler LHS in Mexico (although he shopped for the car in Houston, Texas). Because of these factors, the district court granted the defendants' identical motions for dismissal on the ground of forum non conveniens. Gonzalez now appeals.

II. A

The primary question we address today involves the threshold inquiry in the forum non conveniens analysis: Whether the limitation imposed by Mexican law on the award of damages renders Mexico an inadequate alternative forum for resolving a tort suit brought by a Mexican citizen against a United States manufacturer.

We should note at the outset that we may reverse the grant or denial of a motion to dismiss on the ground of forum non conveniens only "where there has been a clear abuse of discretion." Baumgart v. Fairchild Aircraft Corp., 981 F.2d 824, 835 (5th Cir. 1993).

The forum non conveniens inquiry consists of four considerations. First, the district court must assess whether an alternative forum is available. See Alpine View Co. Ltd. v. Atlas Copco AB, 205 F.3d 208, 221 (5th Cir. 2000). An alternative forum is available if "the entire case and all parties can come within the jurisdiction of that forum." In re Air Crash Disaster Near New Orleans, La. on July 9, 1982, 821 F.2d 1147, 1165 (5th Cir. 1987) (en banc), vacated on other grounds sub nom., Pan Am. World Airways, Inc. v. Lopez, 490 U.S. 1032, 104 L. Ed. 2d 400, 109 S. Ct. 1928 (1989). Second, the district court must decide if the alternative forum is adequate. See Alpine View, 205 F.3d at 221. An alternative forum is adequate if "the parties will not be deprived of all remedies or treated unfairly, even though they may not enjoy the same benefits as they might receive in an American court." In re Air Crash, 821 F.2d at 1165 (internal citation omitted).

If the district court decides that an alternative forum is both available and adequate, it next must weigh various private interest factors. See Baumgart, 981 F.2d at 835-36. If consideration of these private interest factors counsels against dismissal, the district court moves to the fourth consideration in the analysis. At this stage, the district court must weigh numerous public interest factors. If these factors weigh in the moving party's favor, the district court may dismiss the case. Id. at 837.

B. 1

The heart of this appeal is whether the alternative forum, Mexico, is adequate.

The jurisprudential root of the adequacy requirement is the Supreme Court's decision in Piper Aircraft Co. v. Reyno, 454 U.S. 235, 70 L. Ed. 2d 419, 102 S. Ct. 252 (1981). The dispute in Piper Aircraft arose after several Scottish citizens were killed in a plane crash in Scotland. A representative for the decedents filed a wrongful death suit against two American aircraft manufacturers. The Court noted that the plaintiff filed suit in the United States because "[U.S.] laws regarding liability, capacity to sue, and damages are more favorable to her position than are those of Scotland." Id. The Court further noted that "Scottish law does not recognize strict liability in tort." Id. This fact, however, did not deter the Court from reversing the Third Circuit. In so doing, the Court held that "although the relatives of the decedent may not be able to rely on a strict liability theory, and although their potential damage award may be smaller, there is no danger that they will be deprived of any remedy or treated unfairly [in Scotland]." Thus, the Court held that Scotland provided an adequate alternative forum for resolving the dispute, even though its forum provided a significantly lesser remedy. In a footnote, however, Justice Marshall observed that on rare occasions this may not be true:

> At the outset of any forum non conveniens inquiry, the court must determine whether there exists an alternative forum. Ordinarily, this requirement will be satisfied when the defendant is "amenable to process" in the other jurisdiction. In rare circumstances, however, where the remedy offered by the other forum is clearly unsatisfactory, the other forum may not be an adequate alternative, and the initial requirement may not be satisfied. Thus, for example, dismissal would not be appropriate where the alternative forum does not permit litigation of the subject matter of the dispute.

Id. at 255 n.22 (emphasis added)(internal citation omitted).

Citing the language from this footnote, Gonzalez contends that a Mexican forum would provide a clearly unsatisfactory remedy because (1) Mexican tort law does not provide for a strict liability theory of recovery for the manufacture or design of an unreasonably dangerous product and (2) Mexican law caps the maximum award for the loss of a child's life at approximately $ 2,500 (730 days' worth of wages at the Mexican minimum wage rate). Thus, according to Gonzalez, Mexico provides an inadequate alternative forum for this dispute.

B.2

(a) Gonzalez's first contention may be quickly dismissed based on the explicit principle stated in Piper Aircraft. As noted, there the Supreme Court held that Scotland's failure to recognize strict liability did not render Scotland an inadequate alternative forum. Id. at 255. There is no basis to distinguish the absence of a strict products liability cause of action under Mexican law from that of Scotland. n4 Piper Aircraft therefore controls. Accordingly, we hold that the failure of Mexican law to allow for strict liability on the facts of this case does not render Mexico an inadequate forum.

(b) Gonzalez's second contention -- that the damage cap renders the remedy available in a Mexican forum "clearly unsatisfactory" -- is slightly more problematic. Underlying this contention are two distinct arguments: First, Gonzalez argues that if he brings suit in Mexico, the cap on damages will entitle him to a de minimis recovery only -- a clearly unsatisfactory award for the loss of a child. Second, Gonzalez argues that because of the damage cap, the cost of litigating this case in Mexico will exceed the potential recovery. As a consequence, the lawsuit will never be brought in Mexico. Stated differently, the lawsuit is not economically viable in Mexico. It follows, therefore, that Mexico offers no forum (much less an adequate forum) through which Gonzalez can (or will) seek redress. We address each argument in turn.

(i)

In addressing Gonzalez's first argument, we start from basic principles of comity. Mexico, as a sovereign nation, has made a deliberate choice in providing a specific remedy for this tort cause of action. In making this policy choice, the Mexican government has resolved a trade-off among the competing objectives and costs of tort law, involving interests of victims, of consumers, of manufacturers, and of various other economic and cultural values. In resolving this trade-off, the Mexican people, through their duly-elected lawmakers, have decided to limit tort damages with respect to a child's death. n6 It would be inappropriate -- even patronizing -- for us to denounce this legitimate policy choice by holding that Mexico provides an inadequate forum for Mexican tort victims. In another forum non conveniens case, the District Court for the Southern District of New York made this same point observing (perhaps in a hyperbolic choice of words) that "to retain the litigation in this forum, as plaintiffs request, would be yet another example of imperialism, another situation in which an established sovereign inflicted its rules, its standards and values on a developing nation." In re Union Carbide Corp. Gas Plant Disaster at Bhopal, India in December, 1984, 634 F. Supp. 842, 867 (S.D.N.Y. 1986), aff'd as modified, 809 F.2d 195 (2d Cir. 1987). In short, we see no warrant for us, a United States court, to replace the policy preference of the Mexican government with our own view of what is a good policy for the citizens of Mexico.

Based on the considerations mentioned above, we hold that the district court did not err when it found that the cap on damages did not render the remedy available in the Mexican forum clearly unsatisfactory.

(ii) We now turn our attention to Gonzalez's "economic viability" argument -- that is, because there is no economic incentive to file suit in the alternative forum, there is effectively no alternative forum.
The practical and economic realities lying at the base of this dispute are clear. At oral argument, the parties agreed that this case would never be filed in Mexico. In short, a dismissal on the ground of forum non conveniens will determine the outcome of this litigation in Chrysler's favor. n9 We nevertheless are unwilling to hold as a legal principle that Mexico offers an inadequate forum simply because it does not make economic sense for Gonzalez to file this lawsuit in Mexico. Our reluctance arises out of two practical considerations.

- - - - - - - - - - - - - - Footnotes - - - - - - - - - - - - - - -
n9 This fact is not unique to this lawsuit. A survey found that between 1945 and 1985, of 85 transnational cases dismissed on the ground of forum non conveniens, only four percent ever reached trial in a foreign court. See David Robertson, Forum Non Conveniens in America and England: "A Rather Fantastic Fiction", 103 L. Q. REV. 398, 418-19 (1987).
- - - - - - - - - - - - End Footnotes- - - - - - - - - - - - -

First, the plaintiff's willingness to maintain suit in the alternative (foreign) forum will usually depend on, inter alia, (1) whether the plaintiff's particular injuries are compensable (and to what extent) in that forum; (2) not whether the forum recognizes some cause of action among those applicable to the plaintiff's case, but whether it recognizes his most provable and compensable action; (3) similarly, whether the alternative forum recognizes defenses that might bar or diminish recovery; and (4) the litigation costs (i.e., the number of experts, the amount of discovery, geographic distances, attorney's fees, etc.) associated with bringing that particular case to trial. These factors will vary from plaintiff to plaintiff, from case to case. Thus, the forum of a foreign country might be deemed inadequate in one case but not another, even though the only difference between the two cases might be the cost of litigation or the recovery for the plaintiff's particular type of injuries. In sum, we find troublesome and lacking in guiding principle the fact that the adequacy determination could hinge on constantly varying and arbitrary differences underlying the "economic viability" of a lawsuit.

Second, if we allow the economic viability of a lawsuit to decide the adequacy of an alternative forum, we are further forced to engage in a rudderless exercise of line drawing with respect to a cap on damages: At what point does a cap on damages transform a forum from adequate to inadequate? Is it, as here,

$2,500? Is it $ 50,000? Or is it $ 100,000? Any recovery cap may, in a given case, make the lawsuit economically unviable. We therefore hold that the adequacy inquiry under Piper Aircraft does not include an evaluation of whether it makes economic sense for Gonzalez to file this lawsuit in Mexico.

C

Having concluded that Mexico provides an adequate forum, we now consider whether the private and public interest factors nonetheless weigh in favor of maintaining this suit in Texas. As noted, the district court concluded that the public and the private interest factors weighed in favor of Mexico and dismissed the case on the ground of forum non conveniens. Our review of this conclusion is restricted to abuse of discretion.

The district court found that almost all of the private and public interest factors pointed away from Texas and toward Mexico as the appropriate forum. It is clear to us that this finding does not represent an abuse of discretion. After all, the tort victim was a Mexican citizen, the driver of the Chrysler LHS (Gonzalez's wife) is a Mexican citizen, and the plaintiff is a Mexican citizen. The accident took place in Mexico. Gonzalez purchased the car in Mexico. Neither the car nor the air bag was designed or manufactured in Texas. In short, there are no public or private interest factors that would suggest that Texas is the appropriate forum for the trial of this case.

III

For the foregoing reasons, the district court's dismissal of this case on the ground of forum non conveniens is

AFFIRMED.

1. If you had to fashion a dissent to this opinion, what would you say?
2. Would it really be "judicial imperialism" for the US courts here to say that the Mexican judicial system did not provide an adequate remedy for the Gonzalez family?
3. Do you think that U.S.—Mexican relations would be adversely affected if the I.S. court had allowed Mr. Gonzalez to proceed with his lawsuit in the U.S.?
4. To keep court dockets moving in the U.S., should the US have a rule that no foreign plaintiffs can bring lawsuits in the U.S.?
5. If the trial judge had deemed the Mexican judicial system inadequate, and allowed the trial to proceed, and Chrysler appealed, how should the appellate court have ruled? Note: in forum non convenience decisions, wide latitude is given to the trial judge's determinations, which should not be overturned unless there is "clear error."

Similarly, *forum non conveniens* was used to avoid accountability for damage to the health of banana plantation workers.

https://www.uwosh.edu/faculty_staff/palmeri/commentary/banana.htm

Forum non conveniens was also used to delay (and ultimately deny) the major health and environmental damage in Ecuador caused by Texaco's oil operations. See

http://www.counterspill.org/article/ecuador-vs-chevron-texaco-brief-history

The Sequihua case, in Chapter One, is the first instance of a U.S. court dismissing the claims of indigenous people in Ecuador's Amazon region.

APPENDIX A

What IS Corruption and Why Does it Matter?

"Dishonest or fraudulent conduct by those in power, typically involving bribery."

AND

"The process by which something, typically a word or expression, is changed from its original use or meaning to one that is regarded as erroneous or debased."

OR (Mayer's definition)

"The act, intentional or otherwise, of altering (for the worse) a person, an institution, or a set of political institutions for individual or organizational gain."

Examples:

A.	The Roman Empire declined because of internal rot, or corruption. People with their own agendas were not willing to support the integrity of the whole.

If Rome's sheer size made it difficult to govern, ineffective and inconsistent leadership only served to magnify the problem. Being the Roman emperor had always been a particularly dangerous job, but during the tumultuous second and third centuries it nearly became a death sentence. Civil war thrust the empire into chaos, and more than 20 men took the throne in the span of only 75 years, usually after the murder of their predecessor. The Praetorian Guard—the emperor's personal bodyguards—assassinated and installed new sovereigns at will, and once even auctioned the spot off to the highest bidder. The political rot also extended to the Roman Senate, which failed to temper the excesses of the emperors due to its own widespread corruption and incompetence. As the situation worsened, civic pride waned and many Roman citizens lost trust in their leadership.

https://www.history.com/news/8-reasons-why-rome-fell#:~:text=The%20Romans%20weathered%20a%20Germanic,sacked%20the%20city%20of%20Rome.&text=From%20then%20on%2C%20no%20Roman,Western%20Empire%20suffered%20its%20deathblow.

B.	America could decline as well if its citizens and politicians fail to agree on what the Republic stands for. If some forms of public goods and capable government are a necessity for the good society, are we corrupting American governance by repeatedly saying that government can do no good?

"Because since Mr. Reagan, it's been apostasy to suggest that good governance could ever do anything to improve people's lives." Jennifer Boylan, New York Times, Nov. 10, 2020.

See also Zephyr Teachout's book on Corruption:

https://www.amazon.com/Corruption-America-Benjamin-Franklins-Citizens/dp/0674659988

Also, the formidable Sarah Chayes has written extensively about corruption. What follows is a short tribute to her work:

"From the prizewinning journalist, internationally recognized expert on corruption in government networks throughout the world, author of *Thieves of State: Why Corruption Threatens Global Security* ("I can't imagine a more important book for our time,"--Sebastian Junger; "Required reading,"--Tom Friedman; "compelling, fascinating . . . a call to action,"--*The Huffington Post*), a major, unflinching book that looks homeward to America, exploring the insidious, dangerous networks of corruption of our past, present, and precarious future.

Now, bringing to bear all of her knowledge, grasp, sense of history and observation, Sarah Chayes writes in her new book, that the United States is showing signs similar to some of the most corrupt countries in the world. Corruption, as Chayes sees it, is an operating system of sophisticated networks in which government officials, key private-sector interests, and out-and-out criminals interweave. Their main objective: not to serve the public but to maximize returns for network members.

From the titans of America's Gilded Age (Carnegie, Rockefeller, J. P. Morgan, et al.) to the collapse of the stock market in 1929, the Great Depression and FDR's New Deal; from Joe Kennedy's years of banking, bootlegging, machine politics, and pursuit of infinite wealth, as well as the Kennedy presidency, to the deregulation of the Reagan Revolution, undermining the middle class and the unions; from the Clinton policies of political favors and personal enrichment to Trump's hydra-headed network of corruption, systematically undoing the Constitution and our laws, Chayes shows how corrupt systems are organized, how they enforce the rules so their crimes are covered legally, how they are overlooked and downplayed—shrugged off with a roll of the eyes—by the richer and better educated, how they become an overt principle determining the shape of our government, affecting all levels of society."

From a 2020 NPR interview: https://englewoodreview.org/sarah-chayes-on-corruption-in-america-npr-interview/

CHAPTER NINE:

INTERNATIONAL ENVIRONMENTAL LAW

INTRODUCTION:

Concern over environmental matters has increased greatly since the first Earth Day 1970. Only in the 1960s did Americans come to worry about pollution of the air, the land, and the water. The word "ecology" emerged into the public's understanding: the scientific concept that all forms of life on earth were linked, and that living systems must be understood holistically. One of the early and most important environmentalists, Rachel Carson, revealed how the widespread application of DDT — useful as a pesticide — what's causing inordinate harm to wildlife, particularly birds.

https://www.youtube.com/watch?v=ekDeG-BJYnE

After the introduction, the entire episode of American Experience plays. Just watch the introduction, though!

Meanwhile, oil spills were becoming more commonplace, and the health problems from toxic waste in placed like New York's "Love Canal" captured the public's attention. During the Nixon administration, major environmental laws were passed on a bi-partisan basis, including the Clean Air Act, the Clean Water Act, and the National Environmental Policy Act.

In 1972, representatives from many nations met in Stockholm, Sweden and created what was the Stockholm principles for international environmental law.

Declaration of the United Nations Conference on the Human Environment
The United Nations Conference on the Human Environment, having met at Stockholm from 5 to 16 June 1972, having considered the need for a common outlook and for common principles to inspire and guide the peoples of the world in the preservation and enhancement of the human environment,
Proclaims that:

1. Man is both creature and moulder of his environment, which gives him physical sustenance and affords him the opportunity for intellectual, moral, social and spiritual growth. In the long and tortuous evolution of the human race on this planet a stage has been reached when, through the rapid acceleration of science and technology, man has acquired the power to transform his environment in countless ways and on an unprecedented scale. Both aspects of man's environment, the natural and the man-made, are essential to his well-being and to the enjoyment of basic human rights the right to life itself.

2. The protection and improvement of the human environment is a major issue which affects the well-being of peoples and economic development throughout the world; it is the urgent desire of the peoples of the whole world and the duty of all Governments.

3. Man has constantly to sum up experience and go on discovering, inventing, creating and advancing. In our time, man's capability to transform his surroundings, if used wisely, can bring to all peoples the benefits of development and the opportunity to enhance the quality of life. Wrongly or heedlessly applied, the same power can do incalculable harm to human beings and the human environment. We see around us growing evidence of man-made harm in many regions of the earth: dangerous levels of pollution in water, air, earth

and living beings; major and undesirable disturbances to the ecological balance of the biosphere; destruction and depletion of irreplaceable resources; and gross deficiencies, harmful to the physical, mental and social health of man, in the man-made environment, particularly in the living and working environment.

4. In the developing countries most of the environmental problems are caused by under-development. Millions continue to live far below the minimum levels required for a decent human existence, deprived of adequate food and clothing, shelter and education, health and sanitation. Therefore, the developing countries must direct their efforts to development, bearing in mind their priorities and the need to safeguard and improve the environment. For the same purpose, the industrialized countries should make efforts to reduce the gap themselves and the developing countries. In the industrialized countries, environmental problems are generally related to industrialization and technological development.

5. The natural growth of population continuously presents problems for the preservation of the environment, and adequate policies and measures should be adopted, as appropriate, to face these problems. Of all things in the world, people are the most precious. It is the people that propel social progress, create social wealth, develop science and technology and, through their hard work, continuously transform the human environment. Along with social progress and the advance of production, science and technology, the capability of man to improve the environment increases with each passing day.

6. A point has been reached in history when we must shape our actions throughout the world with a more prudent care for their environmental consequences. Through ignorance or indifference we can do massive and irreversible harm to the earthly environment on which our life and well being depend. Conversely, through fuller knowledge and wiser action, we can achieve for ourselves and our posterity a better life in an environment more in keeping with human needs and hopes. There are broad vistas for the enhancement of environmental quality and the creation of a good life. What is needed is an enthusiastic but calm state of mind and intense but orderly work. For the purpose of attaining freedom in the world of nature, man must use knowledge to build, in collaboration with nature, a better environment. To defend and improve the human environment for present and future generations has become an imperative goal for mankind-a goal to be pursued together with, and in harmony with, the established and fundamental goals of peace and of worldwide economic and social development.

7. To achieve this environmental goal will demand the acceptance of responsibility by citizens and communities and by enterprises and institutions at every level, all sharing equitably in common efforts. Individuals in all walks of life as well as organizations in many fields, by their values and the sum of their actions, will shape the world environment of the future.
Local and national governments will bear the greatest burden for large-scale environmental policy and action within their jurisdictions. International cooperation is also needed in order to raise resources to support the developing countries in carrying out their responsibilities in this field. A growing class of environmental problems, because they are regional or global in extent or because they affect the common international realm, will require extensive cooperation among nations and action by international organizations in the common interest.

The Conference calls upon Governments and peoples to exert common efforts for the preservation and improvement of the human environment, for the benefit of all the people and for their posterity.

Principles
States the common conviction that:

Principle 1

Man has the fundamental right to freedom, equality and adequate conditions of life, in an environment of a quality that permits a life of dignity and well-being, and he bears a solemn responsibility to protect and improve the environment for present and future generations. In this respect, policies promoting or perpetuating apartheid, racial segregation, discrimination, colonial and other forms of oppression and foreign domination stand condemned and must be eliminated.

Principle 2

The natural resources of the earth, including the air, water, land, flora and fauna and especially representative samples of natural ecosystems, must be safeguarded for the benefit of present and future generations through careful planning or management, as appropriate.

Principle 3

The capacity of the earth to produce vital renewable resources must be maintained and, wherever practicable, restored or improved.

Principle 4

Man has a special responsibility to safeguard and wisely manage the heritage of wildlife and its habitat, which are now gravely imperilled by a combination of adverse factors. Nature conservation, including wildlife, must therefore receive importance in planning for economic development.

Principle 5

The non-renewable resources of the earth must be employed in such a way as to guard against the danger of their future exhaustion and to ensure that benefits from such employment are shared by all mankind.

Principle 6

The discharge of toxic substances or of other substances and the release of heat, in such quantities or concentrations as to exceed the capacity of the environment to render them harmless, must be halted in order to ensure that serious or irreversible damage is not inflicted upon ecosystems. The just struggle of the peoples of ill countries against pollution should be supported.

Principle 7

States shall take all possible steps to prevent pollution of the seas by substances that are liable to create hazards to human health, to harm living resources and marine life, to damage amenities or to interfere with other legitimate uses of the sea.

Principle 8

Economic and social development is essential for ensuring a favorable living and working environment for man and for creating conditions on earth that are necessary for the improvement of the quality of life.

Principle 9

Environmental deficiencies generated by the conditions of under-development and natural disasters pose grave problems and can best be remedied by accelerated development through the transfer of substantial quantities of financial and technological assistance as a supplement to the domestic effort of the developing countries and such timely assistance as may be required.

Principle 10

For the developing countries, stability of prices and adequate earnings for primary commodities and raw materials are essential to environmental management, since economic factors as well as ecological processes must be taken into account.

Principle 11

The environmental policies of all States should enhance and not adversely affect the present or future development potential of developing countries, nor should they hamper the attainment of better living conditions for all, and appropriate steps should be taken by States and international organizations with a view to reaching agreement on meeting the possible national and international economic consequences resulting from the application of environmental measures.

Principle 12

Resources should be made available to preserve and improve the environment, taking into account the circumstances and particular requirements of developing countries and any costs which may emanate- from their incorporating environmental safeguards into their development planning and the need for making available to them, upon their request, additional international technical and financial assistance for this purpose.

Principle 13

In order to achieve a more rational management of resources and thus to improve the environment, States should adopt an integrated and coordinated approach to their development planning so as to ensure that development is compatible with the need to protect and improve environment for the benefit of their population.

Principle 14

Rational planning constitutes an essential tool for reconciling any conflict between the needs of development and the need to protect and improve the environment.

Principle 15

Planning must be applied to human settlements and urbanization with a view to avoiding adverse effects on the environment and obtaining maximum social, economic and environmental benefits for all. In this respect projects which arc designed for colonialist and racist domination must be abandoned.

Principle 16

Demographic policies which are without prejudice to basic human rights and which are deemed appropriate by Governments concerned should be applied in those regions where the rate of population growth or excessive population concentrations are likely to have adverse effects on the environment of the human environment and impede development.

Principle 17

Appropriate national institutions must be entrusted with the task of planning, managing or controlling the 9 environmental resources of States with a view to enhancing environmental quality.

Principle 18

Science and technology, as part of their contribution to economic and social development, must be applied to the identification, avoidance and control of environmental risks and the solution of environmental problems and for the common good of mankind.

Principle 19

Education in environmental matters, for the younger generation as well as adults, giving due consideration to the underprivileged, is essential in order to broaden the basis for an enlightened opinion and responsible conduct by individuals, enterprises and communities in protecting and improving the environment in its full human dimension. It is also essential that mass media of communications avoid contributing to the deterioration of the environment, but, on the contrary, disseminates information of an educational nature on the need to project and improve the environment in order to enable mal to develop in every respect.

Principle 20

Scientific research and development in the context of environmental problems, both national and multinational, must be promoted in all countries, especially the developing countries. In this connection, the free flow of up-to-date scientific information and transfer of experience must be supported and assisted, to facilitate the solution of environmental problems; environmental technologies should be made available to developing countries on terms which would encourage their wide dissemination without constituting an economic burden on the developing countries.

Principle 21

States have, in accordance with the Charter of the United Nations and the principles of international law, the sovereign right to exploit their own resources pursuant to their own environmental policies, and the responsibility to ensure that activities within their jurisdiction or control do not cause damage to the environment of other States or of areas beyond the limits of national jurisdiction.

Principle 22

States shall cooperate to develop further the international law regarding liability and compensation for the victims of pollution and other environmental damage caused by activities within the jurisdiction or control of such States to areas beyond their jurisdiction.

Principle 23

Without prejudice to such criteria as may be agreed upon by the international community, or to standards which will have to be determined nationally, it will be essential in all cases to consider the systems of values prevailing in each country, and the extent of the applicability of standards which are valid for the most advanced countries but which may be inappropriate and of unwarranted social cost for the developing countries.

Principle 24

International matters concerning the protection and improvement of the environment should be handled in a cooperative spirit by all countries, big and small, on an equal footing. Cooperation through multilateral or bilateral arrangements or other appropriate means is essential to effectively control, prevent, reduce and eliminate adverse environmental effects resulting from activities conducted in all spheres, in such a way that due account is taken of the sovereignty and interests of all States.

Principle 25

States shall ensure that international organizations play a coordinated, efficient and dynamic role for the protection and improvement of the environment.

Principle 26

Man and his environment must be spared the effects of nuclear weapons and all other means of mass destruction. States must strive to reach prompt agreement, in the relevant international organs, on the elimination and complete destruction of such weapons.

One of the things to notice about the Stockholm Declaration is that (1) it is not law, and (2) sovereignty over natural resources is assured. Developing countries wanted to make sure that global environmental restrictions did not restrict their economic growth. In general, the developing countries tended to oppose any global environmental regulations because they would impair the nation's ability to profit from less sophisticated production technologies. For example, Brazil wanted to preserve its sovereign right to exploit the resources of the Amazon rainforest, often called the lungs of the planet. The rapid deforestation of the Amazon has been a great concern to environmentalists around the world and in Brazil. But destruction continues at a fairly rapid pace, as various Brazilian leaders felt compelled to favor "development" over rainforest preservation.

Link to BBC report:
Brazil's rainforest is still plundered as world leaders agree "end to deforestation." There appears to be a "losing battle" against "the Rainforest mafia."

https://www.youtube.com/watch?v=sIhnbsfcXgc

It is fairly commonplace to note that multinational corporations can take advantage of different regulatory regimes: where environmental laws are relatively lax, and extractive industries can operate with minimal interference. Mining operations in Ghana, for example, will have less regulatory interference from the state, and a steel factory will cost millions less to build away from the US, where sophisticated anti-pollution equipment is required.

Many developing countries do not have the economic resources to develop extensive regulatory regimes; also, the older technologies these nations have access to are more likely to be polluting technologies. In many countries, as well, the leaders may be influenced by either bribes or campaign contributions to go easy on costly environmental regulations. Even the United States, many politicians are beholden to fossil fuel money, whether as investors or recipients of campaign contributions. Lobbyists

From MSNBC: Video Reveals Oil Lobbyist Go-To List Of Senators To Undercut Climate Action

https://www.youtube.com/watch?v=xs0xAS2mLtg

But, as we know, pollution and climate change do not respect national boundaries. The E.U. can enact tough regulations that reduce pollution in Europe, or sign on to climate change treaties, but If China and India do not, the rest of the world will be affected. There is also an economic and financial downside to strict environmental regulations in developed, industrialized nations: their goods may be more expensive to produce, putting those nations' companies at a disadvantage with products manufactured in nations with lower environmental standards.

I.   TRADITIONAL INTERNATIONAL REMEDIES

The Polluter Pays Principles

If a business can pass costs along to neighboring property owners, or to the public generally, it stands to make more money. Before looking at "the polluter pays" principle internationally, it might be good to look at how U.S. "domestic" law treats polluters whose activities cause economic harm to its neighbors. Even in a well-developed regulatory regime such as in the United States, we can see in the case of Boomer versus Atlantic Cement Company, below, that making the polluter pay for the true costs of their pollution is easier said than done. Economists agree in principle that pollution can create "negative externalities" (costs incurred involuntarily by third parties who do not participate in the contract between producer and consumer).

As capitalism is said to be based on voluntary exchanges by rational human actors, the involuntary nature of having to pay for another's "negative externalities" is a "market failure" where the legal system should properly make adjustments. But again, as Boomer v. Atlantic Cement shows us, that is are easier said than done. In brief, the old aphorism from Ben Franklin applies here: announce a prevention is worth a pound of cure. (But it is prevention that costs companies up front, so there is naturally some resistance to regulations that force preventative measures.)

Oscar H. Boomer et al., Appellants, v. Atlantic Cement Company, Inc., Respondent. (And Five Other Actions.); Charles J. Meilak et al., Appellants, v. Atlantic Cement Company, Inc., Respondent

Court of Appeals of New York, 1970

JUDGES: Chief Judge Fuld and Judges Burke and Scileppi concur with Judge Bergan; Judge Jasen dissents in part and votes to reverse in a separate opinion; Judges Breitel and Gibson taking no part.

OPINION BY: BERGAN

Defendant operates a large cement plant near Albany. These are actions for injunction and damages by neighboring land owners alleging injury to property from dirt, smoke and vibration emanating from the plant. A nuisance has been found after trial, temporary damages have been allowed; but an injunction has been denied.

The public concern with air pollution arising from many sources in industry and in transportation is currently accorded ever wider recognition accompanied by a growing sense of responsibility in State and Federal Governments to control it. Cement plants are obvious sources of air pollution in the neighborhoods where they operate.

. . . .

Effective control of air pollution is a problem presently far from solution even with the full public and financial powers of government. In large measure adequate technical procedures are yet to be developed and some that appear possible may be economically impracticable.

It seems apparent that the amelioration of air pollution will depend on technical research in great depth; on a carefully balanced consideration of the economic impact of close regulation; and of the actual effect on public health. It is likely to require massive public expenditure and to demand more than any local community can accomplish and to depend on regional and interstate controls.

A court should not try to do this on its own as a by-product of private litigation and it seems manifest that the judicial establishment is neither equipped in the limited nature of any judgment it can pronounce nor prepared to lay down and implement an effective policy for the elimination of air pollution. This is an area beyond the circumference of one private lawsuit. It is a direct responsibility for government and should not thus be undertaken as an incident to solving a dispute between property owners and a single cement plant -- one of many -- in the Hudson River valley.

The cement making operations of defendant have been found by the court at Special Term to have damaged the nearby properties of plaintiffs in these two actions. That court, as it has been noted, accordingly found defendant maintained a nuisance and this has been affirmed at the Appellate Division. The total damage to plaintiffs' properties is, however, relatively small in comparison with the value of defendant's operation and with the consequences of the injunction which plaintiffs seek. (emphasis supplied)

. . . .

The rule in New York has been that such a nuisance will be enjoined although marked disparity be shown in economic consequence between the effect of the injunction and the effect of the nuisance.
. . . .
Although the court at Special Term and the Appellate Division held that injunction should be denied, it was found that plaintiffs had been damaged in various specific amounts up to the time of the trial and damages to the respective plaintiffs were awarded for those amounts. The effect of this was, injunction having been denied, plaintiffs could maintain successive actions at law for damages thereafter as further damage was incurred.

The court at Special Term also found the amount of permanent damage attributable to each plaintiff, for the guidance of the parties in the event both sides stipulated to the payment and acceptance of such permanent damage as a settlement of all the controversies among the parties. The total of permanent damages to all plaintiffs thus found was $ 185,000. . . .

This result at Special Term and at the Appellate Division is a departure from a rule that has become settled; but to follow the rule literally in these cases would be to close down the plant at once. This court is fully agreed to avoid that immediately drastic remedy; the difference in view is how best to avoid it. (Note: Respondent's investment in the plant is in excess of $ 45,000,000. There are over 300 people employed there.)

One alternative is to grant the injunction but postpone its effect to a specified future date to give opportunity for technical advances to permit defendant to eliminate the nuisance; another is to grant the injunction conditioned on the payment of permanent damages to plaintiffs which would compensate them for the total economic loss to their property present and future caused by defendant's operations. For reasons which will be developed the court chooses the latter alternative.

If the injunction were to be granted unless within a short period -- e.g., 18 months -- the

262

nuisance be abated by improved methods, there would be no assurance that any significant technical improvement would occur.

. . .

.

For obvious reasons the rate of the research is beyond control of defendant. If at the end of 18 months the whole industry has not found a technical solution a court would be hard put to close down this one cement plant if due regard be given to equitable principles.

On the other hand, to grant the injunction unless defendant pays plaintiffs such permanent damages as may be fixed by the court seems to do justice between the contending parties. All of the attributions of economic loss to the properties on which plaintiffs' complaints are based will have been redressed.

The nuisance complained of by these plaintiffs may have other public or private consequences, but these particular parties are the only ones who have sought remedies and the judgment proposed will fully redress them. The limitation of relief granted is a limitation only within the four corners of these actions and does not foreclose public health or other public agencies from seeking proper relief in a proper court.

It seems reasonable to think that the risk of being required to pay permanent damages to injured property owners by cement plant owners would itself be a reasonable effective spur to research for improved techniques to minimize nuisance.

. . . .

The present cases and the remedy here proposed are in a number of other respects rather similar to *Northern Indiana Public Serv. Co.* v. *Vesey* (210 Ind. 338) decided by the Supreme Court of Indiana. The gases, odors, ammonia and smoke from the Northern Indiana company's gas plant damaged the nearby Vesey greenhouse operation. An injunction and damages were

sought, but an injunction was denied and the relief granted was limited to permanent damages "present, past, and future" (p. 371).

Denial of injunction was grounded on a public interest in the operation of the gas plant and on the court's conclusion "that less injury would be occasioned by requiring the appellant [Public Service] to pay the appellee [Vesey] all damages suffered by it than by enjoining the operation of the gas plant; and that the maintenance and operation of the gas plant should not be enjoined" (p. 349).

The Indiana Supreme Court opinion continued: "When the trial court refused injunctive relief to the appellee upon the ground of public interest in the continuance of the gas plant, it properly retained jurisdiction of the case and awarded full compensation to the appellee. This is upon the general equitable principle that equity will give full relief in one action and prevent a multiplicity of suits" (pp. 353-354).

. . . .

Thus it seems fair to both sides to grant permanent damages to plaintiffs which will terminate this private litigation. The theory of damage is the "servitude on land" of plaintiffs imposed by defendant's nuisance. (See *United States* v. *Causby*, 328 U.S. 256, 261, 262, 267, where the term "servitude" addressed to the land was used by Justice Douglas relating to the effect of airplane noise on property near an airport.)

The judgment, by allowance of permanent damages imposing a servitude on land, which is the basis of the actions, would preclude future recovery by plaintiffs or their grantees (see *Northern Indiana Public Serv. Co.* v. *Vesey, supra*, p. 351).

This should be placed beyond debate by a provision of the judgment that the payment by defendant and the acceptance by plaintiffs of permanent damages found by the court shall be in compensation for a servitude on the land.

. . . .

The orders should be reversed, without costs, and the cases remitted to Supreme Court, Albany County to grant an injunction which shall be vacated upon payment by defendant of such amounts of permanent damage to the respective plaintiffs as shall for this purpose be determined by the court.

DISSENT: Jasen, J. I agree with the majority that a reversal is required here, but I do not subscribe to the newly enunciated doctrine of assessment of permanent damages, in lieu of an injunction, where substantial property rights have been impaired by the creation of a nuisance.

It has long been the rule in this State, as the majority acknowledges, that a nuisance which results in substantial continuing damage to neighbors must be enjoined. (*Whalen* v. *Union Bag & Paper Co.*, 208 N. Y. 1; *Campbell* v. *Seaman*, 63 N. Y. 568; see, also, *Kennedy* v. *Moog Servocontrols*, 21 N Y 2d 966.) To now change the rule to permit the cement company to continue polluting the air indefinitely upon the payment of permanent damages is, in my opinion, compounding the magnitude of a very serious problem in our State and Nation today.

In recognition of this problem, the Legislature of this State has enacted the Air Pollution Control Act (Public Health Law, §§ 1264-1299-m) declaring that it is the State policy to require the use of all available and reasonable methods to prevent and control air pollution (Public Health Law, § 1265).

The harmful nature and widespread occurrence of air pollution have been extensively documented. Congressional hearings have revealed that air pollution causes substantial property damage, as well as being a contributing factor to a rising incidence of lung cancer, emphysema, bronchitis and asthma.

The specific problem faced here is known as particulate contamination because of the fine dust particles emanating from defendant's cement plant. The particular type of nuisance is not new, having appeared in many cases for at least the past 60 years. (See *Hulbert* v. *California Portland Cement Co.*, 161 Cal. 239 [1911].) It is interesting to note that cement production has recently been identified as a significant source of particulate contamination in the Hudson Valley. n3 This type of pollution, wherein very small particles escape and stay in the atmosphere, has been denominated as the type of air pollution which produces the greatest hazard to human health. n4 We have thus a nuisance which not only is damaging to the plaintiffs, but also is decidedly harmful to the general public. (Notes: There are seven plaintiffs here who have been substantially damaged by the maintenance of this nuisance. The trial court found their total permanent damages to equal $ 185,000.)

I see grave dangers in overruling our long-established rule of granting an injunction where a nuisance results in substantial continuing damage. In permitting the injunction to become inoperative upon the payment of permanent damages, the majority is, in effect, licensing a continuing wrong. It is the same as saying to the cement company, you may continue to do harm to your neighbors so long as you pay a fee for it. Furthermore, once such permanent damages are assessed and paid, the incentive to alleviate the wrong would be eliminated, thereby continuing air pollution of an area without abatement.

It is true that some courts have sanctioned the remedy here proposed by the majority in a number of cases, n6 (omitted) but none of the authorities relied upon by the majority are analogous to the situation before us. In those cases, the courts, in denying an injunction and awarding money damages, grounded their decision on a showing that the use to which the property was intended to be put was primarily for the public benefit. Here, on the other hand, it is clearly established that the cement company is creating a continuing air pollution nuisance primarily for its own private interest with no public benefit.

. . . .

I would enjoin the defendant cement company

264

from continuing the discharge of dust particles upon its neighbors' properties unless, within 18 months, the cement company abated this nuisance.

It is not my intention to cause the removal of the cement plant from the Albany area, but to recognize the urgency of the problem stemming from this stationary source of air pollution, and to allow the company a specified period of time to develop a means to alleviate this nuisance.

I am aware that the trial court found that the most modern dust control devices available have been installed in defendant's plant, but, I submit, this does not mean that *better* and more effective dust control devices could not be developed within the time allowed to abate the pollution.

Moreover, I believe it is incumbent upon the defendant to develop such devices, since the cement company, at the time the plant commenced production (1962), was well aware of the plaintiffs' presence in the area, as well as the probable consequences of its contemplated operation. Yet, it still chose to build and operate the plant at this site.

In a day when there is a growing concern for clean air, highly developed industry should not expect acquiescence by the courts, but should, instead, plan its operations to eliminate contamination of our air and damage to its neighbors.

Accordingly, the orders of the Appellate Division, insofar as they denied the injunction, should be reversed, and the actions remitted to Supreme Court, Albany County to grant an injunction to take effect 18 months hence, unless the nuisance is abated by improved techniques prior to said date.

Case Questions:

1. Did the Court abandon its prior precedents here? (Yes, but why?)
2. How well can a court assess damages to the plaintiffs? Soot, noise, vibration, health? How can these be adequately measured?
3. If Boomer sells his house and land to you, what rights do you have against Atlantic Cement?

Earlier, we saw with the Trail Smelter arbitration that one nation's economic activities must not impair the economic activities of a neighboring nation. But in the absence of a treaty or an agreement to negotiate, you could not force a neighboring nation to arbitrate over their injurious activities. A rare case in which the alleged polluter consented to arbitration involved a Uruguayan pulp mill on the river Uruguay, which forms the border between Uruguay and Argentina. In this case, the International Court of Justice concluded that Argentina had failed to establish environmental infractions under their relevant bilateral agreement.

Case 9 - 1
Pulp Mills on the River Uruguay (Argentina v. Uruguay)
April 20, 2010 – International Court of Justice

On 4 May 2006, Argentina filed an Application instituting proceedings against Uruguay concerning alleged breaches by Uruguay of obligations incumbent upon it under the Statute of the River Uruguay, a treaty signed by the two States on 26 February 1975 (hereinafter "the 1975 Statute") for the purpose of establishing the joint machinery necessary for the optimum and rational utilization of that part of the river which constitutes their joint boundary. In its Application, Argentina charged Uruguay with having unilaterally authorized the construction of two pulp mills on the River Uruguay without complying with the obligatory prior notification and consultation procedures under the 1975 Statute. Argentina claimed that those mills posed a threat to the river and its environment and were likely to impair the quality of the river's waters and to cause significant transboundary damage to Argentina. As basis for the Court's jurisdiction, Argentina invoked the first paragraph of Article 60 of the 1975 Statute, which provides that any dispute concerning the interpretation or application of that Statute which cannot be settled by direct negotiations may be submitted by either party to the Court.

Argentina's Application was accompanied by a Request for the indication of provisional measures, whereby Argentina asked that Uruguay be ordered to suspend the authorizations for construction of the mills and all building works pending a final decision by the Court; to co-operate with Argentina with a view to protecting and conserving the aquatic environment of the River Uruguay; and to refrain from taking any further unilateral action with respect to the construction of the two mills incompatible with the 1975 Statute, and from any other action which might aggravate the dispute or render its settlement more difficult. Public hearings on the Request for the indication of provisional measures were held on 8 and 9 June 2006. By an Order of 13 July 2006, the Court found that the circumstances, as they then presented themselves to it, were not such as to require the exercise of its power under Article 41 of the Statute to indicate provisional measures.

On 29 November 2006, Uruguay in turn submitted a Request for the indication of provisional measures on the grounds that, from 20 November 2006, organized groups of Argentine citizens had blockaded a "vital international bridge" over the River Uruguay, that that action was causing it considerable economic prejudice and that Argentina had made no effort to end the blockade. At the end of its Request, Uruguay asked the Court to order Argentina to take "all reasonable and appropriate steps . . . to prevent or end the interruption of transit between Uruguay and Argentina, including the blockading of bridges or roads between the two States"; to abstain "from any measure that might aggravate, extend or make more difficult the settlement of this dispute"; and to abstain "from any other measure which might prejudice the rights of Uruguay in dispute before the Court".

Public hearings on the Request for the indication of provisional measures were held on 18 and 19 December 2006. By an Order of 23 January 2007, the Court found that the circumstances, as they then presented themselves to it, were not such as to require the exercise of its power under Article 41 of the Statute.

Following public hearings held between 14 September 2009 and 2 October 2009, the Court delivered its Judgment on 20 April 2010. With respect to Argentina's argument that projects had been authorized by Uruguay in violation of the mechanism for prior notification and consultation laid down by Articles 7 to 13 of the 1975 Statute (the procedural violations), the Court noted that Uruguay had not informed the Administrative Commission of the River Uruguay (CARU) of the projects as prescribed in the Statute. The Court concluded that, by not informing CARU of the planned works before the issuing of the initial environmental authorizations for each of the mills and for the port terminal adjacent to the Orion (Botnia) mill, and by failing to notify the plans to Argentina through CARU, Uruguay had violated the 1975 Statute.

With respect to Argentina's contention that the industrial activities authorized by Uruguay had had, or would have, an adverse impact on the quality of the waters of the river and the area affected by it, and had caused significant damage to the quality of the waters of the river and significant transboundary damage to Argentina (the substantive violations), the Court found, based on a detailed examination of the Parties' arguments, that there was

> "no conclusive evidence in the record to show that Uruguay has not acted with the requisite degree of due diligence or that the discharges of effluent from the Orion (Botnia) mill have had deleterious effects or caused harm to living resources or to the quality of the water or the ecological balance of the river since it started its operations in November 2007".

Consequently, the Court concluded that Uruguay had not breached substantive obligations under the Statute. In addition to this finding, however, the Court emphasized that, under the 1975 Statute, "[t]he Parties have a legal obligation . . . to continue their co-operation through CARU and to enable it to devise the necessary means to promote the equitable utilization of the river, while protecting its environment."

In 2015, the international Court of Justice solidified the legal principle of responsibility for transboundary environmental damage. In the following case, however, it did make clear that nations will have to prove that their allegations are true.

Case 9-2
Certain Activities Carried Out by Nicaragua in the Border Area (Costa Rica v. Nicaragua)
Proceedings joined with construction of a Road in Costa Rica along the San Juan River
(Nicaragua v. Costa Rica)
17 April 2013

The geographical context of the dispute is as follows: The source of the San Juan River (the River) is Lake Nicaragua in the far west of Nicaragua. From there, the River runs some 205 kilometers to the east—across the remaining width of the Isthmus of Panama—before emptying into the Caribbean Sea. At the so-called Delta Costa Rica, the River divides into two branches and continues on its way to the Caribbean. The northern branch, the Lower San Juan, flows into the ocean about thirty kilometers south of the delta. The southern (and larger) branch, the Colorado River, crosses into Costa Rica and reaches the Caribbean about twenty kilometers southeast of the mouth of the Lower San Juan at the Barra de Colorado. The 150-square-kilometer area between the Lower San Juan and Colorado River is known as Isla Calero, within which there is a smaller, 17-square-kilometer area known to Costa Rica as Isla Portillos and to Nicaragua as Harbor Head. A large lagoon (Laguna Los Portillos or Harbor Head Lagoon, depending on whom you ask) lies to the north, separated from the Caribbean by a sandbar. The area as a whole includes two wetlands of international importance within the meaning of the Convention on Wetlands of International Importance especially as Waterfowl Habitat (Ramsar Convention): the Humidal Caribe Noreste (Northeast Caribbean Wetland) and the Refugio de Vida Silvestre Rio San Juan (San Juan River Wildlife Refuge).

By way of historical context, the dispute began in 1857 when, following the overthrow of William Walker's filibuster regime in Nicaragua by a coalition of Central American armies, Costa Rica and Nicaragua resolved to set their shared border via treaty. The resulting 1858 Treaty established the border in part as running along the River, with Nicaragua receiving sovereignty over the river itself, subject to certain rights of freedom of commerce and navigation accruing to Costa Rica. Following a Nicaraguan challenge, the Treaty's validity was confirmed in an arbitral award issued by U.S. President Grover Cleveland in 1888. Subsequent to that decision, Costa Rica and Nicaragua agreed to establish two National Demarcation Commissions. U.S. General Edward Porter Alexander was duly appointed. Between 1897 and 1900, he issued five awards, of which the first three were of particular relevance in these proceedings.

The disputes themselves arose out of infrastructure projects undertaken separately by Costa Rica and Nicaragua in and around the border area.[7] On October 18, 2010, Nicaraguan troops entered Isla Portillos as part of ongoing dredging operations along the River. Nicaragua said that it did so in order to clear a historic channel that had become overgrown, thereby restoring the natural flow of the River. It further asserted that Isla Portillos was Nicaraguan territory. Costa Rica disputed this, averring that not only was Isla Portillos Costa Rican territory, but Nicaragua was in fact cutting an entirely new channel where none had existed previously. On November 18, 2010, Costa Rica filed an Application with the Court for the *Border Area* case, relying on the Pact of Bogata and Nicaragua's "optional clause" declaration under Article 36(2) of the ICJ Statute as providing jurisdiction. It also filed what would be the first of several applications (by both parties) concerning provisional measures under Article 41 of the Statute.

For its part, Costa Rica started works in December 2010 for the construction of Route 1856 Juan Rafael Mora Porras (the Road), which was to run in Costa Rican territory alongside the River between Los Chiles in the west and a point just beyond the Delta Colorado in the east– a distance of just under 160 km. On February 21, 2011, Costa Rica adopted an Executive Decree declaring a state of emergency in the area, which it maintained relieved it of the obligation to conduct an EIA in respect of the Road. Nicaragua filed its Application to the Court for the *Road* case on December 22, 2011. It also relied on the Pact of Bogata and Costa Rica's optional clause declaration as furnishing the Court with jurisdiction.

The Court has already found that Nicaragua is responsible for the harm caused by its activities in breach of Costa Rica's territorial sovereignty. What remains to be examined is whether Nicaragua is responsible for any transboundary harm allegedly caused by its dredging activities which have taken place in areas under Nicaragua's territorial sovereignty, in the Lower San Juan River and on its left bank.

Costa Rica submits that Nicaragua has breached "the obligation not to dredge, divert or alter the course of the San Juan River, or conduct any other works on the San Juan River, if this causes damage to Costa Rican territory (including the Colorado River), its environment, or to Costa Rican rights under the 1888 Cleveland Award." According to Costa Rica, the dredging programme executed by Nicaragua in the Lower San Juan River was in breach of Nicaragua's obligations under customary international law and caused harm to Costa Rican lands on the right bank of the river and to the Colorado River.

Nicaragua contends that the dredging programme has not caused any harm to Costa Rican territory including the Colorado River. It argues that the execution of the dredging programme has been beneficial to the dredged section of the Lower San Juan River and to the wetlands of international importance lying downstream. Moreover, Nicaragua maintains that, under a special rule stated in the Cleveland Award and applying to the San Juan River, even if damage to Costa Rica's territory resulted from the works to maintain and improve the river, the dredging activities would not be unlawful.

As the Court restated in the *Pulp Mills* case, under customary international law, "[a] State is . . . obliged to use all the means at its disposal in order to avoid activities which take place in its territory, or in any area under its jurisdiction, causing significant damage to the environment of another State" (*I.C.J. Reports 2010 (I)*, p. 56, para. 101)

In any event, it would be necessary for the Court to address the question of the relationship between the 1858 Treaty as interpreted by the Cleveland Award and the current rule of customary international law with regard to transboundary harm only if Costa Rica were to prove that the dredging programme in the Lower San Juan River produced harm to Costa Rica's territory.

Costa Rica has not provided any convincing evidence that sediments dredged from the river were deposited on its right bank. Costa Rica has also not proved that the dredging programme caused harm to its wetland. With regard to Costa Rica's contention that "the dredging programme has had a significant effect upon the Colorado River", it has already been noted that the Parties agree that at the so-called "Delta Colorado" the Colorado River receives about 90 per cent of the waters flowing through the San Juan River. Nicaragua estimates that the diversion of water from the Colorado River due to the dredging of the Lower San Juan River affected less than 2 per cent of the waters flowing into the Colorado River. No higher figure has been suggested by Costa Rica. Its main expert observed that "there is no evidence that the dredging programme has significantly affected flows in the Rio Colorado. Costa Rica did adduce evidence indicating a significant reduction in flow of the Colorado River between January 2011 and October 2014. However, the Court considers that a causal link between this reduction and Nicaragua's dredging programme has not been established. As Costa Rica admits, other factors may be relevant to the decrease in flow, most notably the relatively small amount of rainfall in the relevant period. In any event, the diversion of water due to the dredging of the Lower San Juan River is far from seriously impairing navigation on the Colorado River, as envisaged in paragraph 3 (9) of the Cleveland Award, or otherwise causing harm to Costa Rica.
The Court therefore concludes that the available evidence does not show that Nicaragua breached its obligations by engaging in dredging activities in the Lower San Juan River.

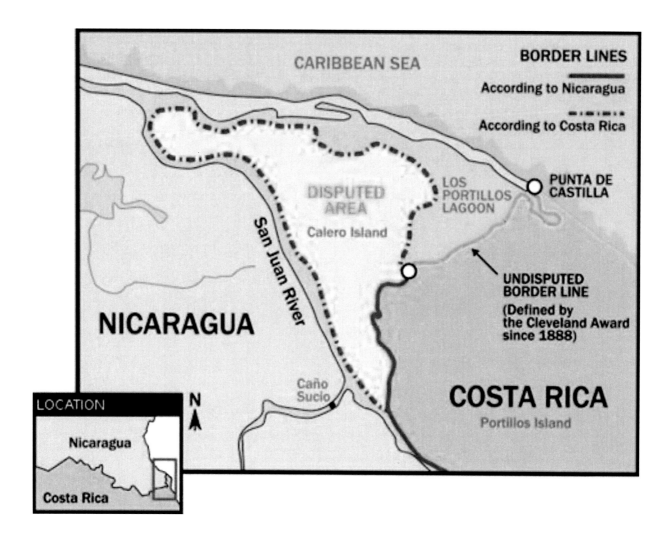

II. Regulation of Products that Violate Environmental Objectives

Consider again the week 4 materials on Tunas and Dolphins, and the WTO dispute settlement in the Shrimp-Turtle case. When it comes to conflicts between free trade and the environment, the WTO will typically come down in favor of free trade. That is why, in 1999, environmentalists (and others) protested the WTO meeting in Seattle. This has sometimes been called "The Battle of Seattle."
https://www.youtube.com/watch?v=-t13R6ej-WQ

Protesters were concerned about environmental issues, but those issues included concerns about the local sustainability of food supplies in a globalized era where large corporations were starting to monopolize food sources, and using TRIPS (see Chapter Six) to patent seeds. Here is renowned scientist/environmentalist/activist Vananda Shiva expressing her concerns 20 years after The Battle of Seattle. https://www.youtube.com/watch?v=kBljGGRcyVY

While the WTO is not entirely "anti-environment," it does seem more likely to protect human health. For example, t has allowed governments to keep out imports to protect human health, such as supporting France in keeping Canadian asbestos out of France.

Case 9-3
Canadian Asbestos Case
5/AB/R40 (Feb. 16, 2001) WTO Appellate Body

Chrysotile asbestos poses significant risks to human health. It is generally recognized to cause lung cancer and other respiratory diseases. Nonetheless, because it has such favorable qualities as resistance to high temperatures, it has been used widely in many industries.

This case involved a ban on asbestos products instituted by the French government, which previously had been a large importer of chrysotile asbestos. This ban entered into force on January 1, 1997. Canada, as the second largest asbestos producer in the world, challenged the prohibition in the WTO. It claimed that the French ban violated several articles of the GATT in addition to the Agreement on Technical Barriers to Trade, which ensures that domestic product standards and regulations do not create unnecessary trade barriers.

The European Commission contended that the ban was necessary to protect both workers subject to prolonged asbestos exposure and members of the general population who could be subject to occasional exposure, and that it was therefore permissible under GATT Article XX(b). Article XX(b) allows domestic measures that affect foreign products if those measures are "necessary to protect human, animal or plant life or health."

The WTO panel concluded that the banned asbestos products and the domestic products used to replace them were "like products." The French ban was accordingly determined to be discriminatory under GATT Article III. The panel concluded, however, that the ban was justified under article XX(b). The panel also found that that TBT agreement did not apply. Canada appealed the panel's decision.
In reading the following excerpt from the appellate body report, Please note that both the panel and the appellate body confirmed France's ability to implement measures to exclude a harmful product, albeit on different grounds.

MESSRS. FELICIANO, BACCHUS, EHLERMANN

It is undisputed that WTO members have the right to determine the level of protection of health that they consider appropriate in a given situation. France has determined, and the panel accepted, that the chosen level of health protection by France is a "halt" to the spread of asbestos related health risks. By prohibiting all forms of amphibole asbestos, and by severely restricting the use of chrysotile asbestos, the measure at issue is clearly designed and apt to achieve that level of health protection. Our conclusion is not altered by the fact that PCG fibers might pose a risk to health. The scientific evidence before the panel indicated that the risk posed by PCG fibers is, in any case, less than the risk posed by chrysotile asbestos fibers, although that evidence did not indicate that the risk posed by PCG fibers is nonexistent. Accordingly, it seems to us perfectly legitimate for a member to seek to halt the spread of a highly risky product while allowing the use of a less risky product in its place.

Canada asserts that the Panel erred in finding that "controlled use" is not a reasonably available alternative to the Decree. The remaining question, then, is whether there is an alternative measure that would achieve the same end and that is less restrictive of trade than a prohibition.

Canada asserts that "controlled use" represents a "reasonably available" measure that would serve the same end. The issue is, thus, whether France could reasonably be expected to employ "controlled use" practices to achieve its chosen level of health protection – a halt in the spread of asbestos-related health risks.

In our view, France could not reasonably be expected to employ any alternative measure if that measure would involve a continuation of the very risk that the Decree seeks to "halt". Such an alternative measure would, in effect, prevent France from achieving its chosen level of health protection.

On the basis of the scientific evidence before it, the Panel found that, in general, the efficacy of "controlled use" remains to be demonstrated. Moreover, even in cases where "controlled use" practices are applied "with greater certainty," the scientific evidence suggests that the level of exposure can, in some circumstances, still be high enough for there to be a "significant residual risk of developing asbestos-related diseases." The Panel found, too, that the efficacy of "controlled use" is particularly doubtful for the building industry and for DIY enthusiasts, which are the most important users of cement-based products containing chrysotile asbestos. Given these factual findings by the Panel, we believe that "controlled use" would not allow France to achieve its chosen level of health protection by halting the spread of asbestos-related health risks. "Controlled use" would, thus, not be an alternative measure that would achieve the end sought by France.

The appellate body concluded that there was no "reasonably available alternative" to Francis chosen method of preventing asbestos caused harm. It upheld the panel's finding that France had acted consistently with international trade law.

For these reasons, we uphold the Panel's finding, in paragraph 8.222 of the Panel Report, that the European Communities has demonstrated a prima facie case that there was no "reasonably available alternative" to the prohibition inherent in the Decree. As a result, we also uphold the Panel's conclusion, in paragraph 8.223 of the Panel Report, that the Decree is "necessary to protect human ... life or health" within the meaning of Article XX(b) of the GATT 1994.

Like asbestos, there are other products that WTO member nations (especially the E.U.) seek to keep out of its market and out of reach of its citizens. For example, GMOs have been a bone of contention, as noted in the following link: https://www.euractiv.com/section/trade-society/news/eu-gmo-ban-was-illegal-wto-rules/